J. Meichardt

Dynamics of Regional Politics

Dynamics of Regional Politics:

Four Systems on the Indian Ocean Rim

W. Howard Wriggins

with

F. Gregory Gause, III
Terrence P. Lyons
Evelyn Colbert

Columbia University Press
NEW YORK

This book was prepared under the
sponsorship of the Institute of War
and Peace Studies, Columbia University.

Columbia University Press
New York   Oxford
Copyright ©1992 Columbia University Press
All rights reserved

Library of Congress Cataloging-in-Publication Data

Wriggins, W. Howard (William Howard)
    Dynamics of regional politics : four systems on the Indian ocean
rim / W. Howard Wriggins, with F. Gregory Gause, Terrence P. Lyons,
Evelyn Colbert.
        p.   cm.
    Includes bibliographical references and index.
    ISBN 0-231-07860-9
    1. Indian Ocean Region—Politics and government.   2. Asia,
Southeastern—Politics and government—1945–   I. Title.
DS341.W75   1992
909'.0965082—dc20   92-9119
                                                           CIP

⊗

Casebound editions of Columbia University Press books are Smyth-sewn and printed
on permanent and durable acid-free paper.

Printed in the United States of America

c   10   9   8   7   6   5   4   3   2   1

For

WILLIAM T. R. FOX,

mentor to so many of us.
He believed there were many roads to an
understanding of world politics.

However useful it may be for certain purposes to focus on relations among the two to five greatest aggregations of territorially organized power, fifty years ago I learned that there is a great deal more to world politics than politics among the first-ranking nation-states.   —William T. R. Fox, 1986

Contents

Acknowledgments

Thanks go first to Enid Schoettle and the Ford Foundation for financing evening seminars that shaped our ideas and for a later grant that made this project possible. Colleagues Warner Schilling, Robert Jervis, Jack Snyder, and Zalmay Khalilzad helped assemble the original proposal, and the first three were available for consultation throughout. My collaborators—Evelyn Colbert, Gregg Gause, and Terrence Lyons—deserve thanks for their patience and persistence, richly textured contributions, and editorial suggestions for the conclusion.

Colleagues who reviewed early formulations and drafts of different parts include Jack Bresnan, Ainslie Embree, Annette and the late William T. R. Fox, Robert Jervis, James Morely, Warner Schilling, Jack Snyder, and Zalmay Khalilzad. I am indebted to Philip Oldenburg, Barnett R. Rubin, and Thomas P. Thornton for their detailed suggestions regarding the South Asia chapter. William Zartman encouraged the enterprise and warned of likely pitfalls. Other friends who usefully criticized parts of the manuscript include Maya Chadda, K. M. de Silva, Selig Harrison, Stanley Heginbotham, Marina Ottaway, Rasul Rais, Bhabani Sen Gupta, and Phillips Talbot. Particularly helpful former students include Mark Dubois, Teg Gettu, Deepa Ollapally, Raja Aziz, and Nandita Aras. Philip Oldenburg and Harpreet Mahajan assisted in ways too numerous to recount. These colleagues, friends, and students gave me much good advice, which I have always considered, though not always taken.

Columbia University's many colleagues associated with the Southern Asian, African, East Asian, and Middle Eastern Institutes have been of great help. They have rightly stressed how the particularities of unique regional contexts and domestic politics often decisively shaped the range of choice that limits what these statesmen (and women) are able to do. The intellectual atmosphere created and the questions raised by colleagues at the Institute of War and Peace Studies and the Political Science Department stimulated the search for links between these particularities and international politics perspectives. The mix this volume strives for therefore reflects many influences.

Jennifer Thorne, Jean Leong, and Jenny Dharamsey managed different parts of the enterprise, for which deep thanks.

Evelyn Colbert wishes to record her indebtedness to Michael Leifer for his exceptionally helpful review of her manuscript.

Gregory Gause would like to thank Fred Lawson, Jack Snyder, and Robert Jervis for comments on earlier versions of his chapter. He would also like to thank Laura Blumenfeld for research assistance during the project.

Terrence Lyons thanks William Zartman for his generous assistance from the beginning. In addition, he has benefited from discussions with Marina Ottaway, Harold Marcus, Michael Schatzberg, Francis Deng, and his colleagues at the SAIS Ph.D. seminar.

W. H. W.

Contributors

W. HOWARD WRIGGINS, Bryce Professor Emeritus of the History of International Relations, Columbia University received his Ph.D. from Yale University in 1952 and joined Columbia University in 1967, where he founded the Southern Asian Institute. Before that he spent ten years in Washington at the Library of Congress, the Policy Planning Council in the Department of State, and the National Security Council staff. His books include *Ceylon: Dilemmas of a New Nation* (Princeton: Princeton University Press, 1960); *The Ruler's Imperative* (New York: Columbia University Press, 1969); *Population, Politics, and the Future of Southern Asia* (New York: Columbia University Press, 1973, with J. Guyot); *Third World Strategies for Change* (New York: Council on Foreign Relations, 1978); *J. R. Jayewardene of Sri Lanka: A Political Biography* (with K. M. de Silva) (Honolulu: University of Hawaii Press; London: Anthony Blond, 1989). He has also written numerous articles on South Asia and the Middle East.

EVELYN COLBERT, a graduate of Barnard College, received her Ph.D. from Columbia University in 1947. In her thirty-five-year career in the Department of State, she served in the Bureau of Intelligence and Research as chief of the Southeast Asia Division and deputy director of the Office of Analysis for East Asia and the Pacific; in the Office of the Director of Central Intelligence as National Intelligence Officer of East Asia and the Pacific; and in the Bureau of East Asian and Pacific Affairs as policy planning adviser and deputy assistant secretary. She has been a Federal Executive Fellow at the Brookings Institution and a resident associate at the Carnegie Endowment for International Peace. She has taught at the Foreign Service Institute and the School of Advanced International Studies of the Johns Hopkins University. Her published works on Asia include *Southeast Asia in International Politics* (Cornell: Cornell University Press, 1977).

F. GREGORY GAUSE III is an assistant professor of political science at Columbia University and member of the university's Middle East Institute. He received his Ph.D. from Harvard University in 1987 and studied Arabic at the American University in Cairo and at Middlebury College. He is the author of *Saudi-Yemeni Relations: Domestic Structures and Foreign Influence* (New York: Columbia University Press, 1990), and of articles in *Middle East Journal, Review of International Studies*, and *Journal of Arab Affairs* among others. He has conducted research in a number of Middle Eastern countries, including Saudi Arabia, Yemen, Jordan, Egypt, and Oman.

TERRENCE P. LYONS is a senior research analyst in the Foreign Policy Studies Project of the Brookings Institution. He received his Ph.D. in 1991 from the Paul Nitze School of Advanced International Studies, Johns Hopkins University. He conducted research in Ethiopia in August 1987 and from November 1988 to April 1989. His publications include "Internal Vulnerability and Interstate Conflict: Ethiopia's Regional Foreign Policy," in Marina Ottaway, *The Political Economy of Ethiopia* (New York: Praeger, 1990) and "The United States and Ethiopia: The Politics of a Patron-Client Relationship," *Northeast African Studies*, 8(2–3) (1986):53–75.

I

The Dynamics of Regional Politics: An Orientation

W. HOWARD WRIGGINS

Scope and Purpose

Regional conflicts have been high on the agendas of superpower diplomacy, but until recently scholars have paid little attention to them. Many "Third World" regions have been cursed by protracted conflicts between neighbors. Since the 1940s and 1950s, when many of the states in these regions gained their independence, each region has suffered from wars between neighboring states, some of which dragged on for more than a decade. At the height of the Cold War, the two superpowers blamed each other for the intensity and persistence of these regional conflicts, and many Third World spokesmen blamed the superpowers. But those with more knowledge understood that most of these conflicts were essentially homegrown and had their roots deep in structural characteristics or historical, ethnic, or other indigenous rivalries. To be sure, outside powers sometimes added to hostility by backing their own protégés, but the sources of the strife were within each region, as our explorations confirm. With the economic and political difficulties besetting the Soviet Union, Cold War rivalry between the powers is subsiding and both are likely to become less concerned about what happens in most Third World regions. How will this affect regional conflicts? Should we expect an intensification of local rivalries as these external powers no longer impose restraints, or will local rivalries moderate as these powers can no longer be counted upon for support? The following chapters suggest that generalizations across Third World regions have limited reliability.

To gain a clearer perception of how newly independent states of the Third World have related to one another since the dismantling of the European empires and to better understand these regional conflicts as they have unfolded, this study explores the international politics of four such regions from the late 1940s to the 1980s. They lie along that great arc that marks the southern rim of mainland Asia and is washed by the Indian Ocean and the South China Sea. It stretches from the Red Sea and the Horn of Africa in the west; across the plains of Iran, Pakistan, and India; and down through the tropical mainland and islands of Southeast Asia.

Most studies of international politics focus on relations among the major powers, whose actions have shaped the global environment in which all states must live. Their missteps or vaulting ambitions in the past have brought on world wars. With nuclear weapons they can in an instant precipitate conflagrations of a magnitude never before imagined. Understandably, generalizations about interstate relations have been drawn mainly from observing these states in Europe, North America, and East Asia.

Since World War II, however, despite the tensions and alarums of the Cold War between the major powers, most interstate conflicts have erupted between former colonies or protectorates. Although each of the regions we examine has been marked by the persistence and intensity of regional rivalries, some states have formed alliances. As we will see in Southeast Asia at least, a group of states has moved remarkably far toward shaping a consultative regime that allows them to mute many of their differences and to deal collectively with states and institutions outside their region.[1] In other ways, too, remarkably varied relationships— quite outside the conventional arenas of international relations study— have formed since the dismantling of the European empires.

Consequently, we believe that there are many reasons for studying the international politics of the less powerful states. One way to do that is to look at regional systems. We focus on the relationships within clusters of states that are thrust together by geography, the unavoidable implications of proximity, their history, the permeability of many frontiers, and the attention and energy they apply to their dealings with each other. Each forms a "system" of states by virtue of numerous action-reaction relationships.[2] Each regional system is different from the others and poses special problems to the leaders who must cope with their imperatives. Nevertheless, within these regional systems similarities exist that are worth examining.

In this book we seek to characterize the patterned relationships that mark each of these four regional systems and each region's links to external states and to understand the forces that have driven the foreign policy choices of the region's states. To this end, we consider three sets of factors. Structural and relational characteristics of each region are among the essential dimensions examined. With Waltz we ask, "What are the relative strengths and foreign policy capabilities of a region's states?" Like Buzan, we believe that their enduring patterns of alignment and conflict are crucial to understanding their relationships.[3] Their interactions generate the environment in which they must all live. Second, domestic political factors are important, including the internal cohesion and capability of the neighboring states, the confidence leaders have in their ability to remain in office, their perceptions and misperceptions, fears and ambitions.[4] How do the domestic strengths or weaknesses of governments and ethnic or other cleavages affect these states' relations with one another? Third, we assess the policies and activities of major outside powers as they affect the evolution of these regional forces.[5] How have outside major powers—the United States, the Soviet Union, and China—become involved in the regions' affairs? What roles have they played and with what result?

There are circularity implications; the patterns of conflict and alignment within each region and the character of the states affect each other. Precarious governments are unable to reach accommodation with neighbors, and persistent conflicts may weaken an already weakening regime. Moreover, relationships between them can influence whether and how the external powers become involved in the region. These external influences, in turn, affect relationships between the region's states.

Our four regions are easy to identify, although the exact boundaries between several of them are not.

The *Arabian/Persian Gulf* remains strategically and economically the most important Third World region. Because it is near the Soviet Union, what happens in the Gulf can directly affect the security preoccupations of the leaders in Moscow. This region also contains the world's largest remaining reserves of inexpensive oil and, consequently, is vital to much of the world economy.

Politically, the Gulf is centered on the triangle of Iran, Iraq, and Saudi Arabia, with the Emirates as small but in some cases financially important participants.[6] To the east of the Gulf, *South Asia*, formerly the foundation of Britain's control of the whole Indian Ocean, reveals the simplest structure, centered on India, the world's second most populous state. It is a region of great asymmetries, divided by the Indo-Pakistani rivalry, with a number of smaller states circling around them. On the southwestern end of the southern Asian rim lies the *Horn of Africa*, centered on Ethiopia, Somalia, and Sudan, with Kenya, Egypt, and South Yemen as important participants. Libya and Saudi Arabia periodically play their parts. At the eastern extremity, the *Southeast Asian* region is more complex. There a major cleavage exists between the states that are members of the Association of Southeast Asian Nations (ASEAN) and the states of Indochina. The former have developed the most carefully institutionalized set of consultative diplomatic relations of any in these four regions.

These regions were chosen because a detailed examination of the diplomacy of relations within such clusters of states can provide useful perspectives on how Third World states deal with one another. Equally important, each region has been an arena of competition between major external powers. This competition often led outside states to give financial and other kinds of assistance. Such assistance often complicated a neighbor's efforts to cope with problems of nascent nationhood and barely institutionalized government, as its leaders sought to come to terms with its regional neighbors. Over the years since independence, these states have been shaping sets of relationships among themselves and dealing with external powers in ways increasingly typical of the wider international system. Such an exploration would provide a useful supplement to more abstract speculation about the international system. To examine relations among the states in these four regions, beyond the better-documented European and East Asian worlds, broadens our field of observation and may enrich our generalizations about international relations.

The activities of external powers have often appeared to derive more from their rivalry than from any real interest in a region. At other times, particularly in the Gulf, they have pursued specific interests. The regional entanglements resulting from these activities have made relationships between the major powers hostage to the relationships between the states of each region. The activities of the powers within a region have in turn affected the way the states of that region have dealt with one another. Moreover, a number of states within these regions have invested substantial economic and organizational resources in improving their international capability. By becoming stronger economically (thereby acquiring the means to earn considerable foreign exchange surpluses) or by strengthening their defense industries and acquiring more sophisticated weaponry, they are becoming more important in the international system. Their domestic affairs will no longer be as manipulable, nor will their governments be as easily intimidated, as in the past.[7] The way the most important states in each region play their roles will make more of a difference to outside powers.

Finally, one-third of the world's population lives in these regions. Few have suffered more from political and ethnic strife, famines, interstate rivalries, partitions, and wars than these peoples. Hard-pressed leaders face many difficulties (some of which will be outlined later). The peoples of this sprawling area deserve to be better understood by those who may have some influence on their future.

Regional Security Systems

We look on these clusters of states as regional anarchies that are of particular interest because they are located in a non-European setting.[8] Their relationships exist in conditions of anarchy—that is, they are characterized by "politics in the absence of central authority."[9] No one state has the legitimate right to manage security relations within any one region. No overall authority protects the weak from the strong. Each must devote a proportion of its resources to protecting itself from potentially hostile neighbors. Typically, however, chaos does not result.

Familiar relationships and traditional strategies can be observed, and in some cases, close consultations and rules of the game moderate the worst effects of unbridled anarchy.

Even where certain cultural traits transcend frontiers, leaders typically eye neighboring states with suspicion. Proximity often generates friction, as Kautilya long ago discerned.[10] Atavistic fears carried by embedded cultural memories whisper warnings and commend distrust. To be sure, political leaders sometimes cooperate with one another, usually when facing a mutual threat or when cooperation is seen as forwarding their country's interests.[11] More typically, however, they act as if they are all in a self-help system in which each must look out for itself.[12]

To better understand the dynamics of these relations the states in each region can be seen as functioning within a *regional security system*. In each of these security systems the states interact so intensely and with such possible consequence for one another that the behavior of any one of them "is a necessary element in the calculation of the others."[13] Prudent leaders can make no major move without considering the actual or probable reactions of their neighbor.[14]

Accordingly, prudent leaders, acting in the name of their state, try to anticipate the actions of other states and to take counteractive measures. In such an anarchic, insecure environment, leaders must be concerned with protecting their own independence. There is no acceptable authority to do it for them.

Since the Treaty of Westphalia in 1648, national sovereignty and independence have been the watchwords of the international system. However, most states have usually been marked by security interdependencies.

In a profound irony familiar to students of the wider international system, each state's leaders seek maximum independence. However, they know that each state is acutely dependent on what other states in the region do.

The anarchic model is suggestive as a first attempt at understanding the concerns of leaders and the resulting relationships. There are, however, significant differences among anarchies; relationships in each region under consideration have a different quality, depending on a number of variables, including the distribution of power among the states, the goals of neighboring leaders, governmental cohesion, and ethnic cleavages within states and across frontiers.[15]

Indeed, the four regional systems examined here show a range of contrasting anarchies. The Horn, most like Thomas Hobbes' model, is the least evolved. Its members are in persistent conflict, and instability is the norm. The ASEAN subregion in Southeast Asia exemplifies a near opposite model. Frontiers have been generally accepted, or if differences exist, they are usually negotiated quietly or set aside. Generally, state structures are capable of maintaining domestic order and controlling the way their peoples impinge upon their neighbors, and basic state goals are compatible. Constant consultation reduces uncertainties, contributing to a high degree of mutual accommodation and stability. Relations in this subregion mirror Europe's early steps toward the community.[16] The Gulf and South Asia lie between these two ends of the spectrum, with the first characterized by an unstable balance of power prone to periodic conflict and the other a nearly ideal type of sharply asymmetrical system with one power claiming hegemony.

Inevitably, a tension occurs between *system imperatives* and the *range of policy choice* open to the leaders of these countries. Each system sets limits to what individual leaders can accomplish, discouraging innovation and inducing propensities in the region's states to act in certain ways.[17] Typical situations of insecurity often evoke foreseeable policy responses; many actions produce likely if not always exactly predictable reactions. As Waltz argues, individual leaders may change, but the states their successors manage often react in much the same ways. There are consistent patterns that help one foresee the range of probable choices.[18] Accordingly, understanding regional security systems can be useful for policy-making and of intellectual interest.

At the same time, the states whose fates are linked within any one of these systems are not mechanistically articulated one to another, interacting by fixed and invariant "laws." Leaders' perceptions, their values, the goals they set, and the assumptions they make about their own political circumstances affect their responses. These and other individual or domestic political considerations can lead statesmen to decisions that run counter to what one might expect from systems-level analysis. This is why one must also consider domestic politics, the room for maneuver they allow, and the incentives they offer for accentuating hostility toward neighbors or for seeking mutual accommodation. Moreover, few direct links connect the degree of conflict or cooperation within a region, on the one hand, and the extent to which statesmen's choices are severely limited by the structure of the system itself or reflect policies drawn from a broad range of alternatives, on the other. Indeed, greater freedom of policy choice can lead either to more conflict between neighbors or to less, depending on circumstances and on the fears and ambitions of the region's leaders.

The ASEAN states, for example, have successfully shaped some rules of the game that restrain their former rivalry and mitigate unbridled competition. If these norms are to survive when no single power can enforce them, however, each must expect that restraint will be reciprocated by others in the system.[19]

To identify these regional systems as "subordinate" misrepresents the extent to which each has a life of its own, driven by domestic and security requirements.[20]

Each regional system defines the parameters within which serious leaders must work. Each is the international environment that matters most to them, creating the most direct external threats and whatever opportunities may exist. This is why we place these systems at the center of our discussion from the outset. Unfortunately, however, for intellectual tidiness, governments define their most serious threats differently and often unpredictably. We also examine the tension between those leaders who seek to maximize regional autonomy and those who call on external influences to help them.

The four regional security systems we examine are not entirely autonomous systems. Usually, each is the most important arena for international political activity for most of the region's statesmen. However, each security system has been linked to two other, analogous systems. One such system has been the one stretching from Eastern Europe to Asia.[21] How the two great states of this region—the Soviet Union and the People's Republic of China—have related to each other has been significant to the states of the southern Asian rim. Following the Sino-Soviet split, for example, their rivalry greatly encouraged Soviet support for India after the Sino-Indian war and intensified their competing support for the Democratic Republic of Vietnam (DRV) regime during the war against America. Similarly, at the highest level, the global interdependent competition between the United States and the Soviet Union added another set of relations with Washington and/or Moscow that affected the behavior of the regional states.[22] When rivalry between any two of these external powers has been intense, typically they have been more ready to become involved in these regional systems. Conversely, when their rivalry has been more relaxed, they have appeared less concerned about the area. In short, their engagement in the regional system is in part derivative of their relations with each other.

The way in which the external security systems have been linked to these different regional systems and the effects of such ties are of great interest and will be explored.

Regional Dynamics

Characteristic policy perplexities can be seen in each of these regions. One is the tension between the balancing process and the search for predominance. Most of the states in each region are concerned with balancing; several are perceived as seeking regional predominance.

The balancing of power has long been considered a necessary concern of leaders, given the anarchic, self-help character of the international system. Heads of state are impelled to assess the possible threats to their state's interests, to judge "the balance" of capability between the threatening state or states and their own, and to choose the policy most likely to meet these necessities.[23] In so doing, they are engaging in the balancing process, which has three distinguishable forms.

By internal balancing they may undertake on their own to improve their state's international capability. They may promote national cohesion, often by dramatizing external threats or by using religion or ideology to galvanize their nations. They may expand and train their forces, import or manufacture weapons. They may improve frontier defenses and establish stricter border controls or take other domestic measures to improve the state's position or prevent it from deteriorating in comparison to its neighbors. In the last twenty years, many states in these systems have tried to improve their situation by such internal measures, including India, Pakistan, Iran, Iraq, Saudi Arabia, and Ethiopia.

Regional balancing occurs when heads of state who have been nervously watching accumulations of power by a hostile state in their region attempt to collaborate. Much diplomatic history in areas more central to the international system, such as Western Europe or East Asia, is best explained as representing this simple strategy.[24] Is this also the case in our regional state systems?

Here conditions have not favored such regional balancing. Long-standing hostilities, as in the Horn, may prevent jointly threatened states from collaborating. Ideologically zealous states or those that have recently undergone a revolution (e.g., Iran, Iraq, or Ethiopia) may not be safe allies. Immediate neighbors often find it difficult to cooperate. When smaller states are too small to contribute to an effective counterweight, they may hope to remain safe by bandwagoning (i.e., by underlining their own weakness or by seeking to be useful to a threatening state).[25]

Where these conditions predominate, the threatened states may engage in a third form of balancing.

External balancing requires appealing to external powers, drawing them in from beyond the region. Typically, as illustrated by Pakistan in the mid–1950s, extraregional powers are invited in by one of the regional protagonists seeking outside backing in its local competition. The more intense the regional rivalries, the more urgent are the invitations to outside powers by hard-pressed regional competitors. To be sure, a determined nonregional state could shoulder its way into most regional systems even when not invited. Nevertheless, were it not for the rivalries that so mark all four of these regional systems, it would have been much more difficult for external powers to become so involved.[26]

External powers may have had *direct* reasons for their involvement, such as a sense of dependence on the reliable flow of oil from the Gulf or worries about the presence of foreign troops near their frontier. However, their readiness to respond to invitations during the period under review may have been *derivative*, more the result of their competition against each other for influence, for facilities, and for allies within these regions than of any interest intrinsic to the particular region. To preempt the other by being first may have been thought to provide important long-term advantages. To outcompete or undermine the other's presence in one state could be seen as weakening the position of one's competitor throughout the region or beyond. A consequential assertion of power by a nonregional state, such as Moscow's strong support for Ethiopia in 1978 or Washington's for Pakistan in 1981, could symbolize that patron's enhanced capability in the international system.

The eagerness of regional states to issue invitations to nonregional powers (the "pull" factor), accordingly, is one dynamic. Rivalry among the nonregional powers for whatever gains these regional states can provide them (the "push" factor) is another.

Balancing connotes caution and a legitimate desire to offset threats from a neighboring state. Seeking predominance suggests an ambition to be the most important state in one's region. For such a state, the balancing activities of others in the region are undesirable. They represent an attempt by the weak to develop counterweights against the one who aspires to assert superior strength. Indeed, the would-be predominant power seeks to substitute hierarchy (with itself in charge) for the more conventional balancing, in which the states of the region may work together to set limits to the most ambitious. To be sure, balancing may be undertaken against a particular state out of exaggerated fear. Another's apparently vaulting intentions may be misconstrued. At the same time, states may be seeking assistance from beyond the region, both to enhance their regional position and to counterbalance another major power. There are examples in our regions in which states are feared because they are perceived as having ambitions to bring the balancing process to an end. India, Indonesia, Iran, Iraq, and Ethiopia at times have each been seen by their immediate neighbors as such states.

As leaders seek security in a dangerous world, they frequently generate an action-reaction effect within each region, conventionally called the *security dilemma*.[27] Often the steps one state takes to reduce its anxieties about its neighbor turn out to be the very ones that intensify that neighbor's sense of insecurity. Because the margin of safety for one state is often seen as the margin of danger for its neighbor, these can provoke defensive efforts that only reinforce the sense of threat. Together, the interacting states generate the security environment in which all the states of that region must live.

Elements of the security dilemma can be seen in all four of our regions—between Ethiopia and its smaller neighbors, between Iran and Iraq, between India and its neighbors Pakistan and China, and between Vietnam and the states of ASEAN. Its requirements suggest that statesmen in an anarchic world are not as much masters of their fate as they would like to believe, although if conditions and leadership are right, cooperation of a sort is possible even under the security dilemma, as Jervis has argued.[28]

Domestic political imperatives may drive foreign policy decisions. A leader's desire to remain in power can affect relations with neighboring states, and the leadership circumstances in many of these states are more likely to cause difficulties than to result in mutual accommodation. Many of these states are so designated more out of courtesy than out of accuracy. Few come close to the European model of a nation-state.[29] The ruler's writ often does not run throughout the realm. Factions, often ethnically or regionally based, compete with the government's monopoly of legitimate violence. Bureaucracies may be unresponsive, both to the ruler and to the people. Where legitimacy is in doubt, the government may be truly insecure. When governments cannot count on surviving a full term or domestic opposition threatens their survival, foreign policies may be influenced by anxiety about the future of the regime.[30] Even otherwise careful statesmen may unwittingly court risks abroad in their effort to quiet unrest at home. Policies adopted more to deal with such domestic difficulties than to deal with regional neighbors may have severe, unintended effects on neighboring states.

The policy goals of leading personalities in important states can also affect the way a region functions. Particularly where political institutions are not well established or where cultural traditions call on a paternalistic leader to make important decisions on his own, the personal fears and ambitions of key personalities can decisively shape foreign policy.[31] Leaders may accept the way things are and live quietly, concerned mainly with affairs at home, or they can set high ambitions, trying to change their state's place in the regional hierarchy or even to transform their region more to their own liking (as we shall see in the Gulf).

Where political institutions commanding the loyalty of the people are not well established, where states are unable to maintain frontier control and public order may be uncertain, governments cannot count on controlling the way their own people impinge on their neighbors. The domestic politics of one can be severely affected by a neighbor's domestic politics. In these and other ways, domestic politics can affect the policies of regional states toward one another, as the states of South Asia and the Horn so clearly demonstrate.

Ethnic identities complicate regional relations. Particularly when regional states share a common politico-religious culture or ethnic links, what happens within one inevitably has repercussions on its neighbor. Nearly all the states have inhabitants who speak different languages and often come from different ethnic or tribal backgrounds. Many ethnic ties transcend international boundaries. Together they affect the structure and international politics of the regions, blurring the distinction between domestic and foreign policy.[32]

National integration may be a government's objective, but retaining one's ethnic identity and cultural distinctiveness is often a top goal for important minorities in these mosaic societies. Secessionist demands complicate the task of central governments and often worsen relations with neighbors, as proponents of secession seek help from fellow ethnics in a neighboring state and a weak or ambitious government fails to discourage such assistance. Ethnic divisions make such conflicts extremely difficult to settle, in part because competing ethnic leaders may seek to outbid each other by inflating promises or enlarging demands.[33] Governments may use the existence of ethnic brethren across a frontier to justify direct aggression. They may use affiliated minorities as proxies to weaken a neighbor or gain influence over a neighbor's foreign policy.[34] Multiethnic states are peculiarly susceptible to unpredictable disorders, and ethnic brethren who cross frontiers can easily transfer disorders from one state to its neighbor.

In a sophisticated but destructive form of ethnic deterrence strategy, prominent in the Horn but noticeable in South Asia too, leaders in one state may threaten to stimulate a neighbor's ethnic troubles unless its foreign policy changes. Or they may do so if that neighbor dares to exacerbate the division in the threatening statesmen's own country.[35] The "balance of ethnic vulnerability" may suggest that one neighbor is far more vulnerable than another so that the normal constraints of reciprocity may not be persuasive.[36] Expectations about such activities influence statesmen's choices in ways that affect the overall functioning of the regional system.

Some Methodological Problems

Major methodological problems in this approach should be noted.

The boundaries between the regions are not entirely clear in every case; the cast of significant actors is not beyond debate. The intimacy of interaction among the participating states becomes less as the edge of one region and the start of the next one is approached. Certain states may be only occasional participants. A number of states are active participants in more than one region. South Asian states play a role in the

Gulf; Afghanistan straddles both regions and only occasionally has been of consequence to its neighbors. Certain Gulf states impinge on the Horn. In some instances, as in Southeast Asia, influences play into a region from outside that are so consequential it is not always easy to distinguish the regional "system" from the external powers that sometimes may seem to be almost part of the region. A state can be under such pressure from insurgent or secessionist movements (as in Ethiopia or Sri Lanka) or from large numbers of refugees who have fled across the frontier that it cannot claim full control over its territory. Indeed, in a number of instances, nonstate actors—dissidents or secessionist groups—can be more consequential to regional politics than the so-called states. Nevertheless, the states within each of these four regions interact sufficiently to justify considering each cluster of states a distinct international political-security system.

However, boundaries are also sometimes difficult to draw between the regional system and phenomena generated by the participating individual states. Interaction between the two levels sometimes can be so close that in specific instances the distinction cannot be drawn easily.[37] For these and other reasons, our four regional systems have limitations as units of analysis for rigorous comparison.

Multiple variables—domestic, regional, and global—affect the behavior of states within these regional systems. There are questions of structure, shaped by the distribution of international capability, by patterns of cleavage and cooperation, and by the capacity of governments to retain coherence against domestic forces favoring political fragmentation or even secession. There are matters of leadership choice among possible foreign policy goals and alternative forms of the "balancing process," focused sometimes against a prospective regional hegemon, sometimes against an intruder from beyond the regional system. Political institutionalization has often depended on leaders' political skills, their longevity, and the fate of coups and revolutions. These can quickly change the ability of any one government to defend its interests, press its case, or impose its will. In addition, external forces play into each region from the central or East Asian and global security systems.

Each of these regions is marked by differing cultural characteristics. Linguistic, religious, or historical traditions may be shared by inhabitants of rival states within the same region and ultimately may provide the foundation for closer collaboration (as we may be witnessing in Western Europe after centuries of strife). For now, however, in most of our regions, they do not seem to provide many means for reducing regional conflict. However, they may justify regional jealousies and political rivalry.[38]

An unduly strong commitment to parsimony at this stage of our analysis would distort the richness and variety of the real world within which these leaders must operate and which sets limits to what they can do. The range of plausible outcomes could be severely constricted if we chose prematurely to focus exclusively on a few variables at the outset.[39]

These regional systems have been highly dynamic. They have experienced remarkable changes since World War II and the retreat of European power and have been marked by disorder, conflict, and the active involvement of external powers. Forty years is not a long time to make the transition from colonial dependency to stable, resilient independent statehood or orderly regional relations. To expect that peaceful regional orders would promptly follow the dismantling of empires is to expect too much (although a subregion of Southeast Asia appears to have reached a close approximation).

Coups d'état and revolutions have overturned regimes in Ethiopia, Iraq, Iran, Yemen, Afghanistan, Pakistan, Thailand, Somalia, Sudan, Bangladesh, Burma, and Indonesia. Wars have been fought between India and Pakistan, Malaysia and Indonesia, Somalia and Ethiopia, Iran and Iraq; and Iraq sought to take over Kuwait. Secessionist groups have struggled for independence in Ethiopia, Sudan, Sri Lanka, India, and Indonesia. Outside powers have been active in this sprawling area—China and India have fought over their Himalayan frontier; early on the United States strengthened Pakistan and later unsuccessfully tried to halt North Vietnam's ambitions in South Vietnam; the Soviet Union became militarily enmeshed in Afghanistan and Ethiopia and provided indispensable support to Vietnam's activities in Cambodia. Moreover, the newly independent states have been changing at very different rates, with economic growth accelerating in some and barely changing in others. The burden of accelerated population growth differs sharply from state to state.

It is therefore bold to claim that one can identify reiterated patterns in this turbulence of conflict and change. The following chapters on each region demonstrate the discontinuities and unpredictable pace of change during this transition. Nevertheless, we hope to show that underlying consistencies can be discerned.

Summary

Each chapter examines the security system in one of these four regions by looking closely at the relationships among these states. Each has been prepared by a specialist in the international and domestic politics of the specific region. The analysis has been made in the light of the preceding considerations and questions. Each considers primarily the regional structure and interactive processes developed within the regional system itself. Each explores how domestic politics affects the foreign policy behavior of the major regional states. It also considers how the activities of the major outside powers, operating either within the central or East Asian or global systems, affect the regional systems.

Chapter 2, by Gregory Gause, examines the Gulf, which has changed dramatically since the British withdrew in the early 1970s. Iran, Iraq, and Saudi Arabia are the principal states. Iran and Iraq have contended for preeminence while Saudi Arabia has tried to balance whichever seemed the most threatening by aligning with the other while seeking support from beyond the region. Because most of the regimes have had an inherited, familial legitimacy, ambitious single-party regimes like Ba'th Iraq and revolutionary Iran were bound to be seen as threatening to Saudi Arabia, calling for subtle security responses that run counter to conventional balance-of-power theories. The Iran-Iraq war, deriving more from domestic than from international concerns, and the attempted seizure of Kuwait have both precipitated change in the regional configuration. While nonregional states' concern with assured supplies of oil draws them to the region, the dynamic within the region is best explained by long-standing rivalries and internal movements within the region.

Chapter 3 considers the South Asian regional system, with India at its center posing the principal international security problem to its smaller neighbors. The relationships the nations of this region develop present New Delhi with sometimes worrisome problems. Indo-Pakistani antagonism has influenced much in the regional system, including Pakistan's search for support in Washington, Beijing, or the states of the Gulf. China's border quarrel with India complicated India's security problems. Ethnic affiliations crossing international frontiers threaten both the integrity of South Asian states and the stability of the regional system.

Chapter 4, by Terrence Lyons, shows how the important states of the Horn are marked by institutional weakness and antistate secessionist movements. Ethiopia's size, central location, and claim to multiethnic legitimacy has been challenged by the national-state conception of much smaller Somalia, whose determination to encompass Somalis in the Ogaden led to a debilitating war. The more symmetrical rivalry between Ethiopia and Sudan and the secessionist movements that beset both states provided ethnic vulnerabilities that each could use against the other. Collapse of governments in both Ethiopia and Somalia and the success of the Eritrean independence movement in 1990–91 epitomized structural characteristics of the region. By comparison with our other regions, the Horn is nearest to the extreme of anarchy, without rules, reliable alignments, or peace.

By contrast, as Evelyn Colbert shows in chapter 5, at least among the ASEAN states, determined and sustained diplomacy has developed a remarkable degree of mutual consultation and accommodation that has muted earlier quarrels and contributed to a notable surge in economic growth. The principal states are each sufficiently powerful that none is likely to be ignored, as happens in more asymmetrical systems. As a result of the close exchange of information, uncertainty is reduced and the states can concentrate on economic performance and the gains to be derived from cooperation. Unlike the nations of the other regions, the ASEAN states often deal as a group with major external markets and sources of security. The Indochina subregion, by contrast, is hierarchically organized, is clearly dominated by Vietnam, and has been on a war footing for forty years. Vietnam's involvement in Cambodia provided an opportunity to the ASEAN states to strengthen the role of their association in international diplomacy.

Chapter 6 identifies important characteristics of these four regional systems and states that limit what individual statesmen (and women) can do. It also considers dynamic factors and instances where leaders' choices make a difference to the functioning of the regional systems. The way in which the policies of the local states contribute to and are affected by the activities of the major outside powers is considered. This chapter concludes with speculation on how the end of the Cold War is likely to affect these regional systems.

NOTES

1. For references on how conflicts in anarchic systems can be changed into cooperation, see articles by Kenneth Oye, "Explaining Cooperation Under Anarchy: Hypotheses and Strategies"; Robert Jervis, "From Balance to Concert: A Study of International Security Cooperation"; Robert Axelrod and Robert O. Keohane, "Achieving Cooperation Under Anarchy: Strategies and Institutions'—all in *World Politics,* vol. 38, no. 1 (October 1985). See also the "regime" literature, particularly the special issue of *International Organization* entitled "International Regimes," vol. 36, no. 2 (Spring 1982), articles by Krasner, Ruggie, and Young.

2. William R. Thompson identifies four conditions for defining a regional subsystem: (a) a "degree of regularity and intensity" exists in relations among the actors "to the extent that a change at one point in the subsystem affects other parts"; (b) "the actors are generally proximate"; (c) the subsystem is recognized "as a distinctive area or 'theater of operations' "; and (d) the subsystem

"consists of at least two and probably more actors." In "The Regional Subsystem: A Conceptual Explication and a Propositional Inventory," *International Studies Quarterly,* 17(1) (March 1973):89–117. Louis J. Cantori and Steven L. Spiegel have a somewhat different definition; see "The International Relations of Regions," in *Polity,* 2(4) (1970):397–425.

3. Kenneth N. Waltz, *Theory of International Relations* (Reading, Mass.: Addison-Wesley, 1979), esp. chs. 5 and 6, stresses the relative capability and anarchic principle ordering their relationships. Buzan adds the "amity/enmity axis" as a further critical dimension, which we have called "embedded cleavages" in our conclusion. See Barry Buzan and Gowher Rizvi, *South Asian Insecurity and the Great Powers* (London: Macmillan, 1986), ch. 1, and *People, States, and Fear* (Chapel Hill: University of North Carolina Press, 1983), ch. 4.

4. Robert Jervis, *Perception and Misperception in International Politics* (Princeton: Princeton University Press, 1976); W. Howard Wriggins, *The Ruler's Imperative* (New York: Columbia University Press, 1969), chs. 3 and 12.

5. Neil McFarland, *Superpower Rivalry and Third World Radicalism: The Idea of National Liberation* (London: Croom Holm, 1985). See also the volume paralleling this one, edited by Robert Jervis and Jack Snyder, *Dominoes and Bandwagons: Strategic Beliefs of Great Power Competition in the Eurasian Rimland* (New York: Oxford University Press, 1991).

6. The larger Middle Eastern region that centers on the Arab-Israeli conflict is not considered here, since the Gulf system is itself reasonably distinct from the Arab-Israeli dynamic and since the former possesses so many unique characteristics, including the special relationship between the United States and Israel.

7. For a discussion of the growing risks and costs of external intervention, see Hedley Bull, ed., *Intervention in World Politics* (Oxford: Clarendon, 1984), esp. ch. 9, pp. 136–39. Saddam Husayn's adventure dramatized both points in 1990 and 1991.

8. The most useful recent study, based on similar assumptions, is that by Barry Buzan and Gowher Rizvi, *South Asian Insecurity,* esp. ch. 1. Our debt to their work is obvious throughout. Buzan calls such an interdependent cluster a "security complex" (p. 8). See also his *People, States, and Fear,* esp. ch. 4; working paper "The Logic of Anarchy: Neorealism Reconsidered," with Rizvi, Charles Jones, and Richard Little (1988); and "Regional Security" (Copenhagen: CPSR, 1989). Also see Raimo Vayrynen's "Regional Conflict Formations: An Intractable Problem of International Relations," *Journal of Peace Research,* 21(4) (1984):337–59; and Thomas P. Thornton, *Challenge to United States Policy in the Third World: Global Responsibilities and Regional Devolution* (Boulder, Colo.: SAIS, Westview, 1986). For earlier detailed discussions of regional analysis, see Louis J. Cantori and Steven L. Spiegel, *The International Politics of Regions: A Comparative Approach* (Englewood Cliffs, N.J.: Prentice-Hall, 1970); William R. Thompson, "The Regional Subsystem"; the important study originally commissioned by the Senate Foreign Relations Committee, by Lloyd and Susanne Rudolph, *The Regional Imperative* (Atlantic Highlands, N.J.: Humanities Press, 1980), which focused on South Asia; and the more inclusive edited

volume by Richard Falk and Saul H. Mendlovitz, eds., *Regional Politics and World Order* (San Francisco: Freeman, 1973). Also see Michael Brecher, "International Relations and Asian Studies: The Subordinate State System of Southern Asia," *World Politics,* 15(2) (1963):213–35; and Leonard Binder, "The Middle East as a Subordinate International System," *World Politics,* 10(3) (1958):408–29. Ferenc A Vali, *Politics of the Indian Ocean Region: The Balances of Power* (New York: Free Press, 1976) showed one way of approaching our set of regions.

9. W. T. R. Fox, "Theories of International Relations," in Fox, ed., *Theoretical Aspects of International Relations* (Notre Dame, Ind.: University of Notre Dame Press, 1959).

10. Kautilya's *Arthasastra,* a collection of statecraft "wisdom" essays, advised Chandragupta Maurya in the third century B.C. that neighbors were generally hostile and that reliable allies are to be found on the other side of one's neighbor—hence, the apothegm "my enemy's neighbor is my friend." R. Shamasastry, *Kautilya's Athasastra* (Mysore: Raghuveer, 1951). See also George Modelski, "Kautilya: Foreign Policy in the Ancient Hindu World," *American Political Science Review,* 58(3) (1964):549–60.

11. Karl Deutsch's discussion of a "security community" explicates the exceptional circumstances, exemplified earlier by the North Atlantic Community, *Political Community and the North Atlantic Area: International Organization in the Light of Historical Experience* (Princeton: Princeton University Press, 1957), 228 pp.

12. Waltz, *Theory,* p. 111.

13. Hedley Bull, *The Anarchical Society* (New York: Columbia University Press, 1977), p. 10. As Buzan put the same point, each region is made up of "states whose major security perceptions and concerns link them sufficiently closely that their national security problems cannot realistically be considered apart from one another" (1986):8.

14. Waltz provides a more thorough explication in *Theory,* ch. 6, "Anarchic Orders and Balances of Power." Thomas Schelling early discussed the problem of "interdependent decision" in *The Strategy of Conflict* (New York: Oxford University Press, 1963), ch. 4.

15. See Buzan et al., "The Logic of Anarchy: Neorealism Reconsidered," working paper (1988); also Robert Keohane, "Theory of World Politics: Structural Realism and Beyond," in his *International Institutions and State Power* (Boulder, Colo.: Westview, 1989), ch. 3.

16. For an analogous comparison, though assessed somewhat differently, see Buzan, "The Southeast Asian Security Complex," *Contemporary Southeast Asia,* vol. 10, no. 1 (June 1988); also see Jervis, "From Balance to Concert: A Study of International Security Cooperation," *World Politics,* 38(1) (October 1985):58–79.

17. Waltz, "Reflections on Theory of International Relations: A Response to My Critics," in R. Keohane, ed., *Neorealism and Its Critics* (New York: Columbia University Press, 1986), pp. 341–43.

18. Waltz, *Theory,* ch. 6; also Buzan et al., "Logic of Anarchy," pp. 26–29.

19. As elaborated by Jervis, "Security Regimes," *International Organization,* 36(2) (Spring 1982):357–78.

20. Brecher exaggerated the subordination; Binder stressed their autonomy. For a discussion, see Oren Young, "Political Discontinuities in the International System," *World Politics*, 20(3) (1968):369–92.

21. Buzan and Rizvi, *South Asian Insecurity*, p. 17.

22. For a discussion of this aspect, see, for example, Anita Inder Singh, "The Superpower Global Complex and South Asia," in Buzan and Rizvi, *South Asian Insecurity*, ch. 8; Karl Kaiser, "The Interaction of Regional Subsystems," *World Politics*, vol. 21, no. 1 (October 1968).

23. See, for instance, Ludwig Dehio, *The Precarious Balance: Four Centuries of the European Power Struggle* (New York: Vintage, 1962); Edward V. Gulick, *Europe's Classical Balance of Power* (New York: Norton, 1967); also see Waltz, *Theory*, ch. 6; Bull, *Anarchical Society*, ch. 5; Martin Wight, "The Balance of Power and International Order," in Alan James, ed., *The Bases of International Order: Essays in Honour of C. A. W. Manning* (London: Oxford University Press, 1973); and Arnold Wolfers, *Discord and Collaboration* (Baltimore: Johns Hopkins, 1962), ch. 8.

24. As Waltz put it, the theory of the anarchic international system "predicts that states will engage in balancing behavior, whether or not balanced power is the end of their acts" (*Theory*, ch. 6). Historical analyses confirm the utility of this proposition, as Dehio argues in *Precarious Balance*.

25. Stephen M. Walt, "Testing Theories of Alliance Formation: The Case of Southwest Asia," *International Organization*, 42(2) (Spring 1988):275–317; see also in Jervis and Snyder, *Dominoes and Bandwagons*.

26. See, for example, Surjit Mansingh, *India's Search for Power: Indira Gandhi's Foreign Policy, 1966–1982* (Beverly Hills: Sage, 1984), pp. 302–303.

27. John Herz, *Political Realism and Political Idealism* (Chicago: University of Chicago Press, 1959), p. 4; N. Spykman described the dilemma without giving it that name in his *America's Strategy in World Politics* (New York: Harcourt Brace, 1942), p. 24; Robert Jervis, *Perception*, pp. 75–76, 80, 82; also see "Cooperation Under the Security Dilemma," *World Politics*, 25(2) (1978):167–214; Glenn Snyder, "The Security Dilemma in Alliance Politics," *World Politics*, 36 (July 1984):461–95.

28. Jervis, "Cooperation," *World Politics*.

29. Joel Migdal, *Strong Societies and Weak States: State-Society Relations and State Capitalism in the Third World* (Princeton: Princeton University Press, 1988); Robert A. Jackson, *Quasi-States: Sovereignty, International Relations, and the Third World* (Cambridge: Cambridge University Press, 1990).

30. Avi Plascov, *Security in the Persian Gulf #3: Modernization, Political Development, and Stability* (London: Gower, for IISS, 1982), chs. 3, 4, 6; Zalmay Khalilzad in Zalmay Khalilzad, Timothy George, Robert Litwak, and S. Chubin, eds., *Security in Southern Asia* (New York: St. Martin's Press, 1984), pp. 60–84, 101. See also Wriggins, *Ruler's Imperative*, ch. 12.

31. Lucian Pye argues that most Asian governments emulate Asian societies' preference for paternalistic authority, as all power tends to be concentrated in the hands of one person. See his ambitious and controversial *Asian Power and Politics: The Cultural Dimensions of Authority* (Cambridge: Harvard University Press, 1986), esp. chs. 2 and 3.

32. The frontiers between Afghanistan and Pakistan, Bangladesh and India; Somalia, Ethiopia, and the Sudan; or Thailand, Kampuchea, and Vietnam have been more zones of movement than demarcated lines of effective separation. For Southeast Asia see Lim Jook-Jok, *Territorial Power Domains, Southeast Asia and China: The Geostrategy of an Overarching Massif* (Singapore: Institute of Southeast Asia Studies, 1985).

33. Maya Chadda, "Domestic Determinants of India's Foreign Policy in the 1980's," *Journal of South Asia and Middle East Studies*, 11(1 and 2) (Fall/Winter 1987):21–36, 25.

34. For a classic discussion of these and other possibilities, see Myron Weiner, "The Macedonian Syndrome: An Historical Model of International Relations and Political Development," *World Politics*, 23(4) (July 1971):665–83.

35. Zalmay Khalilzad has interesting hypotheses on how ethnic politics affects foreign policy making in these regions, in *Security in Southern Asia*, pp. 60–84 and particularly p. 101.

36. Bhabani Sen Gupta, *Ethno-Political Interstate Tensions and Conflicts in South Asia: Prognosis for the Next 15 Years* (New Delhi: Center for Policy Research, 1986), mimeo, pp. 50–59.

37. Buzan explores this problem in both working papers "Logic of Anarchy" (1988) and "Regional Security" (1989).

38. Point suggested by Ponna Wigneraja.

39. See Jack Snyder, "Richness, Rigor, and Relevance in the Study of Soviet Foreign Policy," *International Security*, vol. 9, no. 3 (Winter 1984–85).

2

Gulf Regional Politics: Revolution, War, and Rivalry

F. GREGORY GAUSE III

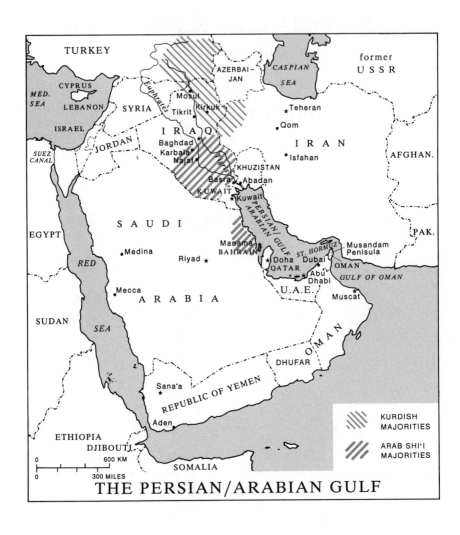

THE PERSIAN/ARABIAN GULF

Introduction

From the 1820s to 1971, the Persian-Arabian Gulf was a sleepy backwater of the British Empire that was rarely considered by global strategists.[1] Although Britain gradually ceded its predominance in the larger littoral countries (Saudi Arabia in the 1930s, Iran in the 1950s, Iraq in 1958), until 1971 it remained the formal protector of the smaller states and the dominant naval power. Kuwait became independent in 1961, with Bahrain, Qatar, the United Arab Emirates, and Oman following ten years later.

Ironically, just as Britain was giving up its formal role, the oil price boom dramatically affected both domestic and interstate politics in the region. International attention focused on the Gulf. The larger states now had the resources to build substantial military forces and to assert their right to be regional "policemen." The United States became much more involved in the region. Although the Soviet Union had always shown some interest in the region because of geographic proximity, that interest increased in response to American moves. Since 1971 the region has witnessed a revolution in oil pricing that shook the world economic system, a spiraling arms buildup, a domestic social revolution of great regional significance, a debilitating eight-year war between its two major powers, major commitments of U.S. naval and land forces, and a full-scale war between a regional power and an American-led international coalition.

In examining the action-reaction dynamics of the states in the Gulf, I first outline the major themes of the analysis and identify important continuities in the international structure and domestic political environment of the region. A thumbnail sketch of each of the regional players is followed by a brief account of the pre–1971 history. Subsequent sections examine in detail Gulf international politics during the 1971–78, 1979–88, and 1989–91 periods. I conclude by considering patterns of conflict and alignment among the regional states and major outside powers.

Patterns of Politics in the Gulf

The Gulf regional system encompasses Iran, Iraq, Saudi Arabia, and the five shaykhdoms on the Arab side of the Gulf—Kuwait, Bahrain, Qatar, United Arab Emirates, and Oman. This area has been profoundly affected by the actions of external powers drawn to it because of oil.

The *distribution of regional power* provides the context in which conflict and cooperation have occurred in the Gulf. Iran and Iraq, the two major powers in the region, have regularly vied for regional dominance. Their rivalry has been constant, but the level of hostility between them has varied from their relatively managed relationship of the late 1970s to all-out war in the 1980s. Saudi Arabia ranks third in power capabilities. It lacks the population and military resources to aspire to regional hegemony. Consequently, it has maneuvered between Iran and Iraq, shifting alignments to protect regime security and to maximize its freedom of action while working to maintain primacy among the smaller Arab shaykhdoms. The smaller states are linked to Saudi Arabia geographically and by similar domestic political systems, but they all (particularly Oman and pre–1990 Kuwait) have attempted to avoid an exclusive relationship with the Saudis by fostering ties with other regional and international powers. The regional power distribution therefore defines two sets of triangular relations within the Gulf—that of Iran, Iraq, and Saudi Arabia, aimed at regional predominance, and that of Saudi Arabia, the smaller Gulf states, and various other powers (including at times Iran, Iraq, Great Britain, and the United States), aimed at predominance on the Arab littoral of the Gulf.

The Balancing Process and Political-Ideological Threats

Examination of the patterns of conflict and alignment in these two triangles reveals the balancing process in operation. Conventional balance-of-power theory cannot adequately explain this process, because it holds that states balance against the potential rival that is strongest in terms of overall military capabilities. Balancing behavior has predominated in the Gulf, but it has not been against military power per se.[2] Gulf states are faced with numerous potential threats of various types.[3] Regimes have opposed and balanced against what they perceive to be the most serious threat to their domestic political stability, even if that meant aligning with another state whose military power could pose a future threat.[4] In the Gulf, two characteristics make political factors appear to local leaders as normally more consequential in security calculations than military capability. The first is the appeal of transnational ideologies in the region. Arab nationalist, Islamic, and separatist-nationalist (particularly Kurdish) political platforms have had ready audiences and have been used to deny the legitimacy of existing regimes and even, in extreme cases, of existing state entities. With these transnational ideologies one state can appeal directly to citizens in other states, over the heads of their governments, in an effort to extend its influence and destabilize other regimes.

The second reason for the importance of ideological-political threats in Gulf politics lies in the domestic political structures of the countries—societies divided along ethnic, sectarian, and regional lines and states still in the process of building administrative capacities and links to society. Ethnic and sectarian loyalties cut across existing state boundaries, in terms both of overarching Muslim and Arab identities and of subnational identifications. Other governments claiming to better represent their interests appeal to restive nationalist, sectarian, or class-based groups. Despite impressive state-building efforts in all the countries, financed by the enormous increase in oil revenues, the problems of suppressing opposition and, most important, of fostering a sense of political identity that could bind the ruled to the rulers continued to face all the states in the region during the period under study. Such domestic political challenges have been as important as those posed by disparities in military capabilities in driving regional international politics. Decisions on war and alliance made by Gulf states can be understood only in light of both kinds of threats.

Links Beyond the Gulf

All the Gulf states have at one time or another attempted to redress unfavorable local balances by aligning with actors outside the Gulf—other regional powers such as Egypt and Pakistan—and great powers beyond. Such ties, particularly with Western powers, were not risk-free, however, for they opened those states to charges of disloyalty to larger Arab and/or Islamic causes. Understandably, whenever possible, the monarchies preferred to keep their Western, especially their American, connections as inconspicuous as possible.

The causes and effects of superpower involvement in the region are a second major theme of this chapter. The roles of the Soviet Union and the United States need to be examined as both *cause* and *effect*. They are causes in that their policy decisions helped determine the outcome of regional conflicts and crises. However, superpower policies are also affected and constrained by regional events over which they have little control, like the Iranian revolution and the Iraqi invasion of Kuwait. Local states sought superpower assistance to further their own interests, not those of the superpower. The agenda of the region was set locally; the superpowers responded to it; those responses at least partially determined the course of regional politics.

Both superpowers had enduring and specific interests in the Gulf. The primary American aim has been the free flow of oil at bearable prices to the industrialized world. To that end the United States has supported friendly local states and opposed the domination of the region by any state, superpower or local power, considered hostile. The Soviets shared a long and at times troubled border with Iran; their goal was to prevent the United States from bringing the area under its exclusive control. The pattern of Soviet and American involvement in the Gulf has changed as their global relationship has changed. Rivalry, driven by the global superpower competition, characterized their relations most of the time, even during periods of détente. With the collapse of Soviet power in Eastern Europe and the worsening of its domestic crises, Moscow's ability to challenge Washington in the Gulf came to an end. During the Iraq-Kuwait crisis of 1990–91, the Soviets followed the American lead and supported the international coalition against Saddam Husayn. That stance, however, proved to be among the last international acts of the now defunct Soviet state.

The Role of Oil

A final theme is oil and its effects on the domestic and regional politics of the Gulf. Each of the Gulf states is an oil state. The region accounts for 25.4 percent of world oil production (1990 average) and 62.5 percent of world oil reserves (as of 1988).[5] Outsiders, particularly the United States, are interested in the region because of oil. The states in the region became attractive allies for outside powers for the same reason. Oil also gave the Gulf states greater bargaining power in their relations with great power allies, permitting them a measure of autonomy they had not enjoyed before the price revolution of 1973–74.

Oil revenues permitted the major states to acquire large and sophisticated arsenals, and in the cases of Iran and Iraq, to increase vastly the size of their military establishments. Such new-found sources of power tempted ambitious leaders like the shah and Saddam Husayn to assert their ambitions for regional dominance. Oil exacerbated the security dilemma in the Gulf, encouraging grandiose dreams and heightening the risks of miscalculation in dealing with one's neighbors. However, it did not give any of the three major regional states an enormous advantage over the others. The oil boom of the 1970s and 1980s also allowed the states to develop extensive bureaucracies, which both distributed benefits to citizens and exercised an unprecedented degree of control over their lives. That does not ensure domestic political stability, as the shah of Iran discovered, but it does give regimes more tools with which to govern their societies. Although challenged by transnational ideological and political appeals, the regimes became better prepared to meet them than they had been in the past. This tension between increasing state strength and powerful sub- and suprastate appeals for political loyalty marks the entire period under study.

The States of the Region

Each of the countries of the region brings particular strengths to the contest for power and security and suffers from specific weaknesses that its enemies have attempted to exploit.[6]

Iran

Iran is the second-largest (in terms of area) and the most populous country in the Gulf, with a population of fifty-two million people. Although approximately three-quarters of that population are of Persian or other Iranic nationalities, there are significant ethnic and linguistic minorities. Turkic peoples make up over 15 percent of the Iranian population, mostly concentrated in the area in the northwest corner of the country called Azerbaijan. Kurds make up less than 5 percent of the population but are concentrated in the north-central area on the Iraqi-Iranian border, across from their fellow Kurds in Iraq. Arabs also constitute less than 5 percent of the population, although Arabic speakers make up a majority of the population of Khuzistan, in the southwestern corner of the country. The vast majority of Iranians are Shi'i Muslims, although there are some Sunni minorities in the eastern part of the country.

Iran is a major exporter of oil, although its oil reserves are not nearly as large as those of Saudi Arabia, Iraq, or even Kuwait. Its daily production capacity is now less than one-half that of Saudi Arabia and is about equal to that of Iraq, although through the 1970s Iranian daily production was greater than that of Iraq. Iranian oil money, however, must be spread over many more people than in the Arab states of the Gulf, and its per capita income is therefore the lowest in the area, probably less than $2,000.[7]

Persian political entities and identity go back millennia. Iranians are very conscious of the historical, racial, and linguistic separation between them and their Gulf neighbors, who are all Arab. At the beginning of the period under study Iran was ruled by the Pahlavi monarchy, which itself had come to power only in the early twentieth century. The Iranian revolution of 1978–79 brought down the monarchy, which was replaced by the Islamic Republican regime of Ayatollah Ruhallah Khumayni.

Iraq

Iraq is the second-largest state in the Gulf, and the largest Arab state, in terms of population (over nineteen million, which before 1990 was supplemented by around two million Arab, mostly Egyptian, migrant workers). It is the third largest in terms of area, although strategically it has been limited by its very short Gulf coastline. The population of Iraq is about 80 percent Arab and 15 percent Kurdish, with the Kurds concentrated in the mountainous northeastern part of the country. The Arab population is divided along sectarian lines; over half of the total population is Shi'i (the Kurds are mostly Sunni). The Arab Shi'a are concentrated in the southern half of the country, from Baghdad south along the Tigris and Euphrates rivers to the Gulf coast.

Iraq has enormous oil reserves, and, unlike Iran, can count on being a major oil exporter well into the next century. Like Iran, and unlike the other Gulf states, it has both a sufficiently large home market and other resources (such as water) to have a more diversified economy, although oil still plays the major economic role. As in Iran, estimates of Iraqi economic strength differ. The 1989 GDP was probably somewhere between $40 billion and $58 billion, yielding a per capita income between $2,100 and $3,050.[8] The massive damage done to the country's economic infrastructure during the allied military campaign of 1991 has not yet shown up in the figures.

Since 1968 Iraq has been under single-party rule. The Ba'th party, an Arab nationalist and socialist party, has adjusted its ideological platform since it came to power to emphasize a more specific sense of Iraqi nationalism. The crisis surrounding the invasion of Kuwait has led the regime to renew its emphasis on the Arab nationalist aspects of its ideology, however. President Saddam Husayn has been a major force in the Iraqi Ba'th since the 1950s, assuming the presidency in 1979. The Ba'th's rule has been characterized both by extremely ruthless internal security measures to suppress dissent and by substantial economic development, at least until 1990.

Saudi Arabia

The kingdom of Saudi Arabia is the largest country in the Gulf region, with a land area about one-fourth the size of the United States. Most of the country is desert, and its population is extremely small for its size, although it is the second most populous Arab state in the Gulf. Population estimates vary, and the government's official figures are considered very high. A reasonable guess would put the total population at ten to twelve million, including two to four million foreign workers and their families.[9] The entire citizen population of the kingdom is Arab, and over 90 percent Sunni. The Shi'i population is centered in the oil-producing Eastern Province, on the Gulf coast.

Oil is the basis of the Saudi economy, and Saudi Arabia has the largest proven oil reserves in the world. It can produce approximately 10 million barrels of oil per day, although in recent years it has usually kept its production much lower than that, to help maintain prices. Its 1989 estimated GDP was $79 billion, which yields a per capita GDP of between $6,600 and $7,900.

Historically, the Arabian peninsula has been hostile to centralized rule. The founder of modern Saudi Arabia, King ʿAbd al-ʿAziz Al Saʿud, brought the territories within the current boundaries under his control between 1901 and 1934, using a mixture of military force, adept tribal politics, religious ideology, and skillful international diplomacy. Since that time oil revenues have helped link the far-flung kingdom and overcome many of the centrifugal forces that had been at work in Arabia. The current king, King Fahd, is one of ʿAbd al-ʿAziz's sons, as are Crown Prince ʿAbdallah and the next in line after him, Defense Minister Prince Sultan.

Kuwait

Kuwait, which received its independence from Britain in 1961, had a population of about two million in 1990, less than one-half of which were Kuwaiti citizens. Of that citizen population, all were Arab, and about 75 percent were Sunni. The largest group of expatriate residents were Palestinians. Since the Iraqi invasion and subsequent liberation of the country, the future population structure, in terms of citizenship and the number and composition of the foreign community, has been a subject of intense debate. Kuwait's economy is based on oil and the revenues derived from investments made with oil revenues. Its 1989 GDP was $23 billion, with a per capita rate of approximately $11,500. The Al Sabah family provides the hereditary amirs (princes) of Kuwait, although their rule is circumscribed by a powerful coterie of old merchant families, who consider themselves the social equals of the Al Sabah, and by the only active parliamentary tradition on the Arab side of the Gulf. Parliament was closed by the rulers in 1986 because of the pressures of the Iran-Iraq war, but popular agitation in 1990 led the Al Sabah to promise to reopen it. In the wake of the war, political tensions between the ruling family and political forces seeking a return to representative institutions resurfaced.

Bahrain

Bahrain received its independence from Britain in 1971. It has a population of approximately 500,000, including at least 100,000 expatriates. Seventy percent of the citizen population is Shiʿi, although the ruling shaykhs, from the Al Khalifa family, are Sunni. Bahrain is the first post-oil economy in the Gulf, for most of its oil reserves have run dry.

However, the country planned for this decades ago by developing industry (aluminum smelting, oil refining, shipbuilding) and by encouraging the service and financial sectors of its economy. It had a 1989 GDP of $3.9 billion (per capita, $7,800).

Qatar

Qatar received its independence from Britain in 1971. It has a population of approximately 420,000, less than one-half of which are citizens (probably closer to one-quarter). Its citizen population is nearly 85 percent Sunni and around 15 percent Shi'i. The ruling Al Thani family is Sunni and professes the same Wahhabi interpretation of Islam as the Al Sa'ud in Saudi Arabia. The state's 1989 GDP was $5.4 billion, for an amazing per capita income of over $17,000.

United Arab Emirates

The United Arab Emirates (UAE) is a federation of seven shaykhdoms: Abu Dhabi, Dubai, Sharjah (al-Shariqa), Ra's al-Khayma, Fujayra, 'Um al-Qaywayn, and 'Ajman. The federation received its independence from Britain in 1971. Its population is approximately 1.7 million, of which about one-fourth are citizens (the remainder, as in all the Gulf states, being a mixture of Westerners, South Asians, other Arabs, and a small number of expatriate Iranians). Of the citizen population, over 80 percent are Sunni and somewhat under 20 percent are Shi'i. The UAE economy, based almost exclusively on oil but also including a thriving reexport trade based at Dubai, had a 1989 GDP of $26 billion (approximately $15,300 per capita). The political structure of the federation is loose, with the shaykhs of the individual states preserving a large amount of autonomy. For example, the shaykh of Dubai does not feel bound by the oil production quota obligations assumed by the central government in OPEC negotiations. The president of the federation, and its guiding force since inception, is the shaykh of Abu Dhabi, Za'id ibn Sultan Al Nahayan.

Oman

The sultanate of Oman has a rich history as a commercial empire, extending its sway in the seventeenth century to Zanzibar and the east African coast. From the mid-nineteenth century until 1971 it was a British protectorate. It has an estimated population of 1.5 million, almost all citizens, and the largest land area of any of the smaller Gulf states. It controls the Arab side of the Strait of Hormuz, leading into the Gulf. Most of the population in Oman profess the Ibadi sect of Islam, a

TABLE 2.1
Elements of State Capability Compared—1989

	Population (thousands)	Military Forces (thousands)	GDP (bil. U.S. $)	Military Expend. (bil. U.S. $)	Mil. Exp as % of GDP
Iran	52,000	504	100	9.9	9.9
Iraq	19,000	1,000	58	12.9	22.2
Saudi Arabia	6,000–10,000 citizens	102	79	14.7	18.6
Kuwait	1,000 citizens	20	23	1.5	6.5
Bahrain	400 citizens	6	3.9	.2	5.1
Qatar	200 citizens	7.5	5.4	.15	2.7
UAE	400 citizens	44	26	1.5	5.8
Oman	1,500	29.5	8.4	1.4	16.7

SOURCE: International Institute for Strategic Studies, *The Military Balance 1990–91*, except for Saudi population and Iranian GDP figures.

branch of the Kharijite movement (neither Sunni nor Shi'i), although there are no current political or religious differences between the Ibadis and the minority Sunnis. Oil was discovered in Oman much later than in the rest of the Gulf, and agriculture is still an important part of the economy. It had a 1989 GDP of $8.4 billion (per capita $5,600). Sultan Qabus ibn Sa'id Al Bu Sa'id, who replaced his reactionary father in 1970, has promoted economic development and a more open policy toward the outside world.

The Gulf Before 1971: British Role and Enduring Structures

Great Britain's involvement in the Gulf was rooted in the imperial strategy of protecting India. Gulf "piracy" disrupted the India trade; a hostile power in control of the Gulf could cut the Suez Canal-India lifeline. Beginning in the 1820s Britain imposed a perpetual maritime truce on the shaykhdoms of the Arab littoral (from which they became known in English as the "Trucial States") aimed at ending such "piracy." Gradually, Britain assumed more responsibilities in the Gulf shaykhdoms, keeping the peace among them, supporting the ruling families against internal political challenges, and protecting them from the periodic pressures mounted by the Saudi dynasty of central Arabia. In exchange, the shaykhs entrusted to Britain the management of their foreign policy and acquiesced in considerable British influence in their domestic and commercial affairs. 'Abd al-'Aziz ibn Sa'ud, the founder of modern Saudi Arabia, avoided this kind of formal submission to Britain, but British power circumscribed the extent of his territorial acquisitions, and his relations with London were central to his foreign policy.

Although they did not enjoy similar legal status on the Iranian side of the Gulf, the British were actively involved in the politics of the declining Qajar Persian Empire. In 1907 they formally agreed to divide Persia into spheres of influence with tsarist Russia, securing a free hand along the Gulf littoral. Although this arrangement was superseded by the Russian Revolution and the subsequent replacement of the Qajar by the Pahlavi dynasty in what is now called Iran, London retained substantial influence in the domestic politics and foreign policy of the country.[10] Britain completed its "encirclement" of the Gulf after World War I, when it acquired the newly created state of Iraq, carved out of the defunct Ottoman Empire, as a mandate from the League of Nations.

During the first decades of the twentieth century, the Gulf became increasingly important to the British because of its oil. Oil was discovered in Iran in 1908, with the Anglo-Persian oil company (later to become British Petroleum) founded to exploit it the next year. As the British fleet was converting from coal to oil, in 1914 the British government acquired a majority share in the company. British interest in Iraqi oil predated the mandate, and in 1927 the British-controlled Iraq Petroleum Company made a major find in northern Iraq. British Petroleum shared control of the Kuwait Oil Company (which began producing oil on a large scale in 1946) with Gulf Oil of the United States, and a subsidiary of the Iraq Petroleum Company developed the oil resources of Abu Dhabi, Dubai, and Qatar after World War II. Strong economic and strategic reasons for continued British involvement in the Gulf continued after the withdrawal from India in 1947.[11]

Yet even at the height of British power London could not completely monopolize the Gulf area. Tsarist Russia was the dominant power in northern Iran until its collapse, and the Soviet Union made efforts after both world wars to reestablish itself there. Britain invited the French national oil company to take a one-quarter interest in the Iraq Petroleum Company to avoid more acrimony in their division of the post–World War I Middle East. American oil companies won lucrative concessions in Saudi Arabia and Bahrain in the 1930s from their British competitors. After World War II, British dominance in the region steadily faded. London gave up the effort to compete with the United States for influence in Saudi Arabia. Both the Soviet pressure on Iran in 1946 and the Mussadiq crisis of 1951–53 found the British unable to meet the test alone, and they were forced to invite Washington to take a larger role in Iran. By the mid–1950s the United States had supplanted Britain as the shah's primary foreign patron. The 1958 Iraqi revolution, which saw the violent overthrow of Britain's client, the Hashemite monarchy, ended Britain's extraordinary influence there.

Although the British acknowledged that the Empire was on the wane elsewhere, they maintained their privileged position in the Gulf, now anchored in the protectorate states of the Arab side. Kuwait negotiated its independence in 1961 but relied on British forces to stave off an immediate Iraqi claim to the new state. Even while they were withdrawing from the Aden colony at the southern tip of the Arabian Peninsula in 1967, the British reaffirmed their intention to remain in the Gulf. There were no serious manifestations of anti-British feeling in the remaining protectorates; the ruling families there were very happy to remain under British protection. Moreover, the only outside power that could challenge that position, the United States, encouraged the British to stay. Yet suddenly in 1968, as a result of domestic financial pressures and parliamentary politics, Prime Minister Harold Wilson was forced to end Britain's imperial presence in the Gulf.[12]

Although the British withdrawal initiated a new strategic era in the Gulf, some aspects of the post–1971 strategic situation had crystallized in the twenty-five years after World War II. Iran and Iraq had settled into a basically hostile relationship. Border issues, particularly over the Shatt al-Arab—the confluence of the Tigris and Euphrates rivers that forms the southernmost part of the border—remained a steady irritant and a barometer of the bilateral relationship. The intensity of hostility between the two states, however, fluctuated, depending on domestic political developments in each country. During the rule of the British-supported Hashemites in Iraq the border issue was held in abeyance and the two monarchies even entered into short-lived military alliances (the Sa'dabad Pact of 1937; the Baghdad Pact of 1954). In both 1958 and 1968 violent coups in Iraq brought regimes to power that espoused republican, Pan-Arab, and pro-Soviet policies, which were anathema to the shah's monarchical, Iranian nationalist, and pro-Western orientation. Tensions between the two countries, including the revival of border disputes, escalated after these two regime changes. In 1969 the outbreak of war seemed imminent, as Iranian troops moved toward the border. Iraq requested Turkey to mediate, and the immediate crisis passed, but Iranian-Iraqi relations were very tense as the British withdrawal occurred.[13]

Another pattern of regional politics established prior to the British withdrawal was the uneasy relationship between Saudi Arabia and the smaller shaykhdoms of the Arab side of the Gulf. Unlike the Iran-Iraq relationship, ideological differences were not involved. The Saudis supported the monarchies in the smaller states, even if they might oppose particular leaders in them. However, Riyadh sought to assert its primacy over them in the realms of foreign policy and border adjustments. An outstanding example was the Buraymi Oasis dispute of the 1950s. Saudi Arabia claimed sovereignty over Buraymi, which lies along what is now the Oman-UAE border in the southeastern corner of the peninsula. Arbitration efforts in the early 1950s collapsed, and troops led by

British officers from Oman and Abu Dhabi forcibly removed a Saudi police detachment from the area in 1955. The Saudis maintained their claim to the area and even supported tribal forces in Oman rebelling against the British-supported sultan. With the departure of the British, the shaykhdoms would lose their protector against Saudi demands and have to develop a new working relationship with Riyadh. British withdrawal also allowed revival of the Iraqi claim to Kuwait and the Iranian claim to Bahrain.

Finally, the basic superpower alignments that characterized the Gulf in the 1970s had been formed in the previous decades. The United States had developed very close relations with both Saudi Arabia and Iran after World War II. Standard Oil Company of California (Socal) had signed an oil concession with the Saudi government in 1933 and later brought in the Texas Oil Company (Texaco) as a partner in its Arabian subsidiary, the Arabian-American Oil Company (Aramco). Discoveries were made before World War II, but major production and export did not begin until the late 1940s. Washington's interest in Saudi oil was strong, and in 1948, with government encouragement, Standard Oil of New Jersey (now Exxon) and Standard Oil of New York (Mobil) bought into Aramco, solidifying American access to the constantly growing Saudi oil reserves.

Interest in Saudi oil led naturally to an interest in the stability of the Saudi regime. The U.S. Air Force established an airbase at Dhahran in the oil-rich Eastern Province during World War II (which was turned over to the Saudi government in 1961). In 1950 Washington altered the tax code for American corporations operating abroad, allowing them to write off foreign tax liabilities against their U.S. taxes. This change had the intended effect of permitting the Aramco partners to pay much higher royalties to the Saudi government and deducting them from their U.S. tax bill, an indirect transfer of funds from the U.S. Treasury to the Saudi regime.[14]

The U.S. commitment to Iran grew out of its strategic location on the southern border of the Soviet Union. Soviet efforts in 1946 to set up client states in the Iranian provinces of Azerbaijan and Kurdistan were one of the first incidents in the Cold War, and the United States supported Iran with diplomatic pressure on Moscow and small amounts of military aid. Washington became more deeply involved in Iranian affairs during the prolonged crisis between the shah and Prime Minister Mussadiq in 1951–53 over the nationalization of the Anglo-Iranian Oil Company. Fearing that a victory by Mussadiq would increase Communist influence in Iran, President Eisenhower ordered the CIA to become involved in a covert plot that unseated Mussadiq and returned the shah to power in Teheran. Following that, U.S. military and economic aid to the shah's government increased, and Washington encouraged American oil companies to join British Petroleum in a new international oil consortium for Iran. Iran joined the Baghdad Pact (later to become the Central Treaty Organization) in 1955, and in 1959 a bilateral Iranian-American agreement was signed committing the United States to come to the aid of Iran in case of aggression.[15]

Soviet involvement in the region before 1971 was much less sustained than that of the United States. The pressure asserted on Iran after World War II backfired, pushing Teheran toward close relations with the United States. Saudi Arabia refused to permit the Soviet Union to establish an embassy in the kingdom. Only with the 1958 Iraqi revolution could the Soviets play more of a role in the Gulf region. The first president of republican Iraq, ʿAbd al-Karim Qasim, looked to the Soviet Union and local Communists for support in his quarrels with Iran, with Nasir's Egypt, and with local Iraqi Nasirists. Qasim's fall in 1963 ended this round of close Iraqi-Soviet relations, but the coup of 1968, which brought the Baʿth party to power, led to renewed cooperation between the two countries.

Thus, as the British withdrew from the Gulf in 1971 (something of an exaggeration, as British political and military influence remained high in Oman and the UAE), some of the patterns of regional politics were set. The United States was aligned with Iran and Saudi Arabia; the Soviet Union, with Iraq. Iranian-Iraqi hostility was obvious, as was the Saudi desire to dominate the newly independent Gulf shaykhdoms (including Kuwait). However, an entirely new set of issues was introduced: How would the Iranian-Iraqi contest over which should be the "policeman" of the Gulf work itself out? Where would Saudi Arabia fit into that contest? Would the shaykhdoms look to Iran and/or Iraq as a counterinfluence to Saudi Arabia? Would either or both of the superpowers seek to "fill the vacuum" left by the British? These tensions would be played out in the context of increased resources available to each of the Gulf states, as profound changes in the world oil market occurred just as the British withdrew.

Regional Politics in the Gulf: 1971–78

The Fate of the Protected Shaykhdoms

The immediate question to be addressed on the British withdrawal was the political status of the nine shaykhdoms (Bahrain, Qatar, and the seven members of the United Arab Emirates) still under formal British protection and their relations to the major regional powers. (It was generally acknowledged that Oman would become an independent state and retain a close political and security relationship with Britain.) British diplomats worked to affiliate all nine into a single independent state. This effort soon faltered over the distribution of power among them. Bahrain, the most populous, demanded that proportional representation govern the institutions of the new state; the others argued for a federal structure that would equalize power among the member states.

The federation project was further complicated by the positions of the regional powers, as it became the first test of influence in the new Gulf order. Iran immediately revived its claim to Bahrain, based on pre-eighteenth-century Persian control of the island and backed up by the fact that a large majority of the island's residents, although Arab, are Shi'i. Saudi Arabia quickly expressed its support for Bahrain and the concept of federation, but it also pressed its border claims regarding the Buraymi oasis against Abu Dhabi.[16] Britain and the United States encouraged Riyadh and Teheran to compose their differences and adopt a joint approach to Gulf security. This mediation was successful, as in October 1968 the two countries settled rival claims to isolated islands in the upper Gulf and agreed to a demarcation of their offshore oil rights. The shah visited Riyadh a month later as a symbol of the two sides' commitment to security coordination.

Although no formal arrangements were announced at this meeting, the subsequent course of events indicates that an understanding was reached on the post–1971 Gulf order. In January 1969 the shah dropped the Iranian claim to Bahrain, in effect recognizing the primacy of Saudi influence in the shaykhdoms. However, he remained insistent that Iran assume control over three small islands near the Strait of Hormuz—Abu Musa, Greater Tunbs, and Lesser Tunbs. The first was under the jurisdiction of Sharjah; the latter two were under that of Ra's al-Khaymah. On November 30, 1971, the day before the formal end of British protection of the shaykhdoms, Iranian forces landed on all three islands. While not publicly endorsing the action, both Britain and Saudi Arabia quietly acquiesced as the price for Iranian cooperation in larger security issues. The islands were of questionable strategic value, but the shah's insistence on forcibly occupying them symbolized his self-proclaimed role of "policeman" of the Gulf. With resignation and some trepidation, Riyadh agreed to the junior role in its de facto alliance with Teheran as the only practical way to secure stability in the Gulf and win Iranian acceptance of Saudi primacy on the Arab littoral.[17]

With the informal Saudi-Iranian security understanding in place, the political status of the shaykhdoms could be settled. Both Bahrain and Qatar opted for independence as separate states. The other seven shaykhdoms federated in the United Arab Emirates (UAE), under the leadership of the two richest members, Abu Dhabi and Dubai.[18] Although King Faysal gave his blessings to the new UAE, he withheld diplomatic recognition until 1974, when the Buraymi dispute was finally settled. The Saudis gave up their claim to the area, but in exchange the UAE recognized Saudi claims to a small stretch of land on the Gulf that separates Qatar from the UAE and to some sections of the western part of the Abu Dhabi shaykhdom.[19]

The Iran-Iraq-Saudi Triangle

While Saudi Arabia and Iran were coming to a strategic understanding, the other major regional power, Iraq, was largely engrossed in other matters. Six months after the British announcement of its intention to withdraw, a coup in Baghdad brought the Ba'th party back to power, a position it had held briefly in 1963, before being shunted aside by the military regime of 'Abd al-Rahman 'Arif. Consolidating its position was complicated by both regional and domestic pressures. As discussed earlier, the regime change in Iraq was followed almost immediately by a serious crisis with Iran over the disputed border. The new regime was also faced in 1969 by a renewal of armed rebellion in the Kurdish areas of northern Iraq, supported by the shah's regime and eventually by the United States and Israel. Though Baghdad was consumed by these more immediate issues, it did try to affect developments in the Gulf. Iraq pressed the case for Arab solidarity against Iran and proposed that the Arab states of the Gulf join in a security pact. However, as Baghdad also expressed hostility to what it considered the "reactionary" Arab monarchical regimes of the region allied to "imperialist" powers, it is not surprising that they did not rally to Baghdad's call.

Left out of the regional security arrangement reached by Iran and Saudi Arabia, Iraq broke diplomatic relations with both Iran and Great Britain in November 1971 over the Gulf islands issue and attempted to rally Arab and world opinion against Iran. Propaganda and subversion against the Arab monarchs continued, as Iraq supported opposition efforts mounted by local Ba'thist groups and the Popular Front for the Liberation of the Occupied Arab Gulf (PFLOAG). In January 1972 the shaykh of Sharjah, who had ceded Abu Musa island to the shah, was killed in a coup attempt linked to Iraq. UAE forces intervened to ensure the succession of the shaykh's brother. In March 1973 Iraqi troops, which had been stationed on Kuwaiti territory since the 1969 border crisis with Iran, occupied a Kuwaiti border post. The Ba'thist regime demanded that Kuwait cede to it the islands of Warba and Bubiyan, which control access to the Iraqi port of 'Um al-Qasr. Saudi troops were dispatched to Kuwait, Iran expressed its support, and the Soviet Union apparently urged Baghdad to be cautious. The Iraqis agreed to negotiate, after what was rumored to be a Kuwaiti commitment of financial aid, although the border issue was not settled and Iraqi troops did not leave the area until July 1977.[20]

External Powers

Despite talk in Washington of "filling the vacuum" left by the British, neither superpower assumed the mantle of "policeman of the Gulf." The United States, which might have been able to take on such a role with some measure of regional support, was too preoccupied with Vietnam to consider any new military commitments. Moreover, Washington's major regional ally, Iran, intended to play policeman itself and did not welcome an increased American presence. It is not certain that the Soviet Union, still in the process of building up its navy, had the means to play a major role, and Moscow faced serious regional constraints. Only Iraq would have been sympathetic to a major Soviet security role in the Gulf, and its access to the Gulf was limited geographically.

Immediately ruling out increased direct involvement, the United States looked to regional allies to ensure the stability and security of the Gulf. This was in keeping with the "Nixon Doctrine" policy of supporting local proxies to limit the growth of Soviet influence and avoiding direct American military commitments in the Third World. American policymakers focused on Iran as the best candidate and an arms supply relationship as the best way to promote that candidacy. Total American military transfers to Iran increased from $103.6 million in 1970 to $475 million in 1971 and $552.7 million in 1972. Although American grant-in-aid to Iran was eliminated as a result of the shah's growing oil revenues, the United States gave Teheran highly preferential terms for the purchase of weapons, including $220 million in Export–Import Bank credits in 1970 and 1971 for advanced F–4E Phantom fighter-bombers. In May 1972, on a visit to Iran, President Nixon personally authorized the sale of F–14 and F–15 aircraft to the shah's regime and, in the words of Henry Kissinger, "added the proviso that in the future Iranian requests should not be second-guessed."[21] Far from being concerned about increases in the world price of oil in the 1970–73 period, officials in Washington were pleased that Iran could now fund, without direct American aid, the military role envisaged for it.

While general strategists in Washington pushed Iran as regional proxy in the Gulf, those in the State Department concerned with Arab affairs were suspicious of Iranian motives and worried about the prospects of Saudi-Iranian tensions. American diplomats played a mediating role in bringing the Saudis and the shah together in a general understanding on regional security. The United States also increased military sales to Saudi Arabia, in dollar amounts much smaller than the Iranian sales, but higher in terms of percentage increase: $15.8 million in 1970,

$81.7 million in 1971, and $312.4 million in 1972. Part of the American commitment to Saudi Arabia was a long-term program to expand the tiny Saudi navy and its shore facilities. An undercurrent of rivalry characterized the Saudi-Iranian relationship during this period, and Saudi military purchases were as much a reaction to the Iranian buildup as to any other threat. American policymakers, having settled on a Gulf policy by 1970, were very careful not to slight the Saudis in their enthusiasm for Iran as regional proxy. The "twin-pillar" aspect of U.S. policy was always emphasized in public, although clearly the Iranian "pillar" was intended in Washington to bear the greater weight of regional military responsibility.[22]

Iraq, alarmed at the military buildup of its two regional rivals and the American commitment that implied, turned to the Soviet Union to bolster its position. Soviet naval forces paid a publicized visit to the Iraqi ports of Basra and Umm al-Qasr in May 1968, before the Baʿthist coup, and followed it with a number of visits in the late 1960s and early 1970s. Between 1969 and 1971 Baghdad and Moscow signed agreements on economic cooperation, the joint development of oil resources in Iraq, and peaceful nuclear cooperation. In April 1972 Iraq and the Soviet Union signed a fifteen-year treaty of friendship and cooperation. Thus, by 1972, the regional alignments that emerged from the process of British withdrawal were solidified by the involvement of the superpowers.

Regional Effects of the Oil Boom

The maneuverings surrounding the British withdrawal from the Gulf occurred while the balance of power in the world oil market was shifting from the consumer nations and their oil companies to the producer governments. A series of unilateral moves and multilateral conferences between June 1970 and June 1973 led to an increase both in the price of Gulf oil (from $1.27 per barrel in 1969 to $2.80 in June 1973) and in the percentage of the sale price retained by the producer government. Despite this increase, world demand continued to rise, setting the stage for the even greater increases following the 1973 oil embargo.[23]

The revenues to the Gulf states that resulted from these increases during the early 1970s, although nowhere near the windfalls they would enjoy after 1973, had a number of international political consequences. First, they smoothed the transition to independence for the smaller states. General prosperity helped reduce social tensions in Bahrain, where the Sunni ruling house was governing a Shiʿi majority. Oil-rich Abu Dhabi was able to maintain the loyalty of the poorer shaykhdoms to the UAE through the judicious use of formal redistribution mechanisms and informal side payments. The stability of the shaykhdoms reduced the opportunities for meddling in their domestic politics by the larger regional powers, and thus the chances of confrontations among them.[24]

Second, the increase in oil revenues allowed the three major regional states to engage in a frantic and fantastic arms buildup, which would continue through the 1970s and, in a different form, to the present. This acquisition of large amounts of sophisticated weaponry might have played some deterrent role during the 1970s, raising the costs of conflict among the regional powers. It was only after the Iranian revolution, when Iran had deliberately isolated itself from its major arms supplier and decimated its officer corps, that Iraq launched its war against Iran. It is clear that the shah's military buildup, which to some extent drove that of the other powers, was deliberately intended to consolidate Iran's role as the dominant political force in the region. However, much of that buildup reflects two other processes not directly related to a rational calculation of power balancing and security needs.

One is the psychological spiral built into potentially hostile international relationships that scholars have termed the "security dilemma": A state's leaders frequently assume both that military preparations made by another country are for offensive use and that its own military moves are clearly understood by all others to be defensive. This kind of reasoning contributes to arms races like the one that occurred in the Gulf in the 1970s. The other process is that of bureaucratic politics. Here demands by military organizations on the budget arise not only from objective security needs but also from more domestic political imperatives: inter- and intraservice rivalries, empire building and pocket lining by the leaders, maintenance of large patron-client networks with local businesses and social groups. Bureaucratic politics becomes especially important when potential political rivals control different military organizations. This has been the case in Saudi Arabia, where Crown Prince ʿAbdallah has headed the National Guard and Prince Sultan, who stands behind him in the line of succession, has been minister of defense.

The third consequence of the oil boom was to give the major regional powers some independence from their superpower patrons. Oil could be bargained with, at least during the 1970s; arms could be bought with hard currency, rather than received as aid from an outside donor. The manifestations of that autonomy are obvious. Iran made it very clear to Britain and the United States that it intended to assume primary security responsibility for the Gulf and would not welcome either a continued British or an augmented American role. It was Iran, in late 1973 and early 1974, that took the lead in driving oil prices up to $11.65 per barrel, by holding an oil auction in December 1973 at the height of the supply squeeze from the Arab oil embargo. Iran, with limited oil reserves, a very large population, and a seemingly unlimited

appetite for military hardware, sought to maximize current prices regardless of long-term effects on global demand. The shah remained a
leader of the "price hawks" in OPEC, despite American demands for
stable prices at lower levels.

Iraq also displayed more independence from its superpower patron,
the Soviet Union. Hard currency freed Baghdad from its sole reliance
on Soviet military supplies. Iraq looked to Western sources, particularly
France, to help upgrade its military. Symbolically, the Iraqis also sought
to distance themselves from Moscow, vehemently criticizing the Soviet
invasion of Afghanistan in December 1979 and seeking to play a high-
profile role in the Nonaligned Movement.

The Saudi assertion of autonomy from the United States was the
most spectacular of the three cases—the oil embargo of 1973–74. The
Saudis were willing to put their American connection at risk to support
Egypt and Syria in their October 1973 war with Israel because of the
changes in inter-Arab politics. Both Anwar al-Sadat and Hafiz al-'Asad
had reversed their predecessors' policy of hostility toward Riyadh, giving the Saudis an important stake in their success. On October 17, as the
tide of the battle in the Arab-Israeli war was turning against Egypt and
Syria, all the Arab oil producers save Iraq agreed to cut oil production
by 5 percent per month until Israel evacuated the occupied territories.
On October 20, Riyadh announced an embargo on the shipment of
Saudi oil to the United States.

The production cut, some have argued, was necessary to support the
increase to $5.12 per barrel imposed by the producer states on October
16, and the war was just a convenient pretext to justify the cut. It is also
clear that the Saudi embargo had only marginal consequences for oil
supply, since the international oil companies juggled their sources of
supply to meet contractual obligations. However, the psychological effect of these combined measures was enormous. Panic buying drove oil
prices as high as $17 per barrel in December; gas lines formed in major
American cities; the NATO allies split publicly on how to deal with the
crisis; and the issue of oil was effectively linked to that of the Arab-
Israeli dispute for the first time. The United States took an active role in
mediating disengagement agreements between Israeli and Arab forces
on both the Egyptian and Syrian fronts, at least in part to lessen the
pressure of the oil embargo, which was lifted in March 1974 (the production cut plan was dropped in December 1973, as diplomatic moves
were getting under way).[25]

All these manifestations of independence from superpower patrons
can be traced, directly or indirectly, to the new power increased oil revenues gave Saudi Arabia, Iran, and Iraq. However, it is important to
realize that the oil "revolution" of the early 1970s did not alter the pattern of local or international alignments in the region, nor did it affect

the local distribution of power. None of the three major states gained relatively compared to the other two, for each benefited enormously from the new windfall. The pre–1973 "balance" continued, although at a much higher level of armaments. Iraq remained the odd man out in the Iranian-Saudi security understanding. After some tensions regarding the oil embargo and price hikes, including public statements by American officials about consideration of the use of force to secure oil supplies, relations between the United States and both Saudi Arabia and Iran were quickly put back on track. In fact, with the increased importance of oil in general and of the Gulf in particular to the prosperity of the capitalist world, those two states became even more central to Washington's regional policy. From the standpoint of Saudi and Iranian security, their alignment with the United States was also more important, because Riyadh and Teheran were now more inviting targets. The Soviet Union remained Iraq's principal foreign supporter, and Iraqi forces continued to rely heavily on Soviet weaponry.

Regional Intervention: The Kurds and the Dhufar Rebellion

Although the consequences of the oil revolution for regional politics were important, it was not the only domestic factor that affected security in the Gulf. Regional rivalries during the early 1970s were pursued in part through outside manipulation of domestic political cleavages, the two most important cases being the Kurdish problem in Iraq and the Dhufar rebellion in Oman.

The Kurds are an ethnically and linguistically distinct people, mostly professing the Sunni version of Islam, who are centered in a band of territory running from southeastern Turkey through northeastern Iraq and into northwestern Iran. The Versailles Peace Conference of 1919 pledged to set up an autonomous Kurdish region in territory of the defunct Ottoman Empire, but the European colonial powers did not fulfill that promise. Kurdish nationalism grew during the twentieth century and at various times has bedeviled governments in Ankara, Baghdad, and Teheran. In Iraq, where Kurds make up about 15 percent of the total population, the challenge of Kurdish separatism has been the most serious. Since 1958, political weakness at the center and the explicitly Arab nationalist basis of many of the postrevolutionary Iraqi governments have combined to encourage the reassertion of Kurdish demands for autonomy.

The Ba'thist regime that came to power in 1968 immediately tried to placate Kurdish leaders, but by early 1969 fighting between government forces and Kurdish irregulars had resumed. Relations between Iran and

Iraq over border issues were tense, and Iraq accused Iran of providing support for the Kurdish rebels. In March 1970 yet another "settlement" of the Kurdish issue was reached, in which Baghdad and Kurdish leader Mustafa Barazani accepted a compromise plan for local autonomy. This agreement kept the peace for less than two years; by November 1971 reports of fighting again surfaced and Iran pledged to support the Kurdish dissidents. Baghdad and the Kurdish leadership alternated between talks and hostilities for the next two years. With border tensions between Iran and Iraq rising once again in early 1974, negotiations broke down between the Ba'th and the Kurds. Openly supported by Iran, the Kurds rose in full rebellion against Baghdad. Israel and the United States provided military supplies to Barazani through Iran, and Syria also supported Kurdish dissidents.[26] During the late 1960s and early 1970s, the shah used Kurdish discontent to pressure Baghdad on the border question, despite the clear risks that Kurdish nationalist sentiment could pose within Iran itself.

In the Dhufar province of southern Oman, what had originally been manageable tribal unrest had by the early 1970s developed into an ideological movement aimed at overthrowing the sultan. The turning point in this process was the victory in 1967 of the Marxist National Front in the fight for control of newly independent South Yemen. With Soviet and Chinese support the National Front encouraged similar elements in Dhufar to take control of the antisultan political movement, which adopted the name "Popular Front for the Liberation of Oman." The secure base and new source of military supplies provided by South Yemen allowed the Front to expand its military operations, so that by 1970 it had effective control of most of Dhufar province.

With the deposition by the British in 1970 of the lethargic and hidebound Sultan Sa'id and the accession of his more vigorous son Qabus, the government in Muscat actively confronted the rebels. Money was allocated for government projects in the region; political and financial inducements were offered to rebel leaders to join the government's side. With the support of British and Jordanian advisers, the sultan's armed forces began to take the fight to the rebels. Iranian forces joined those of the sultan in the fighting. In December 1975 Sultan Qabus declared that the rebellion had been crushed and that his government was in control of all of Dhufar.

Although Iran and Saudi Arabia welcomed the end of the Dhufar threat, they viewed the situation very differently. The shah had used the Dhufar situation to emphasize his role as regional policeman, and Iranian troops remained in Oman after December 1975, at the request of the sultan's government. The Saudis, who saw the peninsula as their area of influence, were not comfortable with an Iranian military pres-

ence on the Arab side of the Gulf. They were, however, even more un-
comfortable at the prospect of the fall of the sultan's government and
therefore reluctantly acquiesced to the original Iranian deployments.
The sultan was playing his own balancing game and tried to maintain
his relationships with Iran, Britain, and America and thereby to preserve his autonomy vis-à-vis Riyadh. A domestic political dispute in
Oman was thus exploited first by South Yemen and then by Iran, in
their efforts to increase their own regional influence.

From the Algiers Accord to the Iranian
Revolution: 1975–78

A major turning point in regional relations occurred in March 1975. Iraq
and Iran, which had been on the brink of war over their various border
and political disputes several times, reached an agreement on all their
outstanding differences. Iraq agreed to recognize Iranian sovereignty
over half of the Shatt al-Arab River, acquiescing to a long-standing Iranian demand. In return, Iran agreed to transfer to Iraq disputed territories along the two states' central frontier and, more important, to end
its support for the Iraqi Kurdish dissidents. The inability of the Ba'thist
regime to suppress the Kurdish rebellion finally led to its willingness to
compromise with Teheran. This diplomatic deal was mediated by a
number of OPEC members, led by Algeria, who worried that Iranian-
Iraqi tensions would adversely affect the organization's unity. The
agreement was announced at the March 1975 OPEC conference at Algiers and has since been known as the Algiers Accord.

As the border issues that were ostensibly settled at Algiers once again
emerged during the Iran-Iraq war, particularly the Shatt al-Arab, a brief
review is in order. The boundary between twentieth-century Iran and
Iraq has been one of the most disputed in history. The Ottoman and
Persian empires battled over it for centuries, as its location shifted with
changes in the military fortunes of the two sides. In 1847 the Treaty of
Arzurum established Ottoman control over the entire Shatt al-Arab, in
exchange for Ottoman recognition of Persian control over what is now
the province of Khuzistan in Iran. Other border issues were also settled,
but the exact delineation of the frontier had not been completed by the
outbreak of World War I. In 1937 Iran and Iraq agreed on Iraqi sovereignty over the whole Shatt, with the important exception of 8 kilome-
ters around the Iranian port of Abadan, where the boundary would be
the river's midpoint, or thalweg. However, increased tensions between
the two states that resulted from the political upheavals in Iraq after 1958
scuttled this agreement. 'Abd al-Karim Qasim reasserted Iraqi sovereignty over the entire Shatt in the late 1950s. In April 1969, with tensions
again intensifying after the Ba'thist coup, Iran unilaterally abrogated

the 1937 treaty and asserted equal rights in the Shatt by providing naval escorts to Iranian shipping.[27] As mentioned previously, although these border disputes were a constant irritant in Iraqi-Iranian relations, their most serious flare-ups occurred after domestic political changes in Iraq led to increased ideological hostility between the two regimes.

While resolution of the border disputes was an important part of the Algiers Accord, a more fundamental agreement—to accept the legitimacy and durability of the other's domestic political regime—underlay the specifics of territorial control and riparian rights. Since the Ba'thist takeover in 1968 both states had taken a number of steps aimed at fomenting domestic political problems for the other. Iran supported an anti-Ba'thist cabal in 1970; Baghdad tried to stir up the Arabic-speaking population of Khuzistan; the shah supported the Kurdish rebels in Iraq. Algiers brought at least a temporary end to these interventions. The accord was explicitly based on "the principles of territorial integrity, border inviolability and noninterference in internal affairs."[28] The shah's support for the Kurds ended; Iraqi propaganda broadcasts into Khuzistan were suspended. In 1978 the Iraqi government expelled Ayatollah Khumayni, who was emerging as the leading figure in the Iranian revolutionary movement, from the Shi'i holy city of Najaf, where he had resided for fifteen years. The Ba'thist government clearly made the greater compromise in ceding its claim to all of the Shatt al-Arab, but in return bought some breathing space for consolidating its hold over the country.

Iraq's willingness to settle its differences with Iran was but one aspect of a general turn in Baghdad's foreign policy away from ideological confrontation and toward state-to-state cooperation. The Algiers Accord was followed in 1976–77 by Iraqi-Iranian cooperation within OPEC and by a number of bilateral economic agreements. Assaults on the "reactionary" Saudi regime gave way to diplomatic exchanges with Riyadh, as Baghdad realized that it could better deal with Iran if it had the support of the other Arab Gulf states. In June 1975 the two states settled the outstanding border dispute between them, agreeing to divide equally the diamond-shaped "neutral zone" carved out by the British in the 1920s. In early 1976 Iraq ended its support for the Dhufari rebels. After an increase in border tensions between Iraq and Kuwait in 1976, the two states agreed in 1977 to mutual troop withdrawals from the border and the establishment of a committee to resolve border issues. In July 1977 Kuwait reopened the border, which had been closed since 1972. In May of 1977 Iraq proposed that the lower Gulf states, which once had been targets of Iraqi-supported opposition groups, cooperate with it on political and security issues.

The easing of Iranian-Iraqi tensions, along with Iraq's more moderate approach to the other Arab states, introduced a new measure of flexibility into regional alignments. Saudi Arabia, which had reluctantly accepted Iranian leadership in the Gulf in the early 1970s for fear of Iraqi intentions, did not align itself with either of the two regional powers. The Saudis, supported by Iraq, resisted Iranian efforts in early 1975 to organize a regional security pact under Teheran's leadership. They also took a much more assertive position in OPEC against Iran. At the May 1976 OPEC meeting Riyadh opposed any price increase, despite Iranian and Iraqi support for one of 15 percent. At the December 1976 meeting in Qatar, Iran and Saudi Arabia publicly split on prices, with the Saudis refusing to agree to the increases accepted by most OPEC members. Riyadh increased oil production in the first months of 1977 to exert downward pressure on prices, despite condemnations by both Iran and Iraq. Iran, suffering from a loss of market share and faced with American unhappiness over its hawkish stance on prices, eventually agreed in April 1977 to compromise with the Saudis on a smaller price increase.[29] Finally, Saudi Arabia worked to achieve a détente between Oman and South Yemen on the Dhufar question that would lead to the removal of Iranian military forces in Oman.[30]

While the Saudis were taking advantage of the new regional fluidity to establish some distance from Teheran, they also attempted to formalize their own primacy among the smaller Gulf shaykhdoms. Saudi pressure was reportedly behind the decision of the shaykh of Bahrain in August 1975 to suspend his country's elected National Assembly. A similar decision by the ruler of Kuwait in August 1976 had its origins in a domestic political crisis, but the Saudis strongly supported the move. In late March and early April of 1976 King Khalid, who had succeeded his half-brother Faysal after the latter's assassination in March 1975, became the first Saudi monarch to visit the Gulf states. Riyadh urged these states to resist Iranian pressure to subscribe to the shah's proposed security plan and pushed its own agenda for bilateral cooperation on internal security.

However, the same environment of regional fluidity that allowed the Saudis to distance themselves from Iran also permitted the two most independent-minded of the smaller states, Kuwait and Oman, to resist Riyadh's efforts to bring them into the Saudi tent. Sultan Qabus, despite promises to the contrary, never completely abandoned his reliance on security ties with Iran. Only with the Iranian revolution did the last Iranian troops leave Oman. In August 1976 Kuwait signed a $400 million arms deal with Moscow, in a clear assertion of independence from Riyadh. Both Kuwait and Oman demurred from Saudi proposals in the fall of 1976 that the Arab monarchies in the Gulf form an organization for internal security cooperation, deflecting Saudi pressures by stressing the need to include Iran (Oman's ally) and Iraq (of special importance to Kuwait) in any such scheme.[31]

The Algiers Accord of 1975 did not end the ongoing contest among the regional powers in the Gulf. The jockeying over competing proposals for a collective security pact is proof enough of that. However, the nature of that contest had changed. Efforts to subvert the regimes of regional rivals had been discontinued. (None of his regional rivals, for example, attempted to exploit the shah's growing domestic difficulties during 1977–78.) From the ruins of the various, more ambitious security plans emerged a sense of shared interest in internal security cooperation, reflecting the general acceptance on the part of all the local parties of the legitimacy of the existing domestic political orders. Consultations among the big three states on internal security matters reached new levels in 1978, amid reports that they were close to signing a formal Gulf security pact.[32] Those plans, and the more stable regional order upon which they were based, were made moot by the success of the Iranian revolution.

Conclusions: 1971–78

A number of patterns regarding regional political alignments and superpower involvement emerge from an analysis of the events of 1971–78. At the regional level, ideological differences and domestic threats to regime security were as important as power considerations in determining alliances and conflicts. The states of the region did not necessarily balance against "power," understood simply in terms of capabilities. Although Iran possessed much greater military and economic resources than Iraq in the early 1970s, Saudi Arabia aligned with the former because of the threatening posture of the Ba'thists toward the Saudi regime. Riyadh began to distance itself somewhat from Teheran in the mid–1970s not because power capabilities among the regional states shifted, but because the Iraqi regime had curtailed its ideological and political attacks on the Saudi regime. Similarly, the enduring irritant of border issues in the Iran-Iraq relationship flared into open hostility only after regime changes in Iraq brought to power ostensibly radical, Pan-Arabist governments (1958, 1968). The Dhufar rebellion in Oman escalated to a major military challenge to the sultan's regime only after a Marxist government had come to power in neighboring South Yemen.

In the regional milieu of 1975–78, where the norm of sovereignty was respected in both word and deed (i.e., where the domestic legitimacy and stability of the actors were not threatened by other parties), more conventional power balancing took place. The Saudis sought to "hold the balance" between Iraq and Iran. Oman played off monarchical Iran against monarchical Saudi Arabia to maintain some room to maneuver. The Kuwaitis used the prospect of Iraqi and Iranian pressure to deflect Saudi efforts to bring them into Saudi-dominated regional arrangements. Kuwait proved willing to appease Iraq in the late 1970s partly in response to Iraqi threats but also because those threats were now balanced by an apparent Iraqi willingness to abandon claims against the regime for tangible benefits like financial aid. General respect for sovereign norms also made regionwide cooperation possible. In 1978 the three major Gulf powers were close to reaching agreement on a security pact, only to be derailed by the Iranian revolution.

Two themes emerge from superpower involvement in the region. First, their competition for regional influence did not abate despite the improvement of their global relations. The British withdrawal from the Gulf occurred at the height of the Nixon-Brezhnev détente, yet there is no evidence of superpower coordination on strategic issues in the region. Rather, American policy was geared to counteracting Soviet influence by supporting local proxies. The Soviet Union then sought to preserve some strategic role by allying with Iraq, the only state left out of the American-supported regional order in the early 1970s. Second, it was not U.S.-Soviet enmity that led to tensions between Iran and Iraq, but rather regional tensions that led each (at least in part) to seek the support of a superpower patron. Washington did take an active role in the late 1960s in overcoming some of the mutual suspicion between Iran and Saudi Arabia, but in the end it was the two regional powers that settled on their strategic alignment. The United States supported that alignment, particularly with military sales, but did not create it. In general, the superpowers worked within the context of existing regional cleavages, alliances and disputes to further their larger strategic goals.

Regional Politics in the Gulf—1979–88: The Iranian Revolution and the Iran-Iraq War

The Iranian revolution profoundly affected the patterns of regional and bilateral alignment in the Gulf. It posed an ideological and strategic threat to all the regimes on the Arab side of the Gulf, causing major changes in their relations with Iran and each other. This essentially domestic political event also reshaped superpower alignment in the region in ways that would not have been predicted by conventional balance-of-power theory. Both superpowers ended up tilting toward Iraq, despite their shared view that Iran was the strategic prize in the region.

The Revolution and Its Immediate Aftermath (January 1979–September 1980)

The Iranian revolution completely reshaped the pattern of international politics in the Gulf, at both the regional and superpower levels. The consequences of the revolution were felt almost immediately, even though it would be nearly two years before Iraq invaded Iran. Both superpowers were drawn into more direct military involvement in the region as a result of the revolution, and Saudi Arabia and Iraq became unlikely allies in an effort to stem the Islamic revolutionary tide.

Neither Iraq nor Saudi Arabia openly confronted the new regime in Teheran immediately. In April 1979 Iraqi President Hasan al-Bakr congratulated Khumayni on the proclamation of the Islamic Republic and called for friendly relations between the countries.[33] In late April 1979 the head of the Saudi National Guard, now Crown Prince, 'Abdallah ibn 'Abd al-'Aziz Al Sa'ud, implied to an interviewer that Riyadh actually preferred the new regime in Teheran to that of the shah.[34] But both capitals were also wary of the revolutionary ideological orientation in Teheran. In February 1979, as Khumayni was coming to power, Iraq and Saudi Arabia signed an agreement to cooperate in matters of internal security; in April 1979 Hasan al-Bakr became the first president of republican Iraq to visit Saudi Arabia. The increasing closeness in Saudi-Iraqi relations was the result not only of the collapse of the shah's regime, but also of events in the Arab world. With Egypt's removal from the Arab political arena after the Camp David Accords and the brief but significant alignment of Syria with Iraq at the beginning of 1979, it appeared that Iraq would come to dominate all the Arab East. Far from acting to "balance" growing Iraqi power at this crucial juncture, the Saudis sought to get on the Iraqi bandwagon.

If the Saudis were balancing in the Gulf, it was against the ideological threat to regime stability posed by the revolution. In 1979 a wave of Shi'i unrest swept Kuwait, Bahrain, and Saudi Arabia, characterized by demonstrations, protests, bombings, and arrests of local Shi'i leaders, particularly in the Eastern Province of Saudi Arabia, the center of the Saudi oil industry.[35] Government forces suppressed the demonstrations, causing a number of deaths. Unrest went beyond the Shi'i community when, in late November 1979, a group of Sunni militants opposed to the rule of the Al Sa'ud took over the holiest shrine in Islam, the Great Mosque in Mecca, and held it for nearly three weeks. Only after heavy fighting, in which Saudi forces were assisted by French military advisers, was the Mosque retaken.

In Iraq, Shi'i opposition and the government reaction to it were particularly violent. Demonstrations followed the arrest of a Shi'i religious leader, Ayatollah Muhammed Baqir al-Sadr, in June 1979. In the spring of 1980 opposition forces tried to assassinate two high-ranking Ba'thist officials (one of whom was Tariq 'Aziz, the highest-ranking Christian in the regime and a close adviser to Saddam Husayn) and undertook other terrorist actions in Baghdad. The regime reacted by arresting thousands of Shi'is, executing Ayatollah al-Sadr and his sister, making membership in the Shiʿi *al-Daʿwa* party punishable by death, and expelling an estimated thirty-five thousand Iraqis of Persian origin to Iran.[36]

These demonstrations of Shiʿi political discontent were founded upon real local grievances and were not attributable simply to Iranian meddling. Both Saudi Arabia and Iraq implicitly recognized the legitimacy of those grievances by increasing government spending in Shiʿi areas. However, it is equally clear that the Iranian revolution helped to spark these local movements. Teheran actively encouraged them materially and ideologically, and in the end sought to use them as instruments of Iranian foreign policy. As early as late 1978 Khumayni deputized Shiʿi figures in Kuwait and Bahrain to represent his interests in those states and organize their communities politically.[37] In October 1979 a leading Iranian clergyman, Ayatollah Sadiq Ruhani, threatened that Iran would revive its claim to Bahrain unless its rulers adopted "an Islamic form of government similar to the one established in Iran."[38] In January 1980 Iranian radio announced in an Arabic language broadcast plans to create a force to help "export the Islamic revolution."[39] After riots in the Saudi Eastern Province in February 1980, Iranian radio stations called openly for revolt against the Al Saʿud.[40] By April 1980 Iran was making explicit threats to unseat the Baʿthist regime in Baghdad.[41]

Domestic changes in Baghdad during this period made it more likely that Iraq would strike back at Iran militarily. In July 1979 Saddam Husayn assumed the presidency of Iraq after the resignation of the more moderate Hasan al-Bakr.[42] Saddam was eager to confront Iran, both to remove the ideological threat and to advance his own plans for Iraqi regional hegemony. In February 1980 he issued the "Arab National Charter" in an effort to rally other Arab states behind Iraqi leadership.[43] The efforts by the Islamic opposition in April 1980 to destabilize the Baʿthist regime were the final straw. Iraqi military preparations in the border areas accelerated.[44] Iraq also sought to establish contacts with opponents of the revolutionary regime both inside and outside Iran, particularly in the Arabic-speaking area of Khuzistan (in the southwest corner of the country).[45]

As regional tensions rose, the superpowers also sought to deal with the fallout from the revolution. The Soviet Union openly welcomed the revolution as a major setback for the United States. The Communist Party in Iran, the Tudeh, backed the Khumayni government, despite obvious ideological differences. But the Soviets were also worried about the spill-over effects of the revolution. Afghanistan was of particular concern. The unstable pro-Soviet regime there was facing growing opposition that was increasingly defined in Islamic terms. In December 1979 Soviet forces invaded Afghanistan, safe in the knowledge that American-Iranian hostility (the hostage crisis had begun just one month earlier) made effective regional or U.S. resistance very unlikely. Teheran immediately condemned the Soviet invasion and began to back Afghan resistance movements in the largely Shi'i western part of the country (independent of the American-Saudi-Pakistani support for other Afghan *mujahidin* groups). In effect, Moscow sacrificed the possibility of supplanting Washington as Iran's major foreign patron by going into Afghanistan, but it did not stop trying to improve relations with the revolutionary regime.

Although the Afghanistan invasion soured Soviet-Iranian relations, it did not push Teheran back into the arms of Washington, as balancing theory would have predicted. Hostility between the two former allies was never higher than immediately after the revolution, as the fourteen-month captivity of American hostages in Teheran (from November of 1979 until January of 1981) consumed the political energies of both the American and Iranian governments. The antipathy of Ayatollah Khumayni for the United States went beyond the obvious resentment of American support for the shah and past intervention in Iranian politics. It also went beyond American support for local states seen as ideological enemies by Khumayni, particularly Israel and Saudi Arabia. Khumayni saw his revolution as both a cultural and a political movement. He considered the main threat to authentic Iranian Islamic cultural norms to be the seductive call of consumerism, materialism, individualism, and sexual liberty represented by Western capitalist societies.[46] The United States personified these values and supplied the products that propagated them in Iran. Opposition to the United States was as much a domestic as a foreign policy imperative for the revolution.

On both sides of the American-Iranian divide domestic politics came to dominate relations. The takeover of the U.S. embassy in Teheran on November 4, 1979, by supporters of the clerical party was aimed as much against Prime Minister Bazargan, who was suspected of trying to normalize relations with Washington, as against the United States. Bazargan, who opposed the takeover, resigned after Ayatollah Khumayni supported the action. From that point control of the hostages became a bargaining chip in Iranian factional infighting, and no politician would allow himself to be outflanked on the issue of anti-Americanism.[47] President Carter became obsessed with the hostage issue.[48] Public opinion was intensely hostile toward Iran in general and Ayatollah Khumayni in particular. Carter's failure to end the hostage crisis contributed to his defeat by Ronald Reagan in the November 1980 presidential elections.

The United States faced a number of crises in the immediate postrevolutionary period that demanded new policy initiatives. Besides the hostage crisis, symbolizing the collapse of the previous American policy of support for Iran, Washington was confronted both with the Soviet invasion of Afghanistan, which raised the specter of Soviet dominance of the region, and with a second oil crisis. During 1979 oil prices doubled, from around $13 per barrel to about $26 per barrel, dealing another shock to Western and Third World economies, which had barely recovered from the inflation and stagnation brought on by the first oil crisis of 1973–74. Prices continued to rise, reaching their peak in 1981 at $34 per barrel.

The underlying cause of this second oil crisis was continuing increases in world demand for oil and limited immediate supply. However, the immediate cause was the disruption in the oil market resulting from the Iranian revolution. Average Iranian oil production fell by more than two million barrels per day between 1978 and 1979 and fell another 1.5 million barrels per day between 1979 and 1980.[49] Moreover, at a critical point in early 1979, Saudi Arabia cut its production by an average of one million barrels per day. Although the cut apparently was due to technical reasons, it came at a time when the new Iranian government was demanding that other producers reduce production, so that it could regain its market share. It took Riyadh five months to return to its original production level.[50] The Saudi decision contributed to panic buying on the spot market, which drove up prices.

The oil price increases of 1979–81, like those of 1973–74, had little effect on the regional balance among Iran, Iraq, and Saudi Arabia. They were all oil producers, and they all benefited from the increased revenues. Both Iraq and Saudi Arabia were able to acquire even more military hardware, and Iraqi self-confidence and regional ambitions increased. In Iran, the oil price increase helped the new revolutionary regime maintain some semblance of a functioning economy and reduced the negative effects of the oil production cuts.

The second oil shock did, however, refocus American strategy on access to Gulf oil. American options for dealing with the new regional realities were limited. The old policy toward Iran was in tatters, and reliance on Iraq as a regional ally was impossible. Baghdad had broken diplomatic relations with Washington over ten years before and had not resumed them. Iraq was considered a close ally of the Soviet Union and was leading the Arab front, which was opposed to the Camp David Accords. That left Saudi Arabia as America's only significant partner in the Gulf. American-Saudi relations were strained. There were differences over the Camp David Accords, and the Saudis felt that, after the fall of the shah, an American connection might create more problems than it would solve.[51] Moreover, given its small population relative to Iran and Iraq, Saudi Arabia could hardly assume the shah's role of "regional policeman."

President Carter presented the American response to these events in his state of the union address in January 1980. He announced that the United States would use all means at its disposal to prevent any "outside force" from gaining control of the Gulf region, a policy that became known as the "Carter Doctrine." To implement this policy, a mobile U.S. military force—the Rapid Deployment Force (RDF)—was established to respond to events in the Gulf. Covert support, through Pakistan, was also given to support Afghan resistance to the Soviet invaders.

The United States found little support in the Gulf for its new policy. Iran saw the RDF as a hostile force (a belief confirmed by the failed U.S. hostage rescue mission in April 1980). Iraq, aiming to replace Iran as the dominant regional power, also did not support an increased American presence. Saddam Husayn's "Arab Charter," issued less than a month after the Carter Doctrine was announced, explicitly rejected any foreign military presence in the region. Saudi Arabia, although it joined the United States in condemning the Soviet invasion of Afghanistan and participated in covert plans to support the Afghan *mujahidin*, refused U.S. requests for access to military facilities needed for the RDF. The Saudis were worried that such an agreement would not only alienate Iraq and Iran, but could crystallize domestic opposition within the kingdom.[52] In the immediate Gulf region, only Oman agreed to grant the United States access to military facilities. Muscat had historically looked to outside powers for support against Saudi hegemony on the Arabian Peninsula and welcomed aid from the United States and other Western powers in its efforts to patrol the Strait of Hormuz.

The Iraqi War Decision (September 1980–June 1982)

Iraq's decision to launch a large-scale attack across its international border with Iran on September 22, 1980, began the longest and costliest (in terms of both human life and money) war in modern Middle East history. Despite the undeniable fact that it was Iraq that escalated the conflict to the level of all-out international war, from an analytical perspective the causes of the Iran-Iraq war can be traced directly to the Iranian revolution. This change at the *domestic* political level best explains the *international* political phenomenon of the war.

The revolution had two direct consequences for regional politics that set the stage for the Iran-Iraq war. First, the very fact of the revolution—mass-based, Islamically inspired, successful political opposition to an authoritarian regime—was a threat to the domestic political stability of all the neighboring Arab states. The strength of its ideological appeal was made all the more threatening by the active rhetorical (and in some cases material) support given by the new revolutionary government to opposition forces within neighboring states, particularly the

Shi'i opposition groups in Iraq. As in other great social revolutions, more moderate leadership elites in Iran, less threatening in the eyes of neighboring states, were quickly swept away, further reducing the possibility of peaceful coexistence.

Second, the chaos that the revolution brought to Iranian politics made the country seem weak in the conventional attributes of national power, and therefore not as potent a military opponent, even as its danger as an ideological opponent was increasing exponentially. Violent factional infighting was the norm in Teheran, and regional separatist movements in Azerbaijan and Kurdistan threatened to tear the country apart. The upper officer corps of the Iranian armed forces was decimated by political purges. The military machine built by the shah, at the cost of billions of dollars, seemed to have collapsed. The revolutionary leadership had willingly, even recklessly, sabotaged Iran's relationship with its superpower ally and weapons supplier, the United States, in pursuit of its ideological goals.

To an ambitious neighbor like Saddam Husayn, these domestic consequences of the revolution created a power vacuum in the region that Iraq could easily exploit. Iranian exiles anxious to return to power confirmed to Saddam that the new government was an easy target. The shift in regional leadership would be confirmed by Iran's rapid defeat.

The Iran-Iraq war cannot be attributed simply to Iraqi ambitions, though Iraq and Saddam were certainly ambitious, nor can it be attributed solely to Iranian meddling in the domestic affairs of Iraq, although that occurred. It can only be understood as the result of a set of political circumstances that made Iran seem both weak militarily and threatening ideologically to the domestic stability of neighboring regimes. And those circumstances trace directly back to the Iranian revolution itself.

On September 17, 1980, Saddam Husayn formally abrogated the 1975 Algiers Accord and claimed Iraqi sovereignty over the whole of the Shatt al-Arab. Five days later the Iraqi air force struck Iranian oil facilities and military bases, and on September 23, 1980, five divisions of the Iraqi army crossed the border into Iran. Having exploited the element of surprise, Iraq looked for a quick end to the hostilities, while it had the upper hand. On September 28 Saddam Husayn indicated his willingness to accept a cease-fire.

Iran, however, refused to consider the possibility. Ayatollah Khumayni, in rejecting a U.N. Security Council resolution of September 28, 1980, calling for a cease-fire, identified Iran's war aims as not only repelling the invasion, but also punishing "the criminal Ba'th leaders."[53] Iran mobilized what was left of its regular armed forces and irregular forces, eventually organized into the Revolutionary Guards (*pasdaran*) and the *basij* (popular militia). The Iraqi attack created an enormous popular response in Iran. It allowed the regime to link Iranian nationalist sentiments to its Islamic revolutionary platform and to brand its domestic opponents not only as enemies of Islam but also as traitors to the nation. The Iraqi advance bogged down shortly after the capture of Khorramshahr and the surrounding of Abadan in late October 1980.

The outbreak of the war created a dilemma for the other Gulf states. They would have been very happy to see Khumayni get his comeuppance, but an even stronger Iraq also presented risks. The continuation of hostilities increased the threat that they would come under attack, either from one of the parties or by the extension of the fighting into the Gulf, which could disrupt oil exports. Two Iranian air attacks on a Kuwaiti border post in November 1980 underscored this danger. Ending the fighting was their top priority, but early mediation efforts failed. The Gulf monarchies could not avoid a stark choice: to support Iraq, which appeared to be winning the war and accept the security risks of eventual Iraqi hegemony in the region, or to act as balance-of-power theorists would predict and back Iran despite the ideological threat the latter's revolution posed.

Saudi Arabia saw the ideological threat from Iran as posing more immediate problems than the longer-run strategic threat of a victorious Iraq. Riyadh maintained a studied silence at the outbreak of the war, but Iraqi ships and warplanes were permitted to take shelter in Saudi Arabia during the first days of the fighting, despite Iranian threats to attack Iraqi forces wherever they were.[54] The Saudis permitted their Red Sea ports to be used for transshipping military material and other supplies to Iraq.[55] Kuwait and Saudi Arabia supported Iraq financially, with loans and oil production undertaken on the Iraqi account.[56] Saudi Arabia and the other Gulf monarchies also attended an Arab summit meeting in Amman, Jordan, in November 1980, boycotted by Syria, Libya, and the PLO, which expressed support for Iraq in the war.

While tilting toward Iraq, the Saudis also took steps to bolster security cooperation with Pakistan, a power on the periphery of the Gulf that presented no immediate threat to either Saudi domestic stability or regional position. Saudi-Pakistani discussions predated the beginning of the war and stemmed from mutual worries about the Iranian revolution and the Soviet invasion of Afghanistan. The Iran-Iraq war added new urgency. The kingdom reportedly committed large sums in aid in exchange for Pakistani military deployment in Saudi Arabia. Although only two brigades were sent, the Pakistani connection indicates that the Saudis actively sought to expand the geographic extension of Gulf politics, in order to bring in a powerful but ideologically and strategically "safe" player to balance both Iran and Iraq.[57] As will be seen, the Saudis also looked to another "outsider," the United States, to bolster their security position during this crisis period.

As the fighting bogged down in early 1981 and the threat of its immediate geographical extension did not materialize, Saudi authorities began to see a silver lining in the dark cloud of the war. With Iran and Iraq engaged, the Saudis could consolidate their leadership among the smaller Gulf shaykhdoms. In the past these states had used Iran and Iraq and foreign powers (principally Great Britain and the United States) to offset Saudi influence. However, the security threat presented by both the Iranian revolution and the Iran-Iraq war underlined their vulnerability; the war removed both Iran and Iraq as possible counterweights to the Saudis. In May 1981 these extraordinary circumstances led the smaller states to put their fears of Saudi dominance aside and to agree to the formation of the Gulf Cooperation Council (GCC).

The GCC consists of Saudi Arabia, Kuwait, Bahrain, Qatar, the United Arab Emirates, and Oman. Although its founding documents stress economic and cultural cooperation, the security threats arising from the revolution and the war are clearly what brought the five smaller states formally under the Saudi umbrella.[58] The security rationale for the GCC became much more apparent in December 1981, when Saudi and Bahraini authorities uncovered a plot to overthrow the Bahraini government. Officials in both countries charged that Iran armed and trained the saboteurs, and the evidence for some Iranian complicity in the plot is strong. Security issues headed the agenda at the GCC summit of February 1982. Kuwait resisted proposals for multilateral internal security cooperation, but coordination on both defense and internal security issues proceeded at both the bilateral and the GCC levels.[59]

Like the Saudis, both superpowers sought to take advantage of the regional upheaval created by the Iran-Iraq war to improve their positions. The United States and the Soviet Union declared their neutrality at the outset of the war, supported the territorial integrity of Iran, and called for an end to the hostilities. Both powers also moved to strengthen themselves with other states in the region. Closed out of both Iran and Iraq, Washington concentrated on the Saudis. The United States responded immediately to Saudi requests by dispatching AWACS aircraft and personnel to aid in the air defense of the kingdom. The new Reagan administration quickly announced its decision to sell AWACS to Saudi Arabia and pushed the sale through a reluctant Congress in October 1981. For their part, Saudi Arabia and the smaller Gulf states increased oil production by three million barrels per day when the war began, making up for the shortfall created by Iraq's inability to export. Oil prices on the spot market surged at the outset of the war but quickly fell back to previous levels.

When confronted with an immediate security threat, the Saudis turned to Washington for support, as they had in the past and would in the future. However, they continued to resist American plans (now dubbed "strategic consensus" by the Reagan Administration) for a formal American military presence in the kingdom, fearing both the opposition of Iran and Iraq and the domestic consequences of increased identification with the United States. They preferred to have the Americans "over the horizon," in the Indian Ocean area and able to respond to military threats, but not on Saudi soil.

The Soviet Union looked to Iran, seeking once again to take advantage of the rupture between Iran and America. Moscow cut its arms deliveries to Iraq, warned Iran of the impending attack, supplied it with jet fuel, and assured the leadership that it would respect their joint frontier, so that more Iranian troops could be deployed against Iraq.[60] There were also reports of a secret agreement, signed by Iran and the Soviet Union in July 1981, under which the Soviets would provide technical military aid and advisers to Iran and train Iranians in the Soviet Union.[61] Iran quickly became dependent upon close Soviet allies as its main weapons suppliers—Syria, Libya, North Korea, and Warsaw Pact countries. The Iranians offered few immediate political returns to the Soviets, but the Tudeh Party continued to operate openly in Iran.

The initial actions of the regional and outside powers occurred while there was a clear Iraqi advantage in the early fighting. However, as the war continued in 1981 the Iranians began to get the upper hand. By June 1982 they had driven the Iraqis out of Iran. At the same time, domestic politics in Iran were again in turmoil. President Abul-Hassan Bani-Sadr, the last major nonclerical player in the Iranian power game, was impeached and removed from office in June 1981, ending a bitter power struggle with the clerical Islamic Republican Party (IRP). Bani-Sadr had been seen by Arab leaders as someone who might be willing to compromise on Iran's war aims. After his fall, the IRP consolidated clerical power by crushing the leftist opposition.[62] In July 1982, with Iraqi troops in retreat and Iran in complete control of previously captured territory, the Iranian leadership faced a momentous choice.

Iran on the Offensive (July 1982 to Summer 1987)

The Iranian revolution had arrived at a turning point. The Iraqi invaders had been routed. Ayatollah Khumayni and his clerical allies were in firm control, having disposed of liberal, leftist, and nonclerical challengers. The revolutionary leadership was in a position to declare victory in the Iran-Iraq war, demobilize the popular militias, and concentrate on domestic economic reconstruction. However, the ayatollah succumbed to much the same temptations that had drawn Saddam Husayn into war in the fall of 1980. Now it was Iraq that seemed an easy target for revived Iranian military power. The opportunity to promote the spread of the Islamic revolution into Iraq and to reconfirm Iranian regional hegemony proved irresistible. On July 13, 1982, Iranian forces crossed the border into Iraq.

High on Iran's agenda was the spread of the message of Islamic revolution. Khumayni brought to an end the debate within Iran about continuing the war on June 21, 1982 in a statement calling for the overthrow of Saddam Husayn.[63] From the outset of the fighting, Khumayni had defined the war in spiritual and metaphysical terms, as a battle of the forces of Islam against those of irreligion and evil. Compromise was impossible in such a framework.[64] As Iran mounted its offensive, it also organized a number of Iraqi Shi'i opponents of the Ba'th into the Supreme Assembly of the Islamic Revolution in Iraq (SAIRI), a kind of proto-government in exile. In September 1983, Khumayni publicly urged SAIRI to aim at setting up an Islamic government in Iraq.[65]

The Iraqi strategy during the next several years of the war was as clear as it was desperate. Baghdad continually expressed its willingness to negotiate as long as there was a cease-fire first.[66] Moreover, it was unwilling to endure a prolonged war of attrition and took a number of steps to escalate the conflict, seeking both to increase the immediate cost of the war to Iran and to involve regional and outside powers more actively in seeking to end it. In February 1984 Iraq extended the war geographically by attacking Iranian oil tankers in the Gulf and escalated the war by launching air attacks on major Iranian cities. In the summer of 1985 the Iraqi air force began a concerted effort to destroy the Iranian oil terminal at Kharg Island, and later extended its attacks to Iranian oil facilities further down the Gulf. It was Iraq that introduced chemical weapons into the fighting and began to use medium-range missiles to attack Iranian population centers.[67] However, until 1987, Iraqi escalation tactics could neither break the Iranian will nor draw the superpowers further into the conflict.

The extension of the war into Iraq increased the military and the ideological threat posed by Iran to the Arab Gulf monarchies. At minimum the war fronts were pushed closer to the Kuwaiti and Saudi borders, and the risks of more direct involvement grew. A military victory by Iran would establish its domination of the region geopolitically and lead to the dismemberment or the satellitization of Iraq. It would also increase the prospects for successful Islamic opposition in the Gulf monarchies.

Direct Iranian attacks on Gulf targets during the war were limited. Teheran feared that confrontation would lead to a larger U.S. military role in the area. In September 1986 Iran did begin to attack Saudi and Kuwaiti oil tankers, but only in response to Iraq's extension of the war to the waters of the Gulf. Periodically, Teheran threatened to close the Straits of Hormuz if Iraqi attacks made it impossible for Iran to maintain its exports.

The threat to domestic political stability resulting from Iranian military successes was more serious and immediate. The Bahrain coup plot of December 1981 occurred as the Iranians were turning the tide on the battlefield. Kuwait was particularly threatened by opposition groups working with the support of members of the Iranian government. In December 1983 a series of coordinated explosions damaged a number of strategic and economic targets in the country. In May 1985 an attempt was made on the life of Shaykh Jabir al-Ahmad Al-Sabah, the ruler of Kuwait. Other politically inspired acts of sabotage and terror occurred in July 1985 and in January 1987, when fires occurred in Kuwaiti oil facilities as the country was hosting an Islamic Conference Organization summit boycotted and condemned by Iran.[68] The domestic political pressures in Kuwait, brought on largely by the war and Iranian-supported dissident activity, led Shaykh Jabir to dissolve the Kuwaiti parliament, the only elected legislature on the Arab side of the Gulf, in July 1986.

Iran also sponsored and encouraged political demonstrations during the annual Muslim pilgrimage to Mecca, aimed at questioning the domestic and international legitimacy of the Al Sa'ud regime. Management of the pilgrimage is at once a source of great pride to the Saudi leaders, part of their claim to Islamic leadership, and a security risk, as Muslims from all over the world gather in numbers so great that they are hard to monitor and control. Ayatollah Khumayni bluntly asserted that the pilgrimage should be as much a political event as a religious one and openly encouraged Iranian pilgrims to use the occasion to forward their political agendas. In 1982 demonstrations during the pilgrimage led to the expulsion of approximately 100 Iranians from Saudi Arabia.[69] The pilgrimage became a barometer of the state of Saudi-Iranian relations.

The policy reactions of Saudi Arabia during the period of Iranian battlefield advantage are the most interesting and important among the Gulf monarchies: interesting because of the shifts in the tone of Saudi policy toward Iran; important because of Saudi size and wealth, the leading Saudi role on the Arab side of the Gulf generally and specifically in the GCC, and the close relationship between Riyadh and Washington. The Saudis continued their political and financial support for Iraq. However, they experimented with a much more conciliatory and open policy toward Iran from mid–1984 to the beginning of 1986. The shooting down of an Iranian fighter over a Saudi island in the Gulf in the summer of 1984, rather than escalating Saudi-Iranian tensions, led to a degree of accommodation. Iran moderated its rhetorical attacks on the Saudi regime; Iranians in the 1984 and 1985 pilgrimages were well behaved. The Saudi foreign minister visited Teheran in May 1985, and the November GCC meeting stressed the need to end the war "in a manner that safeguards the legitimate rights and interests of the *two sides*"(emphasis added).[70]

Clearly, the new Iranian approach to Saudi Arabia was to separate Iraq from its Arab allies. Although the threat of an Iranian military victory seemed much reduced, because of the military stalemate, the Iranians still held the advantage on the battlefield. Balance-of-power logic would have dictated continued Saudi alignment with Iraq. The Saudis were willing to improve ties with Iran, however, because Teheran showed a new, more moderate disposition toward the Saudi regime itself. Propaganda attacks questioning the legitimacy of the Al Saʿud family and labeling monarchy an "un-Islamic" form of government abated. Iranian officials kept the pilgrimage quiet. The Iranian threat to Saudi domestic stability seemed reduced and Riyadh responded by improving relations.

The improvement in Saudi-Iranian relations proved temporary, for in the end it was predicated upon continuing stalemate in the war. In early 1986, Iran achieved its first major victory since the summer of 1982, when its forces captured the Fao Peninsula, a spit of Iraqi land extending into the Gulf. Iraqi counterattacks failed, as did their effort to capture compensating Iranian territory along the central front. An Iraqi military collapse again appeared possible. This Iranian battlefield success was accompanied by a return to a threatening posture toward the Gulf monarchies, militarily and ideologically. Iranian officials publicly warned those states to reconsider their support for Iraq or risk becoming targets.[71] Iranians attempted to disrupt the 1986 pilgrimage, and the 1987 pilgrimage saw clashes between Iranians and Saudi authorities that left more than four hundred dead.[72] Iran renewed sporadic attacks on Saudi oil tankers, and the Saudis supported the increased American naval role in the Gulf that followed the decision to reflag Kuwaiti tankers. Saudi Arabia finally broke diplomatic relations with Iran in May 1988, effectively preventing any Iranian participation in the pilgrimage until relations improved in 1991.

A change in the role of the major outside powers was provoked by Kuwait's 1986 request to the United States and the Soviet Union to re-flag and protect Kuwaiti tankers. Until then neither one had taken a direct role in the hostilities. Moscow's tilt toward Iran ended in the summer of 1982, when the forces of the Islamic Republic crossed into Iraq. The Soviet Union resumed arms shipments, including medium-range missiles, to Baghdad that had been cut off in 1980, and remained Iraq's major military supplier throughout the remainder of the war. Soviet-Iranian relations were further hampered in April 1983, when officials in Teheran, acting on intelligence information passed to them by Western powers, expelled eighteen Soviet diplomats and arrested the leadership of the Tudeh Party. With Iran on the offensive, the United States also publicly tilted toward Iraq. Diplomatic relations between Baghdad and Washington were reestablished in 1984, and the United States provided Iraq with intelligence data and credits for the purchase of technology and agricultural products.[73]

Although the superpower tilt toward Iraq was clear, neither Washington nor Moscow felt the need to inject itself directly into the hostilities. As the battlefield situation restabilized, the fear that Iran would win an outright military victory abated. With the Soviets tied down in Afghanistan, it was extremely unlikely that they could become involved in another military operation. For the United States, the continuing decline of oil prices during the mid–1980s reduced the immediate strategic importance of the Gulf. Shortly after the Iranian military victory at Fao in February 1986, which was the high point of Iranian offensives into Iraq, world oil prices fell to their lowest level since the 1973 price explosion. The war seemed not to threaten either the supply of oil or its price.

The public tilt toward Iraq by both superpowers did not prevent their continued secret efforts to improve relations with Iran. Moscow encouraged the development of economic ties with Iran and permitted a number of its allies, including North Korea and Syria, to supply Soviet-made arms to Teheran.[74] The United States engaged in secret dealings with Iran, involving the sale of American arms, the provision of intelligence information, and the release of American hostages held in Lebanon, over the years 1984–86, in what became known as the "Iran-Contra" affair. For the superpowers, Iran remained the geopolitical prize in the Gulf, and fear that the other would gain a dominant position there inspired efforts by both to maintain some role in Iranian politics.

In the fall of 1986 Iran began attacking Kuwaiti oil tankers in the Gulf, in response to continued Iraqi attacks on Iranian oil facilities and tankers. In November 1986 Kuwait requested assistance from both the

United States and the Soviet Union, to protect its own interests and to involve both superpowers in a strategy aimed against Iran. Initially, the United States did not respond. However, after learning that the Soviet Union had entered into negotiations with Kuwait on the issue, in March 1987 the United States agreed to put American flags on a number of Kuwaiti tankers and to provide them with naval escorts. The Soviet Union also sent naval forces to protect three reflagged Kuwaiti tankers, as did a number of Western European countries.[75]

The United States and the Soviet Union became more directly involved in the Iran-Iraq war, not because of any significant change in the state of the battle or because of notable changes in their policies toward the region, but because of their own global strategic rivalry. Neither Iraq nor its Gulf Arab allies appeared in more danger of Iranian military defeat or attack than previously. In fact, in early 1987 Iraq had repelled a major Iranian offensive in the south, and the battlefront had stabilized. The Soviets saw an opportunity to increase their military presence in an area where the United States had had the upper hand. The United States responded to the Kuwaiti request only when it learned of Soviet intentions. Two aspects of the circumstances of the American decision are especially noteworthy. It came at a time when U.S.-Soviet relations were beginning to improve. The Soviets and the Americans also had similar goals, immediately in protecting Kuwaiti shipping and ultimately in pressuring Iran to accept a cease-fire in the war, yet Washington refused to consider cooperative action with Moscow in this area. Cold War competition dominated each superpower's view of the other in the Gulf, even during the Reagan-Gorbachev detente.

Cease-Fire (Summer 1987 to Summer 1988)

The most important factor leading to the August 1988 cease-fire in the Iran-Iraq war was the changing fortunes of the two combatants on the battlefield. Superpower diplomacy, U.S. military actions, and Iranian domestic political events all contributed to the Iranian decision of July 18, 1988, to accept United Nations Security Council Resolution 598, which called for the cease-fire. However, had Iraq not regained the military initiative, it is difficult to imagine that the Iranian leadership would have given up its stated goal of continuing the war until some domestic political change occurred in Iraq. The threat that continued fighting might lead to new Iraqi gains in Iranian territory, re-creating the situation of 1980–81, led Iran to take the decision that Ayatollah Khumayni publicly likened to drinking poison.

The change in the military tide began in early 1987. Iran mounted a large-scale offensive on the southern front, attempting to follow up its success of a year earlier at Fao. The Iraqis turned that offensive back. Meanwhile, the Iraqi military was receiving and integrating massive new shipments of Soviet weaponry and the advice of thousands of Soviet military advisers.[76] In April 1988 Iraqi forces won their first major victory since the beginning of the war, retaking the Fao Peninsula. An Iranian counteroffensive in June 1988 was thrown back. By July 1988 Iraqi troops had captured some Iranian territory on the central front and had engaged in even deeper probes into Iran. These thrusts were especially nettlesome to Teheran, as the Iraqis were accompanied by fighters from the *Mujahidin e-Khalq*, the major Iranian exile organization opposed to the Khumayni regime.

The Iraqi successes on the ground were preceded by yet another Iraqi escalation in the targets and technology of the fighting. From late February to April 1988 Iraqi medium-range missiles pounded Iranian population centers, including Teheran. Iran responded in kind but could not match either the number of missiles or the capacity to deliver them. This was the first sustained use of missiles against major population centers in the war. News reports from Teheran indicated that the attacks had a major impact on morale in the capital, which until then had been largely insulated from direct attack. Iraq also demonstrated its continuing willingness to defy international law by using poison gas against the Iraqi Kurdish town of Halabja, which had been taken by Iranian troops. A United Nations investigation also found that Iraq had used chemical weapons in the fighting in southern Iraq in June 1988.

The Iraqi successes on the battlefield came in the context of increased international pressure on Iran to end the war. In July 1987 the U.N. Security Council adopted resolution 598, calling for an immediate ceasefire and withdrawal of all forces to international boundaries, the negotiation through U.N. auspices of a comprehensive solution to the disputes between Iran and Iraq, and the formation of an international body to assess the question of responsibility for the initiation of the conflict. Although this last aspect of the resolution was meant to appeal to Iran, which had consistently called for blaming Iraq for the war, the bulk of the resolution was clearly directed against Iran's determination to continue the fighting. The United States was the driving force behind resolution 598 and urged that U.N. sanctions be applied to parties that did not accept it. The resolution, along with the American, Soviet, and European naval deployments in the Gulf, represented a significant international consensus on the need to end the hostilities.

Iraq immediately accepted resolution 598, which was consistent with its calls since 1982 for an immediate cease-fire and return to international boundaries.[77] Baghdad stressed that the resolution should be implemented sequentially, with cease-fire and withdrawal leading to direct

Iranian-Iraqi negotiations on a comprehensive settlement, followed by the convening of the proposed international tribunal for assessing war guilt. Iran, although it did not reject the resolution completely, attacked it as biased and stressed that war guilt would have to be assessed before other parts of the resolution could be implemented.[78]

With the Security Council's adoption of resolution 598, the United States began to increase its diplomatic and military pressure on Iran. Washington redoubled its own efforts to organize an international arms embargo against Iran. The revelations of the secret arms transactions in the "Iran-Contra affair" paradoxically increased the American commitment to its embargo proposal, as the Reagan administration sought to reassure its Arab allies and American public opinion that it was not tilting toward Iran. U.S. naval forces in the Gulf engaged in a number of direct confrontations with Iranian forces. In late September 1987 American ships seized the Iranian ship *Ajr*, which was laying mines in the Gulf. In April 1988 another mining incident escalated into a major clash, in which the United States destroyed two Iranian offshore oil platforms and badly damaged six Iranian ships. Finally, in July 1988, just days before the Iranian decision to accept the cease-fire, the *U.S.S. Vincennes* shot down an Iranian civilian airliner, killing nearly 300 people. While undoubtedly an accident, the incident convinced many in Iran that the United States was willing to take drastic steps to prevent an Iranian victory in the war. The muted international response to this tragedy brought home to the Iranian leadership the extent of their isolation.

While Iraq turned the tide on the battlefield and the United States escalated its diplomatic and military pressure, important events were occurring in Iranian domestic politics that set the stage for the acceptance of the cease-fire. In two rounds of voting, in April and May 1988, Iranians elected a new parliament (*majlis*). The elections led to a temporary closing of ranks at the top of the Iranian political system. Ali Akbar Hashemi-Rafsanjani was reelected speaker of the *majlis* and, reportedly on the suggestion of President Ali Khamanei, was appointed commander-in-chief of the armed forces by Ayatollah Khumayni. The pragmatic Rafsanjani's mandate was to reform and reinvigorate the Iranian military. This goal would take time and required some breathing space from renewed Iraqi attacks. In the longer term, rebuilding Iranian military and economic strength would also require mending relations with (at a minimum) Western European countries, which could be sources of capital, trade, and technology for the Islamic Republic. In early July 1988 Rafsanjani commented that Iranian foreign policy had "incorrectly created enemies" while neglecting to attract friends.[79]

Given the general international consensus on the need to end the Iran-Iraq war, any reassessment of Iranian foreign policy had to begin with its stand on U.N. resolution 598. The shooting down by the *U.S.S. Vincennes* of the Iranian passenger plane presented Rafsanjani with an opportunity to form a consensus among the Iranian leadership on the need to accept a cease-fire. This consensus was then presented to Ayatollah Khumayni, who reluctantly accepted the decision. On July 18, 1988, Iranian President Ali Khamanei announced Iran's acceptance of resolution 598.

Now on the offensive, Iraq hesitated to respond to this unexpected change. Attempting to force Teheran into a public acceptance of its legitimacy, Baghdad demanded that face-to-face negotiations between the belligerents begin before a cease-fire went into effect. Iraqi forces continued to probe further into Iran and encouraged Iranian dissidents to maintain their attacks. However, under pressure from its Arab and international allies, on August 6, 1988, Iraq announced that it would accept a cease-fire if Iran agreed to subsequent direct talks. Iran accepted that compromise formula, and on August 20, 1988, a cease-fire in the eight-year Iran-Iraq war went into effect.

Conclusions: 1979–88

The Iranian revolution had a profoundly destabilizing effect on the international politics of the Gulf, but not solely or even primarily because of specific policies of the revolutionary regime. Rather, the domestic upheaval in Iran led to a reassessment by all the concerned parties of their regional policies and alignments and ended the relatively stable *modus vivendi* that had obtained in the region since 1975. The ideological and strategic threat presented by the revolution led to the unlikely alignment of monarchical Saudi Arabia and Ba'thist Iraq and to the overcoming of the smaller Arab states' fears of Saudi hegemony in the formation of the GCC. The rejection by Iran, on ideological grounds, of close relations with either the United States or the Soviet Union eventually drove each to support Iraq in the war, despite the fact that both superpowers continued to see Iran as the geopolitical prize in the area. However, continuing suspicions of each others' motives (even as the Cold War was ending) prevented Washington and Moscow from converting their parallel policies into a coordinated and cooperative effort to end the war. The commitment of the United States to the security of Saudi Arabia was tested in the Iran-Iraq war, which began during a period of U.S.-Saudi tensions over oil and Arab-Israeli issues and proved again to be an enduring feature of regional alignments.

The long and bloody Iran-Iraq war itself resulted from the regional dislocation caused by the revolution. The new regime in Teheran appeared both more threatening to the domestic stability of the Iraqi

Baʿth than had the shah, because of its revolutionary ideological appeal to Iraqi Shiʿa, and weaker than the shah, because of the upheaval it brought to Iranian society generally, the Iranian military specifically, and Iran's relations with the United States. That combination of increased threat and apparent strategic weakness led Iraq to initiate hostilities in September 1980. In July 1982 the Iranian regime faced analogous circumstances, with the Iraqi military in retreat and the secular Baʿthist regime, the ideological antithesis of the Islamic Republic, weakened. The temptation to gain a strategic and an ideological advantage by taking the war into Iraq was irresistible. The war ended with much of the impetus behind Iranian ideological and military expansion spent and with Iraq militarily powerful and profoundly unsatisfied with its meager gains. The stage was thus set for the next Gulf crisis.

The Iraqi Invasion of Kuwait and the Gulf War: 1989–91

The Iraqi invasion of Kuwait, on August 2, 1990, was both the last act of the Iran-Iraq war and the beginning of a new period in the region's security configuration. Although the Iraqi claim to Kuwait goes back to the formation of the Iraqi state in 1920 and had been asserted on other occasions, the immediate origins of this crisis date from the August 1988 cease-fire in the Iran-Iraq war. Saddam Husayn claimed victory, had an enormous military establishment behind him, and held on to some Iranian territory, but Iraq hardly reaped the fruits that a real victor in a bloody eight-year war would expect.

Far from submitting to Iraqi territorial demands, Iran refused to compromise its claim to half of the Shatt al-Arab waterway. The smaller Gulf shaykhdoms sought better relations with Iran, though improvement in Saudi-Iranian relations was stymied by continuing ideological tension. At the end of the war Gulf financial support to Iraq was severely curtailed. Although Saudi Arabia signed a nonaggression pact with Iraq in March 1989, it also improved relations with Egypt and reaffirmed ties with Syria (strained by the Syrian-Iranian alliance), as counterweights to both Iraqi and Iranian power in the Gulf. Iraq sponsored the formation of an Egyptian-Iraqi-Jordanian-North Yemeni grouping called the Arab Cooperation Council (formed in February 1989), but it never was able to act as a vehicle for the extension of Saddam's influence. Egypt was simply unwilling to play second fiddle to Iraq. Saddam began in 1990 to emphasize anti-American and anti-Israeli themes in his public statements in an effort to rally Arab public opinion to his side,[80] but regional realignments were working against his leadership ambitions.

Frustrated in his efforts to reap the fruits of his "victory" in the Iran-Iraq war, Saddam began to suspect that regional and international forces were conspiring to undermine his regime. Although there is no credible evidence for such a conspiracy, Saddam, whose whole political life had been spent in conspiracies of one type or another, had formed a conspiratorial view of the forces arrayed against him. Despite continued professions of good will on the part of the Bush administration, he interpreted anti-Iraqi resolutions by Congress (spurred by his use of poison gas against Kurds in Iraq) and some anti-Saddam broadcasts on the Voice of America Arabic service as proof of Washington's hostile intent. Increasing disquiet throughout 1989 and 1990 in Israel and in some media quarters in the United States over Iraq's nuclear program fed Saddam's suspicions that his enemies had found a pretext to attack him. To further feed Saddam's view of the conspiracy, in March 1990 Britain and the United States arrested Iraqi agents and accused them of trying to smuggle nuclear and other military technologies to Iraq. This coincided with Iraq's execution of an Iranian-born British journalist, Farhad Bazoft, on charges of spying for Israel.[81]

Saddam also increasingly saw domestic events through the prism of conspiracy. A number of high-ranking generals who had organized Iraq's final victories at the end of the Iran-Iraq war died in mysterious helicopter crashes or were placed under house arrest after the cease-fire. In February 1989 there were reports of a coup attempt against Saddam and the execution of a number of officers in its wake. In May 1989 Iraqi Defense Minister Adnan Khayrallah, Saddam's cousin and brother-in-law, died in a helicopter crash, according to official accounts.[82] Iraqi opposition forces report that Saddam himself killed Khayrallah, after discovering that he was involved in a Saudi-supported plot to overthrow him. The truth of that assertion will never be known, but the report undoubtedly reflects perceptions in Baghdad that would only feed Saddam's fears of a region-wide conspiracy against him.

The events that led to Iraq's invasion of Kuwait took place in this atmosphere. The Iraqi economy was suffering from the relatively low price of oil (around $18 per barrel in July 1990). Saddam was finding it difficult to deliver a "peace dividend" and to get the funds for his ambitious economic and military development plans. Kuwait was exceeding its OPEC production quota by nearly 1 million barrels of oil per day, helping to keep prices down.

Saddam began to rattle his saber against Kuwait in the spring of 1990.[83] Because other OPEC members, including Saudi Arabia and Iran, also wanted the Kuwaitis to abide by their quota, Saddam's rhetoric and his military buildup on the Kuwaiti border were largely discounted. The Saudis and Iranians might even have tacitly encouraged him to keep up the pressure on Kuwait before the July 1990 OPEC meeting. At the meeting, Kuwait agreed to reduce its output to the quota level. Saddam then escalated his demands to include formal Kuwaiti forgiveness of Iraq's debt and border changes. Saudi Arabia and Egypt initiated a mediation process aimed at defusing the crisis by meeting some of the Iraqi demands. Like the regional powers, the United States originally did not take the Iraqi threats to Kuwait very seriously. Its only military response was to order naval maneuvers off the coast of the United Arab Emirates, hundreds of miles from Kuwait. According to a transcript released by Iraq, on July 25, 1990, U.S. Ambassador April Glasbie told Saddam that the United States viewed the Iraqi-Kuwaiti border dispute as an inter-Arab problem that should be solved by inter-Arab means, indirectly expressing support for the Saudi-Egyptian mediation effort.

Saddam Husayn, while fearing a general conspiracy, found very little immediate opposition to his hard line on Kuwait. A quick move against the country, he might have surmised, would not be met with a rapid response. Possession of Kuwait could be a bargaining chip in dealing with his enemies and could strengthen him domestically and in Arab public opinion. A show of strength could preempt the conspiracy against him, either by forcing his opponents to make a deal or by so galvanizing Arab opinion as to prevent other Arab leaders from working against him. The actual rationale for Saddam's decision to invade will likely never be known, but this reconstruction best fits the available evidence. The Iraqi invasion of Kuwait on August 2, 1990, was a preemptive strike against an imagined conspiracy, a strike made attractive by the mild responses of other parties to Saddam's pre-August 2 escalation. The irony of Saddam's strategy was that it made his fear of a domestic–regional–international cabal against him a self-fulfilling prophecy.

The course of events from August 2, 1990, to the end of February 1991 is well known. Saudi Arabia quickly requested military support from the United States and other international and regional powers. President Bush responded by immediately dispatching American forces to the kingdom. Their numbers grew to over 500,000 by the beginning of 1991, and they were joined by sizable contingents from Great Britain, France, Egypt, and Syria and by token forces from numerous other countries, including Morocco and Pakistan. The United States also mobilized world support through the United Nations, orchestrating the passage of over a dozen Security Council resolutions condemning Iraq and calling for its unconditional withdrawal from Kuwait. Resolution 678 of November 1990 authorized the use of force against Iraq if it did not withdraw by January 15, 1991.

With the failure of diplomatic efforts to resolve the crisis, allied air forces began to attack Iraqi targets on the morning of January 17, 1991. Despite intensive propaganda efforts and attacks on Israel meant to draw it into the conflict, Iraq was unable to break the coalition arrayed against it or shake the domestic stability of the Arab regimes opposed to it. Allied ground forces moved against Iraqi positions in Iraq and Kuwait on February 24, 1991. On February 27, 1991, President Bush declared a unilateral cease-fire, with allied forces in control of Kuwait and most of southern Iraq. Devastated by the intense bombardment and the allied blitzkrieg, Iraq was forced to accept the onerous peace terms set forth by the U.N. Security Council, including the supervised dismantling of Iraqi weapons of mass destruction and the payment of a percentage of its oil revenues to be determined by the council as war reparations to Kuwait and other affected states.

The invasion of Kuwait forced other Gulf actors to face hard choices with regard to security. Saudi Arabia had seen Saddam as a worrisome but necessary ally in containing Iranian ideological and military pressures. With the invasion he became the major direct threat to Saudi security and domestic stability. Massing troops on the Saudi-Kuwaiti border, he called on the Saudi people to rise up against their rulers. Faced with such an immediate threat, Riyadh openly called for United States military assistance, despite the dangers this association could present to the Saudis' domestic and regional legitimacy. This decision gave Saddam a powerful propaganda weapon to use against the Saudis in mobilizing support throughout the Arab world, and even within Saudi Arabia. In exchange for American support, Saudi Arabia increased oil production by about 3 million barrels per day, cushioning the shock to the market caused by the removal of Iraqi and Kuwaiti production. It also turned to regional powers outside the Gulf—such as Egypt, Syria, and Pakistan—to counter the Iraqi threat. The Saudis saw these countries not only as balancers against Iraq in the military equation, but also as symbolic supporters that could legitimize to Arab and Muslim public opinion the Saudi invitation to the American military.

Iran also faced a dilemma. It had no desire to see Iraq, with which it had just fought a bloody eight-year war, strengthened. Not only was Iraq a potential military threat, but Saddam's "atheistic" Arab nationalist program was still the major ideological challenge to Iranian-supported revolutionary Islam in the Arab world as a whole. The Ba'thist regime and Saddam himself had been the target of sustained Iranian hostility since the revolution. However, an Iraqi defeat would strengthen the role of the United States—the "Great Satan"—in the Gulf and help preserve the "un-Islamic" Gulf monarchies that had been the target of Iranian ideological attacks. The American-led alliance was certainly more militarily powerful than Iraq, and some in Iran argued that it was the real long-term threat to the Islamic Republic. Iraq desperately tried to draw Iran to its side, capitulating in August 1990 on every outstanding issue from the Iran-Iraq war, including the border in the Shatt al-Arab, and adopting a self-consciously (and hypocritically) Islamic veneer in its propaganda. Iran happily accepted these concessions but continued to oppose the Iraqi annexation of Kuwait. Some officially tolerated food smuggling occurred across the Iran-Iraq border, and Teheran spoke out against the American military buildup in the region. However, the Islamic Republic, by remaining neutral, actually worked against Iraq in the crisis.

For the United States, the massive military commitment in the Gulf was the culmination of a process that began with the fall of the shah. Without a powerful and reliable regional ally to "police" the oil-rich area, Washington was progressively drawn into a more direct role. The Carter Doctrine, with the formation of a Rapid Deployment Force and the search for regional access arrangements, was followed by the naval deployments of 1987–88 and by the ground force commitment of 1990–91. The power that Saddam could have on oil questions—with control of Iraqi and Kuwaiti production, decisive influence over Saudi decisions, and the motive to link oil once again to the Arab-Israeli conflict—proved intolerable for the Bush Administration. Without a strong Gulf ally to confront Saddam, the United States acted directly to reverse the invasion of Kuwait.

However, the American military response was only possible with the end of the Cold War. Since the 1960s Iraq had been one of the closest allies of the Soviet Union in the Middle East. If this crisis had occurred during the Cold War, Moscow would have certainly vetoed efforts to build an international consensus against Iraq in the United Nations Security Council, would have refused to abide by boycotts against Iraq, and would have maintained its military supply relationship with Iraq. The risk of escalation to a superpower confrontation would have tempered the American military response against Iraq. Only the changed superpower relationship allowed the United States to use the United Nations as a political cover for its strategy and to attack Iraq without serious risk. This crisis demonstrated that because of its domestic problems, the Soviet Union had not only reoriented its foreign policy toward the West, but had lost the ability to play a major independent role in the Middle East.

Although Iraq was soundly defeated and forced to withdraw from Kuwait, the Gulf War did not immediately create a new security order in the region. Nevertheless, some changes are clear. Devastated economically and severely weakened militarily, Iraq cannot soon aspire to regional leadership, or even present a credible military threat to its neighbors. With Iraq's defeat, Iran has reemerged, for the first time since the revolution, as the strongest regional actor. America forcefully demonstrated its interest in the territorial status quo in the Gulf, and this will have a deterrent effect for some time on ambitious regional actors. The American-Saudi security relationship, which has been a constant in the region since World War II, was also strengthened by the crisis.

However, a number of questions about the postwar security order in the Gulf remained unanswered as of the end of 1991. The first concerns the future of Iraq and the regime of Saddam Husayn. Belying expectations, Saddam did not fall from power immediately after his defeat. He was able to salvage enough military power to put down popular uprisings among Shi'a in the south of Iraq and Kurds in the north. The United States, worried that the success of these revolts would redound to the benefit of Iran and perhaps lead to the dismemberment of Iraq, drew back from its earlier expressions of support for Saddam's domestic opposition. However, discontent with the Ba'thist regime continued to run high among the general public and the military, where a number of high-ranking officers were relieved from duty with the end of the Gulf War.[84] The regime's efforts to negotiate a new autonomy agreement with the Kurdish opposition had yet to bear fruit. United Nations forces occupied a small zone in southern Iraq, and allied forces remained just across the border in Turkey to protect the Kurds. Economic sanctions had not been lifted, and both British and American leaders indicated that they would remain in place as long as Saddam was in power.

Should Saddam fall, Iraq could become an arena in which other regional powers—particularly Iran, Saudi Arabia, and Syria—would struggle for influence. The character of a post-Saddam regime could substantially affect security perceptions in the Gulf, particularly if Shi'i elements close to Iran were to have a major role. As long as Saddam remains in power, Iraq would be an unacceptable partner for other Gulf states in any security arrangement.

A second unanswered question as of the end of 1991 was how relations among Saudi Arabia, Iran, Egypt, and Syria would develop. In March 1991 the GCC states, Egypt, and Syria agreed in what has become known as the Damascus Declaration that troops from the latter two states would remain in the Gulf as the nucleus of an Arab security force for the region. Meanwhile, relations between Saudi Arabia and Iran were improving dramatically, with the restoration of diplomatic ties, high-level visits, and the return of Iranians to the annual pilgrimage to Mecca in June 1991. Iran saw Gulf security as the responsibility of the

Gulf states alone and opposed a permanent Egyptian and Syrian military role in the region. Egypt and Syria, annoyed at GCC hesitation to implement the Damascus Declaration, withdrew their troops from Saudi Arabia in May 1991, but negotiations among the eight states continued through 1991. How the GCC states, particularly Saudi Arabia, will balance the roles of Iran, Egypt, and Syria in their security calculations had yet to crystallize.

The third issue involved the details of the U.S. role in the Gulf. President Bush repeatedly said that all American ground forces would be withdrawn from the region, and as of the end of 1991 most had been. Yet American forces at that time were still deployed at the Turkish-Iraqi border, and military exercises had been conducted in Kuwait. The Kuwaiti government publicly expressed its eagerness to have a permanent American military presence in the emirate, and reports surfaced in Washington that the headquarters of the U.S. Central Command would be transferred from Florida to the region. Although Saudi Arabia was still reluctant to host an American base, it was clear that military cooperation between the two countries would be even stronger and more intensive than it was before the invasion of Kuwait, with the prepositioning of equipment and frequent joint exercises. The permanent American naval presence in the Gulf, which dates back to World War II, would probably be enlarged and continue to be based in Bahrain. The specifics of the American presence would be extremely important. A highly visible American military profile could complicate relations both between the Gulf states and Iran, which is opposed to a major American role, and between Iran and the United States itself. American bases could also serve as lightning rods of domestic discontent in the Gulf monarchies, as foreign military bases historically have in other Middle Eastern countries.

The final unanswered question related to the domestic political stability of the Gulf Arab monarchies. Upheaval in these countries would significantly affect the security picture in the Gulf, their relations with the United States, and the world oil market. The monarchies proved remarkably stable in this crisis, as they have in past crises, belying the predictions of many experts. Few, if any, Kuwaitis rallied to Saddam after the invasion; even Kuwaiti opposition figures reaffirmed their loyalty to the Al Sabah family. Iraqi propaganda and the presence of millions of American soldiers did not shake the Saudi regime. However, the crisis did bring to the surface manifestations of discontent, particularly in Saudi Arabia and Kuwait, and led to promises by the rulers to widen the scope of popular participation in politics. With the end of the crisis, the Al Sabah and the Al Sa'ud have been slow to redeem those promises. How (if at all) the domestic political orders of the oil monarchies will be affected by the crises remains to be seen.

Conclusions: Patterns of Conflict and Alignment in the Gulf—1971–91

The Regional Powers

Immutable factors of physical and human geography underlay the basic structure of Gulf regional politics—a contest for influence between Iran and Iraq, with Saudi Arabia and the smaller shaykhdoms maneuvering between them. However, the level of conflict in these relationships and the alignments formed among these states were determined as much by their specific ideological content and the exigencies of domestic politics as by the distribution of power among them. Conflicts of interest were more likely to escalate to war in an atmosphere of ideological and political challenge to the domestic security and legitimacy of regimes. Saudi Arabia and the smaller shaykhdoms tended to balance against the regional power that directly challenged their domestic stability and regime legitimacy, even if the other regional actor was more powerful militarily.

The security of the Gulf states and regimes was as threatened by domestic unrest as by invasion, and the former has frequently been a prelude to the latter. Restive national and sectarian groups such as the Kurds and Arab Shiʿa have been exploited by outside powers to pressure and even overthrow regimes. Interference in the domestic affairs of neighbors was facilitated and justified by the powerful attraction to many in the Gulf of transnational political ideologies based on Pan-Arabism and Islam. Gulf rulers saw cross-border appeals to national minorities, sectarian groups, and ideological soulmates as serious threats because (with the possible exception of revolutionary Iran) they had not yet inculcated a strong sense of loyalty among their citizens to their states or, more immediately, their regimes.

These ideological and domestic factors were clear in the Iran-Iraq relationship. Direct challenges to the stability and legitimacy of each other's *domestic political regimes* were the key element distinguishing periods of heightened tension and conflict between Iran and Iraq. During those periods when one or both of the parties put forward ideological claims aimed at destabilizing the other's political system or calling into question the other's control over some part of its citizens or territory, the level of conflict escalated. In 1975, conflict between the two did not escalate to war, as Iran agreed to halt efforts to destabilize the Ba'th domestically in exchange for recognition of its claims in the Shatt al-Arab. In contrast, in 1979–80, neither side would give up its ideological claims against the other (Iraq's Arab nationalist claim to Khuzistan; Iran's Islamic claim against the "atheistic" Ba'th). The result was war.

Iraq's decision to go to war against Iran in September 1980 was based on much more than a border dispute in the Shatt al-Arab. It can be understood only in terms of the dual effects of the Iranian revolution on Iraq—the threat the Iranian revolution posed to the Ba'thist regime's domestic political stability *and* the opportunity an Iran apparently in chaos provided to the ambitious Saddam Husayn to achieve regional dominance. Likewise, Iran's decision to take the war into Iraqi territory in 1982 as the tide of battle turned in its favor was the product of the Islamic Republic's desire to spread its ideological message and its perception that the Iraqi regime did not have the resources to meet Iran's challenge. Domestic and ideological factors were also central to the Iraqi decision to invade Kuwait in 1990. The invasion was made possible by the vast disparities in power between the two states, but such disparities had existed for decades. The key element in explaining why Saddam chose to take advantage of those disparities when he did was his belief that a preemptive strike could break the domestic-regional-international conspiracy he believed was arrayed against him. He thought he could consolidate his victory in Kuwait by appealing to citizens throughout the Arab Gulf states, and the Arab world, to support him against their governments.

Perceptions of threat to domestic regime stability were also central in explaining the alignment behavior of the Arab Gulf monarchies. When they were faced with two potential threats, one based on military capability and the other on ideological challenge, the smaller states of the Gulf aligned with the stronger military power against the militarily weaker but more ideologically threatening state. When the two types of threats combined, as was the case with Iran in the mid–1980s and with Iraq after the invasion of Kuwait, alignment decisions became easy and obvious. In the one brief period, where neither of the two major regional powers presented ideological threats to their domestic regime stability (1975–1978), the Arab monarchies sought out a middle position between the two larger Gulf states. Balancing occurred against threats to domestic stability and security, not against power as such. Those threats were frequently more ideological and political than military.

Iran was by any measure of international power superior to Iraq in the early 1970s, yet Saudi Arabia leaned toward Iran and Oman invited Iranian troops into the country to help deal with the Dhufar rebellion. At the beginning of the Gulf War, most observers expected an easy Iraqi victory, yet all the other Gulf states aligned with it, not with the apparently weaker Iran. Similarly, the end of the war, with Iraq holding the military edge, did not lead to a shift of alignment toward Iran, particularly on the part of Saudi Arabia. Only when Iraq actually invaded Kuwait did the Gulf monarchies align themselves openly against Iraq. It is interesting that the Iraqi conquest of Kuwait was shortly followed by calls from Baghdad for the citizens in Saudi Arabia to rebel against their government. What began as a conventional military security threat quickly became combined with an overt ideological threat to the regime's domestic security.

The success of Saudi efforts to maintain their hegemony over the smaller shaykhdoms varied with the level of military and ideological challenges to their regime stability. During the 1975–79 period, the shaykhdoms, particularly Kuwait and Oman, asserted some amount of independence from Riyadh. Conversely, in the face of the Iranian ideological and military threat in the early 1980s, these states put aside their fears of Saudi domination and joined the Saudi-led GCC. The Iraqi invasion of Kuwait and the accompanying propaganda attacks on "oil shaykhs" pushed the shaykhdoms back toward Riyadh after a brief period, with the end of the Iran-Iraq war, of more unilateral tendencies.

Ideological appeals and domestic subversion could not topple any of the regimes in the region during the period under study. Neither Iranian Islamic revolutionary propaganda nor Iraqi appeals based on Pan-Arabism and anti-Americanism could bring down the Al Saʿud or the other ruling families. Both Saddam's Iraq and revolutionary Iran were able to endure even serious military reverses and maintain their regimes. The capacity of states in the Gulf to control their societies, and thus limit the effectiveness of outside interference in domestic affairs, increased during the 1970s and 1980s, as will be discussed later, in the section on oil. Whether increased state capacity has been translated into greater citizen loyalty and identification with state and regime is an open question, and one that Gulf rulers have been unwilling (with the partial exception of the Iranian revolutionary regime) to ask. It is ironic that, when these rulers have been more able to meet the challenges of transnational ideological appeals and outside interference in their domestic affairs, they continued to base their foreign policies on the primacy of such threats.

Regional-Extraregional Links

All the states of the region sought to mitigate their security worries and build up their local capabilities by maintaining relations with extraregional states that were both militarily powerful and apparently unthreatening to their domestic political orders. The Saudis and the smaller Gulf states looked to Egypt as a possible counterweight to both Iraq and Iran, though between 1979 and the mid–1980s, when the Camp David Accords made association with Egypt a domestic political liability, Egyptian-Gulf ties were downgraded. Iraq also turned to Egypt for military supplies and political support after it was on the defensive in the Iran-Iraq war. Saudi Arabia developed a security relationship with Pakistan, which involved stationing Pakistani troops in the kingdom. With the turn in the battle in late 1987 and the restoration of Saudi-Egyptian ties, the kingdom let its security arrangement with Pakistan lapse, only to renew it during the Iraq-Kuwait crisis.[85]

The superpowers were also courted for military and political support. Saudi Arabia, Oman, and Bahrain maintained continuous military relationships with the United States, and all the Gulf monarchies called for American support after the invasion of Kuwait. Kuwait had earlier called on both superpowers to protect its tankers in 1987. Iraq had strong relations with the Soviet Union in the early 1970s and relied heavily on Soviet military supplies throughout the Gulf War. From 1975 Baghdad also developed arms supply relationships with Western European powers, particularly France. The shah's Iran had particularly close ties with the United States. Only revolutionary Iran disdained close contact with both superpowers and was in the midst of reconsidering that policy by 1991.

Ties to superpowers presented a risk, however. Although neither superpower actively worked to destabilize its local clients during the period under study (the United States did play a role in overthrowing the Mussadiq government in Iran in 1953), the perception of an overly close relationship with a superpower could mobilize domestic opposition to a regime. The most obvious case was the shah's Iran and the important role anti-American feeling had in fueling the revolution. Clearly, Saudi Arabia was worried about the same phenomenon, and worked to keep its relationship with the United States, at least as it is portrayed to the Saudi public, at arm's length unless the kingdom was directly threatened. In the 1973 Arab-Israeli War and immediately after the Camp David Accords, the Saudis chose to distance themselves from the United States, fearing that the negative domestic and regional political consequences of their American tie outweighed its security benefits. Riyadh supported the 1987 American naval deployment in the Gulf only after the failure of its efforts in 1984–86 to cultivate better ties with Teheran. It took the Iraqi invasion of Kuwait for the Saudis to overcome their hesitations about a formal American military presence in the kingdom. Even then Saudi officials continued to stress both the multinational nature of the forces and the fact that all foreign forces would leave the kingdom as soon as the crisis ended.

Outside Powers

Involvement in the region by the superpowers was motivated by enduring aspects of their own national strategies. Geographical contiguity gave the Soviet Union an interest in Iran. Fear that domestic political events in the Muslim Middle East could spill over into Soviet Central Asia accounted for the Soviet interest in the area's domestic politics. Moscow also tried to deny rivals a predominant role in the Gulf, or at least to maintain some role in the area to check the influence of the United States. These interests led to the Soviet-Iraqi relationship of the late 1960s and early 1970s, the efforts to take advantage of the hostility in U.S.-Iranian relations in the 1980s, and the Soviet willingness to arm Iraq when Iran went on the offensive in the Gulf War. It also helps explain why the Soviets invaded Afghanistan in 1979, where it appeared that a friendly Communist government was in danger of collapse.

Under Gorbachev, Soviet policy aimed at reducing tensions with the Gulf monarchies. During his tenure the Soviet Union withdrew from Afghanistan; restored diplomatic relations with Saudi Arabia (severed in the 1920s); extended diplomatic recognition to the governments of Oman, the United Arab Emirates, Qatar, and Bahrain; and opposed the Iraqi invasion of Kuwait. For the first time, Moscow acted as a junior partner in an American-led coalition during the Kuwait crisis. In the past, even when their interests coincided (as at the end of the Iran-Iraq war), the United States and the Soviet Union acted in parallel, and mutually suspicious, rather than in cooperative ways.

Analysis of Soviet policy in the Gulf is now of only historical interest. Whether the new Commonwealth of Independent States, or any of its constituent republics, will play an active role in the area in the future remains to be seen. In a reversal of the centuries-old trend of Russian and Soviet expansion of influence to the south, the Gulf states of Iran and Saudi Arabia, along with Turkey, are now competing to augment their influence in the Muslim republics of what used to be the Soviet Union. These states have a whole new arena in which to play out their rivalries. Middle East politics appears to be moving north.

For the United States, the major rationale for interest in the Gulf has been oil. The continuing importance of oil for the economies of the United States, Western Europe, and Japan, and the central role of Gulf producers in the world oil market will mean continued American involvement. American policy in the Gulf has been predicated on denying any hostile (or potentially hostile) power, be it the Soviet Union or a regional power like revolutionary Iran or Saddam's Iraq, a predominant role in the region. Its preferred strategy for achieving that end has been political and military support for friendly local governments, particularly the shah's Iran and Saudi Arabia. In a crisis it has dispatched its own forces to achieve its strategic aim. It is equally clear that the United States has not used direct military force simply to keep oil prices low. The oil shocks of 1973–74 and 1979–80 did palpable damage to the American economy. There was talk of the use of military force to redress the effects of these crises, but no moves were taken. Rather, the crises led to increased American efforts to strengthen ties with states (e.g., the shah's Iran and Saudi Arabia) that were in some ways responsible for the crises.

These underlying strategic rationales explain superpower interest and involvement in the region. Specific policy choices aimed at forwarding those interests can be explained better by referring to the rivalry between the superpowers rather than by any regional realities, at least until 1990. The British withdrawal in 1971 led both Washington and Moscow to adopt local regimes as clients, as much to check each other as anything else. The American naval deployment in the Gulf in 1987 was not a response to the realities of regional politics. Rather, it occurred when it looked as if Moscow would assume a larger naval role there. It is especially interesting that in both 1971 and 1987 the superpowers were generally pursuing policies of détente. Yet this did not reduce their contest for influence in the Gulf, temper their tendency to predicate their Gulf policies on moves made by the other superpower, or lead to efforts at cooperative management of regional problems. The interest of both superpowers in the region was enduring; the extent of their direct military involvement between 1971 and 1990 depended on the state of their own rivalry. With the end of the Cold War and the Kuwait crisis, the United States appeared more willing to use direct military force in response to local events, not just in reaction to perceived Soviet threats. The collapse of the Soviet Union removes a constraint on unilateral American military action in the Gulf, but also removes at least one reason used to justify American military commitments there.

Oil

Finally, it is important to consider the role of oil in the international politics of the region. Oil defines American, Japanese, and European interests in the region. The oil boom of the 1970s accelerated the process of state building throughout the Gulf, allowing regimes to build large bureaucratic and coercive apparatuses aimed both at linking society to the state through the distribution of revenues and at controlling political dissent. This process did not ensure domestic stability. The revolution in Iran emerged, at least in part, from the social and economic dislocations that accompanied the oil boom and the shah's state-building policies.

However, it is equally true that on the Arab side of the Gulf every regime in power in 1971 remains in power in 1991. Even under military occupation, Kuwaitis demonstrated a remarkably resilient loyalty to their state and their government in exile. The Iraqi regime withstood eight years of war and ideological pressure from Iran, and (as of the end of 1991) military defeat and popular uprisings following its defeat in Kuwait. Shrewdly used, oil did foster regime stability in the Arab states. This fact does not necessarily lead to the conclusion that the Arab regimes have overcome the problem of domestic political stability. In fact, the extension of the state more widely and deeply into society contributes to greater politicization of the citizenry, as the policies of the state come to be seen as more important in the everyday life of average people. This encourages the raising of demands for a say in political decisions. Such demands on the Arab side have remained inchoate up to now. Political opposition in the 1980s was in most cases linked to the Iranian revolution, something with which none of the Arab regimes was willing to compromise. However, with the end of the Gulf War and the increasing "domestication" of the revolution in Iran, it is inevitable that new demands will be made on the Arab Gulf rulers. The pressures generated by the Iraqi invasion of Kuwait led the ruling families in Kuwait, Saudi Arabia, and Oman to promise to establish broader structures for political participation after the crisis. It remains to be seen how far they will go in fulfilling these promises.

The international political effects of the oil boom were also varied and complicated. Oil revenues allowed Iran, Iraq, and Saudi Arabia to acquire massive amounts of sophisticated military hardware and, in the cases of Iran and Iraq, to increase vastly the size of their military establishments. These changes fueled the ambitions of the shah to be the "policeman of the Gulf" in the 1970s and encouraged Saddam Husayn to attempt to play the same role in 1980 and 1990. Oil money allowed Iran and Iraq to fight their long and debilitating war. Oil also freed each of the powers, to some extent, from strategic dependence on their superpower allies. The shah's Iran and Saudi Arabia were more important to the United States in the 1970s and thus could exercise much more freedom on such issues as oil pricing than had been possible in the past. Their strategic relations with the United States shifted from dependence to interdependence. In the 1980s the Saudis diversified their sources of weapons, buying more from China, France, and Great Britain, a luxury available only to states with the hard currency earnings to enter the international arms market. Iraq also was able to buy weapons from the West, particularly France, making it less reliant on the Soviet Union. Saddam's move into Kuwait was an expression of confidence (mistaken, but real) in Iraq's ability to pursue an aggressive and independent foreign policy based solely on Iraqi resources. Revolutionary Iran could thumb its nose at both superpowers during the Gulf War because it had the resources to find alternative military suppliers.

It is important not to overestimate the independence oil gave to the regional states. The Saudis still relied on American political and strategic support; the Soviet Union was still Iraq's major weapons supplier during the Gulf War. Iraq in the end could not sustain its confrontation with the United States and the larger international community. Even revolutionary Iran has given signs of improving relations with both superpowers. However, superpower–local-power relations were markedly different after 1973, with the local powers possessed of much more leverage in the relationships, because of oil.

Although the oil boom significantly affected the military capabilities of each of the region's states and their relations with outside powers, its impact on their *relative* power positions with regard to each other was surprisingly limited. Oil did not catapult one state into a position of dominance over the others, nor did it radically alter the relative regional pecking order that existed before 1973. Iran was the leading power in the region before 1973, and it remained so after. Iraq was its principal rival, with the Saudis and the smaller Gulf states maneuvering between them, as was the case before 1973. There are two major reasons that oil did not substantially alter power relations among the local states. First, money is not the only attribute of international power. Population and geography are constants that continue to give Iran an advantage over the Arab states. Saudi Arabia remains a sparsely populated state with far-flung borders and myriad security challenges. Second, because each of the main Gulf states is a major oil exporter, they all benefited from the oil boom. Oil in the 1970s was a tide that lifted all boats; the downturn in oil prices in the mid–1980s affected all the states of the region in equal proportion, as did the price increases of the 1970s. Oil affected, but did not notably alter, the pattern of power relations among the Gulf states themselves, even as it profoundly changed their domestic polities and the interest of the outside world in the region.

NOTES

1. The body of water separating Iran from the Arabian Peninsula is called the Persian Gulf by Iranians and the Arabian Gulf by Arabs. Rather than take

sides on this issue, and to avoid the clumsy compound "Persian-Arabian Gulf," I will refer to it in this chapter simply as "the Gulf."

2. Kenneth Waltz emphasizes balancing against capabilities as the motor of balance-of-power politics, *Theory of International Politics* (Reading, Mass.: Addison-Wesley, 1979), esp. chs. 5 and 6.

3. Barry Buzan, *People, States, and Fear* (Brighton, U.K.: Wheatsheaf Books, 1983), points out that states where "ideas and institutions are internally contested" are as threatened by what he calls "political" challenges as they are by military ones, "for in such cases the state is likely to be highly vulnerable to political penetration." See pp. 65–77, esp. pp. 76–77.

4. Stephen Walt modifies balance-of-power theory to emphasize balancing behavior against threats rather than against capabilities but does not distinguish among different types of threats. See his *Origins of Alliances* (Ithaca: Cornell University Press, 1987). Steven R. David contends that Third World leaders balance against their most serious threat to regime security, be it domestic, regional, or international. See his "Explaining Third World Alignment," *World Politics*, 43, no. 2 (January 1991):233–56.

5. Production figure calculated from U.S. Department of Energy, Energy Information Administration, *Monthly Energy Review* (March 1991); reserves figure taken from British Petroleum, *Statistical Review of World Energy* (June 1988).

6. For a list of sources on the domestic politics of these states, see subsequent notes and the select bibliography at the end of the book. Statistics on the Middle East generally must be taken as estimates. Unless otherwise indicated, information on population, GDP, and per capita income is taken from International Institute of Strategic Studies, *The Military Balance, 1990–91* (London: Brassey's for IISS, 1990). These numbers were cross-checked for general reliability against those given in Central Intelligence Agency, *The World Factbook, 1989* (CPAS WF 88–001, May 1989); Economist Intelligence Unit, Country Reports for first quarter 1991; World Bank, *World Development Report, 1989* (New York: Oxford University Press for World Bank, 1989); and International Monetary Fund, *International Financial Statistics Yearbook—1990* (Washington, D.C.: IMF, 1990). Information on ethnic and sectarian composition of populations taken from James A. Bill, "Resurgent Islam in the Persian Gulf," *Foreign Affairs*, vol. 63, no. 1 (Fall 1984); and Central Intelligence Agency, *The World Factbook, 1989*.

7. Estimates of Iranian GDP vary wildly: $447 billion (1988–89) in *The Military Balance, 1990-—91*; $361 billion (1989) in the Economist Intelligence Unit Country Report on Iran, no. 1, 1991; $297.6 billion (1987) in IMF, *International Financial Statistics Yearbook--1990*; $93.5 billion (1988) in the Central Intelligence Agency, *World Factbook, 1989*. These discrepancies are due both to the difficulties in getting accurate statistics from Iran and to differentials between the real and official exchange rates of the Iranian rial and the U.S. dollar. The per capita figure cited is based on the latter figure.

8. The 1989 GDP figure in *The Military Balance, 1990–91* is $58.54 billion; the 1988 GDP figure in *The World Factbook, 1989* is $34 billion. The 1989 GDP estimate in the Economist Intelligence Unit Country Report on Iraq is extremely high, $213 billion, probably reflecting both high domestic inflation and conversion at the official, rather than the real, exchange rate.

9. *The Military Balance, 1990–91* reports a population of fourteen million, with five million expatriates. The author has been cited lower figures by Saudi officials.

10. On Britain's role in Iranian politics, see Nikki Keddie, *Roots of Revolution* (New Haven: Yale University Press, 1981); Richard Cottam, *Nationalism in Iran* (Pittsburgh: University of Pittsburgh Press, 1979); and Ervand Abrahamian, *Iran Between Two Revolutions* (Princeton: Princeton University Press, 1982).

11. For an outline of the history of oil and oil companies in the region, see Keith McLachan, "Oil in the Persian Gulf Area," in Alvin Cottrell, ed., *The Persian Gulf States: A General Survey* (Baltimore: Johns Hopkins University Press, 1980); and Daniel Yergin, *The Prize* (New York: Simon and Schuster, 1991).

12. For a full account of the British withdrawal decision, see the author's "British and American Policies in the Persian Gulf, 1968–1973," *Review of International Studies* (UK), 11(4) (October 1985):247–73.

13. For the historical background of the Iran-Iraq border dispute, see Daniel Pipes, "A Border Adrift: Origins of the Iran-Iraq War," in his *The Long Shadow: Culture and Politics in the Middle East* (New Brunswick, N.J.: Transaction Publishers, 1989); and Majid Khadduri, *The Gulf War* (New York: Oxford University Press, 1988), pp. 12, 35–41, 49–52.

14. Yergin, *The Prize*, chs. 20–22.

15. On U.S.-Iranian relations in general, see James A. Bill, *The Eagle and the Lion* (New Haven: Yale University Press, 1988). On the 1953 coup, see Mark J. Gasiorowski, "The 1953 Coup d'Etat in Iran," *International Journal of Middle East Studies*, 19, no. 3 (August 1987):261–86.

16. For an overview of Gulf territorial disputes in general, see Lenore G. Martin, *The Unstable Gulf* (Lexington, Mass.: D. C. Heath, 1984), ch. 3.

17. Nadav Safran, *Saudi Arabia: The Ceaseless Quest for Security* (Cambridge, Mass.: Harvard University Press, 1985), pp. 135–37.

18. For accounts of the negotiations that led to the formation of the UAE and the independence of Bahrain and Qatar, see Ali Mohammed Khalifa, *The United Arab Emirates: Unity in Fragmentation* (Boulder, Colo.: Westview, 1979); John Duke Anthony, *Arab States of the Lower Gulf* (Washington, D.C.: Middle East Institute, 1975); and Rosemarie Said Zahlan, *The Origins of the United Arab Emirates* (London: Macmillan, 1978).

19. J. B. Kelly, *Arabia, the Gulf, and the West* (New York: Basic, 1980), pp. 210–212.

20. For an account of the 1973 incident from a Kuwaiti point of view, see Abdul-Reda Assiri, *Kuwait's Foreign Policy* (Boulder, Colo.: Westview, 1990), pp. 54–56.

21. Henry Kissinger, *White House Years* (Boston: Little, Brown, 1979), p. 1264.

22. For a discussion of American policy in the Gulf before the 1973 oil embargo, see the author's "British and American Policies in the Persian Gulf, 1968–1973," pp. 258–66.

23. For an account of the oil negotiations during this period, see Dankwart Rustow, *Oil and Turmoil: America Faces OPEC and the Middle East* (New York: Norton, 1982), pp. 133–43; and Yergin, *The Prize*, ch. 28.

24. The vast increase in oil revenues had profound domestic political effects in all the countries, particularly in terms of the relationship between the state and social groupings that previously enjoyed a fair amount of autonomy. Neither the Iranian revolution nor the ability of the Arab states to resist the ideological and political pressures generated by the revolution can be understood without considering the effect of oil revenues on these polities. These issues will be discussed in more detail later. Excellent discussions can be found in H. Beblawi and G. Luciani, eds., *The Rentier State* (New York: Croom Helm, 1987); Jill Crystal, "Coalitions in Oil Monarchies: Kuwait and Qatar," *Comparative Politics*, 21(4) (July 1989):427–43; Kiren Aziz Chaudhry, "The Price of Wealth: Business and State in Labor Remittance and Oil Economies," *International Organization*, 43(1) (Winter 1989):101–45; Khaldun Hasan al-Naqib, *al-mujtama^c wa al-dawla fi al-khalij wa al-jazira al-^carabiyya* [Society and State in the Gulf and the Arabian Peninsula] (Beirut: markaz dirasat al-wahda al-ʿarabiyya, 1987).

25. On the 1973 embargo and the surrounding circumstances, see Rustow, *Oil and Turmoil*, pp. 145–79; Safran, *Saudi Arabia*, 151–67; Yergin, *The Prize*, ch. 29.

26. On the Iraqi Kurdish issue during this period, see Phebe Marr, *The Modern Hstory of Iraq* (Boulder, Colo.: Westview, 1985), 222–23, 232–26. On the Kurds generally, see Edmond Ghareeb, *The Kurdish Question in Iraq* (Syracuse: Syracuse University Press, 1981) and Stephen C. Pelletiere, *The Kurds: An Unstable Element in the Gulf* (Boulder, Colo.: Westview, 1984).

27. See the sources listed in note 13.

28. Text in Khadduri, *Gulf War*, pp. 199–200.

29. An excellent account of regional politics in the Gulf during this period can be found in Safran, *Saudi Arabia*, ch. 10.

30. For a full account of Saudi diplomacy on this issue, see the author's *Saudi-Yemeni Relations: Domestic Structures and Foreign Influence* (New York: Columbia University Press, 1990), pp. 113–14, 122–23.

31. Safran, *Saudi Arabia*, p. 269.

32. *New York Times*, June 18, 1978, p. 1.

33. R. K. Ramazani, *Revolutionary Iran: Challenge and Response in the Middle East* (Baltimore: Johns Hopkins University Press, 1986), pp. 58–60; Khadduri, *Gulf War*, pp. 80–81.

34. Safran, *Saudi Arabia*, pp. 308, 353–54.

35. Joseph Kostiner, "Shiʿi Unrest in the Gulf," in Martin Kramer, ed., *Shiʿism, Resistance, and Revolution* (Boulder, Colo.: Westview, 1987), p. 179; Laurie Ann Mylroie, "Regional Security After Empire: Saudi Arabia and the Gulf," Ph.D. dissertation, Harvard University (1985), 252–54, 262–63; Ramazani, *Revolutionary Iran*, pp. 40, 50.

36. Shahram Chubin and Charles Tripp, *Iran and Iraq at War* (Boulder, Colo.: Westview, 1988), p. 25; Marr, *Iraq*, p. 293; Khadduri, *Gulf War*, p. 83.

37. Kostiner, "Shiʿi Unrest," pp. 177–78.

38. Ramazani, *Revolutionary Iran*, p. 49.

39. *Middle East Journal*, 34(2) (Spring 1980):171.

40. Mylroie, "Regional Security," pp. 262–63.

41. Chubin and Tripp, *Iran and Iraq*, p. 34.

42. Khadduri, *Gulf War*, p. 68.

43. Text in Khadduri, *Gulf War*, pp. 119–20.

44. Gary Sick, "Trial by Error: Reflections on the Iran-Iraq War," *Middle East Journal*, 43(2) (Spring 1989):233.

45. Khadduri, *Gulf War*, quoting an October 1980 letter from Iranian President Bani Sadr to U.N. Secretary General Kurt Waldheim, p. 89.

46. On this point, see Afsaneh Najmabadi, "Iran's Turn to Islam: From Modernism to Moral Order," *Middle East Journal*, vol. 41, no. 2 (Spring 1987).

47. On Iranian politics during this period, see Shaul Bakhash, *The Reign of the Ayatollahs* (New York: Basic Books, 1984).

48. There are numerous books and memoirs on U.S. policy in the hostage crisis. Two of the best, from very different perspectives, are Gary Sick, *All Fall Down: America's Tragic Encounter with Iran* (New York: Random House, 1985); and Bill, *The Eagle and the Lion*, chs. 8–9.

49. United States, Energy Information Administration, *Monthly Energy Review* (April 1987):112–13.

50. Lawrence Axelrod, "Saudi Oil Policy: Economic and Political Determinants, 1973–1986," Ph.D. dissertation, Columbia University (1989):124–32; Safran, *Saudi Arabia*, pp. 401–402.

51. Safran, *Saudi Arabia*, pp. 398–406.

52. Safran, *Saudi Arabia*, pp. 406–409.

53. Quoted in Khadduri, *Gulf War*, p. 89. See also Chubin and Tripp, *Iran and Iraq*, p. 38.

54. *New York Times*, October 3, 1980, p. A10; *Foreign Broadcast Information Service*—Middle East and Africa (September 30, 1980), p. i.

55. Safran, *Saudi Arabia*, p. 369; Ramazani, *Revolutinary Iran*, pp. 72–73. There is a dispute in the sources over whether the Saudis allowed Soviet tanks to be landed at their ports for shipment to Iraq; Saudi officials denied the report.

56. Khadduri reports that the Saudi and Kuwaiti "loans" amounted to $1 billion per month for the first two years of the war (*Gulf War*, p. 154). Ramazani estimated in 1986 that the total amount of Arab "loans" to Iraq, coming almost exclusively from Saudi Arabia and Kuwait, was $35 billion, not including 350,000 barrels of oil produced daily for the Iraqi account (*Revolutionary Iran*, p. 76).

57. For details see Safran, *Saudi Arabia*, pp. 363–64, 372, 432, 439–40.

58. On the GCC, see R. K. Ramazani, *The Gulf Cooperation Council: Record and Analysis* (Charlottesville: University Press of Virginia, 1988); Emile Nakhleh, *The Gulf Cooperation Council: Policies, Problems, and Prospects* (New York: Praeger, 1986); Erik R. Peterson, *The Gulf Cooperation Council* (Boulder, Colo.: Westview, 1988).

59. Ramazani, *Revolutionary Iran*, 51, 131–32; Khadduri, *Gulf War*, p. 150; Mylroie, "Regional Security," pp. 339–57.

60. Chubin and Tripp, *Iran and Iraq*, p. 221.

61. Ramazani, *Revolutionary Iran*, p. 83.

62. Bakhash, *The Reign of the Ayatollahs*, chs. 6, 9.

63. Bakhash, *The Reign of the Ayatollahs*, p. 232.

64. Chubin and Tripp, *Iran and Iraq*, pp. 38–41.

65. Ramazani, *Revolutionary Iran*, p. 37.

66. According to Chubin and Tripp (*Iran and Iraq*, pp. 89–90), when Iranian forces crossed into Iraq in July 1982, the top Iraqi governing bodies held an extraordinary meeting *in the absence of Saddam Husayn* and issued an offer for a cease-fire. The offer was rejected by Iran, and Saddam had an opportunity to reassert his control in Iraq.

67. Efraim Karsh, "Military Lessons of the Iran-Iraq War," *Orbis* (Spring 1989); Chubin and Tripp, *Iran and Iraq*, p. 59.

68. Kostiner, "Shi'i Unrest," p. 180.

69. Ramazani, *Revolutionary Iran*, pp. 93–96.

70. Ramazani, *Revolutionary Iran*, pp. 99, 142–43.

71. *Washington Post*, March 13, 1986, pp. A25, A28.

72. Iranian efforts to disrupt the 1986 pilgrimage were revealed in a letter from Ayatollah Montazeri to Ayatollah Khumayni, which was made public during the 1989 leadership struggle in Iran (*New York Times*, May 22, 1989, pp. 1, 8.).

73. Chubin and Tripp, *Iran and Iraq*, pp. 191–94, 222.

74. Chubin and Tripp, *Iran and Iraq*, pp. 223–26.

75. Janice Gross Stein, "The Wrong Strategy in the Right Place: The United States in the Gulf," *International Security*, 13(3) (Winter 1988/89):148–50, 160.

76. James Bill, *The Eagle and the Lion*, p. 306.

77. Chubin and Tripp (*Iran and Iraq*, p. 198) report that Saddam Husayn convened special meetings of the Revolutionary Command Council, the Ba'th party regional command, and the Iraqi National Assembly to approve Iraq's acceptance of the resolution, clearly signaling his hope that it would be a way out of the war.

78. The texts of Security Council Resolution 598 and the official Iraqi and Iranian responses to it can be found in Khadduri, *Gulf War*, pp. 215–22.

79. *Middle East Journal*, 42(4) (Autumn 1988):661.

80. See, for example, his speeches to the Arab Cooperation Council summit on February 24, 1990, reproduced in *Foreign Broadcast Information Service—Near East and South Asia* (February 27, 1990):1–5; and to the Arab summit meeting on May 28, 1990, reproduced in *Foreign Broadcast Information Service—Near East and South Asia* (May 29, 1991):2–7; and his statement that if attacked by Israel, Iraq would "burn half of Israel," *New York Times*, April 3, 1991, p. 1.

81. For indications that the Iraqi leadership saw a conspiracy against them, see the following sources: (a) Saddam's remarks of April 12 to a U.S. Senate delegation headed by Sen. Robert Dole, the transcript of which was published by the Iraqi Embassy in Washington on April 24, 1990; (b) excerpts from U.S. Ambassador to Iraq April Glasbie's account of her July 25, 1990, meeting with Saddam Husayn, in which Saddam lists "evidence" of American hostility against Iraq, *New York Times*, July 13, 1991, p. 4; (c) the remarks by Iraqi Foreign Minister Tariq Aziz on January 9, 1991, after his failed meeting with U.S. Secretary of State James Baker, particularly his contention that the U.S. boycott of Iraq began before August 2, 1990, *New York Times*, January 10, 1991, p. A15.

82. *New York Times*, February 9, 1989, p. A7; May 7, 1989, p. 44.

83. See, for example, *New York Times*, July 18, 1990, pp. D1, D5, where Sad-

dam charged that Kuwait and the UAE were overproducing their OPEC quotas under American influence "to undermine Arab interests and security."

84. The London-based Arabic newspaper *al-Hayat* reported on July 8, 1991, p. 1, three failed coup attempts against Saddam between February and June 1991 and changes at the top of the Iraqi office corps.

85. In May 1991 it was reported that eleven thousand Pakistani troops deployed in the kingdom during the crisis would stay there for the foreseeable future, under a Saudi-Pakistani agreement. *Saudi Gazette*, May 22, 1991, p. 2.

3

South Asian Regional Politics: Assymmetrical Balance or One-State Dominance?

W. HOWARD WRIGGINS

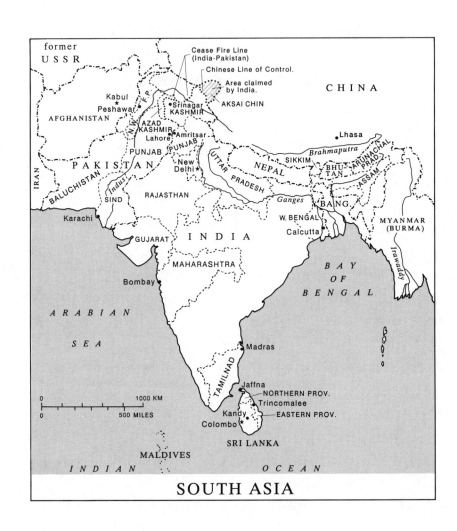

former
USSR

Cease Fire Line
(India-Pakistan)

Chinese Line of Control.

Area claimed
by India.

CHINA

AKSAI CHIN

Kabul
Peshawar
Srinagar
KASHMIR
AFGHANISTAN
AZAD
KASHMIR
Amritsar
Lahore
PUNJAB
PUNJAB

Lhasa

Brahmaputra

SIKKIM

ARUNACHAL
PRAD.

IRAN
BALUCHISTAN
PAKISTAN
New
Delhi
UTTAR
NEPAL
BHU-
TAN
ASSAM

Indus
SIND
RAJASTHAN
PRADESH
Ganges
BANG.

Karachi
W. BENGAL
MYANMAR
(BURMA)

GUJARAT
INDIA
Calcutta

Irrawaddy

MAHARASHTRA
BAY
OF
BENGAL

Bombay

ARABIAN

SEA

Madras

TAMILNAD
Jaffna
NORTHERN PROV.

0   1000 KM
Trincomalee

0   500 MILES
Kandy
EASTERN PROV.

Colombo
SRI LANKA

MALDIVES

INDIAN   OCEAN

SOUTH ASIA

This chapter explores relationships among the states of the South Asian regional security system: India, Pakistan, Bangladesh, Sri Lanka, Afghanistan, and Nepal.[1] It identifies major characteristics of each state that affect foreign policy and analyzes their security goals, their international relations, and the ways in which external powers affect the South Asian system.[2]

It first briefly characterizes the six states and considers fundamental features of the region. It then identifies major events that reveal the action-reaction links that have marked the activities of these states. It notes the rivalry between the two major but unequal states—India and Pakistan—that led to three wars between them. Historical memories, religious affiliations and other differences, and contrasting conceptions of the appropriate organization of the region intensify structural reasons for conflict. The chapter considers how differences in conventional power and other elements of state capability affect relationships. It shows how secessionist movements that are not effectively dealt with can lead to wars, notably the third Indo-Pakistani war in 1971, which led to the creation of Bangladesh, and a secessionist war within Sri Lanka. This deeply engaged New Delhi in Colombo's internal affairs and eventually led to the stationing of some sixty thousand Indian troops, one thousand of whom died at the hands of the Liberation Tigers of Tamil Eelam (LTTE), in the north of the island for more than a year and a half. There is good evidence that Prime Minister Rajiv Gandhi was also a victim of the LTTE. It considers India's and Pakistan's nuclear policies and their special implications in South Asia, the only Third World region thus far to demonstrate a real nuclear capability.

Relations between the major states of South Asia cannot be understood solely by reference to South Asia, however. Each has had profoundly important connections to major states beyond its region—to the United States, the Soviet Union, and China. These relations are explored.

This chapter also examines the ways in which the smaller states of the region are affected by their relations with their larger neighbors. It considers alternative explanations—historical, structural, perceptions and domestic politics—for the intensity of these antagonisms and how they play themselves out. How do the states of this region form a "system" of interactions that links them to one another, and how does that limit their leaders?

Many questions cannot be answered precisely. Often we do not have access to reliable sources, and many of the developments we seek to understand are inherently ambiguous. Nevertheless, the following discussion should shed some light on these and other aspects of the South Asian regional security system.

Regional Characteristics

The States

A number of the states of South Asia share recognizable cultural and other characteristics, but they also have fundamental differences.

India is at the center of the South Asian system, sharing frontiers with nearly every member and separating all but Pakistan and Afghanistan from one another. The world's second most populous state, with 800 million people, it occupies over 1.2 million square miles. It is a federation, with some twenty states and nine union territories. Since 1965 successive Congress party governments have emphasized the centralizing possibilities within the constitution. More variegated than Western Europe, its people speak fifteen officially recognized languages and many other languages and dialects. In constitutional principle a secular state, 82 percent of India's people are Hindus and 12 percent are Muslims. An industrial giant compared to its neighbors, India is a highly contentious democracy that has held ten national elections since independence.

Pakistan, the second most important state of the region, is also second in area, occupying 310,000 square miles. It is third largest in population, with some 102 million people. The creation of a Muslim political movement that culminated in the partition of the subcontinent by the departing British in 1947, Pakistan is also multiethnic and recognizes at least five regional languages. For most of the country's existence it has been governed in the vice-regal tradition, and the bureaucracy and army have been politically dominant. Since 1988 there have been two parliamentary elections.

Bangladesh, with 106 million people crowded into fifty-six thousand square miles (an area the size of Michigan), originally formed the eastern province of Pakistan. It broke away in 1971 over issues of representation, economic policies, and language rights. At the mouths of the great Brahmaputra and Ganges Rivers and beset by annual floods, it has the highest rate of population growth (2.64) in the region.[3] Unlike India and Pakistan, it is culturally relatively homogeneous; nearly everyone speaks Bengali, although about 20 percent of the population is non-

Muslim. Apart from the first years after independence and following elections in March 1991, it had been governed mainly by army officers who seized power in coups d'état.

Afghanistan, on the margin of South Asia, is a mountainous, rugged country of 245,000 square miles, much of it desert, with approximately sixteen million people before the Soviet invasion. Largely Muslim and multiethnic, it has been more a congeries of tribal societies than a state, tenuously held together by a symbolic monarchical rule until the 1978 revolution installed a Communist government and led to a nine-year-long Soviet occupation. Afghanistan was long considered a buffer between the British-ruled subcontinent and growing Russian power in central Asia. Ethnic differences often determined its policies toward its neighbors. After the Soviet army left in early 1989, a virtual civil war continued between the pro-Soviet regime in Kabul and a collection of *mujahidin,* who held sway in the countryside.

Sri Lanka is separated from India by the twenty-five-mile Palk Strait. It has a population of approximately sixteen million people and an area of about twenty-five thousand square miles, part of which is well watered and lush. Most of its citizens are Buddhist and stress their distinctiveness from the population of India. Until Independence in 1948, which was achieved through negotiation, Sri Lanka was a Crown Colony managed directly from London. Unique in Asia, it has had universal adult franchise since 1932 and for many years was seen as a model parliamentary democracy. However, in 1971, thousands of Sinhalese youths organized a movement known as the Janatha Vimukhti Peramuna (JVP) and attempted a one-night seizure of power, which was vigorously put down. Differences between the 70 percent Sinhalese majority and the 9 percent Sri Lankan Tamil minority degenerated since the mid–1950s to the point of a protracted secessionist war. From 1988 to 1990, at the same time, a resuscitated JVP mounted a virtual civil war among the Sinhalese population against the Colombo government. This was successfully repressed in 1990, but the secessionist struggle remained a costly stalemate.

Nepal has a population of about nineteen million. A mountain kingdom occupying some sixteen thousand square miles, it systematically isolated itself until the 1950s. Landlocked and dependent on India for the bulk of its commercial ties, its location along the one thousand miles of frontier dividing India and China made its policies toward China unusually important to New Delhi.

Relations among states of such diverse size and political character were bound to be difficult as the original five groped their way toward mutually acceptable relationships following independence in 1947–48.

TABLE 3.1
Elements of State Capability of South Asian States Compared[4]

	1	2	3	4	5	6	7	8
	Pop., 1988 (mil.)	Pop. Growth Rate, 1985–90 (%)	Armed Forces, 1988 (thous.)	GNP, 1988 ($bil.)	GNP per capita, 1988 ($)	M.E., 1988 ($bil.)	M.E. GNP, 1988 (%)	GDP Growth Rate, 1980– 88 (%)
India	816	1.7	1362	268	329	9.46	3.5	5.2
Bangladesh	110	2.6	102	19	172	N.A.	N.A.	3.7
Pakistan	108	2.3	484	36	338	2.52	6.9	6.5
Nepal	18	2.3	35	3	173	.04	1.1	4.7
Sri Lanka	17	1.5	47	7	415	.32	4.6	4.3
Afghanistan	15	N.A.	55	3	214	N.A.	N.A.	N.A.

Shared Characteristics

Different as the states of South Asia were, however, they all shared certain characteristics. With one-fifth of the world's population, this region is poor. All its states are in the lowest quartile among the less developed countries.[5] Most of these states also display marked contrasts between rich and poor.

In addition to their widespread poverty, the nations of this region have a high rate of population growth, with populations that double every twenty-five or thirty years. This multiplies the burdens of the government, which is faced with more mouths to feed, youths to train, and useful employment to create each year. The explosive growth of the youth cohorts has been particularly important, for when young males cannot find satisfactory life opportunities, they are easily mobilized for violent political action.[6]

Economic relationships among the states of South Asia have been constrained, because their traditional exports, such as tea and textiles, competed with each other. Moreover, each state sought to diversify its economy by protecting infant industries and to insure against undue economic dependence on the other states of the region.[7]

Vulnerable political institutions are not firmly established. Under British rule, certain Western political practices, including periodic elections, were introduced in what is now India, Bangladesh, Sri Lanka, and parts of Pakistan.However, they are sometimes subject to major changes by one leader. Populations have been politically active for several generations and are often volatile, unexpectedly expressing nationalistic or religious zeal that can result in domestic conflict and international difficulties. Understandably, as the most tangible manifestation of sovereignty, key frontier alignments have been bitterly contested.

Bureaucratic structures inherited from the British in India, Pakistan, Bangladesh, and Sri Lanka provided an administration with a more important public role in the states of South Asia than in those of the Gulf or Horn. (Their record in dealing with catastrophic refugee movements is notable.)

National cohesion cannot be taken for granted, since all the societies encompass groups of different cultural backgrounds, languages, and ethnic self-awareness. Ethnic political mobilization has been a marked feature of their histories.[8] In all the states of South Asia there are minorities that feel disadvantaged.

Understandably, the fear that ethnic disorders can destabilize governments and may even lead to separatism haunts the capitals of all the states of the region except Bangladesh. Such differences led to the partition of British India in 1947, to the secession of East Pakistan in 1971, to the recurrent Muslim demand for independence for Kashmir, to the demand for a Sikh state in the Indian Punjab, and for a Tamil state in Sri Lanka in the 1980s.[9]

Ethnic differences that transcend frontiers affect these states' interrelationships.[10] Since ethnic affiliations do not respect national frontiers, members of an ethnic group in one state often seek assistance from their brethren next door, regardless of whether a central government approves. This explains how the internal politics of one state affects the domestic politics of its neighbor.

For the principal protagonists in regional rivalries, the subcontinent does not provide sufficient supporting friends. As a result, a number of states actively participate in the external balancing process, seeking assistance from beyond the region to offset the power of the regional state they fear most.

Together, the interactions of the states in the region and the way these rivalries involve outside states define the direction of the South Asian system. These immediate neighbors, after all, pose the most troublesome and usually inescapable problems.

The Regional System in Action

To oversimplify, for purposes of this chapter two major political dramas are unfolding on the subcontinent:

1. India's effort to assert its predominance and the attempt of other states to offset those ambitions.

2. The tension between leaders seeking to consolidate a "unified" nation and spokesmen for regional and ethnic minorities who oppose the integration so ardently pressed by national governments.

Another important effort is that of consolidating working democracies in lands of traditional political cultures and institutions. Although this is a subject in itself and is as important in human terms, it has less effect on interstate relations and is considered here only as it affects relations between these states.

India and Pakistan: Unequal Rivals

Regional Dynamic: 1

India and Pakistan together shape the most consequential relationship in South Asia, one that affects a number of others. "These two countries were born locked into a complicated rivalry" that defined a central security problem for each of them.[11] Pakistan and India were both obsessed by each other until China's activities in Tibet and their frontier war in 1962 added China to India's major security concerns.

History, Structure, and the Security Dilemma

History casts a long shadow across South Asia. Muslim kingdoms had become well established in various parts of India well before the sixteenth century, when Moghul princes came down from central Asia and established their rule, centered on Delhi. Although Hindus and Muslims lived side by side over the centuries, they came to be seen as historical rivals for control of the Indian subcontinent. At independence in 1947, the protracted three-sided constitutional debate preceding partition left the Muslim minority and Hindu majority more self-aware and fearful of each other than at any time in recent centuries.[12] Muslims feared that within a Hindu majority state, they would be systematically disadvantaged. Hindus feared that the Muslims, long known for their military prowess, would seek to regain the supremacy they had held before the British. Traditional recollections and primordial ethnic fears provided the fundamental assumptions for their relationship, and these were easily played on by competing political leaders, who evoked such fears so that they could develop loyal political followings.[13] These underlying perceptions greatly influenced their postindependence relationships.

Their rivalry can also be seen as partly a reflection of structural problems. From the time of Thucydides, regional systems with only two major states have been marked by hostility.[14] These two populous states, cheek by jowl on the same subcontinent and intimately linked along a historically arbitrary border, lack "natural" frontiers. No buffer state separates them and no balancer checks their rivalry.

The relative size of the two states may contribute another kind of structural difficulty. Had they been more nearly equal, the prudent calculus of reciprocity might have induced the larger to attend more to the anxieties and ambitions of the smaller.[15] Had the latter been substantially smaller, it might have accepted the junior role more readily.

Both states, interlocked in rivalry on their crowded subcontinent, represent a vivid example of the "security dilemma."[16] Without an overarching authority to provide some security, each state focuses its worries on the other. Each attempts to improve its own security, often intensifying its neighbor's anxiety until a costly and risky arms race results.

Moreover, each successor state became committed to different principles of political organization. India opted for a secular state and vigorously opposed a division of the subcontinent on the basis of religion. The leaders of Pakistan, on the other hand, held that although their new state was to be hospitable to all, it was to be especially fit for Muslims of the subcontinent. Each state's constitutional principles were an offense and a tacit or exemplary challenge to the other.

Territorial issues intensified bitterness, and war over the beautiful Vale of Kashmir within weeks of independence made matters worse. In addition, that Pakistan lost out in both Junagadh and Hyderabad (where the leaders were Muslim but the population was Hindu) only confirmed their views that Indian leaders were not to be trusted. In Kashmir the situation was reversed. The population was Muslim but the rulers Hindu. That Pakistan surreptitiously sent Wazari tribesmen into Kashmir to seize the territory and refused to acknowledge their action only confirmed New Delhi's view that its leaders could not be trusted.

In addition, each country's leaders had a different notion of the desirable international order for South Asia. Quite early, Nehru sought to have India recognized as the rightful successor to the British Raj, the predominant regional power.[17] It was natural for many Indian statesmen (or stateswomen) to be acutely sensitive to the relationships their smaller neighbors developed with those beyond former British India. They feared above all that these small neighbors might become the instruments, perhaps unwittingly, of outside powers seeking to use them to intensify India's domestic difficulties for their own purposes. As Surjit Mansingh put Nehru's view:

> Because the source of instability and dissension was identified by New Delhi as the interference of outside powers, India made a discernible effort to have its own superior position recognized by all the other states

concerned. It sought a kind of veto over activities in the region which it judged harmful to its vital interests.[18]

What India's "superior position" was to imply for neighboring states was unclear.[19] The way the princely state of Sikkim, formerly a protectorate, had been integrated into India in 1975 as the twenty-second Indian state, following agitation organized by Indian services, symbolized for her smaller neighbors the extent of Indian ambitions.[20] The Indians liked to cite the Monroe Doctrine as a precedent, but smaller states in the region found India unresponsive to their concerns, and the presumption that they should consult India prior to significant foreign policy initiatives was considered a derogation of their independence.

Both India and Pakistan were concerned about "autonomy," but they had different conceptions of what that implied. For Indian leaders, the autonomy of India required that the whole South Asian region be free of outside influences—an expansive conception of Indian autonomy. In contrast, autonomy for Pakistan required that India not dominate Pakistan's freedom of action. That required seeking support from outside the region. Thus, Pakistan's effort to achieve autonomy ran directly counter to India's prerequisites for autonomy.[21]

Pakistanis saw their role differently. On the western marches of the subcontinent, their state straddles the historical invasion route from central Asia and Iran. Unwilling to play younger brother to elder brother India, Pakistanis stressed the sovereign equality of states, despite differences in size or capability. Their government dedicated a higher proportion of national resources to defense, since it understood that whereas India could overwhelm Pakistan, the reverse was not conceivable, despite occasional tall talk. They also sought countervailing support in association with Iran and among the Arab states of the Gulf. The Indians made much of the privileged status of the Pakistani military, but they could not understand how much the looming shadow of India contributed to legitimize the military leadership they criticized so regularly.

Though suggestive, the security dilemma is not an exact paradigm for Indo-Pakistani relations, because the disparity between India and Pakistan was so great the anxiety of the much larger India often appeared to reflect regional ambitions more than genuine fears. Both states were also determined to defend their territorial integrity—India against Pakistan's ambitions in Kashmir and against China's in the Himalayas, and Pakistan against any attempt by India to undo the original partition or to further divide Pakistan.[22] Each believed the other was seeking to use ethnic vulnerabilities to undermine domestic political cohesion.[23]

Indeed, the great emotional tension in their relationship has helped to generate what appear to outside observers as farfetched anxieties, suggesting the deep fears evoked by their proximity and the policies their leaders espouse. Some Indians see their country as a beleaguered Hindu island in the midst of a Muslim sea that stretches all the way from the Mediterranean to Indonesia. In return, many Pakistanis are persuaded that India's military buildup is designed to overwhelm Pakistan and achieve revenge for centuries of Muslim rule.

As the two states contended against each other, hostility became more deeply entrenched. Expectations of another round fueled an arms race as both responded to the security dilemma they created for each other and to their old fears.

Domestic Politics and Ethnic Regionalism

Each of these two states is affected by developments in the other, and each is ambivalent about the other's difficulties.

India's society is extremely complex. Its peoples, speaking a multitude of languages, are distinguished by hundreds of castes (*jatis*), "little societies" within which individual identities are determined by inherited affiliations.[24] It is a great achievement of India's domestic politics that such large numbers of diverse peoples live and actively participate within one national government. No other polity has managed such a feat. However, deeply felt differences do exist. Efforts of the central government in New Delhi to assert control over states' politics and administrations have intensified regionalist sentiment. Moreover, competition between political rivals tempts would-be leaders to emphasize differences. Despite Nehru's effort to establish a secular India, hospitable to all who live there, demands that India should be recognized as a Hindu state have become more strident. These and the inflexible policies of New Delhi generated Muslim and Sikh responses that have intensified antagonisms. Political violence has increased at each recent election. The assassinations of Prime Minister Indira Gandhi by embittered Sikhs in 1984 and her son Rajiv during an election rally in Tamilnad in 1991 indicate a change for the worse. Affirmative action programs to reserve more government jobs for the lower castes produce deadly riots. Accusations of the "hidden [i.e., foreign] hand" are used to divert attention from local leaders whose political competition contributes to sharpening these differences. Forging a nation from such diversity, therefore, has been difficult; and fear is frequently expressed that India's enemies will misuse its diversity to weaken it.

Moreover, many regional peoples have direct ethnic links to peoples in neighboring states. India's self-conception as the legitimate inheritor of regional preeminence causes it to be concerned about the fate of related peoples next door. Consequently, it calls on the others to "implicitly offer deference," which they are reluctant to show in such a highly status-conscious part of the world.[25]

Since the late 1960s the once great Congress party has declined in its internal organization and its links to the grass roots of state politics. It is less able to act as an aggregator of political demands and mediator among contending factions than in the 1940s and 1950s. Indira Gandhi's efforts to concentrate power in New Delhi weakened local links and encouraged party leaders and her successors to use linquistic and Hindu religious appeals to mobilize support, thus stressing domestic ethnic and religious differences and fueling secessionist movements in both the Punjab and Kashmir. These tactics have weakened the prime minister's power. Nevertheless, out of this diversity the prime minister and a small corps of foreign policy specialists in the bureaucracy have managed to shape a foreign policy with wide public acceptance.

Like India, Pakistan is made up of diverse linguistic and ethnic communities. Punjabis are by far the largest single ethnic group; thus, ironically, the minority peoples of Pakistan—the Sindhis, Pathans, Baluchis, and Muhajirs, people who came from India at partition—resent the domination of the Punjabis in much the same way that the other peoples of the region resent Indian pretensions to regional preeminence. Baluchis have links with their brethren in Iran, as do Pathans with theirs in Afghanistan.

Pakistan has not yet been able to firmly institutionalize representative processes. The one truly free and unintimidated election held before 1988, in 1970, so polarized the electorate along ethnic lines that within a year Pakistan was torn by a civil war and the secession of Bangladesh. Sharply differing views on the appropriate role for Islam have never been resolved, and Pakistan's small but well-connected Shia community carries significant weight. Since 1980, religious zealotry in neighboring Iran caused more contention within Pakistan. No balance between the capital's responsibilities and the powers of the provinces has yet been found. Political violence has been traditional in the tribal areas of the Northwest Frontier Province. However, since the influx of Afghan refugees and the substantial support provided to the resistance movement, weapons are far more widespread than they used to be. The drug trade has worsened urban violence.

On the other hand, Pakistan's highly centralized government and its skillful diplomatic corps have allowed it to implement prompt, and often shrewd, foreign policy decisions and to attract a number of useful allies. The polity is widely thought to be brittle. Its educational system is abysmal, and governments have been subject to mass rejection of a particular incumbent. The army is well entrenched, although widely resented. The 1988 election that led to Benazir Bhutto's prime ministership may have opened a new chapter in Pakistan. Its dismissal within two years by President Ghulam Ishaq was criticized, but the subsequent 1990 election reportedly reflected the will of the electorate in most constituencies.[26]

Both states are vulnerable to ethnic regionalism that can generate separatist movements. Indeed, any assessment of their relative international capability must take into account these sociopolitical vulnerabilities as much as the conventional military balance (to be discussed later). Attempts at centralization can provoke parochial resistance. Competing politicians in both India and Pakistan use linguistic and regional ethnic solidarity to mobilize a local political following or as a ploy to increase bargaining leverage against the central government.[27] There is fear that ethnic and regional agitation could lead to yet another partition, with all its unforgettable horror. That, above all, must not happen again. New Delhi is worried by unrest in Dravidian south India; in the northeastern hill areas along the Bangladesh, Chinese, and Burmese borders; in Assam; and in Kashmir and by more recent demands for an independent Khalistan in the Punjab. Until the late 1970s, restlessness in the Northwest Frontier Province and Baluchistan worried Islamabad. In the 1980s ethnic strife between native Sindhis and *muhajirs* (migrants from India), became much worse. Both India and Pakistan accuse the other of stirring up these troubles. Because of these domestic difficulties, the hostility and distrust voiced by leaders on both sides of the frontier should be seen in part as a means of inducing political cohesion that cannot yet be taken for granted, as well as reflecting rivalry among competing leaders seeking to consolidate voting constituencies.

Some domestic restlessness next door has advantages, for it means that the neighbor is less able to pursue ambitious foreign policy goals. But too much can be a source of real anxiety, as developments in Sri Lanka's Tamil area demonstrated.[28]

Relative Conventional Power

Despite temporary reversals, there has been a change in the power balance that has increasingly favored India. Skillful Pakistani diplomacy and developments in the wider world have at times helped Pakistan and slowed the tipping of the balance in India's favor. The trend has continued, however, as a result of successful Indian efforts that have more than matched Pakistan's.

India has had natural advantages. Stretched along the Indus Valley, the present-day Pakistan is 900 miles long and is only 220 miles across in some places.[29] The major north-south rail and road lines are within easy distance of Indian air power. Lahore, Pakistan's major city and the former capital of the undivided Punjab, is only 15 miles from India's Punjab frontier. Before the secession of Bangladesh, East Pakistan was divided from the western and larger part of Pakistan by one thousand miles of India, leaving it virtually indefensible.

By comparison, given India's more nearly rectangular configuration, Indian troops could trade much space for time and fall back many miles before critical positions would be at risk. India's manpower pool was four times larger than Pakistan's at partition, and after the secession of Bangladesh it was seven times larger. From the beginning, India was endowed with the bulk of prepartition industries and raw materials, enhancing its self-sufficiency and strengthening its international capability. Pakistan has natural gas but not much else.

Pakistan also had to deal with Afghanistan's political agitation on behalf of Pukhtunistan, encouraging demands for autonomy if not independence for Islamabad's Pathan minority. Pakistan, as the smaller and more vulnerable country, sought to compensate for its relative weakness by "internal balancing," by mobilizing a higher proportion of its manpower and spending a substantially larger share of its government budget on defense.

The conventional military balance between the two South Asian states cannot be appreciated, however, without considering how the states of the region have been linked to the broader global system.

External Influences: 1

Pakistan's Search for Makeweights

The most consequential early reach beyond the subcontinent was Pakistan's. In its search for outside backing, Pakistan first sought support among the Middle Eastern Muslim states. However, they found Pakistan's efforts to establish an Islamic state irrelevant to their problems. Following World War II, Nazi documents covering negotiations leading to the Nazi-Soviet Pact of 1938 revealed Stalin's ambitions toward Iran and the Persian Gulf.[31] Pakistan's proximity to the Gulf made it important to those in Washington seeking to implement the containment policy. Not until 1954, however, following the Korean War and Washington's commitment to containing the Soviet Union and the establishment of the Baghdad Pact [later the Central Treaty Organization (CENTO)], did Washington respond to Pakistan's repeated requests for help.[32]

As seen in Washington, Pakistan was a large country (small only by comparison to India), strategically located near the Gulf and south of the Soviet Union, with a good military reputation and willing to align

TABLE 3.2
India and Pakistan Military Establishments Compared[30]

	Armed Forces	Military Expend as % of Cent. Gov. Expend.	Military Exp /GNP
India			
1962	600,000	14.6	2.1
1964	854,000	23.6	4.5
1974	956,000	21.0	3.0
1986	1,492,000	15.0	3.6
Pakistan			
1962	247,700	55.8	3.3
1964	257,000	49.5	2.9
1974	392,000	28.3	5.7
1986	573,000	25.1	6.7

itself with the United States, along with Iran and Turkey in CENTO.[33] American security interests in South Asia were thus largely derivative of these global worries. Some in Washington warned against intruding global concerns into a regional system still torn by its own unsettled differences. But the sense of urgency in Washington was great and the assistance program went ahead.

Over the next decade, the United States provided some $2.5 billion worth of military equipment (including a dozen F–104s, which could outfly anything in the Indian inventory, although the Indians had many more aircraft) and training. Budgetary support reduced the burden of maintaining a 230,000-man army, and commodity assistance helped ease pressures on the urban population. In its turn, Pakistan agreed to join the United States if it was necessary to fight Soviet Communist advances into the Middle East or South Asia. Thanks to American assistance, "Pakistan managed to 'balance' India in the early stages of its security relationship with the United States, but never possessed— probably according to American design—any offensive capability against India."[34]

Thus, Pakistan gained from U.S. concern about the Soviet Union, and Washington profited from Pakistan's rivalry with India and Islamabad's worries about the Soviet Union. In return for military and budgetary aid, Washington gained an electronic listening post and access to Peshawar airport, from which U–2 flights could photograph the Soviet Union. It also gained Pakistan's cooperation in CENTO with Iran and Turkey. With them Karachi generally supported Washington's positions at the United Nations.

New Delhi saw American help to Pakistan as directly threatening India's own security. It strengthened Pakistan, which had not yet given up on Kashmir; it helped consolidate a regime many in India still hoped would disintegrate, and it enhanced the role of the military in Pakistan's domestic politics and foreign policy. Delhi was also offended by the way Washington seemed to "equate" India and Pakistan, rather than recognizing that India had a special destiny.[35] Thus, it dramatized American indifference to Indian interests and increased the cost by raising the level of military technology in the area.

India responded by increasing its defense budget from 1.9 percent to 2.03 percent of GNP.[36] Compared to what happened after the Chinese intrusion, when defense as a percentage of GNP more than doubled, the change does not seem large. But the need to increase defense expenditures was resented by Nehru and many of his civilian associates, even though the military may have privately welcomed the increased budgets.

Transfers of military equipment are often read as much for their symbolic meaning, indicating a change of diplomatic alignment or a consolidation of diplomatic support, as for their immediate military significance. For Pakistan—and for India—Pakistan's military supply relationship with Washington confirmed America's commitment, which would increase Pakistani intransigence on issues between the two and might even embolden Pakistan to "try conclusions" once again in Kashmir.[37] As New Delhi saw it, the relationship with Washington "blinded" Pakistan "to the realities of the power balance in the subcontinent which should have prompted them to accommodation with India."[38]

Although they were collaborating on security matters, Washington and Karachi were preoccupied by quite different threats. For Washington it was the Soviet Union and China to the north. For Pakistan, although it was concerned about Soviet influences in Afghanistan, the most immediate problem was India, a threat from across the Punjab plains, to the east. For some ten years Washington and Karachi-Islamabad cooperated while preparing for very different contingencies, complicating India's security problem. That the American commitment was explicitly limited to a conflict with a Communist power (i.e., the Soviet Union or China) was often forgotten in Pakistan.

India's Search for Makeweights

The Indo-Soviet relationship was another instance of "balancing." Each came to see the other as a useful counterweight to their respective neighboring opponent. Three points deserve attention.

In the mid–1950s, following Stalin's death, Moscow began to court India. It was the largest South Asian state and a major spokesman among the former colonial countries willing to stand against the American containment policy.[39] Moscow's initiative, dramatized by Bulganin's public support for India's position on Kashmir shortly after Pakistan joined the Baghdad Pact (later known as the Central Treaty Organization, or CENTO) in 1955, was quietly reciprocated by India, then eager to obtain diplomatic support for its position in Kashmir against Pakistan and its American supporters. Nehru was also seeking then to dramatize India's "independence from both camps," promoting the self-awareness and solidarity of the nonaligned and working closely with Nasser, Tito, Chou En Lai, and others.

Toward the end of the 1950s, India's security position worsened as a result of differences over Chinese policies in Tibet and over the Sino-Indian frontier. Moscow's sense of rivalry, at first with the United States and subsequently with Mao's China, led it to support India.[40]

Moscow had already supported the Indian position in the Kashmir debates at the United Nations and was proposing to assist the Indian government-run heavy industries, which the United States refused to support. By the spring of 1961 the Soviets had begun a modest military transfer program, and negotiations opened the exciting possibility of coproduction within India of MIG-21s.[41] New Delhi no doubt also saw that military assistance from Moscow would signal to the Chinese that Beijing could not count on Moscow's support if they pursued ambitions at India's expense and to Pakistanis that India had better be left alone. Thus, the South Asian regional system became trebly linked to outsiders: Pakistan and the United States collaborated and post-Stalinist Russia assisted India diplomatically, while China added to India's security worries.

The Chinese Intrusion and Its Effects

The first direct military intrusion of outsiders into postcolonial South Asia was not by the "Western imperialists" but by India's Asian neighbor China.

Indian leaders were shocked by the harshness of Chinese repression in Tibet and angered to discover that during the period of apparently close Sino-Indian friendship, the Chinese had built a military road across Aksai Chin in territory the Indians claimed as theirs, connecting Kashgar in Sinkiang with Lhasa in Tibet. British India and Tibet had never formally agreed on the frontier, and no one controlled the arid, uninhabited plateau effectively.

Chinese road building and other military preparations along the southern edge of the Tibetan plateau made all the more ominous earlier Chinese maps that designated Nepal, Sikkim, Bhutan, and the Northeast Frontier Agency (NEFA) above Assam as part of China's "lost territories." By the late 1950s, India found unacceptable China's suggestion of a pragmatic swap—China would recognize the Indian position on the McMahon line above Assam (which the Indians had all along affirmed as theirs) if India would accept China's position in the Aksai Chin (which India had never recognized). As New Delhi saw it, to agree to this would tacitly acknowledge China's claim to a *droit de regard* over the future of the other areas apparently claimed by China. Consequently, India pushed military defense positions into the mountains further than originally planned or than proved to be prudent.[42] After a number of "firefight" incidents, the Chinese army penetrated deep into Assam, advanced into all the contested areas of Indian-held Ladakh, and took 4,000 prisoners.

India was soundly defeated. To be sure, the terrain and advance preparations were in China's favor, and Indian forces faced nearly impossible logistical handicaps.[43] Nehru's urgent appeal to the United States and Britain for air cover for Indian cities, which was promptly responded to, undermined India's credibility as a critic of those who sought military links with the West.[44] China retained the political initiative by withdrawing unilaterally and promptly returning its prisoners of war.

Allen Whiting argues persuasively that these events may well have resulted from serious misconceptions about the other's intentions on both sides.[45] Indian leaders could not imagine that Delhi's "defensive" steps in the disputed area would provoke a military initiative by China.[46] Moreover, had Indian public opinion been less vehement on the subject of Chinese repression in Tibet or had Nehru's domestic position then been stronger, New Delhi might have been ready to negotiate with Beijing.[47] Or if Mao and his associates had been less worried by severe economic difficulties at home, coinciding with Moscow's increased hostility and the activities of Taiwan and the United States along their sea and southern frontier, they might not have thought it necessary to demonstrate to all parties that China should be taken seriously.

The Sino-Indian conflict that evolved from this frontier dispute helped shape the larger regional system for the next twenty-five years. By showing India's vulnerability, this trans-Himalayan intrusion intensified India's insecurity. For Nehru it represented a disappointment perhaps second only to the tragedy of partition itself.[48] It is not entirely fanciful to suggest that this instance of "betrayal" confirmed for Indian leaders two convictions: (1) No relationship can be trusted that one cannot definitely control; (2) despite its size relative to its neighbors, India lived in a dangerous world.

Thereafter, Indian planners too had to face two ways simultaneously, leading to a radically expanded post-Nehru Five Year Defense Plan.[49] The defense budget increased sharply. Military personnel went from approximately 600,000 to 844,000 in three years, to reach over 1.26 million by the 1980s, the world's fourth largest armed force. Training programs were improved and substantial arms transfers from Moscow and

London were organized, including coproduction with the Soviet Union of high-performance MIG aircraft.

India's buildup sharply increased Pakistan's worries, and the Indo-Pakistani arms race that began after the first Kashmir war was intensified by India's much more serious buildup in response to the perceived threat from China.

The reciprocating character of India's and Pakistan's policies and the role of triangulation were dramatized by the second Indo-Pakistani war of 1965. In the first phase of a challenge to its neighbor before India's ambitious Five Year Defense Plan would tip the regional balance inexorably against it, a Pakistan initiative to the south in the Rann of Kutch ended in Pakistan having the advantage. Emboldened, in a subsequent effort to reactivate the Kashmir dispute while there was still time, Islamabad sent well-trained "irregulars" into Kashmir. India had a ten-to-eight advantage in infantry divisions in place at the start of the three-week conflict, however, and a cutoff of American and British supplies to both antagonists, which worked more to Pakistan's disadvantage, led to a near stalemate in India's favor.[50] The end of the war found Indian troops at the very gates of Lahore. Kashmiris were not ready to revolt in order to join Pakistan, and Pakistan proved unable to seize Kashmir by force. Moscow mediated a settlement at Tashkent in 1966.

Russia, China, and Kautilya

The larger effects of China's energetic moves in 1962 could not have been what Beijing had intended, but the results of these developments were fourfold—and long-lasting. First, as we have seen, they provoked a rapid buildup of India's defense establishment, on the grounds that never again would they show themselves to be so weak militarily.[51]

Second, they also gave a strong push to New Delhi's growing relationship with the Soviet Union. Washington was not prepared to establish the type of coproduction arrangement the Indians desired except with its closest allies, but Moscow eagerly responded, now ready to go further than before the Chinese intrusion. New Delhi believed that China was best balanced by the Soviet Union. By their very existence, their size, and their proximity, China and the Soviet Union checked each other, to India's advantage. As Nehru reportedly said of the Indian and Soviet common interest with respect to China, "we are their second front, and they are ours."[52] To these balancing justifications for India's Moscow connection were added military transfers that in time came to account for some 80 percent of New Delhi's advanced military hardware, generally acquired on favorable repayment terms. For New Delhi, closer ties with Moscow also assured maximum deterrence against a repetition of China's initiative.

Third, the support provided by Moscow encouraged Indian diplomatic firmness toward both Pakistan and China. For the next twenty-five years, India saw no more need to seek a settlement of the frontier difficulty with China than China showed in accommodating to India's position. Simultaneously, in response to these developments, Pakistan and China developed closer balancing relations.[53] Disappointed that the United States had lent military support to India without first insisting on a revision of India's position on Kashmir, Islamabad sought to strengthen its ties with China.

Thus, as India and Pakistan each sought to offset its immediate neighbor, there emerged an eerie reincarnation in the twentieth century of the "checkerboard pattern" of balancing relationships, first discerned by Kautilya. China was a logical ally located to the rear of Pakistan's principal enemy, and the Soviet Union was a similar asset for India. And for China and the Soviet Union, their South Asian clients performed analogous functions.

Both India and Pakistan thus profited from the competition between the United States and the Soviet Union. Pakistan gained military and economic support and India received substantial economic aid from a Washington hopeful that India would see the advantage of not becoming solely dependent on Moscow. Similarly, both also profited from the rivalry between China and the Soviet Union, each receiving more backing than it could otherwise have expected. Russia and China also benefited from the Indo-Pakistani rivalry, since because of it, each of the South Asian states was more willing to respond to its patron's interests.

India countered Soviet efforts to enlist it by refusing certain of Moscow's requests: on naval base rights, on Asian collective security, on the Nonproliferation Treaty (NPT) that was then being sponsored by both Moscow and Washington. Most notably, after the military victory over Pakistan in 1971, it pressed forward with arms purchases from non-Soviet sources, seeking better weapons, especially from France, and made it clear that even though they were partners in a friendship treaty that had clear if only general mutual security commitments, a New Delhi victorious with Soviet assistance was not to be considered a dependency of Moscow.

Regional Dynamic: 2

Pakistan Divided

From 1950 to 1970, a twenty-year period, Pakistan did not acquiesce in India's effort to gain regional predominance. By investing a larger proportion of national resources in defense, maintaining a higher ratio of mobilized manpower, developing links with Iran and Turkey, and gaining military and economic assistance, largely from the United

States and China, Pakistan continued to be a major Indian concern. But developments in 1971 brought an important change in the South Asian configuration.

The third war between these neighbors, in 1971 in East Pakistan, unlike the wars of 1948 and 1965, was both unexpected and unwanted by Islamabad, and it was far more decisive. Ethnic resentments, electoral politics, a failed crackdown by the Pakistan military, and direct Indian military intervention left the structure of South Asia power changed for good.

Ethnic consciousness had been intensifying in Pakistan's eastern wing, separated from western Pakistan by more than one thousand miles. A slight majority of the citizens of Pakistan, the Bengalis resented what they perceived as their virtual exclusion from power. This was reflected in the small share of government revenues and foreign exchange they retained, the central government's preference for Urdu over Bengali, and the Punjabi domination of the bureaucracy. Furthermore, many believed their sophistication far surpassed the essentially "tribal" and "feudal" practices typical in the western wing of the country. Ethnic tensions became so pronounced that when Pakistan's first unintimidated election was held in 1970, the electorate split along ethnic and geographical lines. The overwhelming majority in East Pakistan voted for the Bengali spokesman, Shaykh Mujibur Rahman, whereas the voters in the west preferred Zulfikar Ali Bhutto. Shaykh Mujib won by a slight majority and should have been called to form a government, but Yahya Khan, with the strong support of Bhutto, postponed establishing the new government. Seeing themselves again excluded from their rightful place, the temporarily united Bengali majority called for greater autonomy and mounted huge demonstrations in Dhaka. An ill-starred army effort to repress the movement turned demands for autonomy into a secessionist guerrilla struggle, aroused widespread condemnation abroad, and was supported by India. Over six million refugees, principally Hindus, fled from the fighting into Indian West Bengal, one of India's most volatile states.

The obvious geostrategic opportunity offered by these difficulties was too much for Indira Gandhi's government to ignore. New Delhi first reinsured by concluding a Treaty of Peace, Friendship, and Cooperation with the Soviet Union, presumably as a deterrent against Chinese intervention on Pakistan's behalf and no doubt in part in reaction to the near-simultaneous announcement of the American opening to China that had been effected with the secret assistance of Pakistan. Through clandestine assistance to 100,000 guerrillas and, subsequently, a carefully planned and coordinated military intervention across East Pakistan's western and northern frontiers triggered by a foolish Pakistani air strike in the west, the Indian army roundly defeated Pakistan's forces.[54] This left Pakistan cut in half, the remaining Pakistani army of ninety thousand men in the east as prisoners of war, the reputation of the Indian army restored after the defeat by China ten years earlier, and the myth of the invincible Pakistani "martial races" buried for good.

It also produced a structural change in South Asia. From then on, there would be an additional diplomatic actor on the South Asian stage. More important to India, there would be no more Pakistan military initiatives against India, as had occurred in Kashmir in 1947–48 and in the Rann of Kutch and Kashmir in 1965. However, as long as the two states could not agree on a mutually acceptable ordering of relations in South Asia, their relationship would not change.

India's period of unquestioned preeminence was short-lived. The American opening to China to help balance the Soviet Union could only be seen in New Delhi as strengthening China, India's rival in the Himalayas since the late 1950s, at India's expense. Washington's "tilt" toward Pakistan in 1971 and Kissinger's dispatch of the *Enterprise* task force to the Bay of Bengal while the fighting continued—undertaken to impress the Russians, the Chinese, and the Indians with the seriousness of Washington's commitments to its friends and allies—was seen in New Delhi as a particularly offensive American effort to intimidate India.[55]

Thanks to the first oil price hike in 1971, the shaykhdoms of the Gulf were able to help Pakistan, so that when the ninety thousand prisoners of war were finally returned six months after the 1972 Simla Agreement that formally ended the war, the Pakistani army was already as large as it had been before the war, even though the population had been halved.

External Influences: 2

Pakistan remained acutely dependent on external support from the Gulf states, China, and, after the Reagan administration came to power, Washington. India, however, had become significantly self-reliant in meeting its defense needs. India's industrial base is far more productive and diversified than that of Pakistan. Its arms industry is able to produce nearly all the conventional requirements of its army.[56] It manufactures tanks of considerable sophistication and ever more elements of Soviet MIG fighter aircraft, and in the late 1980s signed contracts to coproduce the latest Mig–29s.[57] Although Pakistan's economy grew more rapidly than India's from the late 1970s until the mid–1980s, Pakistan cannot approach India's capacity to meet its conventional military needs.[58] India's air force has more than twice the number of strike aircraft and seven times the number of air force personnel.[59] Even President Reagan's $3.5 billion in military and economic assistance and the forty F–16s committed in 1982 and half financed by Saudi Arabia could not alter the clear superiority of the Indian air force.

On a more human note, both states have shown sharp improvement in food production. Even in years when the rains have been poor, both have recently been able to feed their people. Not since the drought days of the mid–1960s has either of them had to turn to another country to provide huge transfers of grain to meet the basic food needs of their people. On the other hand, neither set of leaders can forget that their two countries are within the poorest quartile among the world's peoples. Despite this cruel fact, increasingly sophisticated and costly weapons systems face each other across the Indo-Pakistani frontier.

The Middle East Connection

In their preoccupation with one another, Pakistan and India both turned toward the Gulf states for allies. Pakistan developed close relationships with Iran very early and gradually improved relations with Saudi Arabia and Kuwait. In contrast, India found Iraq, squeezed between Iran and Saudi Arabia and befriended by the Soviet Union, as a ready associate.

Pakistan received countervailing support from Iran and in return supplied military and technical specialists for Iran's rapidly expanding military. Following Pakistan's loss of Bangladesh, for example, the shah publicly warned against any further threats to Pakistan's integrity.[60] After the oil price hike, Saudi, UAE, Iranian, and Kuwaiti aid helped Pakistan recover from the loss of foreign exchange earnings and rebuild its depleted army. Many thousands of Pakistanis traveled to the Gulf, with over a million laboring in Saudi Arabia alone, and some twenty thousand Pakistani troops were stationed there until 1988. In return, Pakistan provided both Saudi Arabia and Iran with military advisers and technical staff familiar with the American equipment that they were receiving in large quantities. Indians worried that in the event of another military round, sophisticated American equipment available to Pakistani troops in Saudi Arabia might be transferred to Pakistan, regardless of American policy.[61]

In its relationship with Iraq, by contrast, India could expect no major security support, although the close link to a major Islamic state would help to reduce one of India's deepest fears—a united Muslim backing for Pakistan against Hindu India. Moreover, Baghdad was a rival to both Saudi Arabia and Iran and was then receiving substantial military support from the Soviet Union. As a secular state in the Arab world, it was ready to accept New Delhi as a spokesman for India's Muslim population, unlike the more orthodox Muslim states. It also provided a point of access to the Gulf regional political system for monitoring Pakistani activity and was a reminder to Indian leaders that the Gulf had once been managed (by the British) from Bombay. Despite the general price hike following the 1973 conflict, Iraq provided petroleum to India on concessional terms, and Indian construction, consulting, and trading firms found Iraq a lucrative place to do business.[62]

Here too the pattern is neatly Kautilyan. Once again, however, reality was more subtle—and interesting. Iraq, with ties to the Soviet Union, had always maintained relations with Pakistan, even while being close to India. During the mid-1970s, Iraq began diversifying further, opening tentative relations with the United States, whereas Iran, sensing broader interests in South Asia and beyond, was evolving closer working relations with India.

The increased wealth in the hands of the Gulf states, the increased cost of imported petroleum, and the large number of South Asian workers meant that both India and Pakistan had to be sensitive to Gulf state views that neither relished. New Delhi's efforts to influence the working conditions of Indians in the Gulf were unavailing.[63] Many Pakistanis were worried by President Zia's apparent responsiveness to Saudi Islamic conservatism.

Thus, in part as a result of their rivalry within South Asia, which they were unable to restrict in the name of the region's autonomy, both states sought help from the Gulf. India hoped by its relationships with Iraq and Iran to reduce their backing for Pakistan. Both states found financial support in the Gulf, although Pakistan gained much more.

In the meantime, the navies of the superpowers were becoming more active in the Indian Ocean. The Soviet navy had been markedly expanded after its humiliation during the Cuban missile crisis. Soviet ship visits rapidly increased and a considerable missile repair facility was developed in Somalia at Berbera. The 1973 Arab-Israeli War and the oil embargo and price hike reminded Americans and their allies of their dependence on the sea lanes fanning out from the Gulf. With an eye to the northwest quadrant of the Indian Ocean and the oil flow so critical to Europe, Israel, and Japan, Washington accelerated the development of Diego Garcia, a tiny coral atoll one thousand miles south of Sri Lanka. Its small local population had been removed by the British before they offered Mauritius and the Seychelles their independence, and London had offered it to the United States as an Indian Ocean naval support facility. Pakistan quietly welcomed the American presence as another possible makeweight to the Indian navy, then expanding with help from Moscow, but New Delhi reacted as if the American effort were directed against it. New Delhi preferred that both the Soviet and U.S. navies stay away from the Indian Ocean and leave it to the Indian navy, as in the days of the British Raj. Failing that, it would be better to have them both, even though the Soviet navy was hardly a match for the Americans. Each would check the other's ambitions. The smaller states in South Asia also saw an advantage in having foreign navies in the region. In a truly classic statement of Kautilyan policy, in 1977, Sri Lanka's Prime Minister Jayewardene put it this way:

> It is good to reduce naval competition between you two. But if in your naval negotiations you and the Russians agree that you should go home, that leaves us with the Russians, and we don't like that. But if you agree that you both go home, that leaves us with the Indians, and we don't like that either. So stick around.[64]

Once Soviet-American naval limitation talks in 1978 reassured Moscow that the Americans were not using the Indian Ocean for regular strategic deployment of the American submarine deterrent, Soviet worries relaxed, its naval presence declined, and New Delhi too became less anxious about American intentions.

The subtle relations of India and Pakistan with the states in the Gulf were of course rudely shaken by the revolution in Iran, the Soviet intrusion into Afghanistan, and the Iran-Iraq war. Before we leave the dynamics of Indo-Pakistani actions and reactions, we must consider the nuclear dimension.

Regional Dynamic: 3

The Nuclear Dimension

South Asia is the first region of the Third World where two hostile neighbors are well along in the process of obtaining nuclear capability, despite the risks and cost.

By 1974, India's reprocessing facilities at Trombay had already produced enough weapons-grade plutonium to permit it to explode a subterranean nuclear device, demonstrating that India could join the nuclear powers if it decided to do so. India's pool of scientists and technologists is impressive, smaller only than that of the United States and the Soviet Union. India is able to build its own commercial nuclear power plants. It has three reprocessing plants and is the only Third World country with a fast-breeder program.[65]

Indian leaders measure their nuclear program not by Pakistan's lag but by China's considerable lead. As China before it had sought a nuclear deterrent to the Soviet Union by developing nuclear weapons and a missile capability, so India's leaders have felt obliged to follow China's example, at least in detonating a nuclear device and in conducting early missile experiments.

Pakistan is as haunted by India's nuclear capability on the subcontinent as India has been by China's across the Himalayas. Pakistan sees nuclear weapons as the "great equalizers," compensating for India's advantage in size and quantitative superiority in conventional weapons. Although India has been able to produce at home much of what it has required, Pakistan's program is narrowly based, and Islamabad has had to acquire technologies and equipment from abroad, often through third parties and by subterfuge. Pakistan claims to have achieved uranium enrichment. Periodically there have been unofficial assertions that Pakistan is now able to produce nuclear weapons. By 1988 it "became clear" that Pakistan had achieved a "rudimentary nuclear deterrent."[66] Both states are pushing missile programs.

India faces major disadvantages vis-à-vis China regarding the use of nuclear weapons. Most of China's population centers are far from Indian bases, whereas the heavily populated Ganges plain would be within easy striking distance should China develop missile bases in Tibet.[67] Indian and Pakistani population centers are each vulnerable to strikes from the other, and alert times would be extremely short. Again, however, India holds the substantial advantage. Lahore, for instance, is even more exposed than Bombay, and dispersion of facilities is far easier for India than for Pakistan. Even a limited nuclear exchange against South Asia's concentrated cities could bring unimaginable loss of life to an area where four wars in the past forty years have meant few civilian casualties.

Thus far unwilling to sign the Nonproliferation Treaty (NPT), India has argued that its provisions would perpetuate a two-class international system that would forever make Third World states dependent on the technologically advanced.[68] Of more immediate consequence, so long as China continued to develop its nuclear program untrammeled by international constraints, Indian leaders believed they had no choice but to deter it as best they could. Even an agreement with Pakistan prohibiting nuclear weapons would leave India vulnerable to China. Perhaps as important, nuclear weapons, it is said, form the contemporary currency of international power. Only with them in hand could India sit at the international high table, where, in Nehru's view, it was destined to be.

During the Carter administration, growing U.S. doubts about the safety of nuclear energy and worries about proliferation led the Congress to pass the Nuclear Nonproliferation Act, which forced Washington to cut off all aid to Pakistan in 1979 and required that America's commitment to supply enriched uranium for India's Tarapur reactor until 1993 be canceled. This was one more irritant between the two states, only mitigated by an agreement that France would assume America's former commitment.

Nuclear weapons calculations also tied the South Asian system to the central Asian and the U.S.-Soviet system. Indian planners considered whether their links to Moscow would bring deterrent pressures to bear on Beijing in the event of a renewed Sino-Indian crisis. Similarly, Pakistan assessed whether China's deterrent might induce caution in India or whether America's might induce caution in Moscow or in New Delhi should there be a renewed Indo-Pakistani crisis. The dynamics of this rivalry derived from their mutual relationship; the logic of their reciprocal deterrent calculations led them to weigh the utility of their respective links to states beyond South Asia.

In the fall of 1990, unable to certify that Pakistan was not making nuclear weapons, Washington could no longer postpone applying the Pressler Amendment, which prohibited the administration from transferring technology or military equipment to Pakistan. Pakistan had to choose between continuing with its nuclear program or risking its military and technological links to Washington. It chose the former.

Policy of ambiguity.   Both sides have been pursuing a policy of ambiguity. Both are generally believed to be capable of acquiring a nuclear explosive device, and both assert they are not producing weapons.[69] At the same time, neither would acquiesce to the other being far ahead for long.

Such "part-way" proliferation has been perceived as serving the interests of both parties.[70] If India openly stockpiled nuclear weapons, Pakistan would be compelled to do so too, despite the technical difficulties of matching India. For Pakistan, nuclear ambiguity suggests a capability sufficient to deter a unilateral Indian initiative without provoking New Delhi to go for weapons. According to this argument, ambiguity signals to the other that each has a deterrent that is less threatening than an explicit weapons capability would be but that is serious enough to induce caution.

In 1988 both agreed to abstain from attacking each other's nuclear facilities, and they exchanged ratifications in January 1991. However, unless the two sides can reach some mutual understanding, possibly inspection of each other's facilities, as they encounter uncertainty and temptation, considerable additional tension can be generated by the dynamic of pre–second-strike nuclear weapons systems. How long the two parties can continue the game of ambiguity is difficult to say.[71]

Efforts at Cooperation: 1

Indo-Pakistani accommodation?   Because India and Pakistan have been rivals, policymakers function in an environment of suspicion and ambiguity. They have experienced what each considers the other's long-run hostility and untrustworthiness. Each government is fully aware of its own limited control at home, and in typical—and understandable—misperception, each exaggerates the other's authority. Correctly reading the other's true intentions from across the frontier is sometimes difficult.[72] Restraint on the part of one is often difficult for the other to recognize; each worries that moderation will be seen by the other as weakness. Both can imagine gains from additional forms of cooperation, but the temptation is great to seek unilateral advantage.[73]

On the other hand, the interdependence of these two is a fact of life. Instability or political eruption in one could work against the interests of ruling elites in the other. The costs of maintaining intense regional rivalries are likely to increase. Military equipment is far more expensive and lethal now than it used to be, and nuclear weapons could become an integral part of their arsenals. It is therefore worth considering their experience thus far in the search for mutual accommodation.

On occasion they have attempted modest steps toward cooperation. The following instances of negotiation between India and Pakistan illustrate both the possibilities of and impediments to a more active cooperation.

Negotiations between prime ministers: The 1950s.   In the early 1950s Indian and Pakistani leaders met a number of times. In 1950, following severe strife in both states, Nehru and Liaquat met first in Delhi and then in Karachi, agreeing to strong measures to protect minorities against communal zealots. But within months, the "sweet interval" had been replaced by the old suspicions.[74]

In 1953–54 discussions between Nehru and Pakistani Governor General Ghulam Mohammed and Prime Minister Nazimuddin were interrupted by severe disorders in Karachi that led to Nazimuddin's replacement by Mohammed Ali, Pakistan's ambassador to Washington. The concessions he then made to gain movement on the Kashmir plebiscite inflamed opinion in Pakistan, which intensified when Shaykh Abdulla, leader of the Kashmiri Muslims, was arrested for advocating independence for Kashmir. Thus, popular anger over apparent concessions to India and the accidents of domestic politics in Kashmir caused Karachi to repudiate the recently concluded agreement.

In 1955, when Pakistan announced its military assistance agreement with the United States, New Delhi replied that Pakistan's action had so changed the situation in the subcontinent that there could be no more talk of a plebiscite.

These early efforts led to modest progress on travel permits, trade conditions, and restraints on strident press attacks on each other, but cautious or inflexible leaders and domestic difficulties in both countries impeded accommodation, while Pakistan's search for an external makeweight gave India a justification to withdraw its commitment to a plebiscite. On major issues of relative standing and competing territorial claims, such as that to Kashmir, no progress was made.

The hostility and suspicion hardened. Reciprocity is often commended as a way of encouraging cooperation.[75] But it is not easy to achieve where disparity between the neighbors is so marked, communication has been so limited, and neither party is a unitary actor, as game theorists assume. Moreover, the history of rivalry and conflict has left accumulated evidence of bad faith, if not willful harm. Thus, it is easy for each to expect the worst. To the long preindependence history of Hindu-Muslim hostility has been added forty years of interstate rivalry, including three wars and a forceful division of one of the two. With such a shadow of the past, reciprocity and "tit for tat" can also reinforce existing suspicion and hostility.[76]

The involvement of external powers adds another complication, making prediction even more difficult. Calculations about the other usually involve triangulation, with assessment of how the other's patron is likely to react. Each desires to reduce the other's dependence on external major powers. Expected Chinese or American support for Pakistan or Soviet support for India, for example, might justify concessions, with an eye to reducing that clientilistic dependence. Instead, outside support has been seen as justification for each to urge its patron to greater effort on behalf of his client, permitting each South Asian state to avoid concessions to the other.

Domestic politics has provided few incentives to induce statesmen to seek accommodation. Typically, nation building benefits from a sense of threat next door. Those who undertook to promote cooperation did so despite the risk of generating opposition at home. Quick returns from negotiations sufficient to compensate for such domestic risks were thought unlikely. Nevertheless, leaders of both countries did sometimes take initiatives leading to cooperation.

The less conspicuous their negotiation and the more specific the issues, the easier it was to reach agreements and monitor reciprocal behavior. Of course, these agreements involved smaller issues, which had little to do with major territorial questions or issues of relative standing.

Third-party agreements.   Despite these difficulties, a number of agreements were achieved with the help of third parties.

Indus Waters Agreement.   After prolonged negotiations in 1960, the two protagonists resolved complicated differences over the distribution of the waters in the Indus Valley river system. One can dismiss the agreement as insignificant, since without protracted mediation by the World Bank, sweetened by large Western economic contributions, it is doubtful they would have reached a settlement. On the other hand, the agreement, delaying Indian use of the water New Delhi wanted, gave Pakistan time to develop alternative canal systems to draw replacement water from the Indus instead.[77]

It had been hoped that eliminating this source of friction between the two countries would lead to progress on other differences. But there was no apparent linkage between easing relationships on water issues and, say, the Kashmir dispute or the intensity of the security dilemma reflecting numerous security and other issues.

The Tashkent Declaration.   The 1966 Tashkent agreement ending the 1965 war was also achieved with the help of a third party. As pointed out earlier, the conflict had reached a virtual stalemate, with no clear winner. Without the active mediation of the Soviet Union, it is unlikely that the two could have reached even that agreement by themselves.[78] Tashkent, however, merely restored the status quo ante and did nothing to deal with the issues that led to the war in the first place. It was, in effect, a truce, which held until the secessionist struggle in East Pakistan in 1971.

A bilateral peace accord: the Simla Agreement   The Simla Agreement negotiated in 1972 between India and Pakistan was more conclusive, for it brought the 1971 war over Bangladesh formally to a close without the help of third parties. Unlike previous military encounters, this had been an overwhelming military victory for India. Four points deserve mention: (1) The clearcut victory demonstrated the preeminent position of India. From then on, Islamabad would be chary of risking the kind of military challenge to New Delhi it had attempted three times before. (2) From Mrs. Gandhi's perspective, it was important that in accepting the principle of "bilateralism," Pakistan agreed to no longer seek the support of third parties when India and Pakistan differed. (3) By both parties agreeing to respect the "line of control" as determined by the cease-fire agreement "without prejudice" for the future, downgraded the jurisdiction of the United Nations as the international community's guarantor of the settlement. (4) In exchange for these concessions, Bhutto gained the withdrawal of Indian forces from highly strategic areas of Kashmir and less crucial areas of the Punjab and Sind. Pakistan's POWs had to wait another six months before they were repatriated.[79] The process of normalizing relations thereafter was erratic, which is not surprising, considering the past relationships between the two.[80]

Despite the persisting rivalry, there has been collaboration when it was possible to do it quietly, on a quasi-technical level. Except for the period just before the 1972 conflict, Pakistan and India have been flying over each other's territory, with only the most pro forma permission. For many years, Afghanistan has been sending large numbers of trucks carrying grapes and vegetables across Pakistan to market in India, although New Delhi would like the flow to be better regulated and the road network improved. India and Pakistan collaborate on health measures and pest control; they jointly ensure the unambiguity of border markers, and their survey departments cooperate on perfecting detailed maps and precise delineations. Pilgrimage exchanges involve thousands of devout Muslims moving in both directions, Sikhs visiting the birthplace of Guru Nanak in Pakistan, and so on. These are often governmentally organized group pilgrimages, with well-prepared tent and medical facilities during the pilgrimage seasons. Potentially much more consequential for the longer run, in May 1990, both parties agreed to a number of confidence-building measures, such as a hot line, notification and mutual observation of maneuvers, and other measures to reduce surprise. As both come nearer to an acknowledged nuclear capability, such steps represent a rudimentary beginning of a type of cooperation needed more in the future.

Each of these arrangements, however, is the result of inconspicuous negotiations between officials, usually well out of the public eye.[81]

Leadership styles make a difference.　Different political leaders can alter to some extent the significance of these structures of antagonism.

The Janata government's quiet diplomacy.　In 1977 the Janata government eased the anxieties of India's smaller neighbors. They trusted the restraint and good faith of the new prime minister, Morarji Desai, and his style was different from what had gone before. He assiduously avoided flaunting India's military power; he did not claim India's preeminence. Consulates were opened with Pakistan, visa procedures were eased, a direct telephone link by satellite was established, newspapermen were given new opportunities to visit, and athletic exchanges began. For the first time in twelve years a minister from India visited Islamabad! Once Pakistan withdrew from CENTO in 1979, India supported Pakistan's membership in the Nonaligned Movement.

After Indira Gandhi's return to office in 1980, improved arrangements for dialogue beyond the diplomatic missions were made. A Joint Indo-Pakistan Commission provided regular channels for interministerial consultations on issues of common concern—smuggling, transborder movement of terrorist groups, drug trafficking, and the like. India finally agreed to participate in the South Asian Association for Regional Cooperation (SAARC) proposed by Bangladesh. However, as will be seen, the Soviet intrusion into Afghanistan intensified Indo-Pakistani antagonism, for it revealed how differently they perceived their own security problems.

In sum, one can conclude that the major issues between India and Pakistan were so intractable that there was little room for a satisfying solution to any of them. Suspicion remained high. Until the emergence of the SAARC, communication between elites on both sides had not been enough to assure leaders that they could correctly assess the "seriousness" and "sincerity" of apparently accommodative initiatives proposed by the other. Under such circumstances, venturing toward accommodation appeared to invite serious political risks at home that few public figures were willing to run.

The Other, Lesser States

The South Asian regional system appears very different when seen from New Delhi or the capitals of its smaller neighbors. As noted, India's leaders believed that, as the preeminent regional power, it should keep foreign powers as far away as possible.[82] They also worried others might support those destabilizing ethnic or separatist "fissiparous tendencies" that can weaken state cohesion.[83]

For nearly all the other states, the major external security problem has been India. From the beginning the smaller states have worried about "Indian expansionism."[84] The principal conundrum of their foreign policy has been how to neutralize or at least cope with India's overwhelming presence in ways that would not precipitate direct Indian action against them.[85] Just as the United States is perceived in many Caribbean capitals as a source of threat, India also has been seen as a threatening neighbor. Moreover, regional statesmen could not forget that India had supported the secessionist movement in Bangladesh and finished the job with a conventional military invasion in 1971.[86] At times, India had also tried to affect Nepal's domestic politics by openly supporting B. P. Koirala and the Nepali Congress against the king.[87] In Sikkim, New Delhi had encouraged ethnic groups and factions opposing the Chogyal until the Indian authorities were able to absorb it into India proper.[88] In 1987, India projected its power directly into Sri Lanka as the ethnic conflict worsened there.

For India these were exceptional steps rendered necessary by the exigencies of the moment or long-run historical imperatives. For the smaller neighbors, however, they have been emblematic of India's longer-run aspirations. It is therefore not surprising that from the start Pakistan and the other, smaller states followed classic balancing policies in efforts to deal with their larger neighbor.

Bangladesh

Once Bangladesh was established in 1971, it soon behaved like a normal state in an anarchic world. In the early years, the new state remained acutely dependent on India. New Delhi's economic resources helped in rebuilding the shattered economy; a Treaty of Friendship, Cooperation, and Peace provided for intimate political and economic links between the two states and economies.[89] Close economic exchange soon began, and numerous Indian businessmen and economic officials came to Dhaka to accelerate the process.

There is little thanks in the world of states. Less than three years after the country's liberation with indispensable Indian military help, and with two years of economic aid India could then ill afford, resentment against the close relationship with India became palpable; opposition to the regime grew sharply. A bloody coup d'état in 1975 replaced the government of Shaykh Mujib that India had supported so actively.

A number of specific issues poisoned the relationship.[90] Questions of economic policy and water resources, particularly Indian preemption of water from the Ganges needed by both India for Calcutta and by Bangladesh for agriculture downstream, complicated matters. Numerous Indian entrepreneurs swarmed into the new state. There were frontier differences over islands in the delta that might contain off-shore oil. Moreover, Bengali Muslims had long wanted to assert their distinctive, non-Indian character. Underlying these specific grievances, political dynamics were at work. Shaykh Mujib had been close to India; his successors, like many other new incumbents, reversed course.[91]India, the large, embracing neighbor, was now too close and appeared to threaten the long-run independence of Bangladesh, whereas Pakistan, far on the other side of India, became a natural ally.[92] Despite the bitterness and destructiveness of the secessionist struggle, trade with Pakistan grew rapidly. Like other small states next to a much larger one, as one observer put it, Bangladesh "resorted to the strategy of assiduously cultivating other states to redress the balance."[93]

By the summer of 1974, India was no longer its indispensable friend. Bangladesh had been recognized by many states, including the United States and China, and had been accepted into the United Nations. Moreover, the Muslim states of the Middle East were also providing economic assistance and encouraged Pakistan to recognize Dhaka. China was beginning to provide military assistance to help rebuild the Bangladesh army.[94]

Bangladesh's persisting poverty, population growth at a rate of 2.64 percent, and lack of economic opportunity for its 100 million people in a state the size of Illinois are the sources of one major disruptive force in the region. The migration of thousands of Bangladesh citizens each year into the Indian states of Bengal and Assam periodically provoke grave disorders in what Indians consider to be a strategic frontier area bordering on China and on politically volatile Bengal.

In the long run, Bangladesh's most important contribution may have been its efforts to establish routine consultative mechanisms away from the political limelight to permit the leaders of the South Asian states to improve their understanding of one another's problems and to cope with conflicts before a crisis occurs. For this, its size has made a difference. Because they are so small, neither Sri Lanka nor Nepal would have been taken seriously by the others. Had either India or Pakistan proposed it, the other would have objected to it. Bangladesh, however, was large enough to be taken seriously. The evolution of SAARC is considered later.

Sri Lanka

For the first thirty-five years of independence until the acute ethnic conflict that beset Sri Lanka in the 1980s, the state's role in South Asia reflected typical small-state–large-state relationships. Size alone was a problem—India's population was fifty times larger than Sri Lanka's, and south India, across the Palk Strait, was markedly poorer, which resulted in thousands emigrating annually, until new regulations by Colombo at independence stemmed the flow. Ethnic connections straddled the national frontier between the two, as one-fifth of the island's people spoke Tamil, the language of south India; were mainly Hindu; and typically followed cultural and religious practices akin to those in India.

Unique Indian and Sinhalese cultural memories complicated their relationship.[95] Dark historical memories have been kept alive among the Sinhalese majority by the highly colored and ahistorical Great Chronicle, the *Mahavamsa*, maintained since the third century by Buddhist monks, a source that gives the chronicle an aura of authority. It blames many difficulties of the Sinhalese on successive Tamil invasions from south India between the eighth and twelfth centuries. Moreover, recent Indian political or military initiatives in Bangladesh, Sikkim, and Nepal have been reminders of these ancient anxieties.

Domestic politics also were involved, since the "threat from India" has been a tempting argument for politicians seeking support among the Sinhalese. Political mobilization of the majority around Sinhalese cultural nationalism increasingly seemed to leave little room for the long-established Tamil and Muslim minorities.[96] Because of measures introduced since 1956 (such as the linguistic Sinhalese-only legislation or quotas granting access to university places—and thereby improved economic opportunities—to the Sinhalese majority), young Tamils have become embittered and more inclined to violence and closer links to Madras.

Finally, because Trincomalee Harbor on the east coast was once the key naval station in the Indian Ocean, New Delhi feared Sri Lanka might make it available to the Americans, and Colombo worried that

India's strategic ambitions might tempt it to encourage Tamil independence.[97]

Before the 1983 Ethnic Riots

Until the early 1980s, Sri Lankan-Indian relations accommodated Sri Lanka's desire to affirm its sovereignty, consistent with an awareness of India's most worrisome security concerns.

Personalities affected these asymmetrical, large-state–small-state relations.[98] Sri Lanka was the first practitioner of the "balancing process" in post-British South Asia. The 1948 independence agreements negotiated with the British permitted them to retain naval and air bases to support London's communications with the Far East. As K. M. de Silva put it, writing about D. S. Senanayake, the first prime minister, "a profound suspicion of India was the dominant strand in his external policy." These arrangements were seen as a kind of "reinsurance," as was membership in the Commonwealth and the United Nations.[99]

Unlike his predecessors, S. W. R. D. Bandaranaike, the fourth prime minister, who swept to power in 1956, differentiated himself from his predecessors by aligning himself with Mr. Nehru on most issues and joined the Nonaligned Movement. His widow followed a similar policy, while simultaneously pursuing an active policy at the United Nations and among the nonaligned countries. She also further developed relations with China, which had been first opened by the government of Dudley Senanayake, the second prime minister. He and J. R. Jayewardene followed a policy of warmer relations with other powers, including the United States and Japan.

India's leaders also made a difference to Sri Lankan perceptions. Nehru was admired, but many believed he unthinkingly assumed that India would inherit the raj's overriding regional role. Mrs. Gandhi's imperious style and her part in the secession of Bangladesh confirmed their most active suspicions.[100] Lalbahadur Shastri and Morarji Desai, by comparison, were much more trusted. Had either of them remained in power for any length of time, India's approach to Sri Lanka might well have been more widely accepted on the island. But these were nuances within a widely shared distrust of India's long-term ambitions. For their part, factions of Indian officials read something more sinister than "reinsurance" into Colombo's relationships with states other than New Delhi, although for Colombo, links with China, the United States, Great Britain, and Japan also had direct economic utility.

Sri Lanka usually worked with India at the United Nations and on nonaligned affairs. To India's annoyance, however, Colombo sometimes collaborated with Pakistan. Sri Lanka's airports were used by Pakistan to reinforce its Bengal garrisons during the 1971 secessionist war in East

Pakistan. As the Tamil militancy grew, Pakistan provided military supplies and training for Sri Lanka's army, until the 1987 Indo–Sri Lanka Accord.

Sri Lanka's China connection began during the Korean War, and grew out of economic necessity, as China paid a premium for rubber it could purchase nowhere else and provided scarce rice at below-market prices. After the Sino-Indian conflict of 1962, visible friendship with China took on a political tone, suggesting that little Ceylon not only was dependent on Western countries and India but had a major Asian friend as well.

One issue bedeviled the Colombo–New Delhi relationship: future citizenship rights of "Indian" Tamil estate workers brought to Ceylon beginning in the mid-nineteenth century to work the tea and rubber estates. They had been deprived of their citizenship shortly after independence, and Colombo had sought to have India "repatriate" them, whereas New Delhi considered them Colombo's responsibility. In the meantime they continued to labor on the tea estates, providing Ceylon with its largest single source of foreign exchange. A number of Indo–Sri Lankan agreements increased the proportion of retiring estate workers India would accept, the most notable being the agreement between Mrs. Bandaranaika and Prime Minister Shastri in 1964. Not until the 1980s did those who remained finally receive full citizenship.

Despite their uneasy relationship, New Delhi and Colombo shared certain interests. Both sought to consolidate democratic, constitutional practices and wanted political stability and orderly change. For a time, both took the Nonaligned Movement seriously, although for different reasons. New Delhi considered it was one area in which it could exercise leadership in the global system. Sri Lanka liked it because it provided a collectivity of small states anxious about larger neighbors. Along with London, Moscow, Beijing, and Washington, New Delhi sent help in 1971, when Mrs. Bandaranaike's government appealed for help worldwide following a radical, "Che Guevarist" attempt by youthful Sinhalese militants, the Jathika Vimukthi Peramuna (JVP), to seize power. They would reemerge to make a second attempt in 1988–89.[101]

On the other hand, both states faced a shared difficulty. India wanted to develop enough military capability that nonregional powers would not encroach on its interests in the region. Yet the more India established its own sphere of influence, the more anxious Sri Lanka, like India's other smaller neighbors, became and the more eagerly they sought relationships with outside powers, just as balance-of-power theory would predict.[102] Both parties to these relationships exaggerated the advantages the other was gaining from such arrangements.

After the Summer of 1983

Rising ethnic tensions within Sri Lanka gravely affected Indo–Sri Lankan relations after the early 1980s. Increasingly bitter Tamil youths tried to undermine governmental order in the Jaffna Peninsula. Efforts by Colombo to reestablish order further alienated Tamils, particularly in 1981, when rioting police burned the Jaffna library, a precious repository of Tamil cultural traditions. Government proposals in 1981 to devolve political power to the Tamil areas were considered niggardly by the more militant Tamils, and Sinhalese zealots in the south vigorously opposed them as the first steps toward secession. Anti-Tamil riots in the summer of 1983, in which members of the government were widely thought to be implicated, not only killed hundreds of Tamils and burned hundreds of Tamil businesses and homes, but led to the massacre of some fifty Tamil prisoners in Colombo's high-security prison. Thousands of families fled to Madras, provoking angry protests by Madras politicians and radicalizing many Sri Lanka Tamils who hitherto had stood aloof, believing that a negotiated compromise solution was still possible.

As the violence intensified, competing politicians in Madras outdid each other in backing competing factions with public encouragement, money, office space, and so on. Training camps, organized mainly by India's intelligence service—Research and Analysis Wing (RAW)—and manned by retired officers taught the use of weapons and elementary tactics. In Colombo it seemed as if New Delhi believed that support to the militants would strengthen the Tamils' hand in negotiating with Colombo, win political points for the Congress party in India's southern states, and perhaps even warn Jayewardenee not to become too close to the United States.[103]

Poorly disciplined at first, the Sri Lankan army improved in its discipline, strategy, and tactics as the fighting dragged on; and more modern light arms were purchased abroad. But each improvement seemed to be matched on the other side by more adroit tactics and better equipment, either supplied from India, won from government forces, or purchased with funds from the Tamil diaspora in the west.[104] India sent a number of mediation missions seeking formulas that would meet minimum Tamil aspirations within a united Sri Lanka; and Rajiv Gandhi and J. R. Jayewardene met several times at regular SAARC meetings.

Both governments had limited room for maneuver. Jayewardene faced Sinhalese zealots demanding destruction of the Tamil militants, and rejectionist militants refused Colombo's numerous offers as inadequate. Rajiv Gandhi, beset by a number of defeats in by-elections, could not support the Tamil militants without appearing to back secessionist militancy and thereby encourage it in the Punjab or in India's northeast. Nor could he block Madras' help to Jaffna militants without undermining his political allies in Madras. Somehow the conflict had to be stopped so that moderates in both Sri Lankan communities could shape a mutually acceptable future. A government advance on the Jaffna Peninsula was halted at India's insistence, dramatized by an airlift of relief supplies accompanied by MIG escorts. Unable to defeat the militants or to offer them anything they would accept, Jayewardene saw no alternative but to reach an agreement with Rajiv Gandhi in late June 1987. This brought an end to Indian support for the fighting militants in exchange for the deployment of an Indian Peace-Keeping Force (IPKF) at Jayewardene's invitation, and it specified Indian diplomatic gains.[105]

The accord (1) called on the militants to give up their arms to Indian troops, who would be temporarily stationed in the northern and eastern provinces as a peace-keeping force. For its part, Colombo (2) reaffirmed an agreement between Colombo, New Delhi, and a broad spectrum of Tamil factions confirming that Sri Lanka was a multiethnic society and providing for increased devolution, provincial councils, and elections. In addition, in a side letter, the government of India gained (3) an explicit assertion that Sri Lanka's foreign policy would not oppose India's interests and that a number of policies, such as the agreement to expand the Voice of America facilities or any putative agreement concerning access to Trincomalee, would not contribute to India's worries.[106]

In the event, Prime Minister Gandhi's advisers exaggerated the influence the Indian patron would have over the most extreme faction of the Tamils, the Tamil Tigers (LTTE), who insisted on independence. Instead of laying down their arms, they turned on the IPKF. The Indian force soon grew from the three thousand originally airlifted to some sixty thousand who had to fight an extended guerrilla resistance, losing more than one thousand soldiers over the next two years. Equally serious, Jayewardene underestimated the anger his move would evoke among the Sinhalese. The radical JVP used the obvious challenge to Sri Lankan sovereignty, which touched most sensitive nationalist nerves, to build a terrorist movement directed mainly at the Sri Lankan establishment.

In this way, Jayewardene hoped the government of India would become part of the solution instead of continuing to be part of the problem. In return, New Delhi obtained written recognition of a *droit de regard* over Sri Lanka's foreign policy. Such an open acknowledgment of Indian aspirations, a form of diplomatic overkill, itself seriously complicated the task of the Sri Lankan government. By 1989 the costs to India of its preeminence had never seemed so high. The Tamil Tigers, who managed to survive India's enmity, became the effective rulers of the northern and parts of Eastern Province as the Indian troops withdrew in the spring of 1990 at the insistence of President Premadassa, Jayewardene's successor. Year-long negotiations between the government and the Tigers, aimed at a mutually acceptable devolution, were broken off by the Tamil militants in the spring of 1990 and the indecisive fighting resumed. A costly stalemate ensued.

Afghanistan

In December 1979 Soviet forces numbering some 80,000 troops invaded Afghanistan. This was the first direct intrusion of outside land forces into the subcontinent since the Chinese thrust into Ladakh and India's the Northeast Frontier Agency (NEFA) in 1962. How did the invasion and the protracted conflict in Afghanistan affect relationships in the subcontinent?[107]

India's immediate reaction differed from nearly everyone else's. To be sure, Mrs. Gandhi had just won a grueling election and her government was not yet fully in place. But its initial reaction was so bland that it virtually acquiesced to the Soviet move. In contrast, U.N. resolutions supported by nearly all Muslim and Western states, as well as most of the nonaligned nations, called for immediate withdrawal, and President Carter offered prompt assistance to the anti-Soviet resistance.

Indeed, within eighteen months of the invasion, America again provided security assistance to Pakistan, after a fifteen-year hiatus, with a $3.2 billion military and economic aid package. This time, however, there was no alliance, and the relationship was accurately characterized by the Pakistani foreign secretary as "a handshake not an embrace."[108]

India's muted reaction to the Soviet presence across the Khyber underlined its foreign policy dilemma. New Delhi appeared more worried by the possibility that Washington's response to the Soviet action could strengthen Pakistan than by the Soviet intrusion. As New Delhi saw it, putting "pressure" on Russia to leave would be costly to India and probably would be ineffective. India's equivocation also isolated it from the bulk of its nonaligned friends. Initially, the Soviet move induced India to seek more diverse sources of military support, particularly high-performance aircraft from France and Great Britain. Even before the United States had committed itself to an aid package for Pakistan, Moscow responded by showing how important it considered Indian acquiescence to be by rushing an irresistible offer of $1.6 billion worth of advanced equipment, including high-performance aircraft at bargain prices and highly concessional rates of financing.[109]

At first, the invasion dramatized the Soviet Union's enhanced capacity to project power beyond its frontiers, underlining its claim to strategic parity with the United States, at that time an important Soviet goal. Simultaneously, it damaged Moscow's standing as a friendly and reliable source of political backing for the weak and the nonaligned. As the years dragged on, its inability to defeat the Afghan resistance raised questions about its vaunted military capability.

Did the dramatic change on the western marches of the subcontinent lead the two South Asian antagonists to turn hostility into collaboration?[110] For almost a year this seemed not entirely out of the question. Understandably, however, after India's original bland reaction to Moscow's initiative and its continued reluctance to challenge Moscow openly, Pakistan asked for proof that India's priorities had changed, such as a withdrawal of some Indian forces from the Pakistan border. But New Delhi apparently feared this would send a wrong signal to the Soviets. Thus, little came of these efforts and the two countries reverted to their familiar postures.

Both states perceived the threat in contradictory ways, which prevented closer collaboration. The Indians feared that American, Chinese, and Pakistani efforts to make life in Afghanistan costly for the Russians would only enhance Pakistan's power and make it more difficult for Moscow to withdraw without losing face. The Pakistanis saw India's accommodation to its patron's presence in Afghanistan as a sell-out that could only undermine Pakistan's efforts to induce the Russians to go home.

In addition, familiar domestic politics also mattered. In India, New Delhi feared the rise of a Sunni Islamic fundamentalism, such as that President Zia was encouraging, when Islamic zeal was already a focus of the resistance movement in Afghanistan. Appeals to the anti-Muslim sentiments of Indian Hindus might also help shore up Mrs. Gandhi's political support, complicating the possibility of improved relations with Pakistan. In India, increased Sikh demands for turning the key state of Punjab into Khalistan intensified New Delhi's suspicions that Pakistan was supporting Sikh extremists.[111]

Within Pakistan, the more than three million refugees added heavily to Pakistan's domestic difficulties, although Islamic solidarity, international humanitarian assistance, and support from the Gulf states and Washington cushioned Zia's rule. In addition, the Soviet presence next door temporarily inhibited politicians from organizing rallies that might have triggered severe disorders.[112]

It also provoked a considerable domestic debate.[113] Was it wise to stand so close to the United States, then openly opposing the Soviet presence, when in neither 1965 nor 1971 had the United States proved "reliable"? Some argued it would be better to settle with Moscow, then ready to recognize the Durand Line defining the frontier between Pakistan and Afghanistan. If Moscow offered military assistance to Pakistan, as it had in the late 1960s, that would be likely to reduce its support for New Delhi.[114] Some argued to the contrary, that the most important step should be to mend fences with India and to induce the two countries to bury their differences.[115]

In the meantime, aid to the *mujahidin* increased from many sources, particularly the United States, China, and the Muslim states of the Gulf. To the embarrassment of the Pakistanis, who sought to deny their involvement, the American Congress became more open in its material and rhetorical support to the resistance via Pakistan. The people increasingly felt the consequences, as Afghan and Soviet airplanes periodically attacked refugee centers and life in Peshawar and Karachi became increasingly insecure from ethnic conflict, drug running, and suspected Soviet-inspired provocations. Yet Zia persisted both in supporting the resistance and in negotiating, through the secretary-general, a means of Soviet withdrawal. At the same time, Washington's interest in encouraging Pakistan's resistance to the Soviet presence led it to turn a blind eye to Pakistan's search for a nuclear weapons capability.

Within India, some believed, as Kautilya might have argued, that the Soviet presence on Pakistan's western frontier ought to be welcomed, for it was bound to deter any Pakistani leader tempted to seek revenge against India for the 1971 secession of East Pakistan.[116] Others, following hegemonic principles, supported the government's efforts to defuse the growing tension by urging that all foreign troops be withdrawn and all external support to the *mujahidin* be stopped.[117]

Many saw the Soviet move as working very much against India. Following the 1971 victory over Pakistan and the liberation of Bangladesh, India's position as the preeminent power in the subcontinent had been widely acknowledged, and the truncated Pakistan had been humbled.[118] Before the Soviet invasion, Pakistan had been without economic assistance from Washington for at least a year, because the Americans had ended a modest aid program as a result of Pakistan's efforts to develop a nuclear capability. All that had been changed by the Soviet initiative. Washington was again helping Pakistan, and India's hopes of keeping the superpowers away from the subcontinent had been dashed by its ally, the Soviet Union.

Others felt that the movement of ground troops into Afghanistan had not changed the configuration of power all that much, since Moscow's shadow had loomed over the subcontinent well before 1980 as its military might expanded at home.[119]

The invasion raised doubts in the minds of Indians about the long-term intentions of their superpower friend. Not only had Moscow not consulted New Delhi before acting, but it was not at all responsive to

India's private urging to withdraw its troops. It showed no interest in encouraging India to act as an intermediary, which its new status on the subcontinent might suggest.[120] New Delhi toned down its criticism of Washington and sought to extend commercial and high-tech links, and Washington saw possible advantages in inducing India to depend less on its insensitive patron.

In sum, a deep ground penetration of one superpower into the region's periphery had the following effects: (1) It induced the second South Asian state, the one most threatened and lacking in convincing reassurance from the region's prime power, to seek again counterweights outside the region; (2) it provoked the principal opponent of the intruding major power to renew military support for its former regional ally after a fifteen-year hiatus and to equip the internal resistance movement; (3) it encouraged the prime regional power and the opponent of the intruder to seek opportunities to broaden their relationships.

Once Soviet forces were withdrawn, Afghanistan became less important as a bone of contention, although India still favored a continuation of the Soviet-installed government as more likely to sustain a secular or more moderately Islamic government. Pakistan favored the more extreme Islamic elements among the *mujahidin*. Within Afghanistan, an indecisive struggle dragged on. The Soviet-backed government remained beleaguered in Kabul and the competing leaders among the *mujahidin* were unable to shape a serious government in exile. On the ground in Afghanistan, regional commanders consolidated their hold on specific territories, recapitulating a close imitation of the decentralized, tribally based polity typical of Afghanistan's stormy past.[121]

It was not until the fall of 1990, well after the Russian withdrawal but before a political settlement, that as a result of Pakistan's nuclear program, Washington was obliged by the Pressler Amendment to the Foreign Assistance Act to suspend economic assistance of some $600 million and most weapons transfers to Pakistan. Consequently, the aid program to Islamabad, resumed in 1980 in response to the Soviet invasion of Afghanistan, came to an abrupt end.

Nepal

Like Sri Lanka, Nepal sought to gain some room for maneuver. Landlocked between the two giants—India and China—it depends on India for 70 percent of its imports, including oil, coal, petroleum, and cement. Some 60 percent of Nepal's exports are taken by India, which also contributes over 50 percent of its foreign assistance.[122] Moreover, as many as 700,000 Nepalese are employed in India.[123] Nepal's thousand-mile border with Tibet is critical to the security of India's frontier with China. India can hardly be expected to tolerate policies in Kathmandu that seriously threaten that security.

It is not surprising, however, that Nepal attempted to use a China connection to gain improved terms in its relations with India, and it confirms the lure of the balancing idea.[124] From time to time, India had supported the Nepali Congress, a pro-Indian party modeled on the Indian National Congress, which tended to oppose policies of the monarchy. By an occasional visit to Beijing or by signing a specific agreement, King Mahendra dramatized to the Indians that Kathmandu did have some alternatives. As Sino-Indian relations worsened in the late 1950s and early 1960s, India became more sensitive to Nepal's needs and Nepal was able to diversify its links to the outside world. It welcomed numerous embassies; it sought aid programs from a variety of donors. At the United Nations it found solidarity with other landlocked states, a way of showing it was not as isolated diplomatically as it might seem.

However, India's defeat at the hands of the Chinese in 1962 and Chinese enthusiasm in building the Lhasa-Kathmandu road showed how restricted Nepal's options were.[125] The oversized bridges the Chinese built, reportedly capable of carrying at least medium-sized tanks, reminded Nepal that China might have ambitions that went beyond acting as a counterweight to India in the country's middle valleys.[126]

New Delhi also underlined the limits on Kathmandu's options. Although Mrs. Gandhi no longer provided help to the opposition Nepali Congress, she was able to delay indispensable trade and customs agreements until the monarchy appreciated the limited nature of Nepal's economic autonomy.[127]

The Indian absorption of Sikkim in 1974 provided an object lesson on not pushing India too far, and once again, in negotiations on trade and transit in the late 1980s, India made clear it held the upper hand.

Domestic changes in Nepal seem likely to enhance both China's and India's ability to influence its politics. In 1990, student unrest evoked such widespread protest that King Birendra was forced to establish a constitutional monarchy with an elected parliament chosen by multiparty elections. The first election, held in 1991, returned a slight majority in favor of the Nepali Congress, a party with a tradition of working closely with the Indian Congress.

In contrast, when, in 1988, the Gayoom government in the Maldives appealed to the United States and India for assistance in overcoming an invasion by a group of Sri Lankan Tamil secessionists, New Delhi responded promptly with an airlift of troops, who were quickly withdrawn once the invaders had been subdued.

The balancing efforts of Sri Lanka and Nepal or the brief appeal of the Maldives did little to disturb the basic structure of the South Asian regional system, although internal developments in Sri Lanka following the 1983 riots deeply disturbed New Delhi. Nevertheless, they illustrate the tendency of small states situated near large ones to seek counter-weights wherever they can reasonably be found. Until the ethnic eruption in Sri Lanka, their balancing efforts were irritants to New Delhi, but little more. Once Sinhalese-Tamil relations deteriorated so badly that Madras Tamils became deeply involved in supporting the secessionists, at a time when Sikh agitation in the Punjab threatened India's security vis-à-vis Pakistan, New Delhi responded with actions that deeply involved it in Sri Lanka's internal affairs.

Efforts at Cooperation: 2

We have seen that despite their persisting rivalry and profound mutual suspicions, India and Pakistan have successfully negotiated a number of agreements. Bilateral agreements on repatriation, smuggling control, and other matters have also been worked out between India and Bangladesh and India and Sri Lanka. More recently, force majeure led the Jayewardene government to the unexpected step of accepting the presence of Indian troops as it sought to deal with ethnic difficulties that were closely linked to politics in south India. The emergence of multilateral structures favoring inconspicuous and continuous consultation provides an example of a different sort of mutuality.

South Asian Association for Regional Cooperation

If ASEAN is any guide, mutual accommodation is more likely if there are means for regular consultations through such processes as those established by the South Asian Association for Regional Cooperation (SAARC). South Asia has been remarkable for the lack of such consultation among its leaders. Before the founding of SAARC, there had been more personal consultations between the leaders of the United States and the Soviet Union than between Islamabad and New Delhi.

SAARC was originally called for by President Ziaur Rahman of Bangladesh in 1980 in the improved atmosphere that had been created within the region by the Janata government's more sensitive policies and the worsening regional situation provoked by radical political change in Afghanistan. But the first meeting did not take place until December 1985, in Dhaka.

Initially, both India and Pakistan were skeptical. India assumed SAARC might be what Mrs. Gandhi had always feared, an opportunity for the smaller states to join with Pakistan to "gang up" against India, and Pakistan feared it might be an Indian ploy to gather the subcontinent against Pakistan. On the other hand, the Soviet occupation of Afghanistan lent weight to the argument that the states of South Asia should now, if ever, emphasize what they had in common. India risked isolating itself if it held out when the others were interested. Once the proposal seemed likely to gain headway, both went along, although with caution.[128]

SAARC had obvious advantages for the smaller states. If they could discuss issues that bothered them all with the largest state present, India would be more likely to be responsive. Numerous issues transcend the bounds of bilateral discussions, such as watershed management, deforestation, and other ecological issues; the growing drug trade; and improved regional communications. Moreover, India and Pakistan have such an established history of contention that it may be easier for them to make concessions to each other in a larger regional context than if they had to make concessions to each other bilaterally.

Discussions at the secretarial level defined agreed working principles, by now conventional in regional meetings: Decisions would be made only if they were unanimous; bilateral and contentious issues would be excluded from SAARC deliberations; "cooperation should be based on respect for the principles of sovereign equality, territorial integrity, political independence, noninterference in internal affairs of other states and mutual benefits"; and regional cooperation would not exclude bilateral or multilateral cooperation, nor should it be "inconsistent with bilateral or multilateral obligations."[129] Numerous joint committees have been established to deal with various economic and technical issues. Officials have begun the laborious process of regular consultation to enhance each one's understanding of the other's perceptions and problems. Important, regular meetings require that responsible officials and heads of state prepare positions more carefully and hear firsthand their neighbor's complaints without the publicity that so often generates opposition to any concessions.

The utility of SAARC meetings has already been demonstrated. At Bangalore in December 1986, for instance, Rajiv Gandhi and Zia ul Haq could quietly discuss Indian accusations that Pakistan was harboring proponents of Khalistan. Jayewardene could press India to bear down on the Sri Lankan Tamil's use of Madras as a safe haven and channel for arms, and Delhi could press Colombo to be more accepting of Tamil aspirations. In the end, the Gandhi-Jayewardene negotiations begun on the margins of SAARC produced the controversial Accord discussed earlier. It reflected the nearly desperate position of the Colombo government, the anxieties of New Delhi, and the diplomatic advantages it gained as a result. But without the occasions for inconspicuous personal

relations between the principals, an agreement between the two governments would have been unlikely. Consultations may make it easier for
contending statesmen to perceive ways in which both may gain even
when they see themselves as rivals.

One should not expect too much from SAARC, however, because
the security perceptions of key states differ sharply. Unlike the situation
in ASEAN or the GCC, policymakers in the principal state, India, see
their security interests served best in a hierarchical regional system in
which their preeminence is widely acknowledged. The other states see
India as the principal threat.[130] Indian leaders have not yet been able to
shape their policies to make their nation's obvious preeminence acceptable to its smaller neighbors. The domestic political regimes show
marked contrasts, which may make collaboration more difficult. Finally,
economic interests are not seen as complementary.[131]

The creation of SAARC represents a promising initiative to help
overcome a fundamental structural difficulty. Through improved communication and closer personal connections, South Asia's future leaders
may be more successful than their predecessors in finding mutually acceptable ways of coping with their many difficulties. And younger postindependence leaders who did not experience either the prepartition debates, the horrors of partition, or the bitterness of personal involvement
in direct military regional conflict may be more flexible and able to construct relationships that stress the interests they share rather than the
gains each might make at the expense of the other.

Conclusions

Tracing in this detail the action-reaction relationships of these states, the
effects of domestic politics on foreign policy, and the results of the activities of external states leads to the following conclusions.

Structure of the Regional System

South Asia is a regional system that revolves around India. Geographically central, separating the regional states from one another, and far
and away the largest state, India is the preeminent power. All the smaller
states must deal with it. Indeed, South Asia is largely a system of bilateral relations, as each state has crucial relationships with India and few
security connections to others in the region. The principal armature of
the regional system is the rivalry between India and the second-ranking
state, Pakistan. Together their relations shape the environment in which
all must function.

Relations among the states have been affected by (1) domestic politics, particularly (a) ethnic strife, where national cohesion is uncertain, and (b) the side effects of competition between political figures and factions within each state; (2) major regional states attempting to improve their relative capability; and (3) the effects on local balances of the activities of outside powers.

The Major Rivalry

The intensity of the rivalry between India and Pakistan has deep roots. Incompatible images of past imperial glory cherished by Hindus and Muslims alike, mutual suspicions enlivened by memories of three wars in forty years, familiar problems of the security dilemma (including competitive arms buildups by both states) provide apparently solid justification to both antagonists for continued suspicion and rivalry.

The bipolarity of the region adds further structural difficulties. Because all the other states were so small and the major protagonists had security links to outside states that were also rivals, both regional states could never see one another as possible collaborators against a third that seriously threatened them both.

None of the smaller regional states is substantial enough to be of real help in offsetting the power of the largest. This structural fact best explains why, despite the fears of Indian primacy shared by all the other states, the smaller nations did not find more effective ways of combining to offset India.

Policy purpose was also important. The disparity between the major states has been consciously enlarged by India's determination to develop its own military and industrial capability and to assemble and equip the world's fourth largest army and an expanding navy. Moreover, they are attached to mutually contradictory principles for shaping the desirable public order of South Asia. India seeks a hierarchical arrangement, with itself as the region's security manager. Pakistan, by contrast, holds to the principle of sovereign equality of states. Hegemony and balancing of power are mutually incompatible, and each one's requisites for its conception of autonomy contradict the other's.

Communication between the two major states has been infrequent. Feeling insecure because of their own ethnic and institutional weaknesses, which they fear their neighbors will only exacerbate, the defensive measures India and Pakistan take intensify their neighbors' anxieties. Lacking precise information of the other's intentions, they assume the worst. Each has been unable to take seriously or comprehend the other's fears; each underestimates how the measures it takes to relieve its own anxieties have compounded the anxieties of its neighbor.

The durability of South Asia's hostilities and friendships, therefore, although marked, is not surprising. Even the Soviet invasion of Afghanistan made little difference in these relationships.

Means of Interaction

The states of South Asia have dealt with each other by means of quiet diplomacy; a good deal of public disagreement; a limited but significant manipulation of each other's ethnic vulnerabilities; economic pressures, in the case of India's relations with Nepal; and by the threat and use of force. Diplomacy produced settlements concerning water rights in the Punjab (with the help of the World Bank), the Tashkent Declaration (with the help of Moscow) after the 1965 war, the Simla Agreement following the 1971 conflict, agreements concerning minority nationality problems between India and Sri Lanka, and a number of agreements between India and Nepal on migration, trade, nationality rights, and so on.

There has been open conflict over specific issues, such as frontier alignments, territorial claims, and ethnic secessionist movements. Each specific issue, however, was shadowed by the larger one of relative standing in the region, and reflected differences over the principles by which the region should be organized.

Two of the three Indo-Pakistani wars have been between professional armies with conventional equipment, resulting in few civilian casualties. The third, in Bangladesh, beginning as a popular rebellion, was far more costly in lives and property. Given the level of armaments now available, another round would be far more destructive, as is suggested by the level of civilian destruction in Sri Lanka's ethnic strife and civil wars. If both major South Asian states go nuclear, as is quite possible, renewed hostilities could bring a holocaust.

Regional Communication

There has been remarkably little institutionalized consultation between the leaders of South Asia until recently. Joint commissions dealing inconspicuously at the technical level with such issues as water allocations, communications, frontier security, and the like, do exist. However, until recently, South Asia has had few regular opportunities for politically responsible officials to consult together on a regular and inconspicuous basis. Only in 1983, after efforts since the mid-1970s, did India agree to the establishment of the South Asian Association for Regional Cooperation (SAARC).

A number of important issues already have been dealt with in the corridors of SAARC meetings. Whether closer consultation among the region's leaders can change South Asia into a less conflicted region remains uncertain until the domestic regimes gain greater cohesion and institutional stability and leaders pursue mutual accommodation with greater commitment.

Except for Nepal and Afghanistan, which depend on India and Pakistan, respectively, for access to markets, economic relations between the states of the region have been minimal. Fearing the potential economic leverage interdependence could give to the prime power in South Asia and that their markets would be swamped by India's increasingly diversified economy, the smaller South Asian states insulated themselves as best they could. Moreover, New Delhi's long-term commitment to economic self-sufficiency also inhibited economic connections.

Domestic Insecurities

Internal factors in all the states result in insecurity. The states are all multiethnic and highly permeable; political institutions are not yet reliably established. No leader is confident that his state's cohesion can be taken for granted. Politics in one can easily affect its neighbor. Ethnic loyalties often overlap across frontiers. Each fears that the other is ready to weaken cohesion by encouraging regionalist minorities, of which all have their share. In effect, governments have only limited sovereign control over their ethnic vulnerabilities. As the cases of Pakistan in what became Bangladesh and of Sri Lanka in its northern Tamil-speaking provinces illustrate, ethnic divisions and governmental insensitivity to the aspirations of minorities make the states vulnerable to influences from next door.

Side Effects of Domestic Politics on Foreign Policy

The lack of national unity can provoke difficulties between neighbors as disgruntled minorities seek help from across the frontier. Thus far, to compete successfully in domestic politics, elected leaders have played up issues that intensify interstate antagonisms. Growing Hindu militancy in India, Muslim militancy in Pakistan, Tamil nationalism and Sinhalese Buddhist zealotry in Sri Lanka all threaten domestic tranquility and make concessions between states more difficult.

Under such circumstances, it is politically risky for leaders to advocate accommodation with neighbors. To succeed, such a diplomatic initiative would have to provide visible and quick results; to hold, it would have to be reciprocated unambiguously and quickly, which presently seems unlikely.

External Balancing

Although clearly bounded geographically, South Asia has become intimately linked politically to the central Asian Sino-Soviet competition and, periodically, to the global Soviet-American balance.

The South Asian balancing process expanded well beyond South Asia as the lesser states sought outside support to offset Indian predominance. Pakistan requested help from the Gulf states and from Washington, which gave a temporary boost to Islamabad in response to America's worries about "Soviet expansionism" from the mid–1950s to 1965 and from 1980 to 1990. The still smaller states also had similar concerns. Sri Lanka used British bases as insurance at the outset. Nepal sought to use its geographical position between India and China to extend its room for maneuver, but its dependence on India for transit and trade showed how few options it had.

Even the region's prime power sought to offset its major threats, China and Pakistan, with substantial military equipment from Moscow and coproduction arrangements and high-performance imports from Europe. Following America's opening to China and as the 1971 conflict with Pakistan approached, New Delhi even entered an alliance with Moscow in the hope of deterring the Chinese from directly assisting Pakistan.

Why Join Alliances? The Importance of Triangulation

What appeared on the surface to be bilateral relationships with external powers were in almost every case driven by the actions of third parties. Pakistan sought a Washington connection to obtain diplomatic support, arms, and economic assistance as a by-product of the unresolved Indo-Pakistani rivalry focused particularly on Kashmir and on differing conceptions of an acceptable South Asian regional order. The Sino-Indian conflict over the frontier alignment and over their relative standing in Asia turned India briefly toward Washington during the 1962 war with China and subsequently toward heavy dependence on Soviet diplomatic backing and arms transfers. Similarly, the U.S.-Soviet competition eventually prompted Washington to answer Pakistan's requests and led Moscow to seek friendship with India. India became more important to Moscow in South Asia as a result of China's conflict with the Soviet Union across central Asia. Moscow considered its policy toward India while worrying about China and the United States. Beijing considered its policy toward Pakistan while being concerned principally about its differences with India and the Soviet Union. Each of the two principal states had come to depend on its central Asian patron to deter the patron of its regional rival. These created complex triangular calculations and dependencies.

Accordingly, South Asian states have entered alliances or evolved other arrangements with outside powers (1) to receive security resources—diplomatic, military, and economic—that helped offset the capability of their rival neighbors, and (2) to deter the patron of their regional rival.

Effects of Outside Help

Foreign diplomatic support, security assistance, and economic aid may increase the relative capability of one state vis-à-vis a neighbor. India, Pakistan, and Bangladesh all gained economically or militarily from external help. Their policy, however, was little changed by such assistance. Their policies continued to be defined fundamentally by established rivalries and friendships within the region.

Outside help may make regional states less willing to accommodate a neighbor. Pakistan refused to accept Indian conceptions of the "natural balance" of forces in the subcontinent in part as a result of American and then Chinese assistance, and India felt no need to respond to Pakistan or China in part because of Soviet support. Efforts by Washington and Great Britain in the early 1960s and by the Soviet Union in the late 1960s to encourage India and Pakistan to accommodate one another proved fruitless. These initiatives were usually vitiated by the support the regional power could expect from its external patron. In none of past cases did the external help change the nature of Indo-Pakistani relations.

Outside help to one nation may lead a regional rival to seek help to a degree it had not originally contemplated. American help to Pakistan as well as the Chinese intrusion contributed to India's reach toward Moscow. These moves affected comparative capabilities, but they did not materially alter the character of relationships within the region.

Outside help may also affect the balance of domestic forces, as American support originally strengthened the hand of Pakistan's military at the expense of civilian politicians. In India, Soviet diplomatic and economic support and military equipment flows strengthened successive Congress governments.

Not until 1990 was it plausible to both protagonists that the old days of playing one major power against the other were now over. Whether this would help them to be more accommodating or would only intensify their rivalry remained to be seen.

Sources of System Change

Although diplomatic, economic, and military support from outside the region may have temporarily altered regional balances, it was more fundamental change within the region that brought a degree of system change. Thus, the 1971 defeat of Pakistan was a watershed in one aspect of Indo-Pakistani relations. The secession of Bangladesh with Indian help appears to have undermined Pakistani leaders' hopes of maintaining military parity with India. New Delhi's unambiguous superiority appears to have induced caution in Islamabad. Pakistan's attempt to acquire a nuclear capability, nevertheless, represents an effort to offset the present imbalance.

Change in capabilities also altered Indo–Sri Lankan relationships in the late 1980s. Sri Lanka's growing difficulties in dealing with Tamil secessionists in the north and with Sinhalese radicals in the south gravely weakened Colombo and led Jayewardene to issue his unprecedented invitation to New Delhi. For a time, this sharply expanded New Delhi's direct involvement in Sri Lankan internal affairs.

On the other hand, even the 1980 Soviet invasion of Afghanistan brought little change in the relationship between India and Pakistan. It underlined the lengthening shadow of Soviet power over the subcontinent as Soviet forces appeared near the Pakistan border, and it raised acute questions about the appropriate response to that presence. The policies both governments advocated for coping with the Soviet presence, however, were so mutually contradictory that after nine years of the Soviet occupation, the two appeared as far apart as ever.

The Role of Persons

The interlocking regional system was not entirely mechanistic. It could be influenced by policies of responsible individuals playing key roles.

Generational or other change in political leaders can open opportunities for regional change if successors see the region in different terms, define national interest in a different way, and are strong enough politically to implement changes that hitherto had been impossible. After all, it was not until Stalin's death that Soviet leaders were ready to open policy toward India and the Third World. Gorbachev and his colleagues have turned Soviet policy sharply. It is not inconceivable that the new generation in Islamabad and New Delhi may perceive possibilities the veterans of partition and 1971 could not imagine.

Suppose that Ayub or Bhutto had been more willing to "accept the facts" in Kashmir. They would have faced different domestic risks, but their need for outside support might not have seemed so urgent. Or if Indira Gandhi, the leader of the largest regional state for much of this period, had been less concerned to assert Indian predominance and had been more responsive to India's smaller neighbors, including Pakistan, the system might have functioned differently. Because the Janata government appeared to define India's national interest differently and its style assuaged its neighbor's anxieties, had it managed to contain its own internal rivalries enough to have survived, new possibilities for reduced suspicion and enhanced cooperation might have brought a substantial change in the character of South Asian relationships. The Kautilyan checkerboard might have been less obvious.

Implications of the End of the Cold War

Change in the system could also come from changes in the impact on the region of the activities of external powers. So long as the principal external states saw themselves as rivals for the backing of regional states, the latter could play on that rivalry in their efforts to win external support.

What were the effects in the late 1980s of all three major external powers devoting less attention to developments in South Asia? What were the effects at the end of the 1980s of the withdrawal of Soviet forces from Afghanistan, the domestic upheaval within the Soviet Union, and the normalization of U.S.-Soviet or Chinese–Soviet relations?

Although Pakistan had long considered Washington unreliable, the cutoff of assistance in 1990 in response to Pakistan's continuing nuclear program was deeply disturbing, emblematiac of declining American interest that would inevitably narrow Islamabad's options. Pakistan would once more press for resources from the Gulf states, but the Iran-Iraq and Iraq-Coalition wars together would sharply curtail resources, at least for a period. The emergence of a number of independent Muslim states in Central Asia would open opportunities for Islamabad's diplomacy and worry New Delhi. However, necessarily inward looking until they became well established, these states would be economically poor and not likely to provide useful diplomatic support to Islamabad except, perhaps, for a few extra notes in the general assembly. Long able to count on Moscow's support, Indian policymakers would be deeply troubled that at moments of difficulty neither diplomatic backing nor generous arms supplies would any longer be available from what had been the Soviet Union. That the United States and the Soviet Union were able to collaborate at the United Nations as they did in the Gulf crisis of early 1991 dramatized the anachronism of nonalignment and might have presaged concerted U.S.-Soviet influence if Soviet power had not collapsed. As the Soviet Union disintegrated, China, too, would be likely to find South Asia of less concern, and its lessened worry about India as a client of the Soviet Union would reduce its support for Pakistan.

Thus, while undermining assumptions of both South Asian states, on balance, these changes would work to the greater long run advantage of the already preeminent power, although whether it could take advantage of this possibility would depend heavily upon its success in dealing with its growing ethnic and religious difficulties. Moreover, an India with less reliable support from Moscow but less worried by a Pakistan receiving less support from Washington and Beijing might be able to be more flexible or innovative in dealing with its regional rival. The emergence of younger leaders less committed to established policies might make such changes more possible. If past relationships in the subcontinent are our principal guides, however, such an outcome appears unlikely.

NOTES

1. Bhutan has been omitted as of minimum significance. Sikkim has been briefly noted because of the demonstration effect of developments there. The Maldives, an island "state" with 202,000 inhabitants, scattered on 200 islands on nineteen atolls is generally not active in the region's international politics.

2. The most useful analysis of the South Asian system for our purposes is Barry Buzan and Gowher Rizvi, *South Asian Insecurity and the Great Powers* (London: Macmillan, 1986).

3. United Nations, *World Demographic Estimates and Projections, 1950–2025* (New York: United Nations, 1988), p. 246.

4. *Key:* Column 1: Population, in millions, 1988. From *World Military Expenditures and Arms Transfers* (Washington, D.C.: U.S. Arms Control and Disarmament Agency, 1989).

Column 2: Annual rate of population growth, percent, 1985–88. From *World Demographic Estimates and Projections, 1950–2025* (New York: United Nations, 1988).

Column 3: Armed forces, in thousands, 1988. From *World Military Expenditures.*

Column 4: Gross National Product, billions of dollars, 1988. From *World Military Expenditures.*

Column 5: Per Capita GNP, dollars, 1988. From *World Military Expenditures.*

Column 6: Military expenditures, millions of dollars, 1988. From *World Military Expenditures.*

Column 7: Military expenditures as a percentage of GNP, 1988. From *World Military Expenditures.*

Column 8: Average annual growth rate of GDP between 1980 and 1988. From *World Development Report 1990*.
Note: Because figures in these columns come from various sources, the implicit relationships between them may not hold as expected.

5. World Bank, *World Development Report, 1985* (New York: Oxford University Press, 1985), Table 1, Basic Indicators.

6. Nazli Choucri, *Population Dynamics and International Violence* (Lexington, Mass.: Lexington Books, 1974); Wriggins and James Guyot, eds., *Population, Politics and the Future of Southern Asia* (New York: Columbia University Press, 1973); Wriggins, "Youth Cohorts, Population Growth and Political Outcomes" (Vienna: International Institute for Applied Systems Analysis, July 1989, Working Paper).

7. For a discussion of possible vulnerabilities from certain forms of interdependence, see Robert O. Keohane and Joseph S. Nye, *Power and Interdependence* (Boston: Little, Brown, 1977), pp. 13–14.

8. For discussions, see Joseph Rothschild, *Ethno-Politics: A Conceptual Framework* (New York: Columbia University Press, 1982); Wriggins, *Ceylon: Dilemmas of a New Nation* (Princeton: Princeton University Press, 1960), chs. 4, 7; Myron Wiener, "The Macedonian Syndrome," *World Politics*, 23(4) (July 1971):665–83; Rounaq Jahan, *Pakistan: Failure of National Integration* (New York: Columbia University Press, 1972); Hafeez Malik, "Problems of Regionalism in Pakistan," in H. Wriggins, ed., *Pakistan in Transition* (Islamabad and New York: University of Islamabad Press, 1975), pp. 60–133.

9. For East Pakistan, see Jahan, *Pakistan: Failure*; for Sri Lanka, see K. M. De Silva's *Managing Ethnic Tensions in Multi-Ethnic Societies: Sri Lanka, 1880–1985* (London: University Press of America, 1986); S. J. Tambiah, *Sri Lanka: Ethnic Fratricide and the Dismantling of Democracy* (Chicago: University of Chicago Press, 1986).

10. Bhabani Sen Gupta, *Ethno-Political Interstate Tensions*. See also Zalmay Khalilzad in T. George, R. Litwak, and S. Chubin, *Security in Southern Asia* (New York: St. Martin's Press, 1984), pp. 73–84.

11. Buzan and Rizvi, *South Asian Insecurity*, p. 14.

12. For a useful discussion, see Percival Spear, *India: A Modern History* (Ann Arbor: University of Michigan Press, 1961), esp. chs. 12 and 13; also Kuldip Nayar, *Distant Neighbors* (New Delhi: Vikas, 1972), esp. ch. 1.

13. For a discussion of the importance of passions and fears in international politics, see Michael Donelan, *The Reasons of States: A Study in International Political Theory* (London: Allen and Unwin, 1978), esp. p. 13.

14. See also Dehio (1962); Gulick (1967); Waltz, *Theory*, ch. 6; Bull, *Anarchical Society*, ch. 5; Martin Wight, "The Balance of Power and International Order," in Alan James (1973); and Wolfers (1962), ch. 8. For a thoughtful discussion of Canadian-U.S. relations, an apparent exception, see William T. R. Fox, *A Continent Apart: The United States and Canada in World Politics* (Toronto: University of Toronto Press, 1985).

15. For a useful discussion of the power of reciprocity, see Robert Axelrod, *The Evolution of Cooperation* (New York: Basic, 1984), ch. 9, "The Robustness of Reciprocity."

16. See note 27 in ch. 1.

17. Michael Brecher, *Nehru: A Political Biography* (London: Oxford University Press, 1959), p. 346.

18. Surjit Mansingh, *India's Search for Power*, p. 41.

19. For a useful evocation of what that might mean, see Mansingh, *India's Search for Power*, pp. 278–92.

20. Mansingh, *India's Search for Power*, pp. 280–88; also Asoka Raina, *Inside RAW: The Story of India's secret service* (New Delhi: Vikas, 1981), ch. 7.

21. For Pakistan's views, see G. W. Choudhury, *Pakistan's Relations with India* (Meerut, India: Meeakshi Prakashan, 1971), ch. 7, "Divergent Foreign Policies."

22. Brecher recalls Pakistani worries that the Congress Working Committee's resolution declaring that "the (Working) Committee believe that the destiny of India will yet be realized and that when passions have cooled, . . . a new and stronger unity based on good will and cooperation will emerge" revealed an Indian ambition to undo partition. Brecher, *Nehru*, p. 378. For a sensitive discussion of the "dominant Indian attitude," see Selig Harrison, *The Widening Gap* (New York: Free Press, 1978), pp. 262–63. As Ayub Khan put it, "the cause of our major problem is India's inability to reconcile herself to our existence as a sovereign, independent state," *Friends Not Masters* (London: Oxford University Press, 1967), p. 115.

23. For a more detailed discussion of illustrative ethno-political problems and their effects on India's relations with its neighbors, see the sections below on "Pakistan Divided" and "Sri Lanka."

24. R. L. Hardgrave, *India: Government and Politics in a Developing Nation* (New York: Harcourt Brace, 1970), p. 8.

25. As Mansingh put it, New Delhi "cannot willingly accept a situation in which the outlying states of the subcontinent do not implicitly offer deference," *India's Search for Power*, p. 238.

26. See report of the National Democratic Institute for International Affairs, *1990 Pakistan National Assembly Elections* (Washington, D.C., 1991), p. 2.

27. Maya Chadda, "Domestic Determinants of Indian Foreign Policy in the 1980's," *Journal of South Asia and Middle East Studies*, vol. 11, nos. 1 and 2 (Fall/Winter 1987).

28. See the section on Sri Lanka.

29. Mohammed Ayoob, "India, Pakistan, and superpower rivalry," *World Today*, 38 (1982):194–202. For an evocative analysis of Indian perspectives on these matters, see Baldav Raj Nayar, "Regional Power in a Multipolar World," in J. W. Mellor, *India, : A Rising Middle Power* (Boulder, Colo.: Westview, 1979), pp. 147–88.

30. Force data for 1962 Lorne J. Kavic, *India's Quest for Security: Defence Policies, 1957–1965* (Berkeley: University of California Press, 1967), budget data for 1962 and 1964 from Harpreet Mahajan, *Arms Transfer to India, Pakistan, and the Third World* (New Delhi: Young Asia, 1981), tables 7.2 and 8.3. Other years from IISS, *Military Balance*, London, appropriate years; Budget percentages from ACDA, *World Military and Arms Transfers, 1967–1976* (Washington, D.C.: Arms Control and Disarmament Agency, 1977); and *1974–1986* (1988).

31. R. E. Sontag and J. S. Beddie, *Nazi-Soviet Relations, 1939–1941* (New York: Didier, 1948), pp. 158–60.

32. Wriggins, "The Balancing Process in Pakistan's Foreign Policy," in Lawrence Ziring, Ralph Braibanti, and H. Wriggins, eds., *Pakistan: The Long View* (Durham, N.C.: Duke University Press, 1977), ch. 11. Anita Inder Singh has looked at British and American documentation of the period and confirms Washington's reluctance to respond. Washington's initiatives were not designed to challenge India, as some Indian spokesmen hold, but were to encourage Pakistani cooperation in the event of a Soviet thrust through Afghanistan. See her "The Superpower Global Complex and South Asia," in Buzan and Rizvi, *South Asian Insecurity*, pp. 209–10.

33. George McGee, *Envoy to the Middle World* (New York: Harper & Row, 1983), p. 86.

34. Onkar Marwah, "National Security and Military Policy in India," in L. Ziring, *The Subcontinent in World Politics* (New York: Praeger, 1982), p. 73; also G. McGee, pp. 92 and 96; Buzan and Rizvi, *South Asian Insecurity*, pp. 209–10.

35. The Soviet Union did the same during certain periods, Mansingh, *India's Search for Power*, p. 201.

36. Mahajan, *Arms Transfer to India*, table 7.3.

37. For an Indian view, see K. Subrahmanyam, "Dialogue with Pakistan," *Strategic Analysis* (New Delhi), 6(10) (January 1983):584.

38. Mansingh, *India's Search for Power*, p. 75.

39. For example, Robert C. Horn, *Soviet Indian Relations: Issues and Influence* (New York: Praeger, 1982), p. 13.

40. As Mullick, Nehru's intelligence chief who was very close to the prime minister, put Nehru's view: "The conflict (between Russia and China) had very little ideology in it. The conflict was between the national interests of these two great countries. In this context it was very helpful to India to have friendly relations with Russia, because of all the countries in the world, only Russia could prove useful to India by its policy in regard to the Sino-Indian dispute." B. N. Mullick, *My Years with Nehru: The Chinese Betrayal* (New Delhi: Allied Publishers, 1971), p. 103.

41. Allen Whiting, *The Chinese Calculus of Deterrence* (Ann Arbor: University of Michigan Press, 1975), p. 74. Whiting studied in detail China's and India's efforts to deter the other. For background see chs. 1–5, esp. ch. 3.

42. For detailed accounts, see Mullick, *My Years*, esp. chs. 6–9, 15, 19, and 20; Lt. Gen. B. M. Kaul, *The Untold Story* (Bombay: Allied Publishers, 1967); Allen Whiting, *Chinese Calculus*; Nevil Maxwell, *India's China War* (London: Jonathan Cape, 1970).

43. For details, see Lt. Gen. B. M. Kaul, *Untold Story*; B. M. Mullick, *My Years*; J. P. Dalvi, *Himalayan Blunder* (Bombay: Thacker, 1969). The flood of memoirs and self-defenses makes clear that much more than logistical difficulties contributed to the result.

44. Kenneth Galbraith, *Ambassador's Journal* (Boston: Houghton Mifflin, 1969), chs. 20–23; Whiting, *Chinese Calculus*, p. 149.

45. Whiting, *Chinese Calculus*, pp. 40–41, 166–69; see also Y. I. Vertzberger,

Misperceptions in Foreign Policy Making: The Sino-Indian Conflict, 1959–1962 (Boulder, Colo.: Westview, 1984), pp. 100–102, 121–22, 236.

46. Whiting's analysis highlights the tragic implications of these developments when he discusses the predicament of leaders in both countries as their respective efforts to deter the other failed, esp. pp. 168–69.

47. For this view see R. N. Lebow, *Between Peace and War* (Baltimore: Johns Hopkins University Press, 1981), pp. 184–92.

48. Mullick is eloquent on the subject, as was Nehru himself. In October 27, 1962, as fighting had begun, Nehru wrote to the Chinese Premier, "Nothing in my long political career has hurt and grieved me more than the fact that the hopes and aspirations of peaceful and friendly neighborly relations, which we entertained and to promote which my colleagues . . . and myself worked so hard since the establishment of the People's Republic of China, should have been shattered by the hasty and unfriendly twist given to India-China relations during the last few years" (*My Years*, p. 397).

49. The Indo-Pakistan force level ratio changed as follows:

Year	India	Pakistan	Ind/Pak
1962	596,000	247,700	2.4
1965	844,000	258,300	3.3
1971	980,000	429,000	2.3
1986	1,260,000	480,000	2.6

Sarbjit Singh Johal, *National Power and Regional Cooperation: Indo-Pakistan Relations, 1947–1983* (unpublished Ph.D. dissertation, University of California, Santa Barbara), p. 560. Data from Barnds, Kavic and relevant years of IISS, *Strategic Balance for 1985* (IISS, 1985–86), pp. 122 and 131.

50. See Marwah, "India's Military Power and Policy," Marwah and J. Pollack, eds., *Military Power in Asian States: China, India, Japan* (Boulder, Colo.: Westview, 1980), p. 113.

51. In summarizing Nehru's communications to numerous heads of state after the conflict, Mullick reported the prime minister's view as follows: "What distressed him (Nehru) was that a policy of peace . . . and the friendship which he had been trying to cultivate with China with whom India had much in common and who was a close neighbor had been shattered by this treachery of the Chinese. Henceforward, India could not follow the same path in her foreign relations. . . . She had to face the evil, which, it had been proved to his dismay, could not be conquered by good faith and sweet reason alone, but had to be met with force and the consequences had to be borne" (*My Years*, pp. 397–98).

52. Martin Wight, "The Balance of Power and International Order," in Alan James, ed., *The Bases of International Order*, p. 89.

53. For a careful discussion of this relationship, see Y. I. Vertzberger, *The Enduring Entente: Sino-Pakistan Relations, 1960–1980* (New York: Praeger, 1983, The Washington Papers no. 95); see also Rasul Bux Rais, *China and Pakistan* (Lahore: Progressive Publishers, 1977).

54. For a careful reconstruction of the politico-ethnic background, see Rounaq Jahan, *Pakistan: Failure*. For accounts of India's role in accelerating the

secession, see Pran Chopra, *India's Second Liberation* (New Delhi: Vikas, 1973); also Robert Victor Jackson, *South Asian Crisis: India, Pakistan, and Bangladesh—A Political and Historical Analysis of the 1971 War* (New York: Praeger, 1975), esp. chs. 4 and 5. For a discussion of allegations that India's intelligence organization helped organize and supported the *mukthibahini*, see Asoka Raina, *Inside RAW: The Story of India's Secret Service* (New Delhi: Vikas, 1981), ch. 6, "Special Operations: Bangladesh."

55. For Henry Kissinger's explanation, see his *White House Years* (Boston: Little, Brown, 1979), pp. 885–918.

56. Standing in 1972 at 392,000 compared to India's 980,000, Robert G. Wirsing, "The Arms Race in South Asia: Implications for the United States," *Asian Survey*, 25(3) (March 1985):270–71; also Marwah, "India's Military Power," in Marwah and Pollack, eds., *Military Power*, p. 117.

57. *Far Eastern Economic Review*, September 11, 1986, p. 47.

58. Marwah's assessment is generally consistent with Raju Thomas' "India" in E. A. Kolodziej and R. E. Harkovy, *Security Policies of Developing Countries* (Lexington, Mass.: Lexington Books, 1982), ch. 6.

59. IISS, *The Military Balance, 1985–86* (London), pp. 123, 131.

60. Amir Taheri, "Policies of Iran and in the Persian Gulf Region," in Abdus Amiris, ed., *The Persian Gulf and the Indian Ocean in International Politics* (Teheran: Institute of International Political and Economic Studies, 1975), p. 270.

61. For details, see Wriggins, "South Asia and the Gulf: Linkages, Gains, and Limitations," *Middle East Review*, 18(2) (Winter 1985–86):25–37. Also B. A. Robertson, "South Asia and the Gulf Complex," in Buzan and Rizvi, *South Asian Insecurity*, ch. 6.

62. Visalakshmi, *India and Iraq: From Cordial Political Relations to Close Economic Relations* dissertation prepared at the University of Hyderabad, 1981 (unpublished). Also Wriggins, "South Asia and the Gulf," *Middle East Review*, pp. 25–35.

63. Myron Weiner, "International Migration and Development: Indians in the Persian Gulf,"*Population and Migration Review*, 8(1) (March 1982):1–36.

64. Conversation, Colombo, September 1977.

65. For details, see Leonard S. Spector, *Nuclear Ambitions* (Boulder, Colo.: Westview, 1990), esp. chs. 6 and 7; Rodney Jones, *Nuclear Proliferation: Islam, the Bomb, and South Asia* (Washington, D.C.: Sage Publications, The Washington Papers no. 82, 1981); also Khalilzad et al., *Security in Southern Asia*, pp. 121–33. Lt. Gen. A. I. Akram, "South Asia and the Bomb," *Regional Studies* (Islamabad): 12(1) (December 1985):3–19; Rodney Jones and S. A. Hildreth, *Modern Weapons and Third World Powers* (Boulder, Colo.: Westview, 1984); Marwah, "India's Military Power," in Marwah and Pollack, eds., *Military Power*, p. 137; R. R. Subramanian, *Proliferation in South Asia: Security in the 1980's* (Canberra: Papers on Strategy and Defense No. 26, 1982); Mitchell Reiss, *Without the Bomb* (New York: Columbia University Press, 1988), esp. chs. 1 and 7.

66. Spector, *Nuclear Ambitions*, pp. 70 and 100.

67. Khalilzad et al., *Security in Southern Asia*, p. 128.

68. Mansingh, *India's Search for Power*, pp. 58–60.

69. K. Subrahmanyam captured the "art of ambivalence" as demonstrated by the two sides as follows: "The art of ambivalence is to let the people know

that one has the capability, then to deny that the capability is backed by intention to do what one can, to drop hints that it may have to be done under certain
contingencies, then more hints that such a course has been imposed upon the
party by external circumstances, then again to deny the development, inspire
those not in authority to disclose the possibility of it, allow discussions to take
place on the general assumption of the capability, once again officially deny it,
release some partial but inadequate information about the capability, carry out
actions which tend to reinforce the suspicions, issue statements that confirm
interest in dispelling any suspicion yet vehemently deny having embarked on
the course of action." In "Pakistan's Nuclear Capability," in V. D. Chopra, ed.,
Studies in Indo-Pakistan Relations (New Delhi: Patriot Publishers, 1984), p. 132.

70. For a discussion of such "part-way proliferation" in general, see Michael
Mandelbaum, *The Nuclear Future* (Ithaca: Cornell University Press, 1983), p.
93; for details of both states' programs, see Spector, *Nuclear Ambitions*, chs. 6
and 7.

71. Israel has managed since the mid–1960s. As Raju Thomas summarized
the argument in 1985, "To maintain the option of going nuclear tends to enhance regional stability. To carry out the option may reduce it." Raju Thomas,
"Strategic Consequences of Nuclear Proliferation in South Asia," *Journal of
Strategic Studies*, 8 (December 1985):75. Ken Waltz and K. Subrahmanyam, however, argue the opposite, both holding that stability will be enhanced when
both states have a demonstrable nuclear capability.

72. The anxieties generated by India's "Operation Brasstacks" in the winter
of 1987 are an example. Pakistanis seem to have genuinely feared that India's
largest-ever peacetime exercises in the Punjab plains could be the prelude to a
bold initiative, which called for an equally bold riposte. Prompt involvement of
political leaders on both sides, including President Zia's "cricket diplomacy,"
defused the growing crisis.

73. Those familiar with game theory writings will recognize the Prisoner's
Dilemma, an accurate characterization of many episodes in Indo-Pakistan rela-
tions. See also Jervis, *Perception and Misperception*; and "Cooperation Under the
Security Dilemma," *World Politics*, vol. 30, no. 2 (January 1978).

74. For a description, see G. W. Choudhury, *Pakistan's Relations*, pp.
156–62.

75. Axelrod, *Evolution of Cooperation*; also Axelrod and Robert O. Keohane,
"Achieving Cooperation under Anarchy: Strategies and Institutions," *World
Politics*, 38(1) (1985):245.

76. Also Jervis, *Perception and Misperception*, pp. 62–66.

77. For details, see A. Michel, *The Indus River: A Study of the Effects of Partition* (New Haven: Yale University Press, 1967); also N. Gulhati, *Indus Water
Treaty: An Experience in International Mediation* (Bombay: Allied Publishers,
1973).

78. For a thoughtful analysis, see T. P. Thornton, "The Indo-Pakistan Conflict: Soviet Mediation at Tashkent, 1966," in Saadia Touval and I. W. Zartman,
International Mediation in Theory and Practice (Boulder, Colo.: Westview, 1985),
pp. 141–75. For an account by a participant, see C. S. Jha, *From Bandung to
Tashkent: Glimpses of India's Foreign Policy* (New Delhi: Orient Longman, 1983),
pp. 232–42.

79. For a useful discussion of the negotiations preceding the Simla Accord, see Imtiaz Bokhari and T. P. Thornton, *The 1972 Simla Agreement: An Asymmetrical Negotiation* (Washington, D.C.: Foreign Policy Institute, SAIS, 1988).

80. Mansingh has a brief but incisive discussion, *India's Search for Power*, pp. 226–32.

81. As an example of the difficulties in the way of mutual concessions between India and its neighbors, the author was told by a senior official in Dakha that numerous agreements on border control, telecommunications, and so on, had already been negotiated by officials, but since no political figure dared to sponsor them for fear that the expected anti-Indian backlash would be directed against him by his political opponents, they remained unimplemented.

82. Mansingh, *India's Search for Power*, p. 41.

83. Mansingh, *India's Search for Power*, p. 264.

84. Vijaya Samaraweera, "Foreign Policy" in K. M. de Silva, ed., *Sri Lanka: A Survey* (Honolulu: University of Hawaii, 1977), pp. 355–56.

85. I. A. Chowdhury, "Strategy of a Small Power in a Subsystem: Bangladesh's External Relations," *Australian Outlook*, 34(1) (April 1980):85–98.

86. For a vivid account, see Raina, *Inside RAW*, ch. 6. For a more detailed account of the military preparations and the campaign, see Pran Chopra, *India's Second Liberation*.

87. Leo Rose, *Nepal: Strategy for Survival* (Berkeley: University of California Press, 1971), pp. 243–46; Sen Gupta, *Ethno-Political Interstate Tensions*.

88. Mansingh, *India's Search for Power*, pp. 280–82; also Raina, *Inside RAW*, ch. 7.

89. For a detailed discussion, see I. A. Chowdhury, "Strategy of a Small Power," *Australian Outlook*.

90. The details have been carefully analyzed by Shauhat Hassan, *Indian-Bangladesh Political Relations During the Awami League Government—1972–1975* (Canberra: Australia National University, Unpublished dissertation, 1987).

91. This argument is developed by Gowher Rizvi, "The Role of the Smaller States in the South Asian Complex," in Buzan and Rizvi, *South Asian Insecurity*, ch. 5.

92. I. A. Chowdhury, "Strategy of a Small Power," *Australian Outlook*, p. 85.

93. I. A. Chowdhury, "Strategy of a Small Power," *Australian Outlook*, p. 90.

94. I. A. Chowdhury, "Strategy of a Small Power," *Australian Outlook*, pp. 86–87.

95. For an interesting discussion, see Sivananda Patnaik, "Sri Lanka and the South Asian Sub-system: A Study of Submacro International Politics," *India Quarterly*, 36(2) (April–June 1980):137–55.

96. Tambiah, *Sri Lanka: Ethnic Fratricide*, esp. ch. 6; also Wriggins *Ceylon: Dilemmas*, esp. chs. 6 and 7.

97. For further characterizations of Sri Lanka's sense of threat from India, see Shelton Kodikara, *Foreign Policy of Sri Lanka: A Third World Perspective* (Delhi: Chanakya, 1982), esp. ch. 2.

98. Wriggins, *Ceylon: Dilemmas*, ch. 10; Samaraweera, "Foreign Policy," in K. M. de Silva, ed., *Sri Lanka: A Survey* (Honolulu: University of Hawaii, 1977).

See also Goher Rizvi, in Buzan and Rizvi, *South Asian Insecurity*, ch. 5, particularly pp. 136–41; Patnaik, "Sri Lanka," *India Quarterly*.

99. K. M. de Silva, *A History of Sri Lanka* (Delhi: Oxford University Press, 1981), pp. 507–508.

100. A reported example of some part of the government of India threatening to encourage ethnic unrest in Sri Lanka unless the smaller state followed India's foreign policy position, see Arnold Smith, *Stitches in Time: The Commonwealth in World Politics*, with Clyde Sawyer (Don Mills, Ontario: General Publishing, 1981), pp. 136–38.

101. G. B. Keerawella, "The Janatha Vimukthi Peramuna and the 1971 Uprising," *Social Science Review* (Colombo), vol. 2 (1989); G. Obeysekere, "Some Comments on the Social Background of the April 1971 Insurgency in Sri Lanka (Ceylon)," *Asian Survey*, vol. 33 (1984); Wriggins and Guyot (1973), ch. 10, "Youth Protest in Sri Lanka.

102. Mansingh, *India's Search for Power*, p. 39; see also Bharat Wariavwalla, "Wary Neighbours," *The Illustrated Weekly of India*, June 11, 1989.

103. *India Today*, "Ominous Presence in Tamil Nadu," 9(6) March 31, 1984, pp. 88–94; *Sunday Times* (London), April 1, 1984; *South* (London), no. 53, "Colombo Rides the Tiger" (March 1985), pp. 13–15.

104. For details as seen with the Government forces, Tom Marks, "Counter Insurgency in Sri Lanka; Asia's Dirty Little War," *Soldier of Fortune* 12(2) (February 1987):38–47, 82–84; E. O'Balance, "Sri Lanka and Its Tamil Problem," *Armed Forces*, 5(12) (December 1986):542–43; James Manor (1984), esp. Part II. For a Tamil liberation perspective, see Satchi Ponnambalam, *Sri Lanka: The National Question and the Tamil Liberation Struggle* (London: Zed Books, 1983).

105. See, for example, P. Venkateshwar Rao, "Ethnic Conflict in Sri Lanka: India's Role and Perceptions," *Asian Survey*, 28(4) (April 1988):19–37.

106. For an encapsulation, see Devin T. Hagerty, "India's Security Doctrine," *Asian Survey*, 31(4) (April 1991):351–63; also earlier, Bhabani Sen Gupta, "The Indian Doctrine," *India Today*, August 31, 1983, pp. 20–21.

107. Anthony Arnold, *Afghanistan: The Soviet Invasion in Perspective* (Stanford, Calif.: Hoover Institute, 1985); Lee Caldron, "Afghanistan in 1985: The Sixth Year of the Russo-Afghan War," *Asian Survey* 26(2) (February 1986); Henry Bradsher, *Afghanistan and the Soviet Union* (Durham, N.C.: Duke University Press, 1983), chs. 5–10; Bhabani Sen Gupta, *The Afghan Syndrome: How to Live with Soviet Power* (New Delhi: Vikas, 1982). See also my "Pakistan's Search for a Foreign Policy After the Invasion of Afghanistan," *Pacific Affairs* 57(2) (Summer 1984):284–303.

108. Agha Shahi at a seminar in Islamabad, 1981.

109. Sen Gupta, *The Afghan Syndrome*, p. 136.

110. G. M. Khar, a former provincial governor, explicitly argued this view from exile in London but had little impact at home, *Economist* (London), October 31, 1981. Bhabani Sen Gupta, Pran Chopra, and a few other journalists argued in a similar vein in India. For Sen Gupta's argument, see *The Afghan Syndrome*, esp. chs. 1 and 6. See also Subrahmaniam Swami, "Pakistan Holds the Key to India's Security," *Sunday* (Calcutta), November 13, 1983.

111. For highly plausible reporting, see, for example, "The Pakistan Hand," *India Today*, May 15, 1986, pp. 42–45.

112. Interviews of the author with politicians in Lahore (summer 1982).

113. For a detailed exploration, see my "Pakistan's Search," *Pacific Affairs*; also Amrita Inder Singh, "The Superpower Global Complex and South Asia," in Buzan and Rizvi, *South Asian Insecurity*, pp. 207–31, esp. 219–20.

114. For views critical of the government's policy, see former Ambassador Sajjad Hyder, "Pakistan's Afghan Predicament," *The Muslim*, Islamabad (February 5, 6, 8, and 10, 1984); and Air Marshal (Ret'd) Zulfiqar Ali Khan, "Afghanistan: The Refugees," *The Muslim*, September 5, 1984.

115. G. M. Khar, *Economist* (London), October 31, 1981.

116. Interviews of the writer in New Delhi (summer 1982).

117. Bhabani Sen Gupta, *Afghan Syndrome*, esp. chs. 1 and 6.

118. See John Mellor, *India: A Rising Middle Power*; Baldev Raj Nayar, "Treat India Seriously," *Foreign Policy*, vol. 18 (Spring 1975); and Bhabani Sen Gupta, "Waiting for India: India's Role as a Regional Power," *Journal of International Affairs* (Columbia University, SIA, 1975), 29(2).

119. See also Robert Litwak, "The Soviet Union in India's Security Perspective," *Security in Southern Asia*, particularly pp. 110–23.

120. Sen Gupta, *Afghan Syndrome*, p. 137. For a view more critical of Soviet intervention, see S. Swami, "Pakistan Holds the Key," *Sunday* (Calcutta), November 13, 1983.

121. For a detailed analysis of the evolution of the Afghanistan state, see forthcoming study by Barnett R. Rubin, *Never Content with a Master: The Struggle for the State in Afghanistan*. See also his "Lineages of the Afghan State," *Asian Survey*, vol. 28, no. 11 (November 1988), and "The Fragmentation of Afghanistan," *Foreign Affairs*, vol. 68, no.5 (Winter 1989–90).

122. Gowher Rizvi in Buzan and Rizvi, *South Asian Insecurity*, p. 144.

123. In addition, some twenty thousand Gurkhas serve in the Indian army.

124. See this assessment, in Leo E. Rose and John T. Scholz, *Nepal: Profile of a Himalayan Kingdom* (Boulder, Colo.: Westview, 1980), pp. 129–37.

125. For a discussion of this evolution, see Rose and Scholz, *Nepal* ch. 5, "International Relations: A Root Between Two Stones"; also Rose's earlier study *Nepal: Strategy for Survival* (Berkeley: University of California Press, 1971), ch. 11, "The Politics of Balance, 1963–1970."

126. Leo Rose, *Nepal: Strategy for Survival*, p. 264. Rose also describes the pressures brought on Mahendra the last day of his visit to Peking to approve the building of the road, pp. 239–40; also pp. 129–37.

127. Rose, *Nepal: Strategy for Survival*, pp. 134–36; Mansingh, *India's Search for Power*, pp. 283–85.

128. For detailed discussion, see among others, Imtiaz H. Bokhari, "South Asian Regional Cooperation: Progress, Problems, Potential, and Prospects," pp. 371–90; S. D. Muni, "Building Regionalism from Below," pp. 391–404; and Mohammed Ayoob, "The Primacy of the Political: South Asian Regional Cooperation (SARC) in Comparative Perspective," pp. 443–57, all in *Asian Survey*, 25(4) (April 1985).

129. Muni, "Building Regionalism," *Asian Survey*, pp. 398–99.

130. For a vivid example, analytically argued, see Ashok Kapur, "The Indian Subcontinent: The Contemporary Structure of Power and the Development of Power Relations," *Asian Survey*, 28(7) (July 1988):693–710; for a contrasting per-

spective from Dhaka, see Abdul Kalam, "Cooperation in South Asia," *Regional Studies* (Islamabad), pp. 62–80.

131. For details see Bokhari, "South Asian Regional Cooperation"; Muni, "Building Regionalism"; Ayoob, "The Primacy of the Political," all in *Asian Survey* (April 1985).

4

The Horn of Africa Regional Politics: A Hobbesian World

TERRENCE P. LYONS

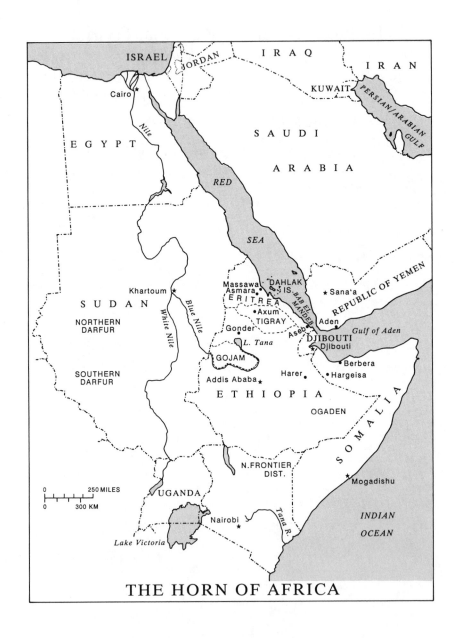

THE HORN OF AFRICA

The Horn of Africa regional security system consists of Ethiopia, the region's largest state, and its immediate neighbors—Somalia, Sudan, Kenya, and Djibouti. These five states form a regional system of relations, compelled to interact by the nature of their contiguity, their common and contentious borders, and their contrasting political structures, state goals, and historic mutual perceptions. As Buzan put it, such states form a "security complex" because their "primary security concerns link together sufficiently closely that their national securities cannot realistically be considered apart from one another."[1] Although the Horn was the most disordered of our four regions, for the forty years we examine in detail, regional relations had a certain, even though highly conflictual, consistency.

Ethiopia is the center of this system. Each of the member states shares a border with it, and the system is organized around a series of bilateral relationships between the core state and its neighbors. The character of these dyads ranges from antagonistic (Somalia and often Sudan) to guardedly cooperative (Djibouti) to strategically allied (Kenya). Although Addis Ababa has important security relationships with all the member states, the other states have weaker links with one another. Somalia and Sudan, for instance, despite their mutual fear of Ethiopia, have not collaborated on security.

Besides being linked by their security concerns, the states of the Horn of Africa form a natural, if currently disjointed and underdeveloped, economic unit. The pastoral mode of production in the southeast is dependent upon pastures on both sides of the Ethiopia-Somalia border. Somalia is potentially Ethiopia's outlet to the sea, and Ethiopia represents Somalia's natural hinterland. These opportunities for economic cooperation have been hampered by nearly incessant warfare. With peace, however, an important productive unit could emerge.[2] The extensive cross-border black market that currently operates indicates that strong economic incentives for trade exist.

Ethiopia, although functionally the center, is not a focus of cohesion or common identity. Instead, the region is characterized by tensions between the central Ethiopian highlands and the Islamic lowland and coastal areas.[3] Ethiopia does not unify the Horn; rather, it represents an isolated state in the middle of a hostile region. The history of the Horn is dominated by Ethiopia's attempts to break its isolation, hold its varied population together, and prevent encirclement by hostile neighbor-

ing forces.[4] Attempts by Ethiopia to improve its security in these circumstances are in turn perceived as threats by the neighboring states.
The system, currently characterized by deep cleavages, is built around
historical hostilities and mutual fears.

The region is also marked by endemic, violent internal opposition to
the governments of a number of the states. The authoritarian, often
brutal governments of the region have driven many inhabitants to resist
them. None of the states has found the means to incorporate its population into a stable—let alone democratic—order in which the government responds to the needs of the people. In many cases, particularly in
Ethiopia and Sudan, resistance to central authority has taken the form
of ethnic and regionally based rebellions. Moreover, the eruption of violence in Somalia in 1991 indicated that insurgency can develop in the
absence of ethnic, cultural, or religious differences when the central
leadership alienates important segments of the society.

In the states of the Horn, the central administration's authority often
does not extend far outside the capital and a few principal cities. In 1991
governments completely collapsed in the face of rebels in Somalia and
Ethiopia, unleashing multisided power struggles to capture central authority or consolidate regional control. State structures remain ill-
formed, institutions of governance are rudimentary, and mechanisms
for resolving competition without violence often do not exist. The
narrow-based, authoritarian regimes of the region, consumed with tactical maneuvers to ensure short-term survival, contribute to the very insecurity that undermines their authority. This insecurity, in turn, leaves
the state vulnerable to intervention from hostile neighbors and leads
hard-pressed leaders to seek assistance from other powers in the Middle
East or from the superpowers. This affects local balances of power, but
the direction of their policies seems scarcely affected by outside influences.

Pervasive poverty adds to the difficulties of the region. Ethiopia, Somalia, and Sudan all rank among the world's poorest states. This underdevelopment is both a cause and a result of political instability. In 1991,
Ethiopia, Somalia, and Sudan were embroiled in civil conflict. The region also suffered from periodic droughts that, when coupled with civil
strife, high expenditures on defense, and counterproductive agricultural
policies, tragically led to famine. Refugee populations proportionately
are the highest in the world, with Sudanese fleeing to Ethiopia; Ethiopians, in turn, seeking safety in Sudan, Somalia, and Djibouti; and Somalis escaping to Ethiopia and Kenya. Even before the upsurge of instability in 1991, more than 350,000 Somalis, 780,000 Ethiopians, and
700,000 Sudanese were refugees.[5]

In 1991, the near-term future and even the number of the states in the

Horn was uncertain. In mid–1991 Somalia collapsed completely, with rival armed groups struggling for authority in the capital and one movement proclaiming a new state in northern Somalia. In Ethiopia rebels seized the capital, and in May 1991, Eritrean secessionists consolidated their control over the northern region and formed an independent transitional government, raising fundamental questions about Ethiopia's future territorial integrity. In Sudan, the government's Islamic fundamentalist policies had alienated large segments of the diverse population and the insurgents in the south were consolidating their zone of control and discussing the option of secession. Tiny Djibouti continued to be tossed about in this turbulent sea, and agitation for more open politics in Kenya challenged the leadership in Nairobi. One or more new states may emerge from this chaos with the potential to fundamentally transform the structure of regional relations.

Nevertheless, our study shows that despite major domestic and regional upheavals, particularly in the late 1970s, regional roles and patterns persisted. Although major changes could occur, historical trends and enduring cleavages are likely to persist and trouble leaders in the future until structures and processes to resolve conflict both internally and regionally are created and become well established.

The Actors: States and Peoples

The Horn is marked by particularly severe instability. The states in this region suffer acutely from a problem that besets many polities on the Indian Ocean rim. Much of this strife derives from the nature of the states and their societies. Each includes diverse peoples, members of distinct ethnic groups, nationalities, and clans, cross-cut with different languages, religions, and cultural systems. An awareness of national identity coterminous with state borders is virtually nonexistent.[6] Leaders in the capital seek to consolidate their rule; people in the outlying areas resist such consolidation.[7] In South Asia we also see instances of this difficulty, particularly in the Punjab, Kashmir, and Sri Lanka. In the Horn, as in these cases, the imperatives of state sovereignty and demands for group autonomy contradict each other in dramatic—and often tragic—ways.

Ethiopia and Sudan represent almost ideal types of this widespread problem, as the Eritreans struggle for independence from Addis Ababa and southerners seek a more equitable relationship with Khartoum. On the other hand, in Somalia the state is smaller than the nation. There Mogadishu has sought to expand its sovereignty so that its boundaries would include all those who see themselves as Somalis. Since many resided in neighboring countries, such ambitions inevitably led to conflict. Across the Horn, nation-building scarcely has begun and many governmental policies recently have exacerbated internal divisions.

Ethiopia

Ethiopia is the key to the structure of the system not only because of its central geographic position and its size, but because of its population of nearly fifty million people and potential military strength. Moreover, as a historically independent state led from 1930 until 1974 by the venerable Emperor Haile Sellassie, Ethiopia was for many years the symbol of African nationalism and the continent's acknowledged leader. The Organization of African Unity (OAU) selected Addis Ababa as its headquarters, in recognition of Ethiopia's leading role on the continent and the prestige accorded the emperor by other African leaders.[8] Despite the recognition of the past, Ethiopia is prevented from dominating the Horn because of its disunity within and encirclement without. The twin imperatives of maintaining internal cohesion and territorial integrity long have been the central emphasis of Ethiopian policy. The threats from domestic disunity and hostile neighbors often became more menacing when rebels and secessionists linked up with surrounding states.

The Struggle for Internal Cohesion

Historically, Ethiopia's territory has expanded and contracted as its power waxed and waned. In the late nineteenth century, under emperors Tewodros and Menilek, the empire expanded as new ethnic groups joined the original Amhara and Tigray inhabitants of the northern high-

TABLE 4.1
Elements of Capability of States of the Horn of Africa Compared (1988*)

	1	2	3	4	5	6	7	8
	Pop., 1988 (mil.)	Pop. Growth Rate, 1985–90 (%)	Armed Forces, 1988 (thous.)	GNP 1988 ($bil.)	GNP per Capita 1988 ($)	M.E., 1988 ($bil.)	M.E. GNP 1988 (%)	GDP Growth Rate, 1980–88, (%)
Ethiopia	47	2.8	300	5	116	.45	8.2	1.4
Sudan	24	2.9	65	7	306	.18	2.4	2.5
Kenya	23	4.2	20	8	354	.29	3.6	4.2
Somalia	8	2.3	47	2	203	N.A.	N.A.	3.2
Djibouti	0.2	N.A.	5	N.A.	N.A.	.04	N.A.	N.A.

*See note 4 in chapter 3 for sources.

lands. The Oromo, facing encroachment from Somalis, migrated into central and eastern Ethiopia. The frontier of the state moved south and east and incorporated the highland Sidama and Gurage, along with such lowland Muslims as the Somali and the Afar.[9] The central regime governed many of these newly incorporated peoples through a system of military overlords but granted others considerable autonomy in exchange for nominal allegiance. At the end of World War II, with the help of the United Nations and the United States, Haile Sellassie attached the former Italian colony of Eritrea to Ethiopia in a federation. The emperor soon dismantled the federal structure in order to consolidate the territory within his domain.

Ethiopia thus became a state of many national and ethnic groups. The central government attempted to assimilate many of the non-Amhara-Tigray elites on the empire's periphery into the central political culture. The governing authorities understood assimilation to mean promotion of Amhara culture and language and Christian religion.[10] In the 1920s and 1930s, to unify the empire, Haile Sellassie tried to strengthen the center at the expense of the hinterlands.[11] He developed a centrally controlled national army and bureaucracy, expanded Ethiopia's transportation and communications network, and tried to reduce the power of the traditional provincial aristocracy by building new political power bases among the urban and educated elite.[12] That effort, however, was far from fully realized.

The inability to unify fully the disparate social groups of Ethiopia posed a grave threat to the regime. Regional political movements, especially those based on ethnicity or nationality, threatened to destroy the social and political structure of the state. The 1943 Weyane Rebellion in Tigay and the 1963 Oromo and Somali uprising in Bale are two prominent examples.[13] Eritrean nationalists began their campaign for independence in the early 1960s. In the government's eyes, to compromise with any of these groups risked the dissolution of the empire. Reflecting his anxiety, Haile Sellassie declared, "woe unto those countries which weaken themselves by dismemberment! . . . Our people from Ethiopia shed blood to save themselves from disintegration."[14] Despite the many ethnic groups and history of rebellion, many Ethiopians have a strong sense of nationalism and commitment to unity, including many who are not from the Amhara heartland. To maintain the unity of the multiethnic state remained an enduring challenge to successive Ethiopian regimes, one that defined the way Ethiopian policymakers typically viewed regional relations.

Haile Sellassie never resolved the problem of forging a unified state administered by a centralized, bureaucratic monarchy. Many of his policies, such as the military suppression of dissidence in Eritrea, further alienated the people over whom he claimed sovereignty. In 1974 the forces unleashed by attempts to modernize, especially in the military and education systems, rebelled in an explosion of political activity. Haile Sellassie's government collapsed after it showed that it could not cope with a severe famine or respond to demands for reform. In September the emperor was deposed by a military committee known as the *Derg*. Initially, the new regime articulated only a vague, nationalist ideology. After a series of often bloody power struggles, however, the revolution became increasingly radical under the leadership of Mengistu Haile Mariam. The *Derg* committed itself to Marxism-Leninism but also to a more energetic effort to incorporate the diverse peoples of Ethiopia into a single national identity within a unified state. The revolution initiated many significant changes in social and political structures, nationalizing land and destroying the power of the old aristocracy and church. Ethiopia's security concerns and its role in regional relations nevertheless endured.

The destruction of the old regime provided fresh opportunities for "dissident nationalists."[15] Some sought secession; others, more political or cultural autonomy; and still others, the replacement of the military leadership. Indeed, efforts by the new Marxist government to pursue the old regime's nationalist goals of consolidating the unity and territorial integrity of the state often provoked the nationalities to more intense resistance to Addis Ababa. In the late 1970s, uprisings in most of Ethiopia's provinces severely limited the government's authority and threatened to shatter the state. The *Derg* tried to rally the populace with slogans calling for the defense of the motherland, reaffirming that the indivisibility of Ethiopia remained a fundamental goal of the new regime, as it had been of the old. Mengistu Haile Mariam combined nationalistic rhetoric with a stepped-up military campaign supported by massive Soviet assistance to beat back but never ultimately defeat the insurgents.

Mengistu introduced a variety of institutions in an effort to consolidate his regime. The Derg established peasant and urban associations to control the population, formed the Worker's Party of Ethiopia (WPE) in 1984 after several failed attempts, and promulgated a new constitution for the Peoples' Democratic Republic of Ethiopia in 1987. This new political structure did not solve Ethiopia's problems of disunity, economic decline, and external dependency.[16] Instead, the harsh system of authoritarian rule from above inspired yet more people to rally to the cause of the opposition.

In May 1989, military officers, frustrated with the inability of Mengistu to end the war in the north, attempted a coup but failed.[17] By mid–1990, the well-armed opposition Ethiopian People's Revolutionary Democratic Front (EPRDF), an umbrella movement dominated by the Tigray People's Liberation Front, advanced almost to Addis Ababa, seeking to depose Mengistu. Although the EPRDF had originally espoused an extremely orthodox form of Marixsm, as their fortunes improved they appeared to endorse more pluralist, democratic principles. In a desperate attempt to hold off the many forces opposed to his rule, Mengistu announced that he had abandoned Marxism-Leninism and would pursue policies designed to encourage a "mixed economy" and multiparty politics.[18] These measures and a cabinet reshuffle in April 1991 proved to be too little too late. Mengistu fled to Zimbabwe in May, marking the collapse of his regime.

The principal opposition movements asked the United States to facilitate talks aimed at ending the fighting and setting up a transitional regime.[19] Anxious to avoid chaos in the capital, if possible, the United States recommended that the EPRDF enter Addis Ababa, which it did on May 28, 1991. In July the interim government, led by Meles Zenawi, formed a broad-based transitional government promising elections, respect for human rights, and economic reforms. The Eritrean People's Liberation Front seized control of Eritrea and began to set up its own independent transitional regime. Ethiopia and Eritrea therefore began a complex and fragile experiment aimed at redefining the basis of politics and even the character of the state itself. Initial indications were that this effort held considerable promise and might lead to greater stability and pluralism, but many fundamental issues and obstacles remained that threatened to derail the process.

Threats from Neighbors

In addition to the conflicts between the center and indigenous groups along the frontier, Ethiopia has faced challenges to its security from outside. Its leaders have seen themselves as surrounded by threatening neighbors, despite the country's apparent power. The memory of attacks from neighboring territories continues to color the perceptions and policies of Ethiopia's leaders. Conflict with pastoral Muslims along their borders has been endemic, and Ethiopians perceive themselves as surrounded by a hostile ring of states, a "Christian island in a sea of pagans."[20]

During the "Scramble for Africa" Menilek wrote to European heads of state that "if Powers at a distance come forward to partition Africa between them, I do not intend to be an indifferent spectator."[21] A sense of confidence and diplomatic and political skills derived from the imperial system allowed Ethiopia's leaders to resist the colonial powers.[22] In 1896 Emperor Menilek militarily defeated Italian forces at Adwa, ensuring that Ethiopian independence would survive the partition of Africa. The Italians, however, invaded once again in 1935, and despite an emotional appeal for help from the international community by Haile Sellassie at the League of Nations, ccupied all of Ethiopia for six years. With the help of British troops, the emperor returned to his throne in 1941.

Statesmen in Addis Ababa also recall that during the colonial period, Italy, France, and Britain attempted to use their positions in neighboring countries to influence Addis Ababa. Traditional precepts of prudent policy have long guided Addis Ababa: Whenever possible, weaken one's neighbors and block hostile alliances that might further isolate Ethiopia. Such policies make the security dilemma more acute and intensify the very hostilities they were supposed to fend off.

The image of an isolated and threatened motherland continued to shape perceptions in Ethiopia. Mengistu labeled the Somali invasion of the Ogaden as an Arab orchestrated *jihad*. He stated that "reactionary" Arab governments "have launched a campaign to turn world Moslems against Ethiopia by misleading them in the name of religion."[23] Until his final days in Addis Ababa he continued to portray his enemies as externally controlled mercenaries.[24]

Despite the volatile politics and social transformation in Ethiopia since 1974, the revolution did not mark a break in Ethiopia's role in the Horn of Africa system. The imperatives inherent in the internal character of the Ethiopian polity and the surrounding regional system are likely to continue to limit Addis Ababa's options. Whatever the outcome of the transition taking place in 1991 in Addis Ababa, the new regime will face challenges similar to those that confronted Mengistu and Haile Sellassie. Ethiopia's size, its enduring problem of nationalities seeking greater autonomy (if not independence), and the perceived threat from encircling neighbors will continue to shape the new government's role in the Horn of Africa.

Eritrea

Two dissident groups that have played important parts in Ethiopia's regional relations—the Eritrean and Ogadeni—deserve attention. The Eritrean groups define themselves territorially rather than ethnically; their goal is an independent state. The people of the territory are a diverse collection of ethnic, religious, and language groups.[25] The uniqueness of the Eritrean case results from the territory's history. Centuries ago, Eritrea formed an important part of such historic Ethiopian empires as Axum. The power of Islam along the Red Sea, however, competed with the Christian empire, and the Eritrean coast became a zone of conflict. The territory lacked defined borders until Italy established a colony there in the late nineteenth century.

Eritrean nationalists assert that this historical experience as a colony outside the control of Addis Ababa led to the development of social forces and aspirations that did not exist in Ethiopia. Eritrean national awareness developed under Italian colonial control and was further shaped by political developments during British occupation after World War II. London encouraged political and labor organizations, and Eritreans enjoyed relative freedom to join political parties and debate issues in a free press.[26]

In 1951 the United Nations voted to federate the former colony with Ethiopia. The liberal Eritrean constitution, however, was an anomaly within the centralized monarchy. In November 1962 the Eritrean National Assembly, allegedly bribed by Haile Sellassie's representatives or intimidated by his forces, voted to end the federation and to bring Eritrea into Ethiopia as its thirteenth province. Haile Sellassie's efforts to integrate the former colony into his empire by forcing cultural conformity and ending the political freedoms of the British occupation understandably intensified Eritrean self-consciousness and desire for independence.

Eritrean dissidents began organizing their protest in the mid–1950s, and in 1958 exiles in Cairo founded the Eritrean Liberation Front (ELF). The ELF began as a moderate nationalist movement anchored in Islam but grew more radical as Christian intellectuals joined. In 1961 the ELF initiated armed resistance against Ethiopian rule. In 1970 internal divisions within the culturally diverse movement led to the creation of the Eritrean Peoples' Liberation Front (EPLF).[27] These movements often won financial support from various states in the Middle East. Although supply routes operated through Sudan, most of their military equipment was captured from the Ethiopian armed forces. Mengistu Haile Mariam sought to assert his authority in Eritrea militarily, further intensifying the dissidence he was attempting to overcome. In May 1991, as Mengistu fled and the EPRDF entered Addis Ababa, the Eritrean movement overran the last government outposts in Eritrea and began to set up its own transitional government throughout the territory. A referendum on independence was scheduled for 1993. Past EPRDF statements had affirmed Eritrea's right to self-determination. The EPLF's control of the entire territory—including Ethiopia's access to the sea—may lead to Eritrean independence. Future relations between the two territories remained a hotly debated question in mid–1991. Regardless of the outcome, Ethiopia and an independent Eritrea will still be closely interlinked and tied to a regional security system.

For decades, by challenging the regime in Addis Ababa, the Eritrean independence movement shaped Ethiopia's policy toward the entire region. The enduring conflict absorbed much of Ethiopia's potential power and provided a means for neighbors, particularly Sudan, to weaken Ethiopia. Although not a recognized state as of mid–1991, the dissident nationalists in Eritrea affect the forces in the regional system as much as if they were.

Somalis in the Ogaden

A second important substate movement that threatened the territorial integrity of Ethiopia is the Western Somali Liberation Front (WSLF), active in the Ogaden region. Emperor Menilek brought the Ogaden under Ethiopian rule in the late-nineteenth century, and Haile Sellassie attempted to incorporate the local Somalis into the state. Somalis, however, claim that the people of "Western Somalia [the Ogaden] have a distinct history and geography, and their ethnic, cultural and linguistic characteristics are completely different from those of Ethiopia."[28] The Ogaden region is historically and culturally one of the homelands of the Somali nation, and many of the political elite in Mogadishu have kin from the area.

Although Somalis have long resisted Ethiopia's rule, as in the Bale uprising in the 1960s, the WSLF was organized and supported by Mogadishu. The movement became active following the Ethiopian revolution, when Somalia saw an opportunity to achieve a Greater Somalia by exploiting its neighbor's weakness. As in the Eritrean resistance, a hostile neighbor exploited ethnic resistance to Addis Ababa's rule to weaken the Ethiopian state. After Somalia's defeat in the Ogaden War, the WSLF split into factions. Many Ogaden Somalis fled back into Ethiopia following the regime collapse in Mogadishu only to face starvation in the chaos after Mengistu's downfall.[29] Some participated in the July 1991 national conference organized by the EPRDF.

Sudan

The government of Sudan also has faced major difficulties in creating a unified state out of diverse components that have been linked weakly to each other. For centuries the central Nile Valley of Sudan has been tied to Egypt, with which it shares a common Arabic culture, language, and religion. The Darfur region in the west and the Red Sea hills in the east generally have been relatively autonomous and culturally distinctive. Because of its divergent colonial experiences and different religions and cultures, the south has been very distinct from the north. As a crossroads state that links Arabia and Africa, the modern state of Sudan has struggled since independence to forge a cohesive national identity out of these heterogeneous parts.[30] Like Ethiopia, Sudan has been weakened by local and mutually hostile groups that have left it vulnerable to exploitation by its neighbors. Its inability to accommodate southern dissatisfaction with the central government has provided Ethiopia with a useful counter to Khartoum's readiness to support Eritrean restlessness against Addis Ababa. Sudanese insecurity, therefore, is linked to Ethiopian actions, impelling Khartoum to play a role in the Horn's regional system.

The north-south cleavage in the Sudan is deeply rooted in the past. During the Turkiya period (1821–85) the Turco-Egyptian rulers viewed the south principally as a source of treasure and slaves. The south remained largely outside of the Islamic state established by the Mahdi (1884–98). Under the Condominium (1899–1955) the British governed the region separately from the north. The "Closed Door" ordinances of the 1920s virtually prohibited all northern Sudanese access to the south.[31]

Since independence in 1956, Sudanese leaders have unsuccessfully sought a basis for stable power. Periods of military and civilian rule in the late 1950s and 1960s failed to establish an enduring basis for national politics and cohesion. The weakness of sectarian and regionally based parties inclined political leaders to exploit differences for short-run tactical gains rather than redress underlying grievances.[32] In May 1969 a Free Officers' Movement, modeled on Nasser's movement, took power in a bloodless coup. Gaafar al-Nimeiri took control, banned political parties, and ruled through a Revolutionary Command Council.

In the search for a viable combination of internal bases of power and international patrons to support his regime, Nimeiri led Sudan through a complicated series of domestic and foreign policy shifts and reversals.[33] He faced twelve coup attempts in his sixteen years of power, and this precarious and volatile domestic political balance and subsequent vulnerability drove Sudan's foreign policy.[34] From 1969 to 1971 Nimeiri included members of the Sudanese Communist Party (SCP) in his cabinet and, with Nasser in Egypt and Qadhafi in Libya, formed a radical Arab bloc aligned with the Soviet Union. In July 1971 the SCP led a nearly successful coup, forcing Nimeiri to move against the communists and diversify his sources of military equipment. Internally, to compensate, Nimeiri sought to build up his constituency by reconciling his regime with southerners in 1972 (see the following discussion) and the conservative National Front in 1977. He strengthened his ties with Egypt and moved, with Sadat, toward the West in the late 1970s. Sectarian politics in Khartoum was dominated by northern parties tied to Islamic groups, requiring competing politicians to cater to fundamentalist demands. In 1983, in an effort to undercut his fundamentalist opponents in the north, Nimeiri adopted Islamic *Shari'a* law, an action that unleashed renewed conflict against the central government in the non-Muslim south.

Nimeiri's ability to stay on top of the volatile politics of Sudan ended with an army coup in April 1985. Because of inflation, corruption, strikes that followed the International Monetary Fund–instigated devaluations, and removal of food subsidies, the economy was nearing total collapse. Important urban professional groups rebelled against Nimeiri's increasingly authoritarian methods, and the military overthrew him. After a short interregnum, it held elections that brought Sadiq el-Mahdi into power. Sadiq, however, still operated within a divided domestic environment, where sectarian Islamic politics severely limited his options.[35] The army's anger over the new regime's inability to resolve the southern conflict or to provide the means to fight it led to Sadiq's overthrow in June 1989. General Omer Hassan Ahmed el-Beshir seized control and established a Revolutionary Command Council of National Salvation. The new regime, however, relied on the fundamentalist National Islamic Front for support and did not demonstrate the ability to break the divisive politics of its predecessors. By 1991, Beshir's authoritarian methods had alienated much of Sudan's beleaguered population.

Leaders in Sudan since independence have not been willing or able to institute policies that reflect the country's historically based cultural diversity. The governments have pursued policies designed to play off various factions for short-term survival rather than attempt, in their weak domestic positions, to encourage an identity that included equitable roles for the many cultures of the vast state and redressed the severe regional deprivation.[36] These actions have exacerbated divisions and resulted in heightened intergroup and especially interregional suspicions and hostility.

The Southern Rebellion

No regime in Khartoum has been able to create a sense of national solidarity and common identity in Sudan to overcome the historical north-south divisions. Southerners fear northern "Arab imperialism" and have resisted Khartoum's authority. The lack of economic development in the south and the perception that the central government favored the Arab north furthered southern alienation. Southern army units rebelled in 1955, the separationist Anya Nya rebel movement opposed central authority in the 1960s, and after a decade of reconciliation, the Sudan People's Liberation Movement and its military wing, the Sudan People's Liberation Army (SPLM/SPLA), continued the struggle into the 1990s.

The most promising steps to incorporate the southern region into central Sudanese politics began with the 1972 Addis Ababa Peace Agreement. Joseph Lagu united the disparate Anya Nya rebels into the Southern Sudan Liberation Front in the early 1970s, and for a period he was able to negotiate in their name. Nimeiri, for his part, needed new domestic supporters following the Communist coup attempt. The Anya Nya were under pressure to settle from their external patrons, Ethiopia and Uganda. The conflict was at a stalemate, and the time for negotiations was ripe. With the All African Council of Churches and Haile Sellassie acting as mediators, Lagu met with Nimeiri's representatives in February 1972 and signed the Addis Ababa Agreement, which granted the south a regional administration and council within a unified state and incorporated some of the rebels into the national army.[37]

The creation of a new autonomous region removed opposition to the north as a unifying force in southern politics. The smaller ethnic groups, therefore, began to fear domination by the largest ethnic group in the region, the Dinka.[38] Ten years of precarious peace and political competition ended in 1983, when Nimeiri, more anxious about political threats from Islamic groups in the north than about retaining his support in the south, unilaterally redivided the southern region. The imposition of Islamic *Shari'a* law on the non-Muslim south in September 1983 intensified the religious antagonism. The collapse of the Addis Ababa agreement led to the next period of rebellion under John Garang and the SPLM/SPLA.[39] During this period, the movement was not secessionist but sought to transform Sudan into a secular state in which all might participate equally, regardless of religion, race, or ethnicity.[40]

In the summer of 1986, following Nimeiri's overthrow, Garang and representatives of most of Sudan's political parties met in Addis Ababa and agreed to the Koka Dam Declaration, which outlined steps to facilitate peace and to initiate a constitutional conference.[41] Sadiq, however, was unwilling to risk alienating the National Islamic Front in the north by discussing an agreement with the SPLM/SPLA. As a result, the Sudanese military, despairing of peace, overthrew Sadiq in June 1989. Beshir's successor government was tied closely to the fundamentalists in the National Islamic Front and was unwilling to agree to the creation of a secular state, a precondition for the SPLA to stop fighting. In 1991 the SPLM/SPLA controlled all but a handful of cities in the south.

The chronic conflict in southern Sudan shapes Khartoum's role in the Horn of Africa. The insurgency weakens the central state, and the southern Sudan rebels' close ties to Ethiopia expands what had been an essentially internal conflict into a regional rivalry. Ethiopia's similar vulnerability from the Eritrean conflict and Sudan's activities in support of that movement further link the security of Addis Ababa and Khartoum. Internal dissidence and regional foreign policy are intertwined in a system that makes it very difficult to resolve conflict.

Somalia

The historical evolution of the Somali state also shapes that country's role in the regional system.[42] During the colonial period the Somali nation was split into five territorial parts: France asserted sovereignty over the hinterlands immediately surrounding the port of Djibouti, Britain and Italy claimed strips along the Indian Ocean, Ethiopia won control over the Ogaden, and Britain maintained jurisdiction over northern Kenya. The goal of reuniting this divided people into a "Greater Somalia" has brought Mogadishu into conflict with all its neighbors and thereby drawn the state into the regional system of interaction.

Unlike most of the rest of Africa, Somalia remains a "nation in search of a state."[43] Somalis have enjoyed a sense of common identity based on a shared culture rather than on a common territory. The roots of Somali nationalism extend back to clashes with Ethiopia and European colonial powers led by such Somali heroes as Ahmad Gran in the sixteenth century and Mohamed ibn Abdullah Hassan (the so-called Mad Mullah) in the early twentieth century. This larger identity, however, overlays a strong clan loyalty that undercuts the shared sense of nationhood. The society of Somalia is segmented; it both encourages solidarity against external threats and generates antagonism between clans.[44]

Traditionally, the Somalis grazed their herds over large areas of the semiarid lowlands without regard to borders. The pastoralists expanded from their home areas in northeast Somalia and the Ogaden and moved to the south and west, where they displaced the Oromo. This migration continued until the early twentieth century, when the Somalis reached the Tana River in northern Kenya. During the scramble for Africa, Europeans and Ethiopians negotiated border agreements, but these administrative lines were meaningless to the pastoralists "for whom there is one frontier only: the furthest limits to their pastures."[45] The lands inhabited and exploited by Somali pastoralists form a single economic and ecological unit, despite the political divisions.

Since independence in 1960, a principal political goal of the leaders in Mogadishu has been the unification of the Somali people into a single nation-state.[46] To remain in power, they had to demonstrate their interest in the welfare of the larger, inclusive Somali nation. Identification with this expanded sense of nationhood had been the legitimizing state principle, and every Somali politician was judged with respect to it.[47] The implications of this sense of nation are clear in a statement by Somali President Adan Abdulla Osman: "God has decreed that the Haud [part of the Ogaden] belongs to the Somalis, although Ethiopia has occupied it."[48] Osman declared in 1965 that "reunification of all Somalis is the very reason of life for our nation." This core value and sense of national identity drove Somalia's leaders to pursue irredentist regional goals during much of the period under review.[49]

From independence until 1969 Somalia had a parliamentary system in which representatives were elected on the basis of clan politics. Although Pan-Somalism played a general unifying and legitimizing role, it was particularly important to the Darod clan, which includes most of the Somalis living in the Ogaden. The two prime ministers between 1960 and 1967 were both members of this clan, as was Siad Barre (1969–1991), a Marehan, a subclan of the Darod. This group therefore had a particularly influential voice in the government and had the most to gain from unification. It is notable that it was under Prime Minister Ibrahim Egal (1967–1969), an Isaq with fewer ties to the Ogaden Somalis, that a period of détente with Ethiopia began.

Egal's attempt at accommodation with Somalia's neighbors was cut short by a military coup. Pervasive corruption, nepotism, a political system unable to meet the demands of the people, and cuts in military spending led to the alienation of important segments of the intelligentsia and members of the armed forces. In 1969 President Abdirashid Ali Shermarke was assassinated by a disgruntled office seeker in a clan dispute. Before the assembly could select a replacement, the military overthrew the government and Major General Siad Barre assumed leadership.

Siad proclaimed "scientific socialism" as his regime's ideology on the first anniversary of the coup, but his program reflected the unique problems of Somalia. Although related to the Ogaden Somalis, Siad Barre at first ignored the clamor for reunification. His military government initially had the power and space to set the political agenda and concentrated its energies on development issues. Siad's regime publicly campaigned to end "tribalism" based on clan identities but in practice relied upon Darods—especially the Marehan, Dulbahante, and Ogaden subclans—for support. Siad attempted to institutionalize his rule in 1976 by disbanding the relatively autonomous Supreme Revolutionary Council and forming the Somali Revolutionary Socialist party, which became a channel for Pan-Somali sentiments.[50]

Following the disastrous Ogaden War (discussed later) and a failed coup attempt in April 1978, Siad altered the focus of his regime. Pan-

Somalism remained an important force, and clashes with Ethiopia continued, but Siad appeared to accept the fact that he lacked the internal means or external support necessary to gain control of the Ogaden. The military defeat in the Ogaden War weakened his legitimacy as the defender of Somali interests, and several opposition groups challenged his authority.[51] The social base of the regime narrowed as a small clique of Siad's relatives received the most important political posts. Dissident groups formed largely on the basis of clan identification and with Ethiopia's financial and material support.[52]

Ethiopia, following normalization of relations with Mogadishu (discussed later), expelled the anti-Siad opposition Somali National Movement (SNM) from its territory. The insurgents, however, moved their campaign against Siad into northern Somalia, where they seized the towns of Hargeisa and Burao in May and June of 1988 and even threatened the port of Berbera. Somali forces retook the towns from the SNM but, in the course of the fighting and subsequent military occupation, destroyed much of northern Somalia.

In 1990–91, Siad's authoritarian methods and increasingly narrow base of support provoked armed rebellions throughout the country. Several groups, building on regionally based clan networks for their support, established rival zones of control and competed for domination in the capital. One of them forced Siad to leave in January and named a new government. But resistance groups, especially in the north, which had fought longer and suffered more, demanded a larger share in the transitional government.[53] In May the SNM dramatized its alienation from the leaders in Mogadishu by announcing the formation of a new independent state in the northern region they controlled.[54]

The viability of this newly declared Republic of Somaliland was unclear in mid–1991. No state had recognized its legitimacy and the Organization of African Unity stated that it would not accept this act of secession. Somalia was in chaos, with several armed movements controlling territory and contesting power; with many of its residents seeking refuge in Ethiopia, Kenya, and Djibouti; and with its always fragile economy shattered. It will be some time before order is reestablished. When a new authority is established, it will have to construct a new basis of politics that recognizes regional autonomy and broadens participation. This new order may replace Somalia's irredentist tendencies, or it may fall back on old nationalist calls to rally the people behind the government.

Since independence, the influence of a sense of Somali identity that extended beyond the territory's boundaries led Mogadishu to pursue irredentist goals. These policies brought Somalia into conflict with Ethiopia, Kenya, and Djibouti, thereby drawing it into the regional system as a source of disturbance, contributing to the insecurity of all its neighbors. The collapse of central authority following the overthrow of Siad Barre in 1991 shifted the focus of politics inward, as various groups used clan bases of support in a political struggle to succeed Siad or build up regional power. The SNM's secessionist policies demonstrate that the breakup of the Somali nation, rather than a concern for Greater Somalia, marks the politics of transition in 1991. Greater Somali nationalism, however, remains as a potential basis of legitimacy that may be adopted by a future regime. This possibility makes Somalia a continuing source of insecurity to its neighbors.

Djibouti

Uncertainty about the future of the independent state of Djibouti has been another source of tension within the Horn. This microstate of some 200,000 people is an important outlet to the sea for Addis Ababa and at one time was considered by Mogadishu as part of Greater Somalia. The former French colony is divided ethnically: The Afar have kinsmen across the border in Ethiopia and Eritrea, whereas the slightly more numerous Issas are ethnic Somalis.[55]

Despite fears in Paris and Djibouti that one of its more powerful neighbors would attempt to annex the territory, Djibouti received its independence from France in June 1977. By forming a multiethnic coalition with an Issa president and an Afar prime minister, the independent government tried to minimize domestic ethnic conflict and avoid entanglement in regional conflicts. The French maintain a sizable military presence that guarantees Djibouti's independence from its regional neighbors. In addition, Addis Ababa's interest in uninterrupted access to the sea through its port ensures Ethiopian resistance to Somali ambitions, whereas Mogadishu's concerns inhibit Addis Ababa from attempting to absorb the territory.[56]

Kenya

Kenya's role in the Horn of Africa is centered on its interest in maintaining sovereignty over the former Northern Frontier District (NFD—now part of the North Eastern Province).[57] In 1962, a survey by British colonial authorities found that Somali pastoralists in the NFD wanted to join their kinsmen in Somalia rather than remain within Kenya at independence. To leaders in Nairobi, however, such an option was unacceptable. To allow Somalis to leave the fragile multiethnic state would lead to similar moves by other dissatisfied groups. Kenya's problem, therefore, paralleled Ethiopia's. The British, anxious to establish good relations with Nairobi's postcolonial leaders, ignored the results of the survey and kept the NFD within Kenya at independence.

Kenyatta's regime militarily defeated a rebellion supported by Mogadishu and wisely opened opportunities in its educational and bureaucratic systems for competent and ambitious ethnic Somalis. Mogadishu's interest in Somalis in Kenya declined, until in the 1980s it renounced Somali claims. Bandit activity in northern Kenya remains a problem for Nairobi, but it has become an issue of internal security, not regional conflict. Recent repression of demonstrators demanding a multiparty democracy suggests that Kenya's relative stability in the region may not last.[58] This rising dissidence, however, is an internal matter unrelated to Somali government interference.

Patterns of Relations on the Horn

It is sometimes argued that the play of superpowers projecting their rivalries into the Horn best explains the difficulties these states face in improving relations with one another. Our analysis suggests that the internal conditions of these states and the fears and ambitions of their governments are at the core of the region's difficulties that have produced such humanly disastrous results. We have outlined the internal security problems and the difficulties all these states have had in trying to build state and nation. We now will examine patterns of relationships among the states of the Horn. We then analyze the relationships of these states with external powers, including the remarkable switch of superpower patrons effected by Ethiopia and Somalia in 1977. Outsiders have played a role, but domestic and regional dynamics are the principal causes of the difficulties.

The internal vulnerability of each state due to disunity exacerbated by government policies, the contradictory state goals and identities, and the fact that state borders do not coincide fully with national and ethnic identities condition the interrelationships of these states. Ethiopia's history and culture led its policymakers to fear encirclement and dissolution and to take actions to reduce its vulnerability. Somali ambition to unify the nation into a single state has caused conflicts with Ethiopia and Kenya. Khartoum's difficulties in its southern region drew it into rivalry with Addis Ababa. Kenya's concerns over its northern region and Djibouti's need to balance relations with its neighbors in order to maintain its independence shaped their respective roles in the regional system.

The political leaders of the various states in the region cannot increase their security against such vulnerabilities in isolation. Actions by

Addis Ababa, Khartoum, and Mogadishu to improve their security typically are perceived by the others as further threats to their own security. Thus, the governments of the Horn are entangled in various forms of the security dilemma; each state's attempts to improve its own security are seen as increasing the insecurity of the others.

Ethiopia-Somalia

The Ethiopia-Somalia conflict is an example of antithetical security goals. Ethiopia's security has been predicated on maintaining territorial integrity and building cohesion for its multinational population. This required maintaining control of the Ogaden. Somalia's security goals have aimed at creating a nation-state that incorporated the Somalis living in the Ogaden. Actions by either of these states in pursuit of their conception of security therefore increased the perceived insecurity of the other.

The origins of the Ethiopia-Somali dispute lie in the distant past. In the precolonial period the peoples of the Ethiopian highlands and the lowland pastoralists competed on the basis of differing modes of production and religious ideologies. Somalis are encroaching nomads, vectors of a *volkerwanderung* that has gradually spread southwestward, ever encroaching toward the settled highlands of Ethiopia and Kenya.

Religious differences also have been important. The royalty of the Axumite empire in northern Ethiopia converted to Monophysite Christianity in the fourth century. From the seventh century forward, Islam spread among the Somali pastoralists. The Ethiopia-Somalia conflict prior to colonialism, therefore, generally took the form of religious holy wars.[59]

During the colonial period the Italians, British, and French used their respective positions in Somaliland to attempt to influence Ethiopia indirectly. After Somalia's independence, the struggle has continued, because the two states have contradictory domestic political structures that parallel the earlier religious rift.[60] Ethiopia, a multinational state, and Somalia, a multistate nation, represent two opposing types of political organization. The conflict, therefore, is structural, for the organizing principles of the two states contradict each other and implicate them so closely they cannot simply ignore each other.[61] The conflict is greatly complicated because the border between Ethiopia and former Italian Somaliland never was demarcated definitively and the maps on which it was drawn are lost.[62]

This tension between opposing principles of statehood and state identities has flared into periodic violence. At the 1963 OAU meeting, the Somali and Ethiopian representatives accused each other of seeking territorial aggrandizement across their common frontier.[63] The Somalis objected to the sanctification of colonial borders and maintained that Somalia had a unique grievance against Ethiopian imperialism that deserved rectification. In early 1964 the two states clashed along their border and engaged in a provocative propaganda campaign. The fighting escalated until Sudan, acting as a third party under the auspices of the OAU, mediated a cease-fire and established a demilitarized zone on both sides of the border. Tensions, however, remained high, and both sides accused the other of border violations.[64]

Following the 1974 Ethiopian revolution, Somalia increased its support to the Western Somali Liberation Front insurgency in the Ogaden. In July 1977 Somalia directly invaded the Ogaden, hoping to exploit Ethiopia's postrevolution weakness to achieve its Pan-Somali goal. Although Ethiopia had a much larger population and army, at that time the balance of forces in the Ogaden seemed to favor Somalia. The Soviets had built up Somalia's army, especially its tank forces, at a far faster rate than the United States had equipped Ethiopia. Moreover, Mogadishu was able to commit all its forces to the Ogaden, while the Derg had to fight simultaneously in Eritrea and against numerous other domestic rebel groups.[65] Nonetheless, Ethiopia successfully repulsed the Somali invaders with the help of massive Soviet and Cuban assistance. (On the superpower role in this conflict see later.)

Since this period of intense military struggle, tensions over the Ogaden gradually abated but have not been eliminated. Mogadishu continued to support Somali separatists, although the WSLF lost much of its power. In return, Ethiopia supported anti-Siad groups such as the Democratic Front for the Salvation of Somalia (DFSS) and the Somali National Movement (SNM).[66] The Ethiopian military, in addition, occupied two Somali border towns.

Despite this enduring conflict, there have been examples of accommodation and conflict management, if not resolution, between the two states. During Egal's regime (1967–69), as already noted, Ethiopia and Somalia initiated a period of détente, in part because of the cost to both parties of the extended stalemate and the freedom of action that the new Egal government enjoyed in domestic politics.[67] Egal began to eliminate specific sore points with Addis Ababa, to demilitarize the conflict, and to start a process in which the major issue, sovereignty of the Ogaden, could be discussed.

The détente, however, proved to be unstable because the core contradiction was not resolved. For reasons unrelated to the Ogaden issue, the Egal government fell to Siad Barre's coup in 1969, and the negotiating process collapsed. In 1977 Moscow and Havana became more deeply engaged on the Ethiopian side of the conflict and tried to broker an agreement, but the gap between the two hostile states remained too large.

By January 1986, both sides concluded that the stalemate benefited neither party and wanted a settlement so that they could concentrate against internal threats. Mengistu and Siad met in Djibouti and established a Provisional Joint Ministerial Committee. An ad hoc ministerial committee met twice in 1986 and again in April 1987 without reaching an agreement. As in the Egal period, the Somalis wanted to concentrate on specific points, such as normalizing relations, whereas the Ethiopians insisted on addressing the core issues of sovereignty, frontier demarcation, and renunciation of Somali territorial claims.

While the deliberations of the ad hoc committee stalled, a military buildup on both sides escalated and border violations threatened to break out into a new round of fighting. In April 1988 Mengistu and Siad again met in Djibouti and agreed to reestablish relations, withdraw troops from the border, exchange prisoners of war, and "refrain from the use or threat of force against the territorial integrity or political independence" of either state. Because of the urgent need to redeploy troops from the Ogaden to face the Eritrean and Tigrayan challenges, Ethiopia apparently gave up its insistence on settling the territorial issue. It withdrew from the two Somali towns and expelled many of the SNM units operating in its territory, although Somali officials accused Ethiopia of continuing their support.[68]

Although the agreement left the major issue of sovereignty and border demarcation unsettled, it could prove to be relatively stable, because neither side has an incentive to violate it. The collapse of the regimes of Siad Barre and Mengistu Haile Mariam in 1991 led to tremendous turmoil in both states. Vulnerable refugees fled on both sides of the border, with some crossing more than once in a fruitless search for safety. The struggle for control of Mogadishu, the SNM's efforts to consolidate their authority in northern Somalia, and the multisided contest for control in Addis Ababa diverted attention from the Ogaden. The underlying conflict, however, remained unresolved and could flare up again once the internal transitions are complete. Furthermore, the explosion of conflict within Somalia that followed the détente with Ethiopia indicates that progress in reducing conflict on the interstate level may contribute to the release of pent-up domestic conflict.

The deeply rooted conflict between Ethiopia and Somalia, which is the result of antithetical state identities and organizing principles and is intertwined with the divisive internal political struggles in both states, thus far has defied resolution. In 1991 the collapse of Siad's and Mengistu's regimes and the subsequent internal political struggles preoccupied the two countries. The Ethiopia-Somalia relationship will remain vital and the two states' security will be linked regardless of the future regimes.

Ethiopia-Eritrea

The Eritrean movement for self-determination has been an internal challenge to Ethiopia's security. Although as of mid–1991, Eritrea had not been recognized as an independent state, as far as Addis Ababa is concerned, it played a role similar to that of Somalia. The insurgents were important to the Horn system because regional actors used them to weaken Ethiopia and because the Eritreans, in turn, used rivalries between regional states to strengthen their position. From Addis Ababa's perspective, any separate Eritrean state was perceived as re-creating the hostile encirclement that has long plagued Ethiopia.[69] Accordingly, the Ethiopia-Eritrea relationship, for many years formally an "internal" matter, was in fact another of the bilateral rivalries that shaped regional relations.

Haile Sellassie made gaining control over Eritrea one of his primary foreign policy goals after World War II. Ethiopia had been attacked from Eritrea twice; in 1895 Menilek defeated the Italians at Adwa, but in 1936 Mussolini's army occupied the entire country. While the United Nations debated the disposition of the former colony, the emperor argued that the area for centuries had been part of the Ethiopian empire and that without the territory Ethiopia would remain landlocked and vulnerable. Eritrean leaders continue to dispute the historical accuracy of Haile Sellassie's claim and to question whether ensuring access to the sea justifies denying self-determination to a former colony. Nevertheless, without access to the sea, Ethiopia would return to being at the mercy of alien littoral powers whose policies have in the past threatened the viability of the state. In addition, the precedent of a successful secession would encourage other dissident nationalists to seek independence at Addis Ababa's expense.

The Eritrean rebels received assistance from Arab states, thereby reinforcing long-standing fears of Arab encirclement. Following the Ethiopian revolution, some of the radical Arab states, most notably Libya, ended their support for the insurgents, but Saudi Arabia and other more conservative Arab states quickly stepped in. In the 1980s Addis Ababa regularly sent delegations to Cairo and Riyadh, believing that persuading the Arab states to halt their support would bring an end to the rebellion. Mengistu sought to paint the Eritreans as mercenaries of reactionary Arabs scheming to achieve the historical goal of carving up Ethiopia. Such policies, however, were bound to fail if leaders did not also recognize that the conflict represented real internal grievances and aspirations, not just external meddling.

Eritrean secessionist groups have based their appeals for independence on international law and African practice. They argued that because Eritrea was in fact a case of former colonial rule, it should have received independence after Italy's empire was dismantled instead of being federated to Ethiopia in 1952. Since then Eritrea has been administered by what they perceive to be an "imperialist" Amhara elite in Addis Ababa whose alien nature became even less acceptable with the creation of the Marxist-Leninist government. The rebels argued that Eritrea is entitled to its rightful decolonization and self-determination.[70]

Like the Ethiopia-Somalia clash, the Ethiopia-Eritrea conflict has been between two contradictory political systems and bases of legitimacy. The Eritreans insisted on self-determination and Addis Ababa asserted the right to maintain its territorial integrity. With both sides of the conflict perceiving their struggles in these antithetical terms, it was difficult to negotiate an end to the violence. Moreover, the long duration and high cost of the conflict to more than a generation of Eritreans made accommodation all the more difficult.

In the early years after the Ethiopian revolution the Eritreans had a promising opportunity to win independence. However, revolutionary ideology also penetrated the Eritrean movements, weakening their struggle against Addis Ababa as the movements split into competing ideological factions.[71] The resulting divisions reduced their effectiveness and the Eritreans yielded some areas they once held, although they regained them in the late 1980s.

Despite the tremendous costs to both the EPLF and the Ethiopian government, not to mention the devastation to the villagers caught in the middle, attempts to end the conflict through a negotiated settlement did not succeed. Abortive negotiations in 1976 and 1980 failed because of Eritrean disunity and Ethiopia's continued attempts to solve the conflict unilaterally by military force. Neither side exhibited any readiness to compromise. The *Derg* offered Eritrea special treatment as an autonomous region under the 1987 constitution, but rebel leaders rejected this as not addressing their commitment to full self-determination. The EPLF demanded a referendum on the status of the region, with independence offered as an option, a condition Mengistu refused.

Former U.S. President Jimmy Carter sponsored talks between the Eritreans and Ethiopian government in 1989, but the process soon derailed on procedural issues. In addition, the rise of the EPRDF had transformed the bilateral conflict into a multisided and still inchoate contest for the future of Ethiopia, thereby greatly complicating peace efforts.[72] An interlinked rebellion in the Sudan further muddled peace talks.

In 1988, the Soviet Union, tired of its costly support of Ethiopia's endless warfare, began to pressure Mengistu to settle the conflict and suggested that military assistance would be curtailed if negotiations did not begin.[73] Moscow supported Washington when, in the fall and winter of 1990–91, Assistant Secretary of State for African Affairs Herman Cohen held talks with EPLF and Ethiopian officials but found no framework for settlement acceptable to both parties.[74] In May 1991, with the EPRDF forces on the outskirts of Addis Ababa, Cohen proposed talks in London to help shape a transitional government in Ethiopia and end the fighting in Eritrea.

When Mengistu fled and the Tigrayan-led EPRDF took control of Addis Ababa, the Eritrean secessionists captured the few remaining government-controlled cities in Eritrea. In May 1991 Isaias Afewerki, the EPLF secretary-general, announced he was setting up a separate provisional government in Asmara.[75] He promised that his organization would do nothing to disrupt the new transitional government in Addis Ababa but that it would not participate. The new Ethiopian regime needed Eritrean cooperation to gain access to the Red Sea ports. Many Ethiopians continue to believe that Eritrea should remain part of a united Ethiopia, but with the EPLF controlling the entire region, it would be difficult to force the Eritreans to remain within the Ethiopian state against their will. In July 1991 the new regime in Addis Ababa agreed to accept a U.N.-supervised referendum in the region after a two-year transitional period in exchange for access to the port of Aseb.

A new phase of the Eritrean struggle clearly had begun. Despite the change of government following Mengistu's overthrow, the fundamental clash between Eritreans who insist on their right to self-determination and independence and the large number of Ethiopians who persist in their conviction that Eritrea must remain part of a united Ethiopia persists. Eritrea may win full independence or join in a reformed and very loose confederation with Ethiopia; relations between Asmara and Addis Ababa may become either cooperative or hostile. Regardless, the two polities will continue to be closely interlinked, with a multitude of security, economic, social, and political interactions, and the Ethiopia-Eritrea relationship will continue to play a vital part in the Horn regional system.

Ethiopia-Sudan

The Eritrean insurgency within Ethiopia profoundly affected relationships between Ethiopia and Sudan. At times, Sudan allowed Eritrean rebels to receive supplies and establish safe havens in camps within its borders; Ethiopia, in turn, periodically offered similar bases and supplies to southern Sudanese rebels. Because the Sudanese backed the Eritreans, Ethiopia perceived Khartoum as one of the encircling powers and one more threat to Addis Ababa. Ethiopia's reciprocal support for the Sudan Peoples' Liberation Army turned the southern rebellion into a regional conflict, making its resolution all the more difficult.

The Ethiopia-Sudan cleavage is not a clash between contradictory political systems, like that between Ethiopia and Somalia, but, ironically, seems to result from their very similarities and common vulnerabilities. Both Khartoum and Addis Ababa must govern incompletely integrated multiethnic populations in weak, poorly institutionalized states. Each is threatened by the other's policy of intervening by proxy in a mutually destructive game of tit for tat.

Despite a series of interventions by proxy during the late 1960s, Haile Sellassie and Nimeiri found the basis for a truce in the early 1970s. Nimeiri needed new domestic partners to shore up his base of support following the Communist coup attempt, and Haile Sellassie hoped to diminish Sudanese support for his opponents. Both leaders gained following the Addis Ababa Agreement, as Ethiopia ended its support for southern rebels and Sudan restricted Eritrean activities. For a period in the early 1970s the intervention by proxy diminished, and Ethiopia-Sudan relations became comparatively peaceful.

By the mid–1970s, however, in the aftermath of the Ethiopian revolution and the subsequent changes in superpower patrons, new domestic political forces and changed relations with external powers led to renewed tensions along the border, and both governments returned to policies of intervention by proxy. In 1976 another coup attempt, led from exile in Libya by Sadiq al-Mahdi, nearly overthrew the regime in Khartoum. Nimeiri called the attempted overthrow a "treacherous foreign invasion" and accused Ethiopia, with good reason, of providing training camps and joining Libya in support of the coup.[76]

By 1977 Nimeiri openly opposed the regime in Addis Ababa, backed the anti-Derg Ethiopian Democratic Union, and revived support for the Eritrean movements. Addis Ababa labeled Nimeiri Ethiopia's worst enemy and accused Sudan of intervening with regular military forces in Ethiopia.[77]

The domestic composition of the two states explains at least part of the persistent and damaging policy of intervention by proxy followed by Ethiopia and Sudan. Both governments have cultural ties with their neighbor's rebels. The southern Sudanese guerrillas are non-Muslim, and supporting them is consistent with Ethiopia's strategy of preventing encirclement by Islamic forces. The Eritrean rebels often stressed their Islamic heritage and appealed to Khartoum on the basis of religious ties. These transborder cultural affinities, however, have not prevented accommodation between neighboring states when both governments found it in their interests and were well enough established at home to restrain their citizens.

The persistence of their mutual intervention results from their very weakness and vulnerability. The weak centers have little power to regulate their borders, and it is perhaps inevitable that cross-border raids and support for neighboring kinsmen will continue at a certain level. The rebel groups, particularly the Eritreans, had a degree of autonomy that made control by their host governments difficult. Sudan and Ethiopia can counter subversion from the outside only by threatening reciprocal subversion in reply. They therefore have been reluctant to cut their ties to neighboring rebel groups. The ability to destabilize one's neighbor, however, has not served as a deterrent to conflict. Instead of limiting intervention, a cycle of spiraling provocation disrupted the Ethiopia-Sudan relationship. State weakness and vulnerability therefore encouraged intervention by proxy.

The parallel problems of Ethiopia and Sudan, both facing internal insurgencies supported by the other, suggest that resolution might have been achieved by both states ending support for their neighbor's rebels. Ethiopian diplomats brokered the 1988 discussions between the Sudanese Democratic Unionist party (DUP) and the southern rebels in the hope of reciprocal assistance from Khartoum to end the Eritrean rebellion.[78] Such four-sided agreements, however, proved exceedingly difficult. The level of influence the respective host countries had over the rebels was not equivalent: Addis Ababa had considerably more leverage over the Sudanese rebels than Khartoum had over the Eritreans, especially in the late 1980s. In addition, both insurgent groups perceived that advantages could still be won by unilateral escalation, indicating that a clear stalemate had not yet been achieved. The precarious hold on power of leaders in both Khartoum and Addis Ababa prevented them from either accepting any agreement their insurgents would also accept, since that would be bound to provoke opposition from their domestic opponents, or delivering on any promises that might constrain their neighbor's rebels.[79]

The takeover of Asmara and Addis Ababa in May 1991 by insurgent movements supported by Khartoum altered this regional competition. The good relations between the new leaders in Ethiopia and the government in Sudan led Addis Ababa to expel the hundreds of thousands of Sudanese refugees and to end SPLM/SPLA access to safe havens in Ethiopia. The EPRDF-led government in Addis Ababa pledged to pursue policies of noninterference with its neighbors and held meetings with Sudanese leader Beshir.[80] If Ethiopia successfully ends the Eritrean conflict and the new leaders in Addis Ababa continue to have cooperative relations with Khartoum, it is possible that the pattern of mutual destabilization will be broken. Leaders in both Addis Ababa and Asmara, however, are suspicious of Sudanese support for Islamic fundamentalist organizations. If regional competition arises again, a return to intervention may tempt leaders in the future.

Ethiopia-Djibouti, Somalia-Djibouti

Djibouti, although a ministate unable to challenge any state in the Horn directly, plays a role in the security system because it is an important outlet for Ethiopia and because its cross-border ethnic affiliations with Somalia heighten Addis Ababa's vulnerability. Concern in Addis Ababa over Djibouti, however, has faded considerably in recent years. Ethiopia developed the Eritrean port of Aseb to provide it with an alternative outlet to the sea. The loss of access to the sea through Eritrea, however, could reawaken Addis Ababa's interest in Djibouti.

Somali interests in Djibouti also have declined. Mogadishu actively campaigned against French control of the territory in the 1960s.[81] Siad, however, accepted as a victory for self-determination the 1976 referendum by which the residents of Djibouti voted for independence. The presence of French troops in the former colony and opportunities in the more important Ogaden region deflected Somali ambitions away from Djibouti. Somalia was the first state to recognize the new government and has dropped its claims to the ethnic Somali residents of the territory.

Neither Addis Ababa nor Mogadishu is willing to risk a regionwide conflict by challenging the status quo. Djibouti is therefore an example of "null possession," whereby both parties abstain from a disputed territory.[82]

Ethiopia-Kenya, Somalia-Kenya

The final member of the Horn of Africa system is Kenya, the only neighbor with which Ethiopia has a fully cooperative relationship. Despite domestic regime changes and rival superpower patrons, Addis Ababa and Nairobi established and have maintained a strategic alliance based on shared fear of Somali irredentism.

The Somalia-Kenya conflict is another instance of a clash between a multistate irredentist nation and a multination state determined to defend its territorial integrity. Kenya's leaders strongly resisted Mogadishu's activities in the Northern Frontier District (NFD) in the early 1960s, arguing that the Somali inhabited region represented "an indivisible part of Kenya."[83] The Somalia-Kenya conflict, like the Ethiopia-Somalia conflict, represented a clash between two contradictory types of state organization.

Somali nationalists in the NFD, with the support of Mogadishu, began a guerrilla campaign against the newly independent Kenyan government, which referred to the rebels as *shiftas*, or bandits. The war continued throughout the early 1960s, with attacks on government outposts and officials. Kenya blamed Somalia for fomenting the rebellion and claimed that "guerrilla terrorism and brigandage . . . covertly sustained" by Somalia had become "an overt undertaking of warfare."[84] In response, as discussed later, Kenya and Ethiopia formed an alliance, one of the few to be found in the Horn.

The Somali-supported *shifta* rebellion declined in the late 1960s. As Kenya gained independence and established its rule, Mogadishu saw its chances of winning jurisdiction over the territory decline. Somali irredentism shifted its focus to the Ogaden, which was of greater cultural and economic importance to the Somali nation. The Somali clans living in northern Kenya were not important components of the political structure of the regime in Mogadishu. Kenya and Somalia negotiated a détente during Egal's regime (1967–1969).[85]

Siad met with Moi at the July 1981 OAU summit and reportedly renounced Somalia's territorial claims on Kenya. Ethnic Somalis have participated in Nairobi's political system, and such access encouraged Mogadishu to deemphasize its agitation for self-determination in northern Kenya. An important test of Siad's intentions toward the Somalis in Kenya occurred in February 1984, when Kenyan soldiers killed several hundred Somalis in the northern region. Mogadishu allowed the matter to pass as an internal problem without making any efforts to assert its role as protector of the Somali nation. Later in 1984, Moi visited Somalia and signed a border agreement. Kenya offered amnesty to the *shiftas* and Somalia encouraged Kenyan exiles to return.

Haile Sellassie and Kenyatta formed an alliance in 1963 to counter Somali irredentism. Kenya gained the protection of the strongest power in the region, which allowed it to deemphasize defense and concentrate on economic development and its relationships with the East African Community.[86] The strategic alliance is important to Addis Ababa because it institutionalizes and reinforces the only significant and enduring breach in the ring of hostile states isolating Ethiopia.

Kenya continued to benefit from the strategic relationship even after the Ethiopian military overthrew the emperor and oriented the country toward the Soviet Union. As Nairobi perceived it, despite denials from Mogadishu, Somali irredentism remained more of a threat than Addis Ababa's Marxist rhetoric or its relationship with Moscow. Kenya diplomatically supported Ethiopia during the Ogaden War, although it did not provide any military help.[87]

In January 1979 Ethiopia and Kenya signed a ten-year treaty of friendship and cooperation. Since then regular Joint Ministerial Consultative Committee meetings have institutionalized cooperative relations. The strong geostrategic rationale for this cooperation has allowed the relationship to survive regime changes, divergent ideologies, and competing superpower patrons.

Relations with Outside Powers

The pervasive weakness of states in the Horn compels their governments to seek relationships with outside powers. They therefore adopt diplomatic strategies to encourage external powers to assist them. Regional states appeal to outside states and organizations for military, financial, and diplomatic support on the basis of ideology, strategic interests, and patron-client exchanges.

Ethiopia and Somalia pursued distinctive diplomatic strategies because of their different natures and the pattern of their conflict. Ethiopia tried to keep the rivalry on the level of state-to-state conflict and concentrated its search for outside support within forums that are made up of other state actors, particularly the OAU, which supports the norm of territorial integrity. Somalia, on the other hand, has sought ties with substate groups such as the Western Somali Liberation Front and the Eritrean movements and suprastate ideological or cultural movements, such as the Arab League and radical Third World solidarity.

Such diplomatic strategies are designed to allow the weak regional states to break out of the constraints of the region and "borrow power" from beyond the system. The support provided by outside powers can help a regional state improve its relative position. It can shift a local balance in favor of the one that draws in major outside support, but it cannot alter the structure of the regional system.

Outside powers have much else to think about besides developments in the Horn. The states of the Middle East, for example, are divided and mutually hostile, and the superpowers during the Cold War competed for global influence. If an outside power intervenes on behalf of one regional state, a competing regional state can often elicit support from the outside power's opponents. In this way, American support for Ethiopia in the 1960s and early 1970s was countered by Soviet support for Ethiopia's neighbors, Sudan and Somalia. After 1977, by the same token, Soviet patronage to Ethiopia encouraged the United States to assist Ethiopia's regional rivals in Somalia and Sudan. Similarly, Libyan support for one regional state generally led to Saudi Arabian intervention on behalf of that state's rivals. To be sure, this pattern of competing support by outside powers is not automatic or precisely equivalent; short-term imbalances are frequent. But in general, nonregional powers manipulate but do not alter regional patterns and indigenous structures.

The decline of Cold War rivalry following the "new thinking" in Moscow modified this pattern. The Soviet Union exhibited little interest in securing clients in the Horn of Africa in the late 1980s and early 1990s, leaving the field open to the United States. The geostrategic rationale for U.S. involvement became less persuasive, allowing Washington to place greater emphasis on human rights, democracy, and conflict resolution in its policies toward the Horn.[88] This change in the international context, however, has not fundamentally changed the regional system of rivalries.

Relations with the Middle East

Egypt

The Middle East states are one source of outside support. Egypt's involvement in the Horn derives from its interests in protecting the sources of the Nile, its historic role in Sudan, and, especially under Nasser, its leadership position in the nonaligned movement and the Arab world.[89]

Egypt has exerted an important influence on Sudan throughout its history, and the two states have many economic, political, and cultural ties. Since Sudan's independence in 1956, periods of cooperation and moves toward integration have alternated with periods of tension and divergent policies.[90] Cooperation in matters of defense, such as the July 1976 joint defense agreement, has been easier than that toward political integration. Political parties in the Sudan are defined in part by their posture toward Cairo, with the Democratic Unionist party favoring cooperation with Egypt and the Umma party opposing such ties.

The close relationship between Khartoum and Cairo has suffered from the volatile politics of the Arab world. The Camp David Accords and the asylum Egypt granted Nimeiri caused some Sudanese to criticize Cairo. Egyptian leader Husni Mubarak, however, held in 1985 that "Egypt and Sudan are bound by one life channel, which is the River Nile, and by the bonds of the womb. Nobody can separate them under any circumstances."[91]

Egypt's diplomatic and military support often has strengthened Khartoum's position in the Horn. The friendly relations with its powerful neighbor to the north have allowed Sudan to concentrate its forces on the threats from Ethiopia, the rebels in the south, and Libya to the west. Some believed that Sudan had become so irrevocably tied to

Egypt in the 1980s that Khartoum had been "Findlandized" and could not take positions that risked antagonizing Egypt.[92] The close ties, however, exacerbated Sudan's internal problems. Southerners feared that close cooperation between Cairo and Khartoum strengthened the Arabic north at their expense, and Sudan's fundamentalist Muslims in the north saw the relationship with Sadat after Camp David as weakening Arab solidarity.

In the late 1980s and early 1990s, Cairo grew frustrated with Khartoum's unwillingness to end the civil war and became alarmed at the rise of Islamic fundamentalism. Egypt endorsed the talks between the southern rebels and the Democratic Unionist party and pressured Sadiq to abandon *Shari'a* law. Cairo feared that a rise in Islamic fundamentalism in Sudan would spill into its territory. Recently, Cairo has lost patience with Beshir's religious policies and his inability to resolve the conflict in the south. Beshir's support for Iraq following Saddam Husayn's invasion of Kuwait also angered Cairo and made relations tense.

The ancient civilizations of Egypt and Ethiopia have interacted throughout the centuries. Until as recently as 1959, coptic religious leaders in Alexandria selected the *abuna* (patriarch) of the Ethiopian Orthodox Church. In the nineteenth century, Ethiopia and Egypt competed for control of the Red Sea, and later, Haile Sellassie saw Nasser's pan-Arabic ideology as a threat to Ethiopia's interest in the Horn. The prospect that a revolutionary ideology such as Nasser's, backed by Egypt's powerful and Soviet-supplied army, would link up with anti-Ethiopian groups in Eritrea and Somalia increased Haile Sellassie's phobia of encirclement by hostile Arab forces. Nasser, however, restrained his interventionist policies after his forces became mired in Yemen and were defeated in the 1967 Arab-Israeli War. In the late 1960s, Haile Sellassie and Nasser reached a modus vivendi, and Cairo reduced its support for anti-Ethiopian movements. Egypt began to perceive that its interests coincided with stability on the Horn.

Saudi Arabia

Before the mid–1970s, Saudi Arabia played only a minor role in the Horn. In the 1960s, the Saudi royal family shared Haile Sellassie's desire for stability and his fear of Nasser and therefore generally supported Ethiopia and the status quo in the Red Sea.[93] Following the Ethiopian revolution and Riyadh's perception that the Ethiopia/Libya/Yemen axis promoted radicalism in the region, Saudi Arabia began to play a more prominent role on the Horn. Riyadh used its growing oil wealth to project its increased power into the region by financially encouraging what it considered to be moderate political developments.

Seeking to counter the radical axis, Saudi Arabia began to encourage cooperation between Egypt and Sudan. Riyadh hoped to promote the "Arabization of the Red Sea" and thereby counter the power of radical Soviet-backed forces in the area.[94] Riyadh played an important role in the negotiations between Somalia and the United States that preceded the 1977 expulsion of Soviet advisers. Djibouti has also won financial aid and political support from Saudi Arabia by joining the Arab League and emphasizing its Islamic heritage.[95]

Saudi Arabia's relationship to the Eritrean movements has been complex. In the mid-1970s, by emphasizing a Pan-Arabic ideology, the Eritrean Liberation Front (ELF) initially won sympathy from Riyadh. The campaign for an independent Eritrea played into Riyadh's Red Sea policy and served as a means to weaken the increasingly radical revolutionaries in Ethiopia. The ELF, however, lost an internal power struggle to the more radical Eritrean Peoples' Liberation Front, which alarmed the conservative Saudis by calling for revolution throughout the region. As a result, support from Riyadh declined.

Saudi Arabia's role in the Horn therefore is based above all on its fear of radicalism and of spreading instability. The upheavals in the Horn in the late 1970s deeply disturbed Saudi leaders.[96] Accordingly, whereas Egypt's intervention has been fairly consistent in support of whichever regime is in control in Khartoum, Saudi Arabian support has shifted as the actors in the Horn have changed their ideologies and the directions of their policies.

Libya

Libyan leader Mommar Qadhafi's radical ideology, ambitions to lead the Arab world, and aggressively expansionist foreign policy have led him to attempt to shape political events in the Horn.[97] At various times, Libya has supported both the governments and opposition groups in Sudan, Ethiopia, and Somalia. The competition between Tripoli and Riyadh for leadership in the Arab world has led these two states generally to support opposing sides of the major cleavages on the Horn.

At first, Qadhafi opposed Haile Sellassie because of the emperor's close ties to Israel and the United States. Libya called for the removal of the OAU from Addis Ababa in retaliation for the emperor's continued recognition of Israel. It supported the Eritreans and Sudan in the early 1970s and endorsed Somalia's claims to the Ogaden.

Qadhafi's policy toward Sudan shifted in response to swings in North African politics. Libya originally advocated closer ties with Egypt and Sudan in the late 1960s and supported Nimeiri during the 1971 coup attempt. Sudan periodically has used relations with Libya to offset the sometimes overbearing Egyptian influence. Growing tensions between Cairo and Tripoli following the 1972 Arab-Israeli war, however, damaged Libya's relations with Sudan as well. Qadhafi provided asylum for Sudanese dissidents in the National Front and encouraged coup attempts in 1974 and 1975. Khartoum broke relations with Libya following a coup attempt in 1976. Libya supported the Sudan Peoples' Liberation Army, even though it was a non-Islamic movement, as a way to distract Nimeiri from becoming involved in other areas that Qadhafi perceived as within his sphere of influence, such as Chad.

Following the overthrow of Nimeiri, Libya changed its stance toward Sudan. Sadiq al-Mahdi had lived in Libya during his exile and to balance Egypt's influence tried to improve relations with Tripoli during his regime. Libya abandoned its support for the Sudanese rebels and began to aid Khartoum's campaign against them. Qadhafi was one of the few world leaders to maintain friendly relations with Beshir's government in the early 1990s.

Following the fall of Haile Sellassie, Libya changed its policy toward Ethiopia. Qadhafi urged the Eritreans to abandon their military struggle and negotiate with the now ideologically friendly Ethiopian regime. Tripoli engineered the Tripartite Pact with Addis Ababa and Aden in 1981 to counter the power of Saudi Arabia, Egypt, Sudan, and other states aligned with the West. This alliance lost much of its importance to Libya with the downfall of Nimeiri and is now moribund. Recent Libyan actions in the region have created suspicion and distrust in Addis Ababa, and relations in the early 1990s were very tentative.

Libya's role in the Horn, therefore, has been above all to challenge Saudi Arabia's influence in the region. These two rivals in Middle East politics compete to shape the development of the Horn to accord with their divergent interests. Like Saudi Arabia, Libya's support for regimes and movements has shifted as the ideology and policies of the actors on the Horn have changed.

Israel

Israel's principal security interest in the Horn is to ensure access to the Red Sea. Accordingly, Israel has intervened in the Horn to prevent any hostile group from gaining decisive control over the Red Sea and the Bab al Mandeb "choke-point." Haile Sellassie and Israel, driven by a common fear of Pan-Arabism, cooperated as regional allies. Vulnerable amid Arab neighbors they perceived as hostile, the two states benefited from an alliance with their enemies' enemy.

Israel provided the Ethiopian army under Haile Sellassie with training in anti-insurgency techniques in an effort to contain the Eritrean guerrillas. This useful relationship, however, subjected Addis Ababa to criticism within the OAU following the 1972 Arab-Israeli War. To reduce pressure from Libya and other states hostile to Israel that were seeking to remove the OAU from Addis Ababa and to weaken Arab support for Eritrean secessionists, Haile Sellassie broke relations with Israel in October 1973.

Throughout the early years of the Ethiopian revolution, however, the strategic relationship quietly continued. Israeli advisers reportedly helped the radical government keep its American-made equipment in repair to counter Arab support for the Eritreans and Riyadh's "Arabization of the Red Sea" policy.[98] Israeli support allegedly continued in the 1980s, partly as a countermeasure to Arab policies in the region and partly in return for concessions from Addis Ababa in allowing Ethiopian Jews to emigrate.[99] In May 1991 the Israelis orchestrated a dramatic airlift of Ethiopian Jews out of Addis Ababa to Israel as the old Ethiopian regime crumbled.

Israel also aided the Anya Nya rebellion in southern Sudan, in an effort to weaken and distract Sudan. In this way it discouraged Sudan from sending troops in support of Egypt's conflict with Israel, as it had in the 1967 Arab-Israeli War.

Yemen

In May 1990 the Peoples' Democratic Republic of Yemen (PDRY-Aden) and the Yemen Arab Republic joined together to form a new state called the Republic of Yemen. In the past, the Marxist-oriented PDRY had played a limited diplomatic and military role in the Horn. PDRY joined other radical Arab states in backing the Eritrean Peoples Liberation Front against Haile Sellassie. Aden ended its support to the Eritreans in 1976, however, and provided Ethiopia with some troops during the fighting in the Ogaden and served as a key transit point for Soviet weapons shipped to Ethiopia.[100] Mengistu once referred to the PDRY as Ethiopia's only "revolutionary friend" in the region.[101] In 1981 PDRY joined Libya and Ethiopia in the Tripartite Pact. The loose coalition based on anti-Western foreign policies benefited Addis Ababa by providing it with another break in the hostile ring that surrounds Ethiopia. Like Haile Sellassie before him, Mengistu played on splits in the Arab world to prevent encirclement.

Relations with Superpowers

Cold War Rivalry

The remarkable diplomatic developments in the Horn between 1974 and 1978 deserve attention, for they vividly illustrate a number of ways that regional and superpower rivalries were linked.

Following the Ethiopian revolution there was a dramatic realignment of great power relations with the states of the Horn. The three most important states swapped superpower patrons—Moscow replaced Washington as the principal supporter of Addis Ababa; Somalia ejected the Soviet Union and, later, opened its ports to the United States; and Sudan expelled Soviet advisers and moved closer to the United States. To understand the complex and interrelated domestic and regional considerations that drove these changes we must first outline the relations between the superpowers and regional states in the 1960s and early 1970s. It was the system of regional relations that drove the reversal of the external alliances and not the reverse, indicating the predominance of the regional over the global system in determining states' behavior.

Both the United States and the Soviet Union had been active in the region in pursuit of their global objectives. The states of the Horn, of course, were but minor actors in the global system, and the superpowers' interest in the region were in the main derivative of their global interests. Nevertheless, the region attracted attention of the great powers because of its strategic location relative to the Red Sea, the Gulf of Aden, and the Indian Ocean and because Ethiopia, its largest state, played a significant role in African affairs. Most important, neither superpower was willing to concede the region to the other.[102]

To the region's hard-pressed states, these outside powers were a source of support—and threat. Patrons from far off provided the sinews of statehood, in some instances permitting governments to survive longer than they might otherwise. The more the regional states were internally fragile and surrounded by hostile neighbors, the easier it was for outsiders to become supporting patrons.

Ethiopia was the early focus of U.S. and USSR interest in the Horn, and even before World War II Addis Ababa sought support from Washington and Moscow to counter European designs. During and immediately after the war, London held the dominant position, since Commonwealth troops had assisted in the liberation of Ethiopia from Italian occupation. As Haile Sellassie became increasingly dissatisfied with London's policies, he turned to the United States.[103]

The United States developed a patron-client relationship with Ethiopia on the basis of an exchange of political, economic, and military goods.[104] Washington supported Addis Ababa's ambitions in the United Nations to federate Eritrea with Ethiopia and supplied weapons, training, and economic development funding. Haile Sellassie, in turn, granted access to the Kagnew communications facility in Eritrea, a critical element in Washington's global communication system until satellite technology made such stations obsolete. Ethiopia also provided troops for U.S.-backed actions in Korea and the Congo. The two states formalized this exchange relationship in 1953 in a series of agreements that represented a trade of military aid for continued and formalized access to Kagnew. Both sides understood that the military assistance was a form of rent or quid pro quo for the use of Kagnew.[105]

Somalia's independence in 1960 presented new opportunities and new problems to both its neighbors and outside powers. Mogadishu's territorial ambitions and its small size relative to Ethiopia led its leaders to seek an external makeweight. In 1963, Washington, Bonn, and Rome offered $10 to $15 million in military assistance, but Mogadishu rejected the offer, since it failed to match U.S. assistance to Addis Ababa, its regional rival. Somali leaders eagerly accepted a Soviet offer of twice as much aid, and following Siad Barre's takeover in 1969, Moscow sharply increased its military support, from less than $10 million to $40 million in five years. By 1974 Moscow had signed a treaty of Friendship and Cooperation and provided Mogadishu with additional arms in exchange for access to naval facilities at Berbera, including a missile servicing depot. Like the United States-Ethiopian bargain, the Soviet-Somalia "arms for access" arrangement was a quid pro quo patron-client relationship.[106] Relations between Somalia and the United States deteriorated rapidly, and by 1974 only a small development assistance program remained.[107]

Table 4.2 indicates the levels of military assistance provided to Ethiopia and Somalia, almost all from either the United States or the Soviet Union. The figures for Ethiopia show the generally steady and relatively low level of military assistance provided by the United States to Haile Sellassie's regime. The Somali numbers indicate the sharp increase in Soviet assistance to Siad in the early 1970s, far outstripping U.S. aid to Ethiopia.

Sudan's policies toward the superpowers reflected the close ties between Khartoum and Cairo and the importance of domestic considerations in Sudan's foreign policy. Nasser's influence and the domestic power of the Sudanese Communist Party led Nimeiri to favor the Soviet Union in the late 1960s and early 1970s. Khartoum was one of the principal recipients of military aid and advice from Moscow in sub-Saharan Africa, and this generosity allowed Nimeiri to expand the size of his military. However, following the 1971 coup attempt by the Sudanese Communist Party, Nimeiri began to distance his regime from Moscow. His economic needs encouraged him to turn toward the West, and after Sadat opened relations with Washington, Nimeiri felt free to move closer to the United States. Washington thus came to have good relations with both sides of the Ethiopian-Sudan cleavage, an arrangement that would not survive long.

All these relations changed rapidly following the 1974 revolution in

TABLE 4.2
Arms Imports, 1961–88 (in millions of current U.S.$)

	Ethiopia	Somalia		Ethiopia	Somalia
1961	9	1	1975	38	70
1962	11	2	1976	50	100
1963	10	2	1977	440	80
1964	6	18	1978	1,500	240
1965	10	12	1979	330	130
1966	11	5	1980	775	200
1967	13	0	1981	430	60
1968	19	4	1982	575	130
1969	12	6	1983	975	70
1970	13	7	1984	1200	70
1971	12	1	1985	775	60
1972	15	7	1986	330	20
1973	10	17	1987	1000	10
1974	14	40	1988	725	30

These figures are from U.S. Arms Control and Disarmament Agency, *World Military Expenditures and Arms Transfers* (Washington, D.C.: Government Printing Office, various years). See also Paul B. Henze, "Arming the Horn, 1960–1980," in Sven Rubenson, ed., *Proceedings of the Seventh International Conference of Ethiopian Studies*, (Addis Ababa: Institute of Ethiopian Studies, 1984), p. 653.

Ethiopia. The overthrow of Haile Sellassie's imperial structure was spontaneous, initially uncoordinated, and not the result of external intervention. The internal transformation of this state that is so central to the region, however, forced outside powers to reevaluate their policies toward the Horn and regional leaders to explore new external alignments.

The United States originally adopted a wait-and-see attitude toward the revolution. Washington hoped to be able to deal with moderates in the Provisional Military Government and feared leaving a vacuum for the Soviets to fill.[108] The *Derg* sent feelers to the Soviet Union for assistance, but Moscow initially remained cautiously noncommittal and continued to arm Somalia. As late as spring 1976, Secretary of State Kissinger agreed to send F–5E jets to Ethiopia and considered a larger military agreement to redress the growing regional arms imbalance resulting from very generous Soviet assistance to Somalia. As the figures in table 4.2 indicate, U.S. assistance jumped from a relatively steady $10 million a year under Haile Sellassie to nearly $90 million over the two-year period following the revolution. During the early years of the *Derg*, therefore, Cold War considerations, the desire to maintain some measure of influence in Addis Ababa, and the perception that the revolution was more nationalist than Marxist led the United States to continue to supply Ethiopia with weapons.[109]

By late 1976, however, this anomalous situation could not continue. Washington criticized the violence and increasing radicalism of the revolutionary government, and the *Derg* had difficulty proclaiming its "progressive" identity and differentiating itself from its predecessor so long as it accepted arms from the "imperialist" power and supporter of the ancien régime. In December 1976 Mengistu signed a secret agreement with the Soviets for $100 million worth of military equipment.[110]

The outgoing Ford administration requested no funding for Ethiopia in its last budget, although sales would continue, and the incoming Carter administration saw no reason to reverse this decision. In April 1977 the embassy notified Addis Ababa that it was ready to negotiate the termination of its access agreement to the now obsolete Kagnew Station. The *Derg* responded by announcing that Kagnew, the U.S. consulate in Asmara, and United States Information Service facilities would be closed immediately and the 1953 agreements abrogated.[111] Twenty-four years of American patronage to Ethiopia came to an end, leaving the field open for the rapid introduction of Soviet arms and influence.

While the United States was withdrawing its support from Addis Ababa, Saudi Arabia and other moderate Arab states encouraged Washington and Mogadishu to reach a modus vivendi. In mid-July 1977 Washington agreed in principle to sell defensive arms to Somalia, an encouragement Mogadishu apparently misinterpreted as a green light to mount an invasion of the Ogaden.[112] Washington quickly suspended the arms discussions and refused to supply Somalia so long as it maintained troops in Ethiopia.

The Soviet Union did not cut its ties immediately with Somalia, but apparently hoped to keep close working relations there while simultaneously helping the revolutionary government in Addis Ababa. Table 4.2 indicates that Somalia received twice the amount of military assistance from the Soviet Union in 1975 and 1976 as Addis Ababa received from the United States. This imbalance in assistance undoubtedly encouraged Siad to try to resolve the Ogaden issue militarily. Throughout the summer of 1977, even while the Somali military was fighting Ethiopian troops in the Ogaden, Moscow continued to unload military supplies in Mogadishu, and in August 1977 Siad visited Moscow.[113]

The well-armed Somali army quickly moved through the Ogaden, and by September 1977 Ethiopia appeared to be on the verge of disintegration. The Somalis captured Jijiga, cut the Addis Ababa-Djibouti railroad, and seemed about to overrun the important city of Harer. In the north, the Eritreans and other rebel groups, many supported indirectly by the Soviets through radical Arab states, intensified their campaigns against the increasingly vulnerable central government. Addis Ababa, therefore, was caught in a vise, created largely by Soviet support for Ethiopia's enemies.

At this dire point for the *Derg,* the Soviets abandoned their effort to straddle the difference and sent a massive airlift of weapons, advisers, and troops to Addis Ababa's rescue. The embattled regime received an estimated $440 million in arms in 1977 and $1.5 billion in 1978, almost all from the Soviet Union. In retaliation, Siad Barre ejected the Soviets from Somalia, and for the moment was left without superpower support. With massive Soviet backing and the assistance of seventeen thousand Cuban advisers and fighting units, the Ethiopian army turned back the Somalis. By March 1978 Somali troops had been forced to withdraw from all Ethiopian territory.

By the turn of the decade, therefore, in one of modern diplomacy's more notable *tours de valse,* Ethiopia and Somalia had both switched external partners, and the external patrons found that their new regional partners were nearly as intractable as the old.

After the Somali defeat in the Ogaden, the United States and the Soviet Union consolidated their positions in their new client states. Addis Ababa and Moscow signed a Treaty of Friendship in November 1978. Despite the level and importance of Soviet support, friction soon developed between the two. Soviet and East German advisers tried to persuade Mengistu to organize a Marxist-Leninist "vanguard" party, but the Ethiopian leaders, fearing the possible political strength of such a party, waited until 1984 to put a party formally in place.[114] Ethiopia and its East Bloc allies also differed on how to deal with Eritrea. Moscow gained access to naval facilities in the Dahlak Islands, but these were not comparable to those lost at Berbera in Somalia.

The United States, concerned about the collapse of Iran and seeking facilities for its new Rapid Deployment Force, negotiated an agreement with Somalia in August 1980 whereby Mogadishu granted access to the port of Berbera in exchange for economic and military aid. However, Washington held up military assistance until Somali troops had withdrawn from the Ogaden. Understandably, under such circumstances, relations between the two states developed slowly and somewhat cautiously.[115]

In the mid–1970s, Nimeiri too altered his foreign alignment and completed his move from Soviet to American patronage. This search for a new makeweight to counter hostile neighbors intensified following the 1976 coup attempt supported by both Libya and Ethiopia. Sudan expelled the remaining Soviet advisers in 1977 and, by presenting an image of a bulwark against Soviet, Libyan, and revolutionary Ethiopian ambitions, won considerable aid from the Reagan administration. The relationship, however, grew more tentative as Sadiq replaced Nimeiri and improved his relations with Libya in an effort to balance Egypt's influence.

Responding to the changes taking place in the regional configuration and the sharp decline in U.S.-Ethiopian relations in the mid–1970s, Washington strengthened its relations with Nairobi. Kenya not only offered a pro-Western ideology and relatively strong economy but also became important strategically as events in the Horn and the collapse of the shah in Iran threatened American interests. The United States and Kenya signed their first military agreement in 1975, and by 1980 Nairobi had received $109 million in military assistance and Washington negotiated access to the port of Mombasa for its rapid deployment forces.[116]

Djibouti had to remain neutral in the threatening Ethiopia-Somalia conflict to avoid domestic ethnic strife and being dragged into the struggle. It needed support from beyond the region to dissuade its neighbors from challenging its independence but could not turn to either of the superpowers without seeming to support one side or the other in the Ethiopia-Somalia conflict. Djibouti therefore requested the French to continue to garrison some four thousand to five thousand troops in the former colony. Outside power thereby was brought in without Djibouti becoming entangled in regional or global conflicts. In addition Djibouti joined the Arab League and Saudi Arabia provided important economic assistance.[117]

This close look at the complex reversal of superpower patronage in the late 1970s suggests a dynamic at work well beyond the control of the United States or the Soviet Union. The precipitant of these changes, the Ethiopian revolution, originated and developed in response to local conditions, not Soviet initiatives. Somalis were tempted by the disorders in Ethiopia to try to realize the dream of a Greater Somalia, in part thanks to the large arms transfers from the Soviet Union but apparently without the endorsement of either superpower. Sudan moved toward the United States in response to internal demands and changed Egyptian policies.

These shifts in superpower patrons, however, did not alter the fundamental regional pattern of relations. The rivalries between Ethiopia and Somalia, Ethiopia and Sudan, and to a lesser extent, Somalia and Kenya are conflicts that superpower interventions seem unable to change. London in the late 1940s, Washington in the early 1960s, and Moscow in the mid–1970s all tried to establish and maintain influence on both sides of the Ethiopia-Somalia cleavage without success. External patrons may change but the structures of regional rivalries endure.

The depth and bitterness of the local differences provided the entry point for outside powers interested in gaining influence within the

Horn, in using regional facilities for purposes having little to do with the region itself, or in blocking their major power competitor. The superpowers were involved by invitation because the prospective client hoped that in this way it could improve its position vis-à-vis its regional rivals.[118]

External support brought a supply of weapons that increased the military character of the indigenous rivalries. Consequently, each encounter became more destructive, and long-stalemated rivalries became far more costly in human terms than before. No doubt, each client hoped the increment of sophistication would give it that margin of advantage it sought. But since each protagonist generally finds some outside support, the stalemate merely continued at a heightened level of conflict.

Decline in Cold War Rivalry

The decline in Cold War competition in the late 1980s resulted in diminished superpower interest in the Horn of Africa. Moscow, preoccupied with internal challenges, signaled its desire to disengage from the region. In 1988 Soviet officials threatened to reduce military shipments to Addis Ababa unless Mengistu participated in negotiations for a "just solution" to the conflict in Eritrea.[119] The United States and the Soviet Union cooperated in supporting the Carter peace initiative and the talks organized by U.S. Assistant Secretary of State for African Affairs Herman Cohen. Moscow, as we saw, stood aside when Mengistu fell in 1991 and remained on the sidelines during the transition process.

Washington also distanced itself from its old regional clients in the late 1980s and early 1990s. Human rights violations throughout the region, chaos in Somalia, the Sudanese government's fundamentalist policies and reluctance to engage in conflict resolution, and Kenya's crackdown on pro-democracy activists convinced Washington that, in the absence of persuasive strategic interests, it could afford to disengage from its former clients. With the exception of humanitarian aid and assistance channeled through such organizations as the United Nations High Commission for Refugees, the United States suspended support to Sudan, Somalia, and Kenya.[120] Without Cold War competition from the Soviet Union, the United States exhibited little interest in becoming heavily involved in these states until their leaders demonstrate their commitment to ending conflict and promoting human rights and greater popular participation.

In Ethiopia, however, U.S. involvement increased significantly in the early 1990s. Washington became convinced that developments within Ethiopia provided an opportunity to promote conflict resolution and humanitarian goals such as human rights, democracy, and famine relief.

Under the leadership of Assistant Secretary Cohen the United States promoted talks between Mengistu and the Eritrean People's Liberation Front (EPLF) in 1990 and early 1991. Following Mengistu's downfall, Cohen chaired a conference in London designed to encourage a smooth transition.[121]

Washington endorsed the EPLF's control of Eritrea and the Ethiopian People's Revolutionary Democratic Front's move into Addis Ababa. Although the United States simply accepted military facts on the ground it could not alter the situation, many Ethiopians objected.[122] United States officials tried to encourage the new leaders to deliver on their promises of reform by linking U.S. assistance to democratization in Ethiopia.[123]

This unfolding experience suggests that the roles external powers will play in the Horn of Africa in the aftermath of the Cold War will differ in important ways from previous patterns. In areas of marginal interest, the absence of Cold War zero-sum competition for global influence will lead the great powers to disengage from states that resist pressures to resolve internal conflicts and introduce reforms to promote democracy and the protection of human rights. The logic that led Washington and others to support authoritarian leaders in the past out of fear that if it did not, Moscow would—and one more state would be lost to communism—no longer motivated policy in the 1990s. The United States, therefore, could disengage itself to a large extent from Sudan, Somalia, and Kenya. In Ethiopia, in contrast, Washington perceived an unusual opportunity to promote its goals of conflict resolution, human rights, and democracy and therefore increased its efforts. External powers such as the United States can encourage such humanitarian policies, but internal dynamics and actions by regional government and nongovernment leaders still will control the timing and the success of such reforms.

Conclusions

The Horn of Africa forms a regional power system centered on Ethiopia and including Somalia, Djibouti, Kenya, Sudan, and several dissident nationalist movements that challenge the central governments' monopoly of power. The system constitutes the environment within which all these actors must maneuver to protect their interests and achieve what security they can. The historical evolution of these states has left them all vulnerable. Geographic proximity coupled with contradictory but intermeshed security goals compel the states to interact.

Ethiopia is the pivotal state in the system, and all the regional actors must concern themselves with this potentially hegemonic power. Ethiopia's neighbors have dealt with their large neighbor by individually seeking outside assistance and attempting to weaken the core power by supporting disgruntled rebel groups. It is notable that Ethiopia's opponents have not formed an anti-Ethiopian defensive alliance among themselves as a balancing strategy. Instead, the region is marked by a series of bilateral relationships between Ethiopia and each of its neighbors.

The Ethiopia-Somalia pair represents an enduring conflict between two states that are based on contradictory principles and overlapping territorial identities. Multinational Ethiopia has claimed the rights of a long-established state to encompass peoples of a variety of cultural, linguistic, and religious backgrounds, whereas Somalia has asserted that all Somali-speaking peoples, including those within the Ogaden, should be within a unified nation-state. The Ethiopia-Eritrea conflict is a clash between the incompatible ideals and norms of self-determination for a distinct people and the territorial integrity of a multinational state. Ethiopia and Sudan are generally in conflict because their respective domestic vulnerabilities and dissident nationalist movements have led each to threaten the other's territorial integrity and legitimacy by supporting regional rebellions. Djibouti enters the system as an important outlet to the sea for Ethiopia and as a part of Mogadishu's goal of creating a Greater Somalia. Kenya's role is that of the only state in the system that has a cooperative relationship with Ethiopia because the two states shared a fear of Somalia. These regional rivalries and roles have endured despite the many changes in government leadership, ideology, and external alignment.

In this contentious and dangerous environment, the states of the Horn employ a variety of means to improve their regional security. All use diplomacy in efforts to promote their interests in the region and to find balancing support by establishing relations with powers in the Middle East and with the great powers beyond the regional system. Some try to build up military power to defend themselves, most frequently by seeking materiel and training support from one or the other superpower. Along with bolstering their own strength, they often seek to weaken their regional rivals by encouraging rebellion next door or intervening by proxy.

Superpower involvement increased the military capabilities of the regional states but did not cause the conflicts. Even though each of these patron-client relationships has been highly asymmetrical, the external power has shown only a limited ability to affect either domestic reforms or the direction of foreign policies if the local regime opposed them.[124] Washington's substantial economic and military assistance gave it only slight influence on Haile Sellassie's internal reforms or regional foreign policy. Similarly, Moscow exchanged military supplies to Mogadishu for access to naval facilities in Somalia but had little control over Mogadishu's irredentist policies. The expulsion of superpower advisers—Soviet Union from Sudan and Somalia, United States from Ethiopia (all in 1977)—demonstrates that client states, if they do not border the patron and have access to alternative sources of support, can ignore pressure and even break ties to their patrons when they perceive it to be in their interests.

The limited ability of external powers to force regional states to take actions contrary to the local leaders' perceptions of their interests is likely to erode further in the 1990s. With the decline in Cold War competition, neither the United States nor the Soviet Union has compelling strategic interests in the Horn of Africa. In the early 1990s, Washington suspended or drastically reduced military support to Kenya, Somalia, and Sudan. Moscow ended its support for Ethiopia, indicating its desire to disengage from the contentious region. Washington's leverage over the transition in Ethiopia following Mengistu's downfall was the result of Ethiopian leaders seeking to interest the United States and gain assistance by acting to promote U.S. humanitarian goals. Until other regional leaders also demonstrate their commitment to reform, external powers are unlikely to become intensively engaged.

The withdrawal of the superpowers, anxious to concentrate on Central Europe, the Gulf, and global economic restructuring, may not reduce conflict in the region. An arms embargo eventually may reduce the level of combat, but the region is currently so awash in military equipment that considerable fighting can continue for some time. In addition, Middle Eastern states have moved in to an extent as Washington and Moscow have withdrawn. This trend may heighten conflict if the political struggles of the Middle East are fought by proxy in the Horn. Finally, the withdrawal of superpower involvement by itself will not resolve any of the conflicts. The complex, intertwined, and enduring disputes are rooted firmly in the nature of the states in the region and their contradictory security needs and aspirations.

Enduring resolution of the conflicts has eluded the leaders of the Horn. Only Djibouti, where a stalemate between covetous neighbors and the presence of French troops has preserved a peaceful status quo, and northern Kenya, where declining Somali interest and Kenyan policies designed to incorporate ethnic Somalis have allowed a quieting of tensions, have avoided conflict in recent years. Transient periods of détente—such as that pursued by the Egal regime in Somalia toward Kenya and Ethiopia, the decade following the Addis Ababa Accords in the southern Sudan, and the current normalization between Ethiopia and Somalia—have broken the pattern of conflict. These periods of reduced tensions, however, rarely addressed the major issues of antithetical state goals or broke the perceptions of zero-sum conflict. Therefore, they usually did not last.

Relations in the Horn of Africa have been dominated by the intensely anarchic character of the system. It has not evolved into either a stable balance of power, an established multilateral system, or a one-power hegemonic system. The Horn forms a system "where each state recognized no other legitimate sovereign unit except itself, and where relations among units took the form of a continuous struggle for dominance."[125]

The system lacks consensus on such basic questions as what constitutes a legitimate participant. Somalia has insisted that the only legitimate actor is the nation-state. But no true nation-state yet exists in the Horn. Somalia is an incomplete nation-state and the other members are all multinational states. Kenya, Ethiopia, and Djibouti do not recognize Greater Somalia as an acceptable basis for legitimacy. Leaders in Eritrea have differed with leaders in Addis Ababa on what should be the proper political unit or basis of sovereignty. Both Sudan and Ethiopia have recognized and assisted dissident groups that the other cannot tolerate. Neither Addis Ababa nor Khartoum have recognized the sovereign right of their neighbor to exercise a monopoly of force and authority over the territory it claims.

Furthermore, large segments of the population of the region do not recognize the legitimacy of the government that asserts its sovereignty over them. The undemocratic and often repressive regimes of the region have tried to rule by force and without the participation of important constituencies. Such policies inspire and feed resistance, often armed rebellion. This pervasive alienation and dissension both weakens the regimes and provides easy opportunities for hostile neighbors to interfere that further undermines the states' authority.

The lack of agreement on the basic definition of the constituent parts of the system has led to a pattern of conflict that often seems to follow no rules. Various states have at times attempted to overthrow their neighbor's government, have aided secessionist groups, have engaged in economic warfare and hostile propaganda campaigns, and have violated each others' borders. They have invited hostile outside powers into the system and allowed their territory to serve as bases of subversion by dissident exile groups. Both the central regimes and various internal insurgencies have used starvation as a weapon in their political struggles and have pursued their conflicts with little regard for the terrible costs to civilians.

Despite this appearance of complete anarchy, a number of observable patterns have shaped expectations in the system. The first might be called a first-stage Kautilya model.[126]

This occurs when a statesman perceives that "my neighbor is my enemy." He may have good reason to think so if his neighbor has in fact been causing him trouble—encouraging dissidence and supporting unrest, raiding across his frontier, threatening to invade. He may also find it useful to make his neighbor out to be more of a threat than he really is. When a leader cannot count on the loyalty of the peoples who make up his state, to raise the cry of the threatening neighbor whenever cohesion seems in doubt may enhance solidarity and draw the population more closely to support the regime. Regional opposition leaders adopt the same strategy: Calls against Arab imperialism in the southern Sudan and Amhara domination in Eritrea create a sense of common identity in a diverse population by depicting the central government as the common enemy.

At least in South Asia and in the Gulf, when states perceive that their neighbors are their enemies, their neighbor's neighbor becomes their friend. This second-stage Kautilya pattern creates a kind of checkerboard, wherein each state is hostile to its immediate neighbor but friendly to the next adjoining state.[127] Such a pattern increases cooperation on one level while dividing the region into competing blocs on another.

It is emblematic of the character of the Horn as a system that Ethiopia is the only state that has successfully joined in second-stage Kautilya relationships with its neighbors. The Ethiopia-Kenya alliance, for example, is based on shared hostility to their common neighbor, Somalia.[128] Ethiopia, Libya, and the PDRY also joined into a defensive Kautilyan relationship in the 1980s. This alliance of Sudan's and Somalia's neighbors with the central power of the system helped Ethiopia leap over the hostile ring surrounding it.

The other members of the Horn of Africa regional system have not created a second-stage Kautilya alliance to balance the central power despite their common fear of Ethiopia. This is partly explained by Somalia's irredentist goals. The dream of Greater Somaliland threatened Kenya and Djibouti, two of Ethiopia's neighbors, and thereby made them loathe to cooperate in an alliance with Mogadishu. Furthermore, Mogadishu's irredentism was considered illegitimate by the other states in the region and the OAU, because, if successful, it would bring into public doubt numerous other African frontiers.

For the Horn of Africa system to evolve into a less violent, more cooperative system, agreement must be reached on the definition and identity of the constituent parts. The legitimacy of actors and recognized borders must be established. Such agreement will require the development of solutions to internal political conflicts and the institutionalization of systems of government that encourage participation and inclusion, rather than resistance and alienation. Regimes and states recognized as legitimate by both their own people and neighboring states will reduce each state's vulnerability and provide each with a cushion of security to encourage them to run the risks implicit in cooperating where distrust has been enduring and intense.[129]

Along with the resolution of internal political struggles and the creation of more stable, legitimate states, the Horn of Africa needs a regional order that includes shared rules and expectations. At present the member states are involved in a nearly continuous and violent struggle to establish the organizing principles of the region. If rules could be agreed on to define limits to acceptable regional behavior, as has developed in the ASEAN region, for example, then insecurity from next door would be substantially reduced. The Intergovernmental Authority on Drought and Development includes all Horn of Africa states and has served a useful function coordinating some development initiatives and providing the venue for leaders to meet, but it has not expanded to serve as an organization that really shapes or constrains regional relations.

In 1991 the governments of Somalia and Ethiopia fell and rival insurgent groups struggled for control. Kenya experienced serious unrest, although not armed rebellion, and Sudan's government lost control of large segments of the countryside. The constituent member states appeared to be facing collapse. It was possible that the emergence of new states, notably Eritrea, would transform the structure of the regional system. Alternatively, the persistence of the regional system of relations, despite many regime changes and internal transformations, such as the Ethiopian revolution, suggests that the same security dilemmas and other difficulties may continue to face future regimes.

The Horn of Africa system, therefore, is a regional system in an early stage of evolution. The states have a long history of intensive interaction, but the volatile nature of their domestic politics and institutions and the lack of consensus on rank and rules of behavior have prevented more stable regional relations. It is therefore a system marked by endemic conflict in which the most vulnerable individuals—refugees, small farmers, pastoralists, and workers—suffer the most. The geographic, social, and political ties among the members of the system prevent any one of the major actors from opting out of the system. Decreasing conflict will therefore require not reducing the level of interaction but regularizing relations, making them more predictable and restraining the temptation of each to attempt to manipulate the internal affairs of his neighbor.

NOTES

1. Barry Buzan, *People, States, and Fear: The National Security Problem in International Relations* (Chapel Hill: University of North Carolina Press, 1983), p. 106.

2. Mesfin Wolde-Mariam, "The Horn of Africa: Ethnoconflict Versus Development," paper presented at the International Symposium on the African Horn, University of Cairo, January 1985.

3. Christopher Clapham, "The Horn of Africa," in Michael Crowder, ed., *The Cambridge History of Africa*, vol. 8 (New York: Praeger, 1977), p. 458, and Christopher Clapham, "Ethiopia and Somalia," *Conflicts in Africa*, Adelphi Paper no. 93 (1972), p. 2.

4. I. William Zartman, *Ripe for Resolution: Conflict and Intervention in Africa* (New York: Oxford University Press, 1985), p. 77.

5. United States Committee for Refugees, *World Refugee Survey, 1991* (Washington, D.C.: U.S. Committee for Refugees, 1991).

6. Atieno Odhiambo, "The Economics of Conflict Among Marginalized Peoples of Eastern Africa," in Francis M. Deng and I. William Zartman, eds., *Conflict Resolution in Africa* (Washington, D.C.: Brookings Institution, 1991), pp. 292–96.

7. Donald Rothchild and Naomi Chazan, eds. *The Precarious Balance: State and Society in Africa* (Boulder, Colo.: Westview, 1988).

8. See S. K. B. Asante, *Pan-African Protest: West Africa and the Italo-Ethiopian Crisis, 1934–1941* (London: Longman, 1977) for a discussion of the symbolic importance of Ethiopia to such diverse African nationalists as Kwame Nkrumah, Leopold Senghor, and Jomo Kenyatta.

9. Donald Donham and Wendy James, eds., *The Southern Marches of Imperial Ethiopia: Essays in History and Social Anthropology* (Cambridge: Cambridge University Press, 1986) includes several excellent essays on this process.

10. On Amhara political culture see Donald N. Levine, "Ethiopia: Identity, Authority, and Realism" in Lucian W. Pye and Sidney Verba, eds., *Political Culture and Political Development* (Princeton: Princeton University Press, 1965); Christopher Clapham, *Transformation and Continuity in Revolutionary Ethiopia* (Cambridge: Cambridge University Press, 1988), pp. 195–201.

11. For a detailed study on how this worked on a microlevel in northern Ethiopia, see James McCann, *From Poverty to Famine in Northeast Ethiopia* (Philadelphia: University of Pennsylvania Press, 1987).

12. Harold G. Marcus, *Haile Sellassie I: The Formative Years, 1892–1936* (Berkeley: University of California Press, 1987); John Markakis, *Ethiopia: Anatomy of a Traditional Polity* (Oxford: Clarendon Press, 1974), p. 337.

13. Gebru Tereke, "Rural Protest in Ethiopia, 1941–1970: A Study of Three Rebellions," Ph.D. dissertation, Syracuse University, 1977.

14. Haile Selassie, *Important Utterances of H.I.M. Emperor Haile Selassie I, 1963–1972* (Addis Ababa: Imperial Ethiopian Ministry of Information, 1972), p. 6.

15. The phrase is from John Markakis, *National and Class Conflict in the Horn of Africa* (Cambridge: Cambridge University Press, 1987), p. xvii.

16. For discussions of Ethiopia's postrevolution politics see Clapham, *Transformation and Continuity in Revolutionary Ethiopia*; John W. Harbeson, *The Ethiopian Transformation: The Quest for the Post-Imperial State* (Boulder, Colo.: Westview, 1988); Edmond J. Keller, *Revolutionary Ethiopia: From Empire to People's Republic* (Bloomington: Indiana University Press, 1988).

17. "Ethiopia: A Blow-by-Blow Account," *Africa Confidential* 30(11) (May 26, 1989):1–3.

18. "Text of Mengistu's Speech to WPE Committee," *The Ethiopian Herald*, March 8, 1990, reprinted in *Foreign Broadcast Information Service Daily Report (Sub-Saharan Africa)*, April 6, 1990, pp. 5–21. See Alain Gascon, "La Perestroïka à l'Ethiopienne: Le Pari de Mengistu," *Politique Africaine*, 38 (June 1990): 121–26.

19. Clifford Krauss, "Ethiopia and 3 Rebel Groups Look Toward U.S.-Led Peace Talks," *New York Times*, May 14, 1991, p. A6; Michael Binyon, "West Acts as Midwife at Birth of New Leadership," *Times* (London), May 14, 1991, p. 9.

20. Menilek's 1891 circular letter to European heads of state printed in Richard Greenfield, *Ethiopia: A New Political History*, (London: Pall Mall Press, 1965), pp. 464–65.

21. Menilek's 1891 letter printed in Greenfield, *Ethiopia*, pp. 464–65. On Menilek's diplomacy see Harold G. Marcus, *The Life and Times of Menelik II: Ethiopia, 1844–1913* (Oxford: Clarendon Press, 1975), pp. 135–73.

22. Sven Rubenson, *The Survival of Ethiopian Independence* (New York: Africana, 1976), p. 409; Donald N. Levine, *Greater Ethiopia: The Evolution of a Multiethnic Society* (Chicago: University of Chicago Press, 1974), p. 87.

23. "PMAC Chairman and the World Press" (Addis Ababa: Ministry of Information and National Guidance, 1978), p. 20. Mengistu used similar images in conversations with Kurt Jansson, the director of the United Nations Relief Operation in Ethiopia. See Kurt Jansson, Michael Harris, and Angela Penrose, *The Ethiopian Famine* (London: Zed, 1987), pp. 28, 50.

24. "President Mengistu Addresses Nation," *FBIS, Africa*, April 26, 1991, pp. 5–18.

25. G. K. N. Trevaskis, *Eritrea: A Colony in Transition* (Oxford: Oxford University Press, 1960).

26. Lloyd Ellingson, "The Origins and Development of the Eritrean Liberation Movement," in Robert L. Hess, ed., *Proceedings of the Fifth International Conference on Ethiopian Studies*, Part B (Chicago: University of Chicago Press, 1977); Bereket Habte Selassie, *Conflict and Intervention in the Horn of Africa* (New York: Monthly Review Press, 1980).

27. For information on the various Eritrean movements see Haggai Erlich, *The Struggle Over Eritrea, 1962–1978* (Stanford, Calif.: Hoover Institution Press, 1983).

28. Abdurahman Jama Barre, *Salient Aspects of Somalia's Foreign Policy: Selected Speeches* (Mogadishu: Ministry of Foreign Affairs, 1978), p. 37.

29. Clifford Krauss, "Ethiopians Have New Rulers, but Famine's Specter Lingers," *New York Times*, June 14, 1991.

30. Francis Mading Deng, "The Identity Factor in the Sudanese Conflict,"

and John O. Voll, "Northern Muslim Perspectives," in Joseph E. Montville, ed., *Conflict and Peacemaking in Multiethnic Societies* (Lexington, Mass.: Lexington Books, 1989); Dunstan Wai, "Revolution, Rhetoric, and Reality in the Sudan," *Journal of Modern African Studies*, 17(1) (March 1979):71–93.

31. See P. M. Holt and M. W. Daly, *A History of the Sudan: From the Coming of Islam to the Present Day*, 4th ed. (London: Longman, 1986); John O. Voll and Sarah Potts Voll, *The Sudan: Unity and Diversity in a Multicultural State* (Boulder, Colo.: Westview, 1985); Peter Woodward, *Sudan, 1898–1989: The Unstable State* (Boulder, Colo.: Lynne Rienner, 1990).

32. Woodward, *Sudan, 1898–1989*, pp. 115, 117.

33. For a concise review see Nelson Kasfir, "One Full Revolution: The Politics of Sudanese Military Government, 1969–1985," in John W. Harbeson, ed., *The Military in African Politics* (New York: Praeger, 1987).

34. Samuel M. Makinda, "Sudan: Old Wine in New Bottles," *Orbis*, 31(2) (Summer 1987):218.

35. See Ann Mosely Lesch, "A View from Khartoum," *Foreign Affairs*, 65(4) (Spring 1987):807–26; and Marina Ottaway, "Post-Numeiri Sudan: One Year On," *Third World Quarterly*, 9(3) (July 1987):891–905.

36. Kamal Osman Salih, "The Sudan, 1985–9: The Fading Democracy," *Journal of Modern African Studies*, 28(3) (1990):199–224; Woodward, *Sudan, 1898–1989*, p. 115.

37. Hizkias Assefa, *Mediation of Civil Wars: Approaches and Strategies—The Sudan Conflict* (Boulder, Colo.: Westview, 1987). For an important firsthand account see Abel Alier, *The Southern Sudan: Too Many Agreements Dishonored* (Exeter, England: Ithaca Press, 1990).

38. Nelson Kasfir, "Peacemaking and Social Cleavages in Sudan," in Montville, ed., *Conflict and Peacemaking in Multiethnic Societies*.

39. Francis Deng and Prosser Gifford, eds., *The Search for Peace and Unity in the Sudan* (Washington, D.C.: Wilson Center Press, 1987).

40. Ann Mosely Lesch, "Confrontation in the Southern Sudan," *Middle East Journal*, 40(3) (Summer 1986):410–28. It is not as clear, however, that the majority of the SPLA endorses Garang's national goals.

41. See the discussion in Abdel Ghaffar M. Ahmed and Gunnar M. Sorbo, eds., *Management of the Crisis in the Sudan: Proceeding of the Bergen Forum, 23–24 February 1989* (Bergen, Norway: University of Bergen Centre for Development Studies, 1989).

42. I. M. Lewis, *A Modern History of Somalia: Nation and State in the Horn of Africa* (London: Longman, 1980); David D. Laitin and Said S. Samatar, *Somalia: Nation in Search of a State* (Boulder, Colo.: Westview Press, 1987).

43. Laitin and Samatar, *Somalia*, p. 129.

44. Laitin and Samatar, *Somalia*, pp. 30–31. See also I. M. Lewis, "The Ogaden and the Fragility of Somali Segmentary Nationalism," *African Affairs* 88(353) (October 1989):573–84.

45. John Drysdale, *The Somali Dispute* (London: Pall Mall Press, 1964), p. 7.

46. Negussay Ayele, "Somalia's Relations with Her Neighbors: From 'Greater Somalia' to 'Western Somalia' to 'Somali Refugees' to . . . ," in Sven

Rubenson, ed., *Proceedings of the Seventh International Conference of Ethiopian Studies* (Uppsala: Scandinavian Institute of African Studies, 1984), pp. 659–60.

47. Saadia Touval, *The Boundary Politics of Independent Africa* (Cambridge, Mass.: Harvard University Press, 1972), p. 34; A. A. Castagno, "Somali Republic," in James S. Coleman and Carl G. Rosberg, Jr., eds., *Political Parties and National Integration in Tropical Africa* (Berkeley: University of California Press, 1964), p. 553.

48. "Somalia: President Osman Visits Northern Region, Speech in Burao," *Foreign Broadcast Information Service*, September 12, 1962, p. 1.

49. Republic of Somalia, *Somalia: A Divided Nation Seeking Reunification* (Mogadishu: Ministry of Information, 1965), p. 48. See the similar statement by Prime Minister 'Abdillahi 'Ise cited in Lewis, *A Modern History of Somalia*, p. 161.

50. Marina Ottaway, "Superpower Competition and Regional Conflicts in the Horn of Africa" in Craig Nation and Mark V. Kauppi, eds., *The Soviet Impact in Africa* (Lexington, Mass.: Lexington Books, 1984), p. 175.

51. David Laitin, "War in the Ogaden: Implications for Siyaad's Role in Somali History," *Journal of Modern African Studies*, vol. 17, no. 1 (1979).

52. Harry Ododa, "Somalia's Domestic Policies and Foreign Relations Since the Ogaden War of 1977–78," *Middle Eastern Studies*, vol. 21, no. 3 (July 1985).

53. "Somalia: Where Do We Go From Here?" *Africa Confidential*, 32(3) (February 8, 1991):1–2.

54. "Part of Somalia Declares Its Independence," *Washington Post*, May 20, 1991.

55. Virginia Thompson and Richard Adloff, *Djibouti and the Horn of Africa* (Stanford: Stanford University Press, 1978); Nancy A. Schilling, "Problems of Political Development in a Ministate: The French Territory of Afars and Issas," *Journal of Developing Areas*, 7(4) (July 1973):613–34.

56. Alain Fenet, "Djibouti: Mini-State on the Horn of Africa," in *Horn of Africa: From "Scramble for Africa" to East-West Conflict* (Bonn: Forschungsinstitut der Friedrich Ebert Stiftune, 1986):59–69.

57. A. A. Castagno, "The Somali-Kenya Controversy: Implications for the Future," *The Journal of Modern African Studies*, 2(2) (July 1964):165–88; see also Drysdale, *The Somali Dispute*.

58. For a pessimistic assessment see "Kenya: How Long Can Moi Survive?" *Africa Confidential*, 31(14) (July 31, 1990):1–2.

59. J. Spencer Trimingham, *Islam in Ethiopia* (Oxford: Oxford University Press, 1952).

60. See Mesfin Wolde Mariam, *The Background of the Ethio-Somalia Boundary Dispute* (Addis Ababa: Berhanena Selam, 1964); Mesfin Wolde Mariam, *Somalia: The Problem Child of Africa* (Addis Ababa: Artistic Printing Press, 1977); and Drysdale, *The Somali Dispute*.

61. Buzan, *People, States, and Fear*, p. 78.

62. Zartman, *Ripe for Resolution*, pp. 75–76.

63. I. William Zartman and W. Scott Thompson, "The Development of

Norms in the African System," in Yassin El-Ayouty, ed., *The Organization of African Unity After Ten Years* (New York: Praeger, 1975).

64. Ted Gurr, "Tensions in the Horn of Africa," in Feliks Gross, *World Politics and Tension Areas* (New York: New York University Press, 1966), pp. 316–65.

65. Robert F. Gorman, *Political Conflict in the Horn of Africa* (New York: Praeger, 1981), pp. 66–68.

66. Ahmed I. Samatar, "Somalia's Impasse: State Power and Dissent Politics," *Third World Quarterly*, 9(3) (July 1987):871–90.

67. Touval, *Boundary Politics*, p. 235. See also Zartman, *Ripe for Resolution*, pp. 89–90.

68. See the comments by Somali Prime Minister Mohamed Ali Samantar printed in Foreign Broadcast Information Service, *Daily Report*, February 10, 1989 and the Economist Intelligence Unit, *Country Report: Uganda, Ethiopia, Somalia, Djibouti*, no. 4 (1988), p. 31.

69. J. Boyer Bell, "Endemic Insurgency and International Order: The Eritrean Example," *Orbis*, 18(2) (Summer 1974):430.

70. See Basil Davidson, Lionel Cliffe, and Bereket Habte Selassie, eds., *Behind the War in Eritrea* (Nottingham: Spokesman, 1980) and Bereket Habte Selassie, *Conflict and Intervention in the Horn of Africa*.

71. Erlich, *The Struggle Over Eritrea*, p. 83.

72. Marina Ottaway, "Eritrea and Ethiopia: Negotiations in a Transitional Conflict," paper presented at a conference on Negotiations in Internal Conflicts, Johns Hopkins University/SAIS, Washington, D.C., March 1990.

73. "Ethiopia's Leader Regaining Control," *New York Times*, May 21, 1989; "Soviet's Press Ethiopia to End War, Envoys Say," *Washington Post*, April 21, 1989.

74. Clifford Krauss, "Conflicting Peace Plans Offered in Ethiopia Strife," *New York Times*, February 24, 1991, p. A11. See Terrence Lyons, "Post–Cold War Superpower Roles in the Horn of Africa," paper presented at the Second Conflict Reduction in Regional Conflicts Conference, Bologna, Italy, May 1991.

75. Blaine Harden, "Eritrean Rebels to Form Own Rule, Separate from Ethiopian Government," *Washington Post*, May 30, 1991.

76. *African Research Bulletin, Political, Social, and Cultural Series*, July 1976, pp. 4092–94. See *Horn of Africa*, vol. 8, no. 1 (1985).

77. "Progressives, Patriots Called on to Join Forces to Defend Motherland, Revolution of the Masses," *Ethiopian Herald*, January 30, 1977.

78. See the statement by the Ethiopian prime minister in "Ethio-Sudan Joint Communique, *Ethiopian Herald*, December 22, 1988.

79. For analysis on host-insurgent relations see I. William Zartman, "Introduction," in I. William Zartman, ed., *Negotiations in Internal Conflict* (forthcoming).

80. "Good-Neighborliness: For Stability and Mutual Progress," *EPRDF News Bulletin*, 1(14) (October 30, 1991):1.

81. For a presentation of Somalia's case see The Republic of Somalia, *French Somaliland: A Classic Colonial Case*.

82. Zartman, *Ripe for Resolution*, p. 102.

83. Republic of Kenya, *Kenya-Somalia Relations: Narrative of Four Years of Inspired Aggression and Direct Subversion Mounted by the Somali Republic Against the Government and People of the Republic of Kenya* (Nairobi: Government Printer, 1967), p. 6.

84. Republic of Kenya, *Kenya-Somalia Relations*, p. 61.

85. For a detailed account of these negotiations see Touval, *Boundary Problems*, pp. 212–45.

86. Samuel M. Makinda, "From Quiet Diplomacy to Cold War" *Third World Politics*, 4(1) (January 1982):308.

87. See the editorial in *Daily Nation* (Nairobi) January 18, 1978, cited in *Africa Research Bulletin*, January 1978, p. 4702.

88. See the address by Deputy Assistant Secretary of State for African Affairs Irvin Hicks to the African American Institute 1990 Forum Series, November 18, 1990.

89. Mohamed Hassanein Heikal, "Egyptian Foreign Policy," *Foreign Affairs*, 56(4) (July 1978):715.

90. John Waterbury, *Hydropolitics of the Nile Valley* (Syracuse: Syracuse University Press, 1979).

91. *Africa Research Bulletin*, July 15, 1985, p. 7672.

92. Muhammad Beshir Hamid, "The 'Findlandization' of Sudan's Foreign Policy: Sudanese-Egyptian Relations Since the Camp David Accords," *Journal of Arab Affairs*, 2(2) (1983):202.

93. William B. Quandt, *Saudi Arabia in the 1980s: Foreign Policy, Security, and Oil* (Washington, D.C.: University Press of America, 1983):44.

94. Erlich, *The Struggle Over Eritrea*, pp. 67–68.

95. John Creed and Kenneth Menkhaus, "The Rise of Saudi Regional Power and the Foreign Policies of Northeast African States," *Northeast African Studies*, 8(2–3) (1986):1–22.

96. Quandt, *Saudi Arabia*, p. 45.

97. On Libya's foreign policy see Mary Jane Deeb, *Libya's Foreign Policy in North Africa* (Boulder, Colo.: Westview, 1990).

98. Peter Schwab, "Israel's Weakened Position on the Horn of Africa," *New Outlook* 21(2) (April 1978):21–27. See also Legum and Lee, *The Horn of Africa in Continuing Conflict*, pp. 69, 95.

99. Larry Cohler, "House Memo Charges Israel Arms Ethiopian Regime," *Washington Jewish Week*, July 12, 1990.

100. See Robin Bidwell, *The Two Yemens* (Essex: Longman, 1983).

101. "PMAC Pledges Democratic Rights to Masses; Mammoth Rally Here Denounces Enemies of Unity, Revolution," *Ethiopian Herald*, February 5, 1977.

102. Shimshon Zelniker, *The Superpowers and the Horn of Africa* (Center for Strategic Studies Paper No. 18, Tel Aviv University, September 1982), pp. 35–38.

103. Harold G. Marcus, *Ethiopia, Great Britain, and the United States: The Politics of Empire* (Berkeley: University of California Press, 1983).

104. Terrence P. Lyons, "The United States and Ethiopia: The Politics of a Patron-Client Relationship," *Northeast African Studies*, 8(2–3) (1986):53–75.

105. John H. Spencer, *Ethiopia at Bay: A Personal Account of the Haile Selassie Years* (Algonac, Mich.: Reference Publications, 1984), p. 262.

106. Richard B. Remnek, "The Soviet-Somali 'Arms for Access' Relationship," *Soviet Union/Union Soviétique*, 10, part 1 (1983):59.

107. Donald K. Petterson, "Somalia and the United States, 1977–1983: The New Relationship," in Gerald J. Bender, James S. Coleman, and Richard L. Sklar, eds., *African Crisis Areas and U.S. Foreign Policy* (Berkeley: University of California Press, 1985), p. 195.

108. On the question of U.S. relations with Ethiopia following the revolution, compare Negussay Ayele, "The Horn of Africa: Revolutionary Developments and Western Reactions," *Northeast African Studies*, vol. 2, no. 2 (1980–81), 3(1) (1981):1–29 with Donald Petterson, "Ethiopia Abandoned? An American Perspective," *International Affairs*, 62(4) (Autumn 1986):627–45.

109. Terrence Lyons, "Reaction to Revolution: United States–Ethiopian Relations, 1974–1977," Ph.D. dissertation, Johns Hopkins University, 1991.

110. Robert G. Patman, *The Soviet Union in the Horn of Africa* (Cambridge: Cambridge University Press, 1990), pp. 150–203; Bruce D. Porter, *The USSR in Third World Conflicts: Soviet Arms and Diplomacy in Local Wars, 1945–1980* (Cambridge: Cambridge University Press, 1984), pp. 182–215.

111. David Korn, *Ethiopia, the United States, and the Soviet Union, 1974–1985* (Carbondale: Southern Illinois University Press, 1986), p. 28.

112. Korn, *Ethiopia, the United States, and the Soviet Union*, p. 36, argues that it was not U.S. policy to encourage Siad. See also Zartman, *Ripe for Resolution*, p. 105.

113. Richard Remnek, "Soviet Policy in the Horn of Africa: The Decision to Intervene," in Robert Donaldson, ed., *The Soviet Union in the Third World* (New York: Praeger, 1981).

114. Marina Ottaway, "State Power Consolidation in Ethiopia," in Edmond J. Keller and Donald Rothchild, eds., *Afro-Marxist Regimes: Ideology and Public Policy* (Boulder, Colo.: Lynne Rienner, 1987).

115. See the statement by the Somali minister for information cited in Ododa, "Somalia's Domestic Policies and Foreign Relations," p. 295.

116. Harry Ododa, "Continuity and Change in Kenya's Foreign Policy from the Kenyatta to the Moi Government," *Journal of African Studies*, 13(2) (Summer 1986):52.

117. Osman Sultan Ali, "Djibouti: The Only Stable State in the Horn of Africa," *Horn of Africa*, 5(2) (1982):48–55.

118. S. Neil MacFarlane, "Africa's Decaying Security System and the Rise of Intervention," *International Security*, 9 (Spring 1984):129–30, and Colin Legum, "Communal Conflict and International Intervention in Africa," in Colin Legum, I. William Zartman, Steven Langdon, and Lynn K. Mytelka, *Africa in the 1980s: A Continent in Crisis* (New York: McGraw-Hill, 1979), p. 55.

119. See Terrence Lyons, "Post–Cold War Superpower Roles in the Horn of Africa," paper presented at the Second Conflict Reduction in Regional Conflicts Conference, Bologna, Italy, May 1991.

120. Neil Henry, "Massacre in Somalia Spurred Shift in U.S. Policy," *Washington Post*, February 19, 1990; Peter Grier, "US Rethinks Africa Aid," *Christian Science Monitor*, July 12, 1990.

121. For more details on this conference see Terrence Lyons, "The Transition in Ethiopia," *CSIS Africa Notes*, no. 127 (August 27, 1991).

122. Daniel Teferra, letter to the editor, *Washington Post*, June 12, 1991; Jennifer Parmelee, "Angry Ethiopians Go On Anti-American Rampage," *Washington Post*, May 30, 1991.

123. Statement of Assistant Secretary of State for African Affairs Herman J. Cohen before the House Foreign Affairs Subcommittee on African Affairs hearing on the Political Crisis in Ethiopia, June 18, 1991. See also Michael Binyon, "West Acts as Midwife at Birth of New Leadership," *Times* (London), May 29, 1991.

124. Marina Ottaway, "Foreign Economic Assistance in the Horn: Does It Influence Horn Government Policies?," paper presented at the Woodrow Wilson International Center for Scholars Conference on Crisis in the Horn of Africa: Causes and Prospects, Washington D.C., June 1987.

125. Buzan, *People, States, and Fear*, p. 96. Buzan calls such systems "immature anarchies."

126. See George Modelski, "Kautilya: Foreign Policy and the International System in the Ancient Hindu World," *The American Political Science Review*, 58(3) (September 1964):549–60; I. William Zartman, "The Political Analysis of Regionalism" (unpublished paper).

127. See Zartman, "The Political Analysis of Regionalism."

128. Geography, not being as regular as checkerboards, makes Ethiopia and Kenya not only their neighbor's neighbor but also neighbors themselves. The driving force behind the alliance, however, is not their common border but their common hostile neighbor.

129. See Robert Axelrod and Robert Keohane, "Achieving Cooperation Under Anarchy: Strategies and Institutions," *World Politics*, vol. 38, no. 1 (1985).

5

Southeast Asian Regional Politics: Toward a Regional Order

EVELYN COLBERT

SOUTHEAST ASIA

In Southeast Asia, differences and rivalries between neighbors are subordinated to maintaining subregional ties. In the Association of Southeast Asian Nations (ASEAN), these ties are maintained by common consent. In Indochina, they have been maintained by the exercise of Vietnam's superior strength.

ASEAN members include Brunei, Indonesia, Malaysia, the Philippines, Singapore, and Thailand. Inaugurated in 1967, ASEAN has moved only slowly and always by consensus to engage its members in a widening range of common positions. Indochina as a subsystem dominated by Vietnam came into existence only in 1979, when Vietnam extended over Cambodia the hegemony it already exercised over Laos.[1] Although ASEAN seems likely to remain a permanent feature of the Southeast Asian scene, the future links among the countries of Indochina are uncertain.

This chapter seeks to identify the factors that have drawn the states of Southeast Asia into these two subsystems and influenced their relations. It examines both the external challenges and the national characteristics and policies that have evoked voluntary cooperation in one case and imposed subordination in the other.

As a region, Southeast Asia is as diverse as any other. Differences in religion and ethnicity abound, in many cases crossing national borders. Social and political institutions differ, and states contrast sharply in size and power potential. Colonial rulers arranged boundaries in accord with their own interests, and the Spanish, Dutch, British, French, and Americans left differing imprints on the countries they ruled. National rivalries and antagonisms, predating the colonial era, survive to affect present-day relations. This chapter considers how, despite these diversities and differences, six of the ten states of Southeast Asia have been able to shape relationships strongly marked by collaboration and accommodation.

More particularly, it characterizes the six ASEAN states and the three in Indochina and their ethnocultural, historical, and colonial differences. It contrasts the recent historical experience of the Indochina states, a Cold War battleground for many years, with that of the rest of the region. It assesses the long-run sources of ASEAN threat perceptions, which focus both on major powers external to the immediate region and on internal instabilities. It traces the processes by which the once quarrelsome ASEAN states evolved their unusual cooperation and shows how they have used their collaboration to deal jointly with the outside world.

It contrasts these relationships with those within the Indochinese grouping and traces the efforts of the victorious Vietnamese to consolidate control over the others, the role of China in attempting to impede these ambitions, and the consequences in Cambodia.

The changing relations between the two subsystems as they responded to altered threat perceptions and priorities as well as changes in the international environment are also examined. In addition, the chapter considers how the rivalry between the external powers—at first between the Communist states and the United States and then between Beijing and Moscow—affected relations within the region. The chapter concludes with some speculations on how relations among the states of the region are likely to be affected by the collapse of the Soviet Union and unfavorable trends in the global marketplace.

Characteristics of the Region

Southeast Asia is a region of great diversity, a characteristic shared by most of its constituent states. Major religious differences—the Islam of Brunei, Indonesia, and Malaysia; the Theravada Buddhism of Burma, Cambodia, Laos, and Thailand; the Hinayana Buddhism of Vietnam; the Roman Catholicism of the Philippines; the Confucianism of Singapore—are only the most easily distinguishable of the differences in fundamental belief systems among and within states. Ethnic, linguistic, and other institutional diversities are equally great.

Southeast Asia's size and its geographic configuration have encouraged diversity. Its land area, almost as great as South Asia's, is much more far-flung. The seas lapping the region's long and deeply indented mainland coasts and separating its ten thousand islands cover much more space than its land area, at least half of which is within 150 miles of tidewater. But as the Indonesians say, "The land divides; the sea connects." And not only the sea. The region's abundant monsoonal rains support an elaborate network of rivers, and similar life-styles and work patterns throughout the region have evolved from the tropical climate and dependence on wet-rice cultivation and water-borne trade.

Southeast Asia's central location on important trade routes opened the region to a multitude of major external influences from earliest times. Merchants and religious teachers, not conquerors or colonizers, brought Hinduism, Brahmanism, and Buddhism from India. Mingling with autochthonous institutions, they helped shape political and religious patterns and village life almost everywhere in the region, bringing common features to an extraordinarily diverse landscape.

The two major exceptions to what is conventionally referred to as the Indianization of Southeast Asia were the Philippines and Vietnam. The kingdoms that grew up elsewhere in the region had no parallel in the Philippine archipelago, where the Arab-inspired consolidation of small tribal communities into Islamic sultanates was halted by Spain's expanding control and the rapid spread of Christianity.

Vietnam alone in Southeast Asia came under strong Chinese influence, Chinese colonial rule (maintained until A.D. 939) leaving a heritage of Confucianist and bureaucratic institutions the Vietnamese carried with them as they expanded southward to the Mekong Delta. Elsewhere in Southeast Asia, trade and tributary relations with China were important, and Chinese traders were part of the region's motley merchant community. Although China's cultural influences were not very important, its image as an imperial giant, intermittently expanding southward and always requiring deference and tribute from its smaller neighbors, remains a potent influence on present-day attitudes and politics.

Lured by the region's wealth in spices and its central location on the trade routes, Arab merchants brought still another ingredient to the Southeast Asia mix. Their contribution to the spread of Islam in the archipelagic areas of the region brought similar ideas and institutions to the coastal trading states, distinguishing them from the Buddhist rice-growing kingdoms of the mainland.

The Europeans, with their own mix of commercial ambition and missionary zeal, began to establish their presence toward the end of the fifteenth century. They encountered in Southeast Asia many kingdoms and principalities—some large and powerful, some very small, some the direct ancestors of present-day states, although not yet defined by current boundaries. Like their predecessors, the Europeans found advantage in taking sides in local competition and quarrels. But, unlike their predecessors, they brought with them not only their competition for trade and converts but also policies within Southeast Asia shaped by their power struggles in Europe. Thus, just as after World War II preoccupation with the balance of power in Europe led the United States to support France in Vietnam, so Britain supported the return of the Dutch to Java, fearful that Napoleon's defeat had not precluded renewed French imperialist drives. Anglo-French rivalry also helped preserve the independence of Thailand. The two European countries concluded that their interests would be served best by preserving a buffer state between their respective colonial possessions.

Consolidated only in the second half of the nineteenth century, Western colonial rule had all but disappeared from the region by the mid–1950s. Brief as it was, however, Western rule had a major impact on Southeast Asia. The peoples of the region were absorbed into the empires of the West, their contacts with one another were diminished, and their economies were organized to serve Western interests. Even independent Thailand maintained its principal external contacts with Western patrons, primarily Britain but also the United States.

Within the new fixed colonial boundaries, the authority of the center penetrated outward from the capital cities as never before and helped strengthen the sense of national identity that fueled anti-colonialism. At the same time, colonial administration reinforced ethnic differences and local particularism. The colonial sovereign typically protected the hill peoples against the lowland majorities, sometimes favoring them over lowlanders because of their greater inclination toward both military service and Christianity. Accordingly, when nationalist leaders asserted their authority to rule over all the territory of the former colony, they frequently encountered tribal demands for autonomy or independence that contributed heavily to postindependence turbulence.

Under colonial rule an already complicated ethnic mix became still more complex as labor was imported on a large scale to meet the manpower requirements of new mines and plantations. Existing foreign Asian communities (mostly Chinese but also Indian) were vastly enlarged and assumed important roles in the economy. These too were to outlast the colonial era; the Overseas Chinese, in particular have been resented for their conspicuous entrepreneurial success and feared as a potential weapon of the colossus to the north.

Modernization under European auspices also exposed Southeast Asians who had access to higher education to common concepts of progress and democratic government as well as to Marxist influences, thus stimulating a certain like-mindedness among the postcolonial elites. But differences in the national channels through which Western concepts flowed—Spanish, French, Dutch, British, and American—also had their differing impacts on those who were exposed to them.[2]

Japan's rapid expulsion of Western power from Southeast Asia and the heightened nationalism evoked by the Japanese occupation set the stage for the decolonization process that was to dominate regional attention for more than a decade after the war. The direction and speed of the Japanese campaign—the military occupation of northern Vietnam in 1940, which expanded to all Vietnam in 1941 and spread to the rest of the region in 1942—was to bolster the credibility of the domino theory in Southeast Asia and support the conviction that control of Vietnam was the key to control of all Southeast Asia.[3]

Decolonization, an uneven process, came early and peacefully to the

Philippines in 1946 and to Burma in 1948. Completion of a similarly peaceful transition in Malaya and Singapore was delayed until the late 1950s with the agreement of all concerned that Britain should not leave until two objectives had been achieved: the establishment of viable cooperative arrangements between Malaya's two principal communities—the indigenous Malays and the almost equally numerous ethnic Chinese—and the suppression of an insurgency (the Emergency) initiated in 1948 by the ethnic Chinese Malayan Communist party. In Indonesia, independence in 1949 followed a bitter armed struggle with the Dutch. In Indochina armed struggle was only temporarily suspended by the Geneva Accords of 1954, which gave independence to Laos and Cambodia and left Vietnam juridically divided between North and South.

Initially, independence did little to replace colonial relationships with new ties to neighbors. The manifold problems of nation building and regime consolidation focused attention inward; at the same time, domestic problems fostered continued reliance on external assistance. Given the weakness of equally problem-ridden neighbors, such help could only come from outside the region. Accordingly, relations with former metropoles or other external enemies or friends continued to be more important to Southeast Asian countries than those with their neighbors. These, moreover, were frequently troubled by the revival of ancient antagonisms as the regional order imposed by the Western powers disintegrated. Meanwhile, the rivalry among external powers, briefly suspended by the consolidation of colonial empires, also resumed. Cold War considerations were now the principal motivating force, encouraging generous aid and assurances of protection by the competing great powers.

The Cold War was especially relevant to Southeast Asia. The region was unique as a theater of war. Nowhere else in the Third World did East and West compete so fiercely and for so long with so great an investment in their regional clients as in the Indochina wars. In Southeast Asia, the China factor was also uniquely important, combining domestic and foreign concerns. The unification under Communist auspices of this huge, neighboring, traditionally feared country raised the frightening possibility of linkages that would be equally dangerous, whether between Beijing and ideologically compatible opposition groups or between China's rulers and Southeast Asia's imperfectly assimilated and economically powerful Overseas Chinese communities. That China initially seemed so closely aligned with the Soviet Union made the prospect even more alarming, since Russian help could compensate for Chinese weaknesses.

The non-Communist governments of the region had no doubt that their countries had been targeted for takeover by international Communism. In 1948, the more or less simultaneous outbreak of Communist insurgencies in Burma, India, Indonesia, Malaya, and the Philippines in the wake of a Soviet-sponsored youth conference in Calcutta confirmed their fears. These were fed also by Soviet and Chinese statements that made much of insurgent achievements and treated the leaders of the newly independent states with hostility and contempt.

On the eve of ASEAN's establishment in 1967, the external relations and security policies of the states of Southeast Asia had settled into patterns largely reflective of the Cold War. With the massive involvement of U.S. ground troops beginning in 1965, Indochina had become a central theater of the East-West struggle, and the two Vietnams had become even more heavily dependent on extraregional allies for military and economic support. The neutrality of Cambodia and Laos, internationally affirmed at Geneva in 1954 (and, in the case of Laos, reaffirmed in 1962) was under constant threat from the belligerents in Vietnam. Laos, in fact, was already an active theater of the Second Indochina War; Cambodia was soon to become one. Except for Burma, which was totally committed to isolationism, the other states of Southeast Asia were all associated with the West, whether formally or otherwise. Economic ties—trade and aid—were of great importance to them all. Cultural relations were active. Defense agreements linked the Philippines and Thailand with the United States and Malaysia and Singapore with Britain. The Southeast Asia Treaty Organization (SEATO), established in 1954, provided still another tie between its regional members—Thailand and the Philippines—and the United States and the other Western members. However, this intense involvement with extraregional powers had not precluded intermittent interest in regional cooperation. Little had come of such interest until 1961, when the Association of Southeast Asia (ASA) was established by Malaya, the Philippines, and Thailand. Its suspension two years later by quarrels between Kuala Lumpur and Manila seemed only to demonstrate the futility of such efforts. Nevertheless, ASA at least survived as part of the history of ASEAN.[4]

ASEAN: The Subregion

The ASEAN subregion accounts for five-sixths of Southeast Asia's land area; its population of 270 million is four-fifths of the region's total. It includes both the world's fifth most populous state, Indonesia, and one of its microstates, Brunei. Its members are among the most economically successful and politically stable countries of the Third World.

The subregion is rich in raw materials and tropical products. Building on this base, its countries have relied on trade and foreign investment to speed economic development. In most of them, the manufacturing sector now produces a significant share of exports, but primary products and fuels still dominate the subregion's trade. Japan is ASEAN's principal customer and supplier of foreign investment; the United States is second. Together, the two countries account for about half of ASEAN's foreign trade.

In the 1960s, Japan's demand for Southeast Asian commodities to support its own rise to economic eminence initiated the high growth rates characteristic of the ASEAN countries. During the fifteen years between 1965 and 1980, for example, annual growth averaged 7.4 percent for Malaysia and Thailand, 7.9 percent for Indonesia, and 10.4 percent for Singapore. Although these remarkably high national growth rates were probably more of an obstacle than otherwise to the development of meaningful economic cooperation within ASEAN, they helped to validate concentration on economic goals and to strengthen national self-confidence in ways conducive to cooperation in other areas.

In all the ASEAN countries, governments play an important role in planning and directing the economy. However, their policies have been pragmatic, flexible, responsive to market forces, and free of ideological compulsions. Western-trained economists and technocrats have played influential roles while the business and professional class, of which ethnic Chinese constitute an important component, has become markedly larger in the postcolonial era.

The importance of trade in their economies has made the ASEAN countries very vulnerable to global market conditions. Fluctuations in world prices for primary products, declining growth rates in the West, and the rise of protectionism and trading blocs have deeply concerned ASEAN governments, whose ability to foster growth has been a major ingredient of legitimacy. Increasingly, economic and trade issues have assumed center stage in foreign policy making, and the extent of domestic interests affected has stimulated broader public concern with foreign policy decisions.

Despite the emphasis on national integration (with education an important tool in this regard), ethnic tensions and local particularism are still problems. Poverty also remains an issue. Except in Singapore, urban and rural poor still bulk large in the total population. Resentments are aggravated by the corruption and political favoritism that help the wealthy few at the expense of the rest. Poverty and disparities between rich and poor have reached explosive proportions in the Philippines, where they have contributed heavily to a revived and serious Communist insurgent threat. Elsewhere in ASEAN, the fruits of economic

growth have been sufficiently distributed in rising incomes and in public amenities, health care, education, and the like, to bring overall improvement in living standards.

With the Philippines again a recent exception, the ASEAN countries
have also maintained relatively high levels of political stability and leadership. Memories of acute internal disorder in the years after the Pacific
War are still vivid. Leaders with their roots in that era are convinced that
national survival and progress continue to require the subordination of
freedom to order. Accordingly, in most, constitutionally prescribed regular elections and other attributes of democracy have been accompanied
by restrictions on political organization and participation and on freedom of expression.

Impatience with the constraints of paternalistic government seems to
be increasing, particularly among the burgeoning middle class and the
growing numbers of educated youth. In the Philippines, Marcos's
twenty-year role came to an end in 1986 in an essentially peaceful revolution. Persistent social and political ills, however, have dampened the
high hopes accompanying the rapid restoration of constitutional democracy. Elsewhere in ASEAN, governments have tended to resist pressures for a more open political forum. Such pressures, however, do not
yet pose significant threats to the established order.

The ASEAN Countries

Historic experience, size, location, and deeply rooted social and institutional characteristics have all helped to perpetuate significant differences among the policies pursued by ASEAN states, much as they have
been brought together by association in ASEAN.

Indonesia[5]

With some 180 million people, Indonesia is ASEAN's largest state.
Sprawling over three thousand miles from west to east, the archipelago
contains eight major islands and around three thousand smaller ones.
Achieving the "unity in diversity" proclaimed in the national motto has
been a formidable task in a country where, despite preponderantly Malay origins, different cultures, traditions, and languages abound and
where the postindependence dominance of the Javanese—45 percent of
the total population—has been resented by Outer Islanders, who have
their own traditions of ancient independence and power. Although 90
percent of Indonesia's population is Muslim, religion has been divisive,
on occasion to the point of inspiring rebellion. Islam, in fact, has pitted
the orthodox—especially strong in Sumatra and elsewhere in the Outer

Islands—against an essentially secular regime in Jakarta dominated by Javanese who, although nominally Muslim, are much more influenced by a unique blend of Hinduism and animism of pre-Islamic origin.

Indonesia's huge and fragmented expanse and the variety of its people have been both an obstacle to cohesion and a source of national pride. Where other Third World countries turned to neutralism out of a sense of weakness and vulnerability, Indonesia's "independent and active foreign policy" reflected confidence in its inherent international importance, which, Jakarta's leaders theorized, would only be diminished by a fixed alignment with either side in the global Cold War competition.

Indonesia's search for unity in diversity and an independent foreign policy has taken several forms. Until 1959, weak, unstable, and short-lived coalition cabinets pursued economic development as the necessary foundation for national integration. Accordingly, they looked to the West—the source also of Indonesia's parliamentary institutions—for aid and technical assistance. Parliamentary government was displaced in 1959, under assault from a politically potent military, the ambitions of the charismatic President Sukarno, and secessionist trends in the Outer Islands. Sukarno became the dominant power, balancing a powerful but factionalized army and a very large Communist party (PKI).

Under Sukarno, attention was diverted from economic development to self-assertion on the international and regional stage, pursuit of remaining claims against the Dutch, and leverage with the West through ever-closer relations with Beijing and Moscow. The confidence that size and strategic location alone would ensure international attention proved well founded. These attributes and the president's superlative rhetorical and mass mobilization talents became the principal weapons of a country conspicuously lacking in economic and military power.

In mid–1965, in the wake of an abortive coup attempt in which the Communist party and Sukarno were implicated, the army took over with considerable support from civilians and student groups and under the leadership of General Suharto. Skilled at balancing the rivalries of his subordinates, his prestige enhanced by membership in the generation of 1945, who fought against the Dutch, by his role in eliminating the PKI, and by the economic successes that have been achieved under his auspices, Suharto stands at the apex of the military elite structure and dominates the political scene. The problem of succession is growing, however; Suharto, already in his seventies, will end his fifth term as president in 1993.

Under Suharto, Sukarno's intensely nationalist, romantic, and emotional themes have been replaced by a more sober emphasis on national development while Indonesia's independent foreign policy accommodates a decided tilt to the West—the principal source of the aid and trade that have underwritten substantial economic growth. Increasingly, it appears that Sukarno's foreign policy pretensions were largely the product of his own revolutionary romanticism rather than of some deep-seated, nationwide urge. Indeed, as Indonesia under Suharto has moved much further toward achieving its potential than under his predecessor, and as economic prowess has everywhere become a determiner of national prestige, Sukarno's transports of self-assertion have no longer been required to ensure that Jakarta receives the respect that Suharto and the military, no less than Sukarno, regard as Indonesia's due.

Malaysia[6]

Malaysia, with some 16 million people, became a state in 1963, as the British were divesting themselves of their remaining responsibilities in the Malay world. The eleven states of the Malay Peninsula had already been joined in the Federation of Malaya, independent since 1957; Singapore was almost fully self-governing and was soon to become independent; and Britain was anxious to cede responsibility for its last Southeast Asian dependencies—Brunei, Sarawak, and Sabah (formerly North Borneo), which shared the island of Borneo with the Indonesian province Kalimantan. The federation's prime minister, Tunku Abdul Rahman, feared the growth of PRC influence in an independent, largely Chinese, and already left-leaning Singapore. To prevent this by a union between Malaya and Singapore was politically inadmissible, since this would produce a Chinese majority in the larger federation. Only the addition of the Borneo states would prevent such an imbalance. However, Malaysia, as finally organized, did not include Brunei, which rejected membership at the eleventh hour. Within two years, Singapore was expelled amid growing discord between the Tunku and Lee and growing racial tension.

Singapore's separation in August 1965 expressed in dramatic form the sensitivity of the Malaysian balance in which the politically dominant Malays do not enjoy a large majority.[7] The economically dominant Chinese make up one-third of the population, and each group distrusts the other. Only once in Malaysia's history, however, has this troubled relationship erupted in significant violence—the Kuala Lumpur race riots of May 1969. By current world standards, the rioting was on a small scale (the government reported only 200 dead) and order was quickly restored. Nevertheless, the impact has been traumatic and long-lasting. Indeed, more than twenty years later, May 1969 remains for all communities the most potent and frequently recalled symbol of the vital importance of containing ethnic tensions.

TABLE 5.1
Elements of State Capability Compared—1988

	1	2	3	4	5	6	7	8
	Population, 1988 (mil.)	Population Growth Rate 1985–90 (%)	Armed Forces 1988 (thousands)	GNP 1988 ($bil.)	GNP per Capita 1988 ($)	M.E. 1988 ($bil.)	M.E. GNP 1988 (%)	GDP Growth Rate, 1980–88 (%)
			ASEAN					
Indonesia	184	1.6	284	76	414	1.40	1.8	5.1
Philippines	63	2.1	105	40	639	.68	1.7	.1
Thailand	54	1.7	273	56	1,031	1.70	3.1	6.0
Malaysia	16	1.9	108	32	1,972	.91	2.8	4.6
Singapore	3	1.0	56	24	9,367	1.32	5.3	5.7
Brunei*	.3	2.7	4.4	3.2	11,000	.23	7.31	N.A.
			Indochina					
Vietnam	65	2.0	1,000	13	200	N.A.	N.A.	N.A.
Cambodia	7	2.0	60	N.A.	N.A.	N.A.	N.A.	N.A.
Laos	4	2.3	56	.5	N.A.	N.A.	N.A.	N.A.

*Brunei figures for columns 3, 4, 5, 6, 7, and 8 are from London, IISS, *Military Balance,* 1990 and earlier.
    Key: Column 1: Population, in millions, 1988. From *World Military Expenditures and Arms Transfers* (Washington, D.C.: U.S. Arms Control and Disarmament Agency, 1989). Figures for Brunei are from *World Development Report 1990* (Washington, D.C., International Bank for Reconstruction and Development, 1990).
    Column 2: Annual rate of population growth, percent, 1985–88. From *World Demographic Estimates and Projections 1950–2025* (New York: United Nations, 1988.
    Column 3: Armed forces, in thousands, 1988. From *World Military Expenditures.* For Brunei from IISS, (London) *The Military Balance* 1990.
    Column 4: Gross National Product, billions of dollars, 1988. From *World Military Expenditures.* For Brunei, from *The Military Balance.* For Laos, from *World Development Report,* 1990.
    Column 5: Per Capita GNP, dollars, 1988. From *World Military Expenditures.* For Brunei, from *The Military Balance.*
    Column 6: Military expenditures, millions of dollars, 1988. From *World Military Expenditures.* For Brunei, from *The Military Balance.*
    Column 7: Military expenditures as a percentage of GNP, 1988. From *World Military Expenditures.* For Brunei, *The Military Balance.*
    Column 8: Average annual growth rate of GNP between 1980 and 1988. From *World Development Report.* For Brunei, *The Military Balance.*
    Note: Because figures in these columns come from various sources, the implicit relationship between them may not hold as expected.

The acceptance by all Malaysians of the ethnic organization of national politics and of Malay dominance within the ethnic structure has been remarkably durable. It has provided the underpinning of a political system characterized by almost unbroken constitutional continuity, an ethnically based multiparty system, and regular free elections. With a per capita GNP second in Southeast Asia only to Singapore's, economic well-being has also contributed to Malaysia's political stability. At the same time, however, governments have not hesitated to use the coercive power of the state to head off challenges to their authority.

The centrality of the ethnic balance in Malaysian domestic politics has been paralleled by the importance attributed to the People's Republic of China in Kuala Lumpur's foreign policy. The conservatism of its leaders, its own experiences with the Malay Communist party, and its initially heavy dependence on British protection during the Emergency all dictated an anti-Communist stance internationally. But the possibility that an aggrieved China might exploit the ethnic balance to Kuala Lumpur's disadvantage eliminated confrontation as an option. Accordingly, the newly independent Federation of Malaya refused to join the anti-Chinese SEATO, and in 1974, Malaysia responded more rapidly than its ASEAN partners to Beijing's interest in cordial state-to-state relations.

Singapore[8]

With a remarkably small land base—239 square miles—and a population of 2.7 million, Singapore's economic success has made it a member of the group of Asian economic prodigies (known as the Gang of Four) that also includes Hong Kong, South Korea, and Taiwan. Singapore's success has been closely associated with the leadership of Lee Kuan Yew, its prime minister from 1959 to 1990. He and his People's Action party (PAP) have played an extremely important part in planning, directing, and regulating the island's economy and in the distribution of its returns. Employment, social service, public housing, and educational policies have given Singapore's citizens the highest standard of living in ASEAN. Housing policies, in addition, have brought apartment ownership to a very large segment of Singapore's working class. Lee remains a formidable influence, although he has been succeeded in the prime ministership by his protégé, Goh Chok Tong.

Despite their accomplishments, Lee and his associates have retained a strong sense of Singapore's vulnerability, which in their eyes justifies continued tight regulation of economic, political, and social life. Strenuous efforts to encourage Singaporean identity have yet to overcome the basic ethnic divisions among Chinese, Malays, and Indians and the additional division of the Chinese majority into dialect groups.

Singapore sees its ethnic composition as posing two potential threats. A self-styled Chinese island in a huge Malay sea, it fears not only the hostility of its neighbors but also PRC powers of attraction. Location along strategic lines of communication, although bolstering Singapore's international importance and prosperity, is seen also as likely to involve Singapore to its disadvantage in conflicts among great powers. Even its economic prowess is seen also as a vulnerability because of its heavy dependence on foreign resources and markets. The deep conviction that its security depends on the maintenance of a favorable global military balance and access to foreign resources and very large foreign markets lies at the root of Singapore's strong support for a continued Western—mainly U.S.—security presence in the region, its membership in the Nonaligned Movement notwithstanding.

Thailand[9]

Thailand, with some 54 million people, is ASEAN's third largest state. From the days of the early kingdoms Thailand's security and foreign policies have been heavily influenced by its extensive borders with neighboring states, borders with Burma, Cambodia, Laos, and Malaysia that extend today for two thousand miles. Moreover, although Thailand shares no borders with Vietnam and China, their proximity and local influence have traditionally made them important in the calculations of Thai leaders. As a competitor for control of the Mekong Basin, Vietnam has historically played an adversarial role equivalent in the east to that of Burma in the west.

During the colonial era, Thailand's location proved to be an asset. It helped to preserve the country's independence as a buffer between the expanding French and British empires, whereas Burma and Vietnam were reduced to colonial status and temporarily eliminated as threats to Thailand. In the postcolonial period, relations with Burma have frequently been troubled, but preoccupation with threats from Hanoi has played a more central part in shaping Thailand's external policies. Early in the postwar period, this preoccupation with Vietnam and with Hanoi's ties to Beijing led Thailand into a close and continuing alliance with the United States. More recently, it has caused Bangkok to look to China as a counterweight against the Vietnamese, even though it shares its neighbors' fears of Chinese pretensions to predominance and to the loyalty of Overseas Chinese.

For a number of reasons, and despite the recurrent coups that have changed governments in a military-dominated political system, Thailand has been basically stable. One reason for this stability has been the absence of serious ethnic conflict. The Lao, a majority in the northeastern provinces, are, in fact, members of the Thai ethnic and linguistic community. Ethnic Chinese (although their disproportionate economic power causes resentment) have become increasingly well assimilated, with Chinese ancestry no bar to high office. The members of the one frequently restive ethnic minority, the Malays, or Pattani Muslims, are localized in Thailand's four southernmost provinces, and although they predominate there, they constitute only 4% of the country's total population. Religious homogeneity is even more striking, with 95 percent of the population professing Buddhism. Thus, whereas the phrase "To be a Malay is to be a Muslim" emphasizes the separation between Chinese and the indigenous "sons of the soil," or *bumiputra*, the equally well-worn phrase "To be a Thai is to be a Buddhist" defines a major element of national cohesion. The mystique of the throne as the central element of Thai nationhood also fosters national cohesion. The present ruler, King Bhumibol Adulyadej, is an important influence in Thai politics, reflecting both the strong official emphasis on royal symbolism and the king's own talents, vigor, and dedication.

In the past decade, movement toward parliamentary government under civilian control has quickened as the business community has become much larger, more self-confident, and more assertive; technocrats and academicians with strong public interest concerns have become more numerous and influential; farmers and workers have become better organized and more demanding; and literacy has much improved, so that it is becoming universal. Nevertheless, the assent of the military remains essential to the survival of any government. As demonstrated in February 1991, change of government by military coup had not yet become obsolete.

The Philippines[10]

The Philippines has a population of more than sixty million. It stands out in Southeast Asia as a state without a great tradition of its own. Under Western rule longer and more influenced by the West than the other countries of the region, it has maintained a uniquely close postindependence relationship with the former metropole. It is frequently seen by its neighbors (and by Filipinos) as lacking any real Southeast Asian identity, constituting instead an amalgam of the not necessarily compatible cultures of Spain and the United States.

The Roman Catholicism that is Spain's most enduring and important legacy has contributed immeasurably to national integration in a country of sixteen major and more than seven thousand smaller islands, eight major languages, and a multitude of minor dialects. The relative receptivity of ethnic Chinese to Christianity and the intermarriage facilitated by conversion smoothed the way for the high level of Chinese assimilation in the Philippines.

The Americans left the Philippines with a political system formally modeled on that of the United States, widespread public education, fluency in English, and an enduring fascination with American-style pop culture. When Ferdinand Marcos replaced the democratic system with his authoritarian New Society in 1972, many Filipinos welcomed the change. Spiraling political violence was brought under control, development-oriented economic policies were adopted, and more attention was given to improving agricultural conditions. By the end of the decade, however, an economy run for the benefit of Marcos' friends and supporters—the "crony capitalists"—had lost much of its international competitiveness and was saddled with an enormous foreign debt. The already great gulf between the wealth of the few and the poverty of the many had widened; corruption and human rights abuses were rampant; and the army, now heavily politicized, was responding ineffectively, but frequently brutally, to an expanding Communist insurgency.

In February 1986 Marcos was forced from office by a broad-based peaceful revolution that had drawn its inspiration from the regime-inspired murder three years earlier of Marcos' charismatic opponent, Benigno Aquino. His widow, Corazon, became the first president of a reconstituted representative democracy. Since then, the gap between the extravagantly high hopes that accompanied her inauguration and political reality has grown markedly. The political forum remains dominated by elite families and patron-client relationships, and corruption continues high. GNP growth and rising investment notwithstanding, poverty is endemic, and the ability of the central government to deliver services to the countryside is very limited. The Communist insurgents have suffered some serious setbacks, but the war against them is far from over and continues to generate human rights abuses by the military and by government-sponsored vigilantes. Meanwhile, intermittent military coup attempts have been another source of instability.

The relationship with the United States has been disturbed more than ever by the debate over renegotiating the American base presence. In the wake of the Pacific war, a continued U.S. military presence seemed to serve the interests of both countries. For a devastated Philippines, the disadvantages of being insufficiently independent seemed outweighed by the extent of Filipino need for continued help from the United States, whose past rule, although not immune to criticism, seemed to have created permanent and generally affectionate ties. More recently, however, this inevitably unbalanced relationship has increasingly come to be described by Filipinos and Americans alike as unhealthy. In their debate over the base presence, Filipinos were caught between their desire to assert their independence and their uncertainty over the implications of a new, more distant relationship with the United States. Despite the 1991 agreement on an early U.S. withdrawal, Filipinos remain preoccupied with their American relationship. Their tendencies to look to the United States as both responsible for Filipino problems and obligated to solve them will not quickly fade away.

Brunei[11]

On a per capita basis, Brunei—with an area of two thousand square miles and a population of 240,000—is ASEAN's wealthiest member, deriving $3.2 billion in 1988 from its oil and natural gas exports.

It is an absolute monarchy, and many of the principal government officials are members of the royal family. It is also something of a welfare state, at least for its Malay subjects (64 percent of the total), who pay no income taxes and receive free education and health care, subsidized loans for cars and housing, subsidized food, and jobs in the public service. The members of the ethnic Chinese community—about 20 percent of the population—are mostly noncitizens who do not share in these government benefits and suffer other discriminations, but have nevertheless largely dominated commerce and the service industries.

Brunei remained under somewhat reluctant British protection until January 1984, when it assumed full control of its foreign policy. Its late entry into ASEAN reflected not only the sultan's reluctance to abandon British protection but also some tensions with Kuala Lumpur. Mutual irritation over the terms offered the sultan for membership in Malaysia played some part in this, but a more persistent grievance concerns Brunei's claim to the Limbang area—1,000 square miles of territory separating Brunei into two parts and incorporated into Sarawak by its British rajah in 1890. Within ASEAN, Brunei's closest relations are with Singapore, its leading trading partner,where the royal family has maintained very large investments.

Overcoming Obstacles to Cooperation

Cohesion among the ASEAN states today reflects much more their appreciation of the advantages of membership in ASEAN than natural or historic ties. Progress toward today's levels of cooperation has been slow. Nevertheless, subordinating national rivalries and disputes to regional cooperation may have been less difficult in ASEAN than in other parts of the world. Among the ASEAN six, relatively few bilateral conflicts reach down into primordial passions. The most deeply embedded bilateral antagonisms in Southeast Asia are not within ASEAN but between Vietnam and Cambodia, and between Thailand and each of its four non-ASEAN mainland neighbors—Burma, Cambodia, Laos, and Vietnam.

Among (and within) the ASEAN states, differences of religion and ethnicity, although responsible for friction, do not often arouse the uncontrollable passions that have caused so much bloodshed and turmoil in other parts of the world. Nor have transnational ethnic or religious affinities often been employed by governments to interfere in the affairs of their neighbors.

Common domestic priorities have also facilitated conflict avoidance. For ASEAN leaders, typically market-oriented and pragmatic, the ability to promote economic growth has been a major ingredient of legitimacy and the modernization of their societies more important than pursuing grievances or dominating their neighbors. Indonesia under the romantic revolutionary Sukarno was the exception; his replacement by the development-oriented Suharto removed a major impediment to regional association.

Moreover, similarities in the political practices of member countries have been important. Continuity in political leadership has made for mutual understanding and mutual accommodation, whether such continuity has resulted from the longevity of individual leaders (as with Suharto, Lee, and until 1986, Marcos) or from the durability of the accepted path to leadership, as in Thailand and Malaysia. Foreign policy has been very much the prerogative of the prime minister or president and his close circle of advisers. The bureaucracy involved in foreign policy is small and professional. Only rarely have issues arisen that have excited the interest of the public, the press, or even the parliament. Except in Thailand and, once again, in the Philippines, controls over the press limit its investigative or adversarial role on foreign policy or other sensitive issues.

Until 1965, however, differences between a number of the states soon to join together in ASEAN seemed strong enough to ensure that efforts at regional cooperation would fail. Sukarno's campaign against the establishment of Malaysia—Confrontation, or *Konfrontasi*—the Philippine claim to the sovereignty of Sabah, problems along the common border between peninsular Malaya and Thailand, and Sinic Singapore's fears of its Malay neighbors were all sources of friction.

The Sabah claim was based on the Philippines' undisputed status as the juridical successor of the sultan of Sulu, whose suzerainty had extended to Sabah until 1878 when it came under British rule. The Philippines contended that in the treaty of 1878 the sultan had merely leased the territory; London and Kuala Lumpur claimed an unequivocal cession. The Philippine proposal that the issue be submitted to the World Court having been rejected, the Philippines joined Indonesia in opposing Malaysia and in breaking relations with Kuala Lumpur.

Differences over dealing with problems on their common border also seemed strong enough to block cooperation between Thailand and Malaysia. Historic Thai expansion deep into the Malay Peninsula and subsequent boundary agreements with Britain had left a Malay Muslim minority, some 700,000 strong, in Thailand's four southernmost provinces. These "Pattani" Muslims, resenting their subordination to the Thai Buddhist state, sought at least greater respect for their ethnic identity. At their most extreme, they advocated separation from Thailand, by arms if necessary. Also in the same region were several thousand Malaysian Communists, mostly ethnic Chinese, so-called Communist

Terrorists (CTs), who fled into Thailand as the Emergency was suppressed, establishing bases there for periodic raids into Malaysia. Malaysia resented the safe haven the CTs found on Thai soil and looked to hot pursuit into Thailand to destroy their camps as the only sure remedy. Bangkok, however, suspected that its Pattani opponents were being supported from Malaysia, at least with official connivance, and feared that a Malay troop presence in predominantly Pattani areas might well increase Thai problems there. Kuala Lumpur, while seeking to dispel Thai suspicions, was fearful that outright disavowal of the Pattani cause would anger Muslims at home and in the Islamic world.

These difficulties paled, however, compared to the obstacles to cooperation created by Sukarno. On the one hand, any regional grouping that Southeast Asia's largest country refused to join could not expect to be taken very seriously. On the other, such participation seemed most unlikely. One barrier was the complex of radical domestic and foreign policies underlying Sukarno's dismissal of the Association of Southeast Asia (ASA) as a neocolonialist device. The other was the *Konfrontasi* campaign, involving Indonesian clandestine operations and cross-border attacks into the Borneo states from Kalimantan and, in later stages, troop landings on the Malayan Peninsula and the infiltration of saboteurs into Singapore.

Konfrontasi reflected a mix of traditional Indonesian emotions and aspirations, vigorously fanned by President Sukarno. The extreme nationalist claims that Indonesia should include not only all the Netherlands East Indies but also Malaya, Singapore, British Borneo, Portuguese Timor, and eastern New Guinea had not survived independence. But an abiding sense of entitlement made for resentment that Indonesia had not been consulted about the organization of the new state, an important regional development affecting the Malay world and including territory contiguous to Indonesia's own. Attitudes toward Kuala Lumpur's ruling elite also affected Indonesian behavior. The Tunku and his colleagues were dismissed as feudal survivals who had not had to fight for their independence and were resented for their presumed support of the Sumatra-based rebellion of the late 1950s. Domestic factors also played a part, for the two principal rivals for power under Sukarno, the army and the Communist party of Indonesia (PKI), each saw opportunities for political aggrandizement in enthusiastically supporting *Konfrontasi*. Paradoxically, what appeared to the British as a prudent and honorable decolonization plan was attacked by Sukarno as a device for perpetuating British colonial rule; in fact, it was his own campaign that perpetuated Britain's major military role in Malaysia's defense. Also paradoxically, although Sukarno boasted of what he called the Beijing-Hanoi-Jakarta axis, he also attacked the union of Malaya and Singapore as opening the path for Chinese domination of Southeast Asia.[12]

In other respects, Sukarno's Indonesia was the odd man out among the five states that were to join together in ASEAN. Politically, the other four were fundamentally conservative, their Communist parties outlawed, and leftist trends carefully watched and controlled. The Indonesian Communist party, with two million members and eleven million in party-controlled mass organizations, was the largest in the non-Communist world. Thanks to Sukarno, moreover, it was increasingly important in internal affairs. The economic contrast was also striking. Among the four, development-oriented policies heavily reliant on international trade were already producing impressive economic growth rates. Under Sukarno, Indonesia's foreign reserves were exhausted, its infrastructure was worn down, and inflation was rampant.

In foreign policy also, Indonesia's radicalism contrasted with the conservatism of the other four. Thailand and the Philippines, of course, were American allies, both hosts to important U.S. military installations, and Thailand was a combatant in Indochina. Malaysia and Singapore maintained security linkages with Britain, Australia, and New Zealand. Both supported the American effort to protect South Vietnam's independence—Malaysia quietly, Singapore very vocally. Indonesia, the recipient of $1 billion in Soviet military assistance, had increasingly aligned itself with the PRC, and Sukarno had become the self-appointed leader of radical Third World confrontation with the West, going so far as to take Indonesia out of the United Nations in January 1965. Even the Philippines, although it too was opposed to Malaysia, was alarmed at the lengths to which Jakarta was willing to go in courting British retaliation. Manila was also fearful of Jakarta's close ties with the PRC and the USSR, a concern shared by Bangkok, which had been antagonized by the way Indonesia had rebuffed Thai mediation efforts.

Clearly demonstrating that dramatic domestic political changes can override apparently well-established structural rivalries, Sukarno's downfall in the wake of the August 1965 Communist coup attempt removed a major obstacle to regional cooperation. It brought to power army leaders who wanted to end *Konfrontasi*, rebuild Indonesia's economy, and, especially because of the acute need for aid that only the West could supply, restore their country's international respectability, and reorient its foreign policy. For the new leadership in Jakarta, joining with like-minded neighbors seemed a useful contribution to these goals as well as a way of demonstrating that Indonesia had indeed changed. To Malaysia, an ASA founder, its revival and expansion seemed one way of ensuring against a revival of Sukarnoism. Nevertheless, especially because Indonesia's New Order was still fragile, it was important to avoid charges by the new regime's domestic critics that Indonesia was subordinating itself to its smaller neighbors by merely joining an organization they had already created. Hence, although ASA was formally revived, negotiations were soon under way to replace it with a new and broader grouping.

As a hopeful portent for the future, the principal negotiators were all experienced officials of very high standing who continued to occupy influential positions long after ASEAN was inaugurated. Representing Indonesia, Adam Malik was a member of the Generation of 1945, closely associated with the military in pre–1965 efforts to curb the influence of the PKI. Formerly ambassador to the Soviet Union and minister of trade, he was appointed foreign minister in 1966, a post he held until 1978, when he became vice president of the republic. Representing Malaysia, Deputy Prime Minister Tun Abdul Razak was a longtime prominent politician close to Tunku Abdul Rahman, whom he was soon to succeed. Representing Thailand, Thanat Khoman was one of the region's most prominent and articulate statesmen. A member of the Free Thai movement during World War II, he was later ambassador to the United States and had served as foreign minister since 1958.

ASEAN's founding document, the Bangkok Declaration of August 1967, was very brief and signed by only the foreign ministers. It confined ASEAN's commitment to economic, social, and cultural cooperation. Embarking on a new experiment that many expected to collapse under the weight of bilateral differences, ASEAN's founders viewed these subjects as less delicate and contention-ridden than publicly acknowledged security or political ones. Moreover, domestic sensitivities aroused by *Konfrontasi* were still strong enough to make it difficult for Malaysia, Indonesia, and Singapore to announce that they were embarking on a course of close political cooperation. Uncertain but pessimistic over the outcome in Indochina, the ASEAN leaders were also anxious to avoid burdening future relations with Hanoi by even the suggestion of a confrontational posture that might be read into any specific focus on political objectives or common defense.

To outside observers ASEAN's economic emphasis constituted almost a guarantee of futility, since there seemed little room for useful collaborative enterprise among five countries whose economies, still in the early stages of development, were much more competitive than complementary. However, even in its uncertain beginnings, the ASEAN relationship had advantages for the participants that were to become increasingly evident. Each member, although low on the global power scale, possessed attributes complementary to those possessed by the others. A constructive Indonesia could contribute its potential standing as a major state, as well as the international consideration attracted even now by its size, resources, and strategic location. At the same time, the tremendous imbalance between its size and that of its partners was significantly corrected by the imbalance between their generally flourishing economies and Indonesia's economic disarray and by the enormity of the obstacles Indonesia's size posed to the achievement of national unity and political coherence. For its part, Indonesia, confronted by poverty, underdevelopment, and the uncertainties of a new political era, could only benefit by its association with its rapidly growing and relatively stable neighbors. Thailand could contribute the prestige it enjoyed as the one Southeast Asian state that had escaped colonial rule and the skill and expertise of its long-established diplomatic corps. Moreover, if Thailand's status as a truly independent state could be challenged by critics of its junior partnership with the United States—and this was even more true of the Philippines—their membership in ASEAN served the other members, giving them a link with the American security system without compromising their nonalignment. This was true also of the continuing defense ties of Malaysia and Singapore with Britain, Australia, and New Zealand; Lee Kuan Yew's international prominence was also to make him a useful spokesman for ASEAN. The different allegiances of its members were helpful in other ways; the nonaligned could speak for ASEAN interests in the Nonaligned Movement, the Muslim states in the Islamic world.

Each ASEAN participant also had its own national stake in the survival of the association. Since the international community considered regional cooperation desirable, each member would gain prestige from a successful regional enterprise. Malaysia enjoyed the satisfaction of seeing its own regional initiative, ASA, perpetuated in the goals and structure of this larger organization. It could hope that association with its neighbors would encourage Indonesian persistence in the moderate course Suharto had set for it. Indonesia and Thailand also gained prestige from the prominent role played by their foreign ministers. For Indonesia, ASEAN provided an opportunity to dispel old antagonisms and create new and more congenial relationships without sacrificing pride or status. Especially because its enormous economic requirements dictated conspicuously heavy reliance on the West, association with its Third World neighbors in an organization avoiding Cold War entanglements would help quiet domestic suspicions that Indonesia was abandoning its independent foreign policy. The Philippines found in ASEAN a way of strengthening the Asian identity undermined by its Spanish and American acculturation. Singapore, although the most skeptical of the prospects of the new organization, was fully aware that, having been invited, it must seize the opportunity to identify itself as Southeast Asian, not Chinese. The least it could hope for was that association with the other four would reduce the prospect of some joint threat from Malaysia and Indonesia; the most it could expect was that ASEAN would become a common market to Singapore's particular profit.

The Common Threat: Definition and Response

Beneath the bland Bangkok Declaration, a shared view on security issues was the driving force behind ASEAN's organization. Common threat perceptions, although not enunciated as they would be later, were already firmly established in the minds of ASEAN's architects.

They had shared experiences of the colonial and postcolonial periods. Weakened by internal divisions and struggles among its rulers, Southeast Asia had been easy prey to the Western colonial powers. In the postcolonial era, Indochina had become a Cold War battleground, and the rest of Southeast Asia not only a scene of domestic disorder and bilateral disputes but also an arena in which the great power contenders assisted local antagonists they regarded as allies. Thus, although the ASEAN founders saw internal disorder as the principal threat to their countries, they linked such disorders to prospects for foreign, especially Chinese, intervention. Quarrels between themselves were also seen as providing occasions for external intervention to the detriment of national independence and regional order.

The remedy, as it was perceived in the minds of ASEAN founders, lay in the development of what the Indonesians came to call "national and regional resilience." National resilience—the combination of political, economic, and social strength necessary for self-reliant national survival in an uncertain world—required more than police measures and authoritarianism. Economic development was to be the driving force, helping to strengthen the ties between government and the governed, reducing the appeal of Communist doctrine, and helping to bring ethnic minorities into the national fold.

Regional resilience was the necessary complement to national resilience. Cooperation among members and strict noninterference in each others' affairs would minimize quarrels and fears and maximize resources for nation-building tasks. As ASEAN nations became stronger, more self-reliant, and more closely linked, pretexts for intervention from outside the region would be reduced and the region's capacity to order its own affairs and deal with the outside world would be increased. Or, as Suharto said in 1966, "A cooperating Southeast Asia, an integrated Southeast Asia" would "constitute the most strongest [sic] bulwark and base in facing imperialism and colonialism of whatever form and from whatever quarter it may come."[13]

Although ASEAN's leaders aspired to regional autonomy, they had no illusions about equidistance. Their shared orientation toward the West, stemming from historic experience and postindependence requirements for help of all kinds, was strengthened by experience with Communist insurgency and deep suspicion of Soviet and Chinese intentions.

The ties of Malaysia, Singapore, and the Philippines to their former metropoles remained strong, reinforced, especially in the early postwar years, by pressing needs for external help. The Philippines, devastated by war and liberation, needed large doses of the economic assistance that only the United States could provide and wanted protection from a possibly resurgent Japan and the forces of international Communism. For Malaysia and Singapore, the utility of a continued British role had been amply demonstrated as British forces bore the principal defense burden both in the Emergency and during *Konfrontasi*. For all three leaving expenditures for defense largely to the former metropoles had obvious advantages.

Thailand too had long-established ties with the West, now focused on the United States as its ally against the DRV, the heir in Thai eyes to traditional Vietnamese expansionism in Laos and Cambodia. Suharto's Indonesia also had good reasons to turn to the West: the massive economic aid the West was prepared to supply and the conviction of military leaders that the PRC had played an important role in the coup attempt.

In sum, in 1967, the ASEAN states had no wish to relinquish Western security protection or lose their claim as allies and friends to the economic assistance needed to fulfill their domestic objectives. At the same time, however, they did not want to be involved in Cold War issues not affecting their own local interests. The circle was neatly squared: On the one hand, ASEAN itself was defined as strictly nonaligned, with three of its members in due course joining the Nonaligned Movement; on the other, the Bangkok Declaration definition of the foreign military presence as "temporary" and "remaining only with the expressed concurrence of the countries concerned" left undisturbed major American bases in the Philippines and Thailand and a smaller Commonwealth military presence in Malaysia and Singapore.

In fact, the concern of the ASEAN powers in the 1960s was not that the Western role might be excessive but that it might wither away, leaving Southeast Asia unprotected against the Russians and Chinese. By 1967, the domestic pressures that were to force American withdrawal from Vietnam were already evident, and in July, Britain had given notice that it was planning to eliminate its military presence east of Suez. A year earlier, Lee Kuan Yew had warned,

> We must never believe that the happy situation we are in will go on forever, that the Americans consider South Vietnam fundamental to their prestige and to the security of the whole of Southeast Asia, and that the British are a necessary backstop in the region from allowing the whole area to be undermined militarily and otherwise, and that therefore they will just do this forever and ever.[14]

Despite abstract appreciation of the importance to regional association of self-restraint and sensitivity to the interests of fellow ASEAN members, political leaders were not yet ready to moderate their policies on disputed issues. Indeed, persisting quarrels were all too evident.

Sabah remained a source of friction between Malaysia and the Philippines. In 1968 diplomatic relations between the two countries (and ASEAN meetings) were temporarily suspended following the revelation that Filipino Muslims were being trained for armed infiltration into Sabah under the auspices of President Marcos. Again, during the 1970s, discord increased as Sabah, with the active participation of its chief minister, became a conduit for Libyan arms for Muslim rebels in Mindanao. Malaysian-Thai frictions also flared, with each side quick to see violations by the other of border cooperation agreements. In 1968 Singapore's execution of two Indonesian marine infiltrators captured during *Konfrontasi*, despite President Suharto's personal appeals for clemency, caused bitter Indonesian press attacks on Singapore, the sacking of its embassy, and temporary suspension of trade. In 1969 the anti-Chinese riots in Kuala Lumpur added still another element to Singapore's fears of Malaysia.

Less evident than this friction, however, but ultimately more important, was the fact that through ASEAN the members were getting to know one another. Significantly, this process began at the top with political leaders and senior officials and gradually expanded to lower levels and the private sector. If it seemed slow, the gap to be filled was extraordinarily wide. Until 1972, for example, Lee Kuan Yew's only visit to another ASEAN country had been a brief stopover in Bangkok in 1966 en route to India. Slowly, foundations were being established for a period of more rapid development in the early 1970s, as ASEAN leaders developed greater confidence in themselves and each other and a changing international atmosphere made evident the need for new adjustments.[15]

The Indochina Connection

The Subregion

Late in the nineteenth century, when the French brought their diverse but contiguous Southeast Asian dependencies into the Indochinese Union, this historically unprecedented connection reflected nothing more than French administrative convenience. Although they shared the same political borders, the components of the Union were much divided jurisdictionally and no organic links were established among them. Moreover, the colonial arrangements did not stimulate a sense of

Indochinese identity to soften the considerable differences between Lao and Khmer, on the one hand, and Vietnamese, on the other.[16] In Indianized Cambodia and Laos, as in Thailand and Burma, Therevada Buddhism prevails; only the Sincized Vietnamese share Hinayana Buddhism with Northeast Asia. Reinforced by these and other sociocultural differences, resentment of Vietnamese pretensions goes back to the precolonial era, when large parts of the once flourishing Lao and Cambodian kingdoms were absorbed by the expanding Vietnamese.

French administrative practices perpetuated the image of the Vietnamese as overbearing and arrogant. Vietnamese filled the lower administrative, police, and military ranks and dominated local commerce throughout Indochina. France considered Vietnam the center of its Indochina empire; Cambodia and Laos were its backwaters. Meanwhile, the internationalism preached by the Comintern had little impact on the Vietnamese Communists, who made up the entire membership of the early Indochinese movement and who viewed their neighbors as too primitive to absorb Marxist-Leninist doctrines.

With the end of French rule in 1954, formal connections among Laos, Cambodia, and Vietnam ended, and Vietnam itself remained divided until 1975. Despite common opposition to the Communists, no new links developed among the governments in Saigon, Vientiane, and Phnom Penh. Indeed, the relations between Cambodia and South Vietnam were all too often bitter. At the same time, however, the Vietnamese Communists, their Lao Dong party now in control of North Vietnam, continued to strengthen their links with the much smaller Communist movements of their neighbors that they had found it profitable to develop during the war against the French. This linkage, formed and nourished during decades of almost uninterrupted hostilities, was to provide the basis for the Indochina Special Relationship— an imposed unity of Communist states with Vietnam as the dominant partner.

Significantly superior size reinforced the dominance of a united Vietnam, with its 65 million people vastly outweighing the 7 million of Cambodia and the 4 million of Laos. Among Cambodians, however, this disparity intensified resistance to Vietnamese rule, direct or indirect, as a threat not only to their country's political identity but to its social and cultural identities as well.

The Indochina Countries

In comparison with the ASEAN states, those of Indochina are impoverished and markedly underdeveloped. Like socialist countries elsewhere, they are moving erratically toward market-based policies. Governing Communist parties in Vietnam and Laos, however, continue to insist on their preeminent political role, and there has been little progress toward more open politics.

Laos[17]

Sandwiched between Thailand and Vietnam and bordering China and Cambodia as well, tiny Laos has figured in postwar international affairs to an extent out of all proportion to its poverty and size. At the same time, exceptionally great ethnic diversity and deep-rooted localism have denied governments in Vientiane the ability to manipulate to national advantage the country's strategic importance to competing outside states.

Within its very small expanse (less than 100,000 square miles) Laos suffers from a singularly rugged terrain that has limited its agricultural and economic development and isolated settled communities from one another. The fragmentation imposed by geography has been reinforced by a population structure in which the politically dominant lowland Lao outnumber only slightly the diverse tribal groups of the uplands. Competition for political advantage among locally based leaders and antagonisms between lowland Lao and the hill tribes survived unification under the royal house of Vientiane. After the Pacific war, newer divisions among rightists, neutralists, and Communists were added to the old, destroying any prospect that Laos could insulate itself from the struggle in neighboring Vietnam.

Leadership of the present government, the Lao People's Democratic Republic (LPDR), proclaimed in December 1975, rests largely in the hands of long-time Communist veterans, some with ties to the movement that go back at least to World War II, and all linked to the Vietnamese by ideology, indebtedness for help over many years, and sometimes blood or marriage. The interlocking nature of this relationship has ensured consistency between the policies of the two countries where Hanoi's basic interests are involved.

Within these bounds, Lao relations with Thailand seem often to move to a rhythm of their own, reflecting the singular affinities between the two countries. More ethnic Lao live in Thailand's neighboring northeast region than in Laos itself, and the refugee flow has increased their number. Easy movement across the one thousand–mile Mekong border makes Thailand and Laos natural trading partners, and Thailand provides Laos with its principal access to the sea. Moreover, although Thailand has been expansionist at Lao expense, it also has served Laos as a counterweight to the Vietnamese, and Laos has served Thailand as a protective buffer.

Laos is desperately poor and is now joining other nations of the socialist world in adopting more flexible market-oriented economic policies. Its ability to manage change, however, suffers from the exodus of much of the commercially important ethnic Chinese community and of over 300,000 tribespeople and ethnic Lao. The latter constitute most of the small class of professionals and technicians.

Cambodia[18]

Cambodia, like Laos, has derived its postcolonial importance in Southeast Asia largely from its location. Its borders with Thailand and Vietnam have involved it in both their rivalry and, more important, the Vietnam struggle. Of its four postwar rulers—Prince Norodom Sihanouk, General Lon Nol, Pol Pot, and Heng Sam-rin—only Sihanouk was able to preserve Cambodia's peace amidst the competing forces surrounding it.

Sihanouk's adroitness in playing rival regional powers and their extraregional patrons against one another was fortified by his authority at home, the respect his royal descent inspired in a population some 90 percent ethnic Khmer, his role in achieving independence for his country, and his compelling personality. In 1970, however, resentment of his acquiescence in the ever-growing North Vietnamese use of Cambodian territory, combined with the ambitions of his right-wing rivals, led to his overthrow. His successor's alliance with the United States and South Vietnam threw Cambodia full scale into the Second Indochina War. The ruthlessness and fanaticism of Pol Pot's anti-Vietnamese policies helped to precipitate the Third. Pol Pot's replacement by a Vietnamese-dominated leadership brought no peace to a Cambodia still enmeshed in the Cold War and the Sino-Soviet confrontation. Civil war between government forces, Vietnamese and Khmer, and an internationally supported resistance coalition, in which the Khmer Rouge mounted the major military effort, continued to inflict death and destruction on the Khmer population. Even so, the government was able to function at least minimally in most of the country.

Phnom Penh was repopulated and became the scene of lively commerce in consumer goods from Thailand and Singapore. The educational system was restored, although at a very low level, and rice production recovered somewhat. In the late 1980s the government abandoned many of its ideologically based policies. Buddhism was reinstated as the national religion. Private ownership was reestablished, and foreign investment encouraged.

The peace settlement achieved in October 1991 by the Paris Conference on Cambodia has brought new opportunities without resolving old problems. Ideally, with genuine cooperation among the three major factions and with extensive U.N. and other international involvement, Cambodia under a restored Prince Sihanouk will move peacefully toward representative government, political stability, and economic recovery. However, dark shadows are cast over this prospect by deep-rooted factional hostility and continued Khmer Rouge strength and revolutionary dedication.

Vietnam[19]

Vietnam is one of the more homogeneous Southeast Asian states. Ethnic Vietnamese make up more than 85 percent of the population. Their differences of origin in Tonkin, Annam, and Cochin China give rise to some local particularism but do not diminish a strong sense of national identity. Indigenous minorities, perhaps 12 percent of the population, include a variety of mountain tribes whose restiveness under Vietnamese domination has been a problem for Communist and non-Communist governments alike. Ethnic Chinese, the only significant alien minority, have been reckoned at about 3 percent of the total population, with most located in the south; their numbers have been much reduced by the exodus of the postwar "boat people." Roman Catholics constitute a significant religious minority.

Vietnam has been almost constantly at war since 1945. During the first two Indochina wars, the cohesion of its leaders, its single-minded drive for the independence and reunification of Vietnam, and its victories over France and the United States all brought the DRV a large measure of international prestige and sympathy. International respect for Hanoi's military and political prowess was mirrored in the confidence of its battle-seasoned leaders, many of them among Ho's early associates. Its occupation of Cambodia, however, put Vietnam into opposition with almost all of the nonsocialist world, helped to transform Hanoi's relations with Beijing from alliance to enmity, deepened Vietnamese dependence on the USSR, and undermined Vietnam's reputation for military effectiveness. Cambodian requirements and the need to maintain a formidable military force on the Chinese border placed a heavy burden on domestic resources, contributing to a significant decline in public and military morale and intensifying Vietnam's economic problems.

These remain grave. Vietnam's per capita GNP has been one of the lowest in the world; among the 164 countries ranked in this respect by the United Nations, it stands 161st. For more than a decade after the fall of Saigon, economic policies, which were in the grip of elderly leaders, were erratic and marked by ideological rigidity and unrealistic goals.

They were administered by a Communist bureaucracy described by the regime itself as riddled with incompetence, rigidity, arrogance, low morale, and corruption.

Those within the party who advocate addressing economic problems with reduced state controls and greater scope for private enterprise have won some important victories in recent years. The central planning structure has been largely abandoned, as have subsidies to a number of state industries; a liberal foreign investment law is now in effect; and private enterprise and ownership have been legalized. Improvements in some areas of economic activity have been marked. Private ownership of land and the removal of price controls, for example, have resulted in significantly increased rice production.

Overall, however, Vietnam's economic problems remain serious. The Soviet Union, which formerly provided aid estimated at $1 billion annually, later required hard-currency payments at world market prices and called for repayment in hard currency of a $4.5 billion debt. Barriers to trade and foreign investment have been reduced since the end of the Cambodian hostilities. But bureaucratic practices and acute infrastructure weaknesses are important impediments to economic progress.

Although economic pressures and the need for foreign investment and development assistance played a role in encouraging greater Vietnamese flexibility on Cambodian settlement issues, there has been no parallel development on the political front. There halting steps toward liberalization ended as the disintegration of Communist control in Eastern Europe and mass student demonstrations in China persuaded Vietnamese leaders of the dangers involved in loosening controls. The continuing power of the ideologues was reflected in the pronouncements of the June 1991 Seventh Party Congress, which emphasized the importance of faithful adherence to the doctrines of Marxism-Leninism and socialism.

Hanoi's Strategic Perspective

In their drive to win power, the Vietnamese Communists had to adjust their strategies to the involvement of their struggle in the Cold War and the Sino-Soviet dispute and to the involvement of their Indochina neighbors.

Soviet and Chinese aid, indispensable in the struggle against France and the United States, brought the dangers of domination and betrayal. For some time, Hanoi could make good use of the competition between its quarreling patrons. But with the growing enmity between Beijing and Hanoi, Vietnam lost some of its maneuverability, becoming wholly dependent on the Soviet Union to achieve its goals in Cambodia, strengthen itself against China, and keep its economy afloat. The perils of its heavy dependence became evident in the Gorbachev era, when external considerations ceased to inspire Soviet generosity and domestic economic problems precluded it. In 1954, at the end of the First Indochina War, the DRV's dependence on its allies had forced it to accept terms well short of its aspirations. In the final years of the Second Indochina War, Vietnam had assets that enabled it to resist Soviet and Chinese pressures for a more gradual strategy. After almost a decade of the Third, Soviet pressures on Hanoi to rein in its ambitions combined decisively with other problems generated by Vietnam's military involvement in Cambodia.

This involvement was nothing new. However artificial the French-created Indochina linkage, it survived for Hanoi and for Hanoi's enemies long after the formal ties disappeared. For both sides the war in Vietnam required military use of Lao and Cambodian territory and efforts to shape political developments in the two smaller states. Victory in Vietnam brought victory for Hanoi's clients in Laos. But Hanoi came to believe that to ensure the security of a reunited Vietnam, the Khmer Rouge would have to be destroyed. Pursuit of this objective was then to blight Vietnam's relations with its non-Communist neighbors and most of the rest of the world.

Allies: Constant and Inconstant

When Ho proclaimed the founding of the Democratic Republic of Vietnam, Moscow was more concerned with French Communist party interests than with the Lao Dong struggle, and the Chinese Communists were still in the throes of their own revolution. In 1959, however, when the People's Liberation Army reached China's border with Vietnam, Vietnamese Communist military capabilities were transformed. By 1954, forty thousand Vietnamese troops had been trained in China. Some ten thousand Chinese support troops and large quantities of Chinese equipment played an important part in the Viet Minh victory at Dien Bien Phu.

In the Second Indochina War both the USSR and China contributed heavily to DRV capabilities. From 1965 to 1974 the Soviet Union provided assistance worth some $3.5 billion, including a complete air defense system and the heavy and mobile weapons indispensable to the large-scale conventional offensives of the last years of the war. The Chinese contributed 50 percent of Viet Cong and 80 percent of PAVN requirements for small arms, and fifty-five thousand to sixty thousand PLA railway troops worked to maintain and repair lines of communication damaged by U.S. air attacks.[20]

After the end of the Second Indochina War, Hanoi had to look more than ever to the USSR for help. Soviet logistic support, arms, and ammunition were all important to Vietnam's military operations in Cambodia. Thanks to the USSR, Vietnamese troops on the border with China became better armed than the Chinese troops facing them. And it was Soviet and Eastern European trade and aid that fended off the complete collapse of the Vietnamese economy.

The perils of dependence became fully evident early in the DRV's struggle. In the 1954 Geneva negotiations, Hanoi had to rely heavily on the diplomacy of its allies, since its military prowess was its only international credential. It correctly concluded that its gains on the battlefield had been partly sacrificed to the Soviet interest in détente and China's desire to avert an American military presence in mainland Southeast Asia. Again in the name of détente, in the early 1970s, Hanoi was pressed by both allies to compromise its settlement terms, abandon large-scale offensives, and return to its earlier strategy of protracted war. In this period, however, the DRV's military successes and its international standing, together with the declining American commitment to South Vietnam, made Hanoi's leaders less vulnerable to the pressures of their allies and even more certain that they were the best judges of their own requirements. Meanwhile, the depth of their split precluded united Sino-Soviet pressure and increased for each the value of a loyal ally.

Nevertheless, the split was not without its dangers. The unity of the Lao Dong party could be threatened, like that of other parties, as Moscow and Beijing competed for Communist support. Moreover, even if Lao Dong unity remained undisturbed, Hanoi's leaders, heavily dependent on both contestants, could not afford to lean too far in one direction. Most serious of all was the potential threat to Hanoi's supply lines, since much of what the Soviet Union provided came overland through China. However, although the movement of Soviet supplies was blocked briefly during the Cultural Revolution, this was an exception. In fact, the competition between Beijing and Moscow enhanced their generosity, with Hanoi's enormous prestige among Communist parties and in left-wing and liberal circles a particular impetus to continued loyal support. Therefore, Hanoi was largely able to pursue its own strategy, whether or not it accorded with the views of its allies.

Hanoi's ability to maintain its own autonomy while extracting maximum assistance from its divided allies survived until the last days of the Second Indochina War. Then, Beijing, no longer a generous aid giver, became entangled in the conflict between the Khmer Rouge and Vietnam. In an action-reaction spiral, China responded to Pol Pot's call for help; Hanoi became increasingly convinced that Beijing was using Khmer-Vietnamese divisions and Khmer Rouge border forays as the spearhead of a campaign to impose Chinese control over Vietnam; and Moscow's response to Hanoi's appeals reinforced Beijing's conviction that the Vietnamese were yet another instrument of the Soviet effort to encircle China. Thus, the compulsions of Vietnam's struggle with the Khmer Rouge, the revival of the Sino-Vietnamese differences that had been set aside during the war, and long-standing negative attitudes toward one another combined to precipitate armed hostilities between the former allies and bring about the long-avoided Vietnamese dependence on a single power.

This dependence, however, did not deprive Hanoi of all bargaining power. Although the Soviet presence in Cam Ranh Bay provided Vietnam with some protection against an overly adventurous Chinese policy, Vietnam was also strengthened by the strategic importance that pre-Gorbachev Moscow placed on its unprecedented military presence in Southeast Asia. But even before the Gorbachev era, Vietnam's value to the USSR as an ally against China began to decline in 1982 as the USSR and China initiated their slow movement toward rapprochement. As Gorbachev reduced defense expenditures and sought more amicable and profitable relations with non-Communist countries in Asia and the West, access to Cam Ranh Bay came to weigh less in the balance of Soviet policy than the economic and political costs of supporting Vietnam's Cambodian venture. Still heavily dependent on the USSR but now lacking some of its previous assets, Hanoi became more vulnerable to Soviet pressures, and Moscow became less inhibited in exerting them.

The Single Battlefield and the Special Relationship

Early in the First Indochina War the Vietnamese Communists came to appreciate that the newly active nationalists of the neighboring states could be useful against the French and that support for Lao and Khmer Communists could pay worthwhile dividends. With French and DRV forces both operating without regard to national boundaries, General Vo Nguyen Giap's 1950 definition of Indochina as "a single strategic unit, a single battlefield" was describing a military reality. When he declared that no one Indochina country could be liberated unless the others were also and defined Vietnam's mission as helping "to liberate all of Indochina," he was asserting political principles of continuing importance in Indochinese Communist doctrine. However, with the reunification of Vietnam under Lao Dong auspices remaining the preeminent objective, practical considerations made the Lao Communists much more important to Hanoi than their Khmer counterparts.

The vital importance of the Ho Chi Minh trail to the movement of North Vietnamese troops and supplies into South Vietnam was reason enough for generous assistance to Lao Communist campaigns against the U.S.-supported Royal Lao Government in Vientiane. Thus, the Lao Communists, when they gained complete control in 1975, had good reason to be loyal to Hanoi beyond the presence of a large Vietnamese military force.

Beginning in the late 1960s, Hanoi's investment in logistic routes, base areas, and safe havens in Cambodia became substantial. But DRV interests were better protected in Cambodia by cultivating Sihanouk than by supporting his opponents. The Khmer Rouge thus received little support or even encouragement from Hanoi until Lon Nol staged his coup against Sihanouk and cast his lot with the United States and South Vietnam. However, the substantial assistance the DRV began to provide did not compensate, in the eyes of the Khmer Rouge, for earlier neglect or outweigh deeply ingrained Cambodian hatred of the Vietnamese and strong suspicion of their motives.

Thus, in 1975, when Communist victory in all three countries seemed to create the opportunity to move from a party-to-party to a formal state-to-state relationship, it quickly became evident that Pol Pot wanted no part of a special relationship with Hanoi. He considered that this would inevitably subordinate Cambodia to Vietnam. Accordingly, just when Vietnamese-Chinese relations were deteriorating badly, he turned to China for support and protection. The single battlefield remained. But now the Chinese "expansionists and hegemonists" had succeeded the "Japanese fascists, French colonialists, and U.S. imperialists."[21] With Pol Pot's cross-border forays now viewed in Hanoi as an instrument of Chinese aggression, the defense of Vietnam required the elimination of his regime. This task Hanoi accomplished in January 1979, in defiance of Chinese warnings and armed with Soviet support.[22]

Having placed its client Heng Samrin in power in Phnom Penh, Hanoi was at last able to achieve a formal trilateral arrangement based on treaties signed with Laos in 1977 and with Cambodia in 1979 and embodying what was described as the Indochinese Special or Strategic Relationship. For some years, the Special Relationship concept was given considerable prominence, providing the framework for a tripartite summit in 1983 and for semiannual foreign ministers' meetings. In due course, subsidiary arrangements developed in the form of tripartite meetings of government officials and other specialists. These gatherings aside, however, no organizational structure emerged, nor did it appear that the Special Relationship was playing any real part in joint policymaking or in enforcing Hanoi's will on its partners.

During its most active period, the Special Relationship was significant largely in the Cambodian negotiating context, its foreign ministers constituting a counterpart to ASEAN's in articulating policy positions that seemed mostly designed to perpetuate the stalemate. As genuine negotiations got under way, however, the Special Relationship began to fade. By the opening of the 1990s, official references to it (or to the single battlefield) had become rare, and Vietnamese officials, speaking informally, have occasionally disowned it.

In the context not only of the Cambodian negotiations but also of Hanoi's drive to improve its relations with ASEAN and the West, the concept of Indochinese unity has had distinct disadvantages. It has not succeeded in obscuring Vietnam's domination of Laos and Cambodia. Instead, it has helped keep alive the charge that maintaining control over Cambodia and Laos is a central and permanent Vietnamese objective. It has undercut the emphasis Hanoi and Phnom Penh have put on the independence of the Phnom Penh government and its commitment to permanent peace and neutrality. As an economic partnership, it is largely irrelevant; there is little mutual aid to be found in impoverished Vietnam, Laos, and Cambodia.

No formal action has been taken to break the Special Relationship tie, which remains available for reinterpretation. Nor has trilateralism disappeared from the political vocabulary of the Indochina states. Both trilateral and bilateral relationships—particularly those of the smaller two with Hanoi—are singled out for praise on anniversaries and similar occasions. Similarly, the debt of all three governing parties to Ho Chi Minh's leadership and their common origin in the Indochinese Communist party are frequent themes. It is hard to imagine that Hanoi will cease to be concerned with the policies of its Indochina neighbors, particularly their external policies. There also may be mixed views in Laos and Cambodia. Both would welcome independence from Hanoi's control. But they will not want to be cut off completely from a relationship that can, as in the past, balance relations with an economically expansive Thailand.

ASEAN: Dynamics of Subregional Relationships

The 1970s: Increased Solidarity in a Changing World

In the 1970s changes in the global and Asian systems altered the context in which ASEAN cooperation developed. Fulfilling Lee Kuan Yew's predictions, Britain and the United States were reducing their involvement. Britain had set 1971 as its target for military withdrawal East of Suez. The Paris Peace Talks were under way; American troops had begun to withdraw from Vietnam in June 1969; and in July, President Nixon's Guam Doctrine warned America's Asian allies and friends that their future defense against nonnuclear threats would rest largely in their own hands. Helping to balance these disturbing changes were elements of reassurance. Fear of Sino-Soviet cooperation against non-Communist states had all but evaporated, and Moscow and Beijing were now competing vigorously for friendly government-to-government relations with non-Communist Asian states. At the same time, emerging East-West détente was signaled by the opening of U.S.-Soviet SALT I negotiations in November 1969 and the resumption of U.S.-PRC talks in Warsaw two months later.

For Southeast Asian leaders, the signals were mixed. Reduced Cold War tensions globally could be expected to reduce regional tensions as well. But the great powers, in adjusting their own relations, might well ignore Third World interests or even undermine them. The developing American détente with China, for example, might accelerate U.S. withdrawal from Southeast Asia. China's declining preoccupation with People's War and its greater interest in cordial diplomatic relations with neighboring governments might prove as impermanent as China's mid–1950s shift to support for peaceful coexistence. Meanwhile, still to be taken into account were China's ties to local Communist parties and its presumed potential for manipulating Overseas Chinese communities or intervening on their behalf. Soviet competition with China in Southeast Asia was less dangerous than their collaboration in hostile policies but might involve the region in still another great power confrontation. More active diplomatic and economic relations might expand Soviet opportunities for espionage and subversion, and balanced relations with Beijing and Moscow would be required to avoid charges of favoritism from either.

Faced with these interacting changes and prospects on the international scene, the ASEAN countries had little choice but to make their own adjustments. They responded individually with varying degrees of favor to Soviet and Chinese overtures, moving toward greater diversity in their great power relations without turning away from the United States. Collectively, they sought to reassure Hanoi of ASEAN's friendly intentions and to emphasize hopes for the eventual neutralization of Southeast Asia.

Normalization with the USSR proceeded relatively rapidly. When ASEAN was inaugurated, Moscow had diplomatic relations with only two of its members—Thailand and Indonesia; by 1972 Malaysia, Singapore, and the Philippines had joined the list and the USSR had become a somewhat more active presence in Indonesia and Thailand.

Normalization with the PRC began later, slowed both by the Cultural Revolution and, until Beijing replaced Taipei in the U.N. in October 1971, by the awkwardness of the choice between the PRC and the U.S.-supported Republic of China. In 1974, Malaysia was the first ASEAN state to establish relations with Beijing, followed by Thailand and the Philippines in 1975. Difficult and, in some cases, prolonged negotiations reflected the depth of ASEAN concerns about PRC connections with local Communist parties and Overseas Chinese. The agreements reached with Malaysia on these two subjects became standard Beijing formulations. The PRC agreed that ethnic Chinese settled abroad should be encouraged to adopt local citizenship and, in doing so, would automatically forfeit Chinese nationality. In a much less satisfactory response on local Communist parties, Beijing pledged noninterference in internal affairs while insisting that relations between China's Communist party and fraternal parties elsewhere were completely separate from state-to-state relations. Jakarta's continuing obsession with ties between the PRC and the PKI postponed the restoration of relations until 1990. Singapore, having fulfilled its own pledge to await Indonesia's action, quickly followed suit, adding diplomatic relations to its already extensive commercial ties.

If the adjustment of diplomatic relations between ASEAN states and the Communist powers was no more than a practical recognition of declining global bipolarity, the promulgation of the Zone of Peace, Freedom, and Neutrality (ZOPFAN) expressed, however vaguely, aspirations for greater autonomy within the changing international system. It was also ASEAN's first step toward avowed political cooperation—a very tentative step, initially attributed not to the organization but to the five foreign ministers.

The ZOPFAN idea originated with Tun Abdul Razak, who became prime minister of Malaysia in 1970. His original concept involved a series of steps, beginning with an Indochina settlement and culminating in great power guarantees of Southeast Asian neutrality. As an ideal, genuine neutrality had some resonance, but as a guide to policy in the here and now, Razak's proposal had few supporters. The Philippines and Thailand were not ready to abandon their security arrangements with the United States. Singapore argued that the Southeast Asian countries could do no more themselves than reduce opportunities for actual great power intervention while seeking to ensure a balance favoring their own interest in the inevitable great power presence. The Indonesians tended to share Singapore's view and rejected the great power guarantees proposed by Razak as a new form of colonialism and as unlikely to be reliable. As Adam Malik said, "neutralization that is the product of 'one-way' benevolence on the part of the big powers, at this stage, would perhaps prove as brittle and unstable as the interrelationship between the major powers themselves."[23]

Razak, however, had invested his prestige in the proposal, which had attracted a good deal of international attention. In this context it was not difficult for the ASEAN foreign ministers to sign on to a very vague formulation—the ZOPFAN Declaration of November 1971—which did no more than pledge their countries to further efforts to exclude external influence and advance peace and stability in Southeast Asia. Vague as ZOPFAN was, it went considerably beyond the ASEAN Charter in clarifying ASEAN's integrating security concept, the determination in Razak's words "that this region will no longer be a theater of conflict for the competing interests of major powers."[24] It was useful also in identifying ASEAN with Third World nonalignment and in providing a feature on which Moscow and Beijing could focus their approval as they departed from their earlier hostility toward ASEAN.

1975: The Shock of Saigon

The Communist victory in Indochina in April, 1975, although initially causing deep shock and uncertainty, stimulated closer ASEAN cooperation and more open political ties. The speed of the southern military collapse caught even Hanoi by surprise. ASEAN concern with Vietnamese military might—now augmented by vast quantities of captured American weapons—was strengthened, as were fears that some of this military equipment might find its way to Communist insurgents still active in ASEAN countries. Thailand and Malaysia were of particular concern. Thailand was unprecedentedly volatile in the wake of an October 1973 student revolt against military rule, with a fourteen-party civilian cabinet holding a very thin parliamentary majority. In Malaysia Razak's sudden death in January 1976 brought Datu Hussein Onn to the prime ministership. Untested outside the domestic arena he faced a seemingly reinvigorated Communist campaign focused on urban terrorism. Meanwhile, it seemed probable that a divided and demoralized United States would withdraw from Southeast Asia, leaving the field to others less well disposed toward the ASEAN states.

Whether optimistic that Vietnam would turn its efforts to the arts of peace, opening the way to a new era in Southeast Asia, or pessimistic that it would be tempted to direct its power against its neighbors, ASEAN members recognized the vital necessity of unity and confidence in dealing with Hanoi.

To demonstrate such unity, however, the ASEAN countries had first to agree among themselves at a time of maximum uncertainty and of differences about how to proceed. The search for consensus was lengthy. In the period between April 1975 and February 1976, when the heads of government met in Bali, there had been innumerable meetings among ministers and senior officials. Heads of governments also met with one another with unprecedented frequency. And on the eve of Bali, Tun Razak's funeral brought all the leaders together in Kuala Lumpur.

Whether the Indochina countries should now be invited to join ASEAN and whether ASEAN should become a security organization were the principal issues. Malaysia, wanting to avoid a two-bloc Southeast Asia and hopeful that Hanoi would focus on domestic development, was a strong proponent of an invitation. Thailand and the Philippines, both seeking to distance themselves from their past support of Saigon, were similarly inclined. Singapore and Indonesia had no such optimistic expectations, and Singapore's Foreign Minister Rajaratnam, pointing to "the possible adverse consequences of the emergence of revolutionary Indochina," had argued that ASEAN should "not give the impression of weakness by pleading with others to join."[25] The case for the negative was strengthened by Hanoi's own statements, which made it evident that an invitation would be rejected. Agreeing at Bali that there should be no such invitation, ASEAN agreed that its members individually should seek friendly relations with the countries of Indochina in the hope of encouraging them to identify their interests with Southeast Asia rather than with the PRC or the USSR.

Arguments in favor of a security role for ASEAN were accorded much less weight than fears that joint security arrangements could solidify Southeast Asia's division into two hostile blocs. Instead, the leaders agreed that each of the ASEAN countries would improve its military capabilities, that the developing network of bilateral security ties would be strengthened and expanded, and that the ASEAN states would encourage the United States to retain its "over-the-horizon" military presence and its interest in Southeast Asia, the disastrous American experience in Indochina notwithstanding.

The 1976 Bali consensus on major immediate issues was accompanied by two formal agreements, the Declaration of ASEAN Concord and the Treaty of Amity and Concord. The Declaration was the first forthright public statement of ASEAN's political role. Hitherto shared but not publicly acknowledged objectives—political solidarity, cooperative political action, the elimination of subversive threats—were now openly emphasized while recommendations for security cooperation outside ASEAN were balanced by calls for the early achievement of ZOPFAN.

The Treaty of Amity and Concord was significant in two respects. It gave the principles of the Bangkok Declaration the force of treaty obligations. And because it was open to signature by all Southeast Asian states, it was in effect an invitation to Hanoi and a symbolic step toward ZOPFAN.[26]

By meeting together at Bali, ASEAN leaders had signaled a commitment beyond any that could be made by periodic foreign-ministerial meetings. That they could do so reflected not only the urgency of the moment but also the extent to which earlier strains had been reduced and greater intimacy established in ten years of consultation.

Fear of Indonesian reversion to a disruptive role in the region had subsided, with Indonesia now firmly under Suharto's control. Progress in relations between Singapore and Indonesia was evidenced in 1973, when Lee Kuan Yew, making his first official visit to Jakarta, apologized for the execution of the marines by sprinkling flower petals on their graves. Suharto's crucial contributions to the achievement of the Bali consensus demonstrated both the importance he attributed to the organization and the willingness of the smaller partners to show Indonesia appropriate deference.

Intraregional differences had not been fully resolved, but they had been very much subordinated to the interests of regional unity. The Philippine claim to Sabah and suspicions of a Malaysian role in the Muslim revolt had not been abandoned. But exchanges on the subject were infrequent and low key, and the Philippines could count on Malaysia and Indonesia for efforts to moderate the response of the Organization of the Islamic Conference to Filipino countermeasures against the Muslim rebels. Thai-Malaysian border cooperation was moving into what was to be a fairly steady upward trend in the wake of a serious incident in the spring of 1976. In the following year, the ASEAN spirit was embodied in agreements among Singapore, Malaysia, and Indonesia on navigation safety in the Malacca and Singapore straits, involving compromises by each party in the interests of retaining control in littoral hands and excluding outside users, particularly Japan, from participation in regulation and management.

In international meetings, ASEAN consultations and joint positions were becoming commonplace. In 1975, seeking improved bargaining power on economic issues, ASEAN began to establish its so-called dialogue relationship with each of its principal trading partners—the European Community, New Zealand, Australia, Canada, Japan, and in 1977, the United States. Testifying to the regard in which it was now held, ASEAN's August 1977 Kuala Lumpur Summit, although not noteworthy for any new decisions, was immediately followed by a conference (the Five plus Three) with the heads of government of Australia, Japan, and New Zealand.

Since then, ASEAN's cohesion has been further consolidated not only as the result of its widely applauded role with respect to Cambodia, but also because of proliferating agreements and cooperative ties among its members in such normally disputatious areas as fishing rights in overlapping jurisdictions at sea and resource development in contiguous land areas. Military cooperation among ASEAN members has evolved also from the early joint measures against insurgents and smugglers on common land or sea borders to a complex of bilateral and trilateral arrangements for air, sea, and land exercises as well as for intelligence and training exchange. The significance of these arrangements has been enhanced by improvements in national defense capabilities.

Although the state of political and security cooperation seems to be regarded with general satisfaction within ASEAN, dissatisfaction with the extent of economic cooperation is widespread.[27] Over the years such cooperation has been blocked by fears of loss of control over significant elements of national policy, concern over possibly unbalanced distribution of advantages and disadvantages, awareness of the unimpressive record of such cooperative ventures as ASEAN has undertaken, and the unwillingness of the foreign ministers to share authority with their economic colleagues. However, the subject is now being approached more seriously as ASEAN statesmen have become preoccupied with the economic threats to their security from moves by their principal trading partners toward protectionism and the formation of trading blocs. Economic officials and businessmen argue that these trends make it more necessary than ever that ASEAN exploit its own market of 270 million people and the economies of scale that could be achieved jointly. The Manila Declaration, issued by the Third ASEAN Summit in December 1987, dealt at length with prospective areas of economic cooperation, but few practical steps were taken between that meeting and the Fourth Summit in Singapore early in 1992. There a number of proposals developed by the economic ministers were approved by the leaders, including plans for the phased establishment of an ASEAN free trade area.

The ASEAN Process and Rules of the Game

Although the pressures posed by international developments and internal weaknesses provided the impetus for cooperation in ASEAN, domestic factors and ASEAN structure and procedures help explain why the association has survived and flourished for more than twenty years. As already noted, the impulse to preserve regional peace was strengthened by the high priority in national policy accorded to economic development. Success in the pursuit of regional peace owed much to the high caliber of national leadership—both political and bureaucratic—and to the authority, longevity, and largely unchallenged control over foreign policy enjoyed by political leaders.

With neither a large bureaucracy nor formally codified procedures, ASEAN has developed forms of consultation that employ existing national institutions and that have given its leaders an unusually clear understanding of one another's interests and needs. These are served also by well-understood rules of the game. Under these rules, decisions are made only by consensus; issues on which consensus is unlikely are not addressed, and collective movement is at the pace of the slowest member. Interference in one another's internal affairs is precluded, and public criticism of one by another is discouraged. Public discussion of policy differences, if it occurs at all, is conducted in a low-key and non-confrontational manner.

Agreement among national leaders puts the final seal of approval on ASEAN decisions and understandings, but the foreign ministers and senior national officials are responsible for the frequently prolonged efforts on which these understandings rest. There have been only four summits to date. Leaders, however, exchange bilateral visits with some frequency. ASEAN foreign ministers meet frequently, both on a regularly scheduled annual basis and on other occasions as the situation dictates. Between such meetings, the work of coordination and consultation continues to be carried on by foreign ministerial staffs, ambassadors and embassy personel, and a variety of special committees. Economic and planning ministers also meet regularly but have been unable to gain equal status with the foreign ministers. A Senior Officials Meeting (SOM) brings together officers at the apex of the national bureaucratic structures and does key preparatory work for the meetings of the foreign ministers. These senior officials, in turn, rely heavily on their own domestic bureaucracies rather than on the very small ASEAN secretariat headquartered in Jakarta.

ASEAN's reliance on national bureaucracies, rather than on its secretariat, has had mixed results. Because of their important role in the ASEAN process and the consequent extent of their contacts, the national bureaucracies have developed both ASEAN consciousness and a stake in the success of the association's activities. Moreover, since the small and weak secretariat cannot compete with its national counterparts, there is little of the tension that exists elsewhere between national and regional establishments. On the other hand, the weakness of the secretariat may have inhibited ASEAN planning and minimized its investigative capabilities and put ASEAN at a disadvantage in its dealings with such generously staffed organizations as the European Community. Concern with these weaknesses has led to proposals to expand the size and functions of the Secretariat and to strengthen the role of the economic ministers.

Relations Between the Blocs

Relations between ASEAN and Hanoi have followed an uneven course. Hanoi's victory in 1975 led to conciliatory gestures on both sides, but in the wake of Vietnam's occupation of Cambodia, these were quickly replaced by a confrontation lasting for almost ten years.[28] In the late 1980s another transition began toward the elimination of Cambodia as an issue between ASEAN and Hanoi and the development of active and cordial bilateral relations between the states of the two subsystems.

For Hanoi, relations with ASEAN became of concern only in the mid–1970s; until then the DRV ignored ASEAN or dismissed it as a SEATO in disguise and Thailand, in particular, as a tool of American imperialism. In contrast, from ASEAN's earliest days, it was preoccupied by Indochina. Apprehensions aroused by the extent of great power intervention there were mixed with concern about Hanoi's future policies should it achieve its goals in Indochina in alliance with the PRC and the USSR.

In the late 1960s and early 1970s fears of a Communist victory and U.S. withdrawal heightened. Seeking to lay the groundwork for a tolerable future relationship with Hanoi, ASEAN emphasized that, as an organization, it was neutral, nonconfrontational, focused on economic cooperation, and looking forward to an Indochina settlement and peaceful relations thereafter. Despite their growing pessimism over the final outcome, ASEAN members hoped for a breathing space long enough to enable them to build the strength they might need to cope with a Communist Indochina. Accordingly, their national policies, carefully distinguished from those of ASEAN, favored the United States and South Vietnam, with Indonesia being the only state even to maintain relations with the DRV.

In the interval between the Second and Third Indochina Wars, ASEAN countries at the Bali Summit tried to persuade Hanoi of their good will, while Hanoi seemed unable to decide whether to treat ASEAN as friend or enemy. On the one hand, the new Socialist Republic of Vietnam (SRV), proclaimed in 1976, established relations with the ASEAN countries and pledged peaceful coexistence. On the other, Hanoi depicted ASEAN as an instrument of U.S. "neocolonialist" policy, and revolutionary themes were conspicuous in Vietnamese propaganda addressed to Southeast Asia.

By mid–1978, however, as Vietnam moved toward its invasion of Cambodia, its new alliance with the USSR, and its final rupture with the PRC, it began to cultivate ASEAN goodwill. Its prime minister and others visited the ASEAN capitals, not only once again pledging respect for peaceful coexistence and national boundaries but also expressing a more positive view of ASEAN.

The ASEAN countries, however, had their own suspicions that Hanoi's courtship and that of Moscow and Beijing were linked to the gathering storm in Cambodia. Moreover, distrust of Vietnam's intentions was now coming from an additional source as the flow of "boat people" to ASEAN shores led statesmen to suspect Hanoi of exporting its own ethnic Chinese minority problem in a possibly deliberate assault on domestic stability in their states.

It was very quickly evident that Vietnam's invasion late in December 1978 was no mere escalated repeat of the earlier cross-border intrusions.

The speed with which the Vietnamese forces drove to Cambodia's western border and the early establishment in Phnom Penh of the Vietnamese-dominated People's Republic of Kampuchea (PRK) demonstrated Hanoi's determination to remain in control in Cambodia, relying on a large military presence to enforce its will and on the Soviet Union for material assistance and protection against the Chinese. For ASEAN a not unwelcome quarrel absorbing the energies of two Communist neighbors had escalated into a threat to Thailand's security, an affront to the principles of respect for national sovereignty and peaceful settlement of disputes (to which Vietnam had only recently pledged itself), and an invitation to renewed external intervention in Southeast Asia.

Thailand had earlier lost its Lao buffer, with tens of thousands of Vietnamese troops stationed there. It was now faced by a still larger Vietnamese force on its border with Cambodia, only a short distance from Bangkok and the Thai heartland. Surviving Khmer Rouge forces had also regrouped in the border area, and armed conflict was already spilling over into Thailand. Hundreds of thousands of fleeing Khmer, seeking refuge in the border area or in Thailand, added to the problems posed by both the cross-border fighting and the ever-growing Vietnamese refugee presence.

Recognizing that their carefully nurtured political ties were now being tested, the ASEAN countries stood firm behind Thailand. Recalling the Japanese advance from Vietnam and then, through Thailand, into all of Southeast Asia, ASEAN leaders saw Bangkok's vulnerability as their own. Acquiescence to Vietnam's aggression against Cambodia could encourage Hanoi to support nearby insurgencies and to pursue by armed force Lao territorial claims to northeast Thailand, Thai-Cambodian border disputes, and claims to islands in the South China Sea, also claimed by Malaysia and the Philippines. Meanwhile, Vietnam had violated principles—nonintervention, respect for sovereignty, and peaceful settlement of disputes—that were at the very core of ASEAN concerns.

ASEAN's initial uncertainty over how to respond to the Vietnamese move was quickly replaced by unqualified opposition. Its abandonment of its traditionally conciliatory approach to Hanoi reflected not only the seriousness of the challenge, but also the confidence ASEAN drew from the extent of its international support. However, although ASEAN very quickly became established as the international community's voice on Cambodia, Hanoi was slow to take it seriously, for some time dismissing its stance as "crude interference" and "brazen meddling." Even after Hanoi accepted the necessity of responding to ASEAN's periodic statements with elaborations of its own position, each side remained unmoved on central issues well into the 1980s.

For ASEAN the basic premise was simple: Vietnam had committed aggression and perpetuated its offense by a military occupation and a puppet government. Accordingly, it must withdraw its troops completely, unconditionally, and under international supervision. It must also agree to the establishment under international supervision of a new government that would represent the freely expressed wishes of the Cambodian people, adopt a neutral and nonaligned posture internationally, and pose no threat to the security interests of any of Cambodia's neighbors.

Hanoi's position was equally clear: It rejected the very principles of international interest and responsibility on which ASEAN's position was based. Vietnam's troops had entered Cambodia in defense of their country and to help the Khmer rid themselves of the genocidal Khmer Rouge. They remained there at Khmer request; they would leave when the Hanoi and Phnom Penh governments agreed that it was safe to do so. The new political situation in Phnom Penh was "irreversible" and not a suitable subject for international negotiations.

For a considerable period each protagonist was sufficiently confident of its ability to outlast the other to stand firm on its basic positions. Hanoi had good reason to believe that, as in the past, time was on its side. Although Vietnam's forces were unable to suppress the Cambodian resistance, Vietnamese control was not threatened. Meanwhile, the Vietnamese-sponsored Heng Sam-rin regime was building an administrative structure, an army, and a presence in the countryside. The Vietnamese were distinctly unpopular, but the possibility that their failure might return Pol Pot to power strengthened the will of Hanoi's Khmer allies. Although China remained deeply hostile, Vietnamese troops on the border were now better armed than their PLA opponents, and China showed no inclination to go beyond periodic border skirmishes to repeat its 1979 invasion. The Soviet Union, although a grumbling ally, continued to underwrite a faltering economy and prolonged hostilities, accepting this and the antagonism of ASEAN as a reasonable price for its ability to maintain an ever-growing military presence in Vietnamese territory.

ASEAN, however, also had reason for confidence. With the passage of time, the relative position of the two blocs had been reversed. ASEAN, preoccupied in 1975 with Hanoi's seemingly much greater strength, had come to see itself as outranking Vietnam in most important respects. Hanoi's own self-image had been dimmed by its massive economic failures, the drain on its resources imposed by its Cambodian policies, the extent of its dependence on the Soviet Union, and the loss of its former international prestige. Strongly supported by the West and much of the Third World, ASEAN had succeeded in blocking Vietnam's efforts to turn de facto success into de jure recognition; each year in the General Assembly the very large majority supporting the ASEAN position grew larger and the diplomatic skill of the ASEAN spokesmen strengthened the association's reputation. Support for the ASEAN position was also evident outside the U.N. Since 1979, the U.S. secretary of state had joined the foreign ministers of the other dialogue partners in meeting annually with their ASEAN counterparts, an important symbol of the solid backing of the West, as was the economic embargo imposed on Vietnam by the advanced countries. The United States had reaffirmed its Manila Pact commitment to Thailand, which had also received assurances that China would respond to a Vietnamese attack. Meanwhile, although Thailand faced severe problems along the frontier and the refugee burden grew markedly, the ASEAN countries were not otherwise seriously challenged. Economic growth continued apace, and political stability was the order of the day.

The Khmer resistance was also a useful instrument, although a dubious one. Its three factions—the Khmer Rouge, the Khmer People's National Liberation Front (KPNLF) of former Prime Minister Son Sann, and Prince Sihanouk's FUNCINPEC (National United Front for an Independent, Neutral, Peaceful, and Cooperative Cambodia)—were unlikely collaborators. In mid–1982 their agreement to establish the Coalition Government of Democratic Kampuchea (CGDK) with Sihanouk as president endowed the resistance collectively with somewhat greater legitimacy and respectability. But forced on the factions by their ASEAN and Chinese allies, the coalition had little impact on the quarrels among them, and they continued to carry on their separate wars, sometimes against each other rather than against the Vietnamese enemy. Moreover, the coalition gambit, however useful in U.N. debates and in adding to the pressures on Hanoi, merely postponed the issue of how the crimes of the Pol Pot regime should ultimately be dealt with and what role the Khmer Rouge should play in an international settlement.

By the late 1980s, formal exchanges between ASEAN and Hanoi had begun to give way to genuine dialogue as, on both sides, changing international circumstances and domestic concerns were reducing Cambodia's priority and confrontation over Cambodia was becoming an obstacle to the achievement of more important objectives.

The retreat from hard-line positions began in 1987 with the gradual abandonment of the mutual rigidity that had excluded the Phnom Penh Khmer and the opposition factions from participating directly in the dialogue. The process was initiated in 1987 by Indonesia's proposal for an informal gathering of the Khmer contestants and by Sihanouk's November meeting with PRK Prime Minister Hun Sen. The new emphasis on national reconciliation resulted in mid–1988 in a meeting in Jakarta (the Jakarta Informal Meeting, or JIM I) at which, for the first time, representatives of ASEAN, Hanoi, the Phnom Penh regime, and the resistance factions met together. JIM I reflected significant changes in Vietnamese and ASEAN positions. By accepting national reconciliation as a major goal, ASEAN had come closer to Hanoi's position that the Cambodian problem originated in civil war, not foreign occupation. By accepting the principle of free, internationally supervised elections, Hanoi had abandoned its initial insistence that "the political situation in Cambodia is irreversible" and that resistance factions could play no part in Cambodia's future. Hanoi had also accepted some of its ASEAN-ascribed responsibility by agreeing to participate in negotiations with the CGDK and Sihanouk. ASEAN, abandoning its insistence that negotiations must be first and foremost with Vietnam, the principal culprit, had acquiesced in this blurring of the issue. It had also abandoned its own earlier objections to any negotiations with the PRK.

At the same time, Hanoi's earlier partial troop withdrawal claims (dismissed at the time as propaganda or camouflaged redeployments) began to assume a new reality. By the end of 1988 Vietnamese troops in Cambodia had fallen to 50,000 to 70,000 from a high of 170,000 to 200,000.[29] Late in 1989, Hanoi's announcement that its withdrawal had been completed was generally accepted, even though the movement had not been internationally monitored. By this time, the now more promising negotiations had largely moved to a new forum, the Paris International Conference on Cambodia, under the auspices of which the five permanent members of the Security Council were to assume an increasingly central role in the effort to devise a Cambodia settlement.

Hanoi's slow retreat from hard-line positions responded to both domestic and international pressures. The burdens of its military role in Cambodia were becoming less bearable as casualties mounted and domestic morale declined. Exclusion from Western trade and investment was a major obstacle to new plans for economic restructuring through a more open market and a greater role for foreign capital. Dependence on Soviet aid was galling enough. But even worse was the approaching significant decline as Moscow became ever more impatient with its Vietnamese economic burdens and more absorbed in major changes in its own foreign policy. Under Gorbachev, the pace of Sino-Soviet rapprochement had quickened, détente with the West had become an overriding concern, a closer relationship with non-Communist Asia had become a more pronounced interest, and the reconstruction of the Soviet economy was being given priority over military expenditures. All these considerations disposed Moscow toward an early Cambodian settlement, and its willingness to put pressure on Hanoi was enhanced by the much reduced value in the new circumstances of its military access to Vietnamese territory.

Although the extent of Vietnam's problems forced serious consideration of the negotiating option, agreement to pursue it may have been eased by the fact that Hanoi still had cards to play: Moscow's residual interest in retaining its "fraternal ties," the strengthened international credibility of the regime in Phnom Penh, the possibility of taking advantage of divisions in ASEAN or of the international weariness with the issue, and mounting international preoccupation with the prospect that the Khmer Rouge might regain power.

If Hanoi's moves toward compromise were prompted by its weaknesses, the reverse was true of ASEAN. In the long years of Cambodian stalemate, ASEAN's firmness in dealing with Vietnam and in standing behind a threatened member had become matters of record. Meanwhile, the threat to Thailand and potentially to ASEAN had receded. Vietnam's reputation for invincibility had suffered badly, and its manifest economic weaknesses and political isolation had made its military power seem much less significant. However, although fortified by its own accomplishments, ASEAN had to be concerned that time would erode international support for a further prolonged Cambodian effort. And there were the concerns aroused by recurring Cambodian-related differences within ASEAN that were a source of strain and bruised egos among its members and of alarm on the part of its supporters.

Periodic differences about Cambodian negotiating policy were less over principle than over tactics—determining the most effective combination of pressures and inducements in dealing with Hanoi and with differing threat perceptions of China entering into differing conclusions. Concern with China as the ultimate threat made Indonesia and Malaysia the most persistent advocates of more conciliatory policies toward Vietnam as a potential barrier against the extension of Chinese influence into Southeast Asia. Thailand's fears, however, were centered on Vietnam. With bitterly anti-Vietnamese China a welcome ally, Bangkok's emphasis was much more on pressure than on conciliation. However, as Thailand was relieved of the presence of Vietnamese troops on its border and as it developed real prospects for joining NIC ranks, economic opportunities began to displace military threats as its principal concerns with dealing with the countries of Indochina.

The Thai shift began even before Chatichai Choonhaven became prime minister in mid-August 1988. But it was most dramatically expressed in Chatichai's public emphasis on turning Indochina "from a battlefield into a marketplace" and in his January 1989 invitation to Hun Sen to visit Bangkok. The latter move, although described as unofficial, alarmed both Chatichai's foreign ministry and the ASEAN partners, who feared that Hun Sen's presence in Bangkok would legitimate the Phnom Penh regime and weaken ASEAN's negotiating position and who resented Chatichai's failure to consult before taking such an important step.

However, as the shock subsided, it became evident that once again, as in the past, an originally aberrant position was being absorbed into a new ASEAN consensus. The precedents were numerous. In the early 1980s the Indonesian-Malaysian Kuantan Doctrine acknowledging Hanoi's legitimate security concerns in Cambodia, although originally seen as dangerously soft, was quickly absorbed into the ASEAN position. In the mid–1980s, initially criticized Malaysian and Indonesian proposals for involving the Khmer factions in the negotiations (seen in much the same light as Chatichai's invitation to Hun Sen) became building blocks for JIM I and the many meetings that followed. In the same period, Indonesia's seeming courtship of Hanoi under the auspices of elements of the military leadership caused serious concern within ASEAN. Harmony was restored, however, by ASEAN recognition of Indonesia's "two-track" policy—one track strictly bilateral, the other concerned with Cambodia where, within the ASEAN consensus, Indonesia served as ASEAN's designated interlocutor.

By the beginning of the new decade all the ASEAN states were in full pursuit of the two-track policy, significantly expanding bilateral contacts with the Indochina states while continuing to speak with one voice in the formal negotiating arena.In this arena, ASEAN and Vietnam came to be less dominant participants. The role of the Khmer factions took on a life of its own, their obduracy becoming the last major obstacle to settlement. The internationalization of the negotiating process, as the five permanent members of the Security Council and Australia and Japan became more heavily involved, both reduced ASEAN's role and made it easier for the individual Indochina and ASEAN states to deal with one another bilaterally.

With Cambodia, whatever its continuing internal problems, largely removed as an issue between ASEAN and Hanoi, the door has now been opened to the closer cooperation between the two subregions that both espouse. However, progress toward a formal regionwide grouping is likely to be slow. The ASEAN countries will want to test Vietnam's behavior—the extent of its movement into a market economy compatible with theirs, its behavior toward its neighbors, and its ability to adjust to ASEAN's consensual procedures. Hanoi may also have misgivings. Will Vietnam wish to become a freshman member of an organization established by other, mostly smaller states twenty-five years ago? Will it be willing to abandon Indochina as an artificial construct imposed by the French or will it want to retain the division of Southeast Asia into two distinct subregions, even though they may be joined together in a cooperative relationship?

Conclusions

Regional Structure

The states of Southeast Asia form two distinct subsystems until recently sharply divided from one another by opposing ideologies, opposing external ties, and confrontation over Cambodia. In both subsystems, preoccupation with threats posed by outside great powers in the Cold War context has been an important ingredient of two major and somewhat conflicting compulsions: on the one hand, to look outward for help and protection to the more sympathetic or less threatening of the Cold War competitors; on the other, to join with neighbors to reduce dependency on extraregional powers and diminish pretexts for their intervention in regional affairs.

The ASEAN subregion is notable for the complementary assets of the six participating states. Their differing strengths—Indonesia's enormous size and potential, Singapore's international financial and commercial role, the economic prowess of Thailand and Malaysia, Brunei's oil wealth, Thai and Filipino security ties to the United States—make them important to one another and enhance the attractions of cooperation. A degree of symbolic deference to Indonesia has been reflected in the selection of Bali as the site of the first ASEAN Summit and Jakarta as the headquarters for the small ASEAN secretariat. But otherwise, the weight of any ASEAN member within the organization tends to vary with circumstances. Thus, as long as the Thai were faced with large armed forces across their borders with Cambodia and Laos, Thailand was accorded front-line status and its views on the Cambodia issue were given particular importance.

In contrast, the Indochina subregion has been dominated by Hanoi, to whose support the Communist governments in Cambodia and Laos owed both their existence and survival. This dependence has been reinforced by the gross disparities in size, population, and mobilization capabilities between Vietnam and its small partners: a Vietnamese population over eight times larger than Cambodia's and sixteen times that of Laos; one of the world's largest armies; and an economy that, however run-down, has attained a higher stage of development than its Indochina neighbors are likely to reach. However, Vietnam's much superior strength has not precluded armed nationalist resistance to Vietnamese domination in Laos and to a much greater extent in Cambodia.

ASEAN

Sources of Readiness to Collaborate

ASEAN's members generally give priority to the preservation of subregional comity over the assertion of superior authority or the imposition on the group of a particular national point of view. The increasingly evident benefits its members enjoy from their cooperation have come to outweigh the satisfactions that might result from vigorous pursuit of bilateral quarrels. The existence of accepted norms, even if they are not always observed, encourages mutual confidence and minimizes unpleasant surprises.

Common security objectives directed toward strengthening national, subregional, and regional autonomy, and common threat perceptions have constituted the cornerstone of ASEAN collaboration, despite early emphasis on economic and social cooperation as ASEAN's major mission. Threat perceptions have changed with the times.

In the 1960s and early 1970s they focused on the problems posed by externally supported insurgents and dissidents and the dangers of outside intervention in these disorders and in the disputes of member states. In the mid–1970s, stimulated by Communist successes in Indochina, they shifted toward heightened concern with the intentions of a heavily armed, united Vietnam under Hanoi's triumphant control. In the 1980s they shifted again to emphasize unfavorable trends in the global market as Vietnam lost its invincible reputation and movement toward détente accelerated.

Limits on Collaboration

Neither the preeminence of their security concerns nor the importance they attribute to economic growth as an essential ingredient of national security has led the ASEAN states to sacrifice elements of their sovereignty to a supranational organization. Instead, when the member states have acted together in their ASEAN capacity, it has been through diplomatic channels and on a case-by-case basis.

Gains from Collaboration

As a "diplomatic community"[30] ASEAN has brought to its members the heightened standing derived from belonging to a long-lived and stable grouping whose members together command a very large population, major resources, a prominent role in the global economy, and a strategic location on major lines of communication. Their concerted voice has helped them defend their interests in the EC, Tokyo, Washington, and international forums such as the United Nations. Their collaboration has reduced their mutual apprehensions, encouraged predictability, and allowed them to maximize their attention to their domestic development. Collaboration in ASEAN has also brought to all its members advantages from the links some of them maintain with other countries or organizations.

Ethnicity and Religion

Multiethnicity is accepted by ASEAN nations as a characteristic they all share in some degree, one that must be taken into account in both domestic and foreign policy. Within ASEAN the activities of ethnic groups that straddle national boundaries have not been a significant source of conflict in recent decades. The only ethnic antagonism that is truly important in relations between ASEAN states is that toward their Overseas Chinese communities. The suspicion with which these communities are regarded spills over into relations between Sinic Singapore, on the one hand, and Malaysia and, to a lesser extent, Indonesia, on the other. This is sometimes to the detriment of ASEAN comity.

In foreign policy, great sensitivity to China's role mirrors domestic concerns with the Overseas Chinese. Beijing's presumed willingness and ability to manipulate Overseas Chinese communities to its own advantage is another ingredient in the preoccupation with China as a potential threat that is characteristic of all Southeast Asian countries. Although common concern with China contributes to collaboration, the question of how to deal with China can be divisive, as was evident in the anxieties caused to its partners by Thailand's close cooperation with China in supporting the Cambodian resistance.

Religion, closely identified with ethnicity, plays an important part in the domestic politics and in the foreign policies of those states whose populations are predominantly Muslim. Except insofar as Islam is an indivisible part of the ethnicity that pits Malays against Chinese, religious differences have not been disruptive of relations between ASEAN states. Malaysia and Indonesia both have their extremist Muslim groups, but in neither country are they the dominant element, nor are they likely to become so. Sympathy for Muslim dissidents in the Roman Catholic Philippines exists in Indonesia and Malaysia. But especially in Indonesia, the other governments want, for their own domestic reasons, to avoid acts that suggest tolerance for secessionist movements. Meanwhile, Indonesian and Malaysian membership in the OIC has helped shield the Philippines from the anger of other Islamic countries.

The ASEAN Process and Rules of the Game

Lacking a large bureaucracy and formally codified procedures, ASEAN has relied on frequent consultation, with the foreign ministers at the apex of the process but with lower political and bureaucratic levels and private interests also actively involved. Out of these consultations has evolved an unusual degree of regional awareness and readiness to cooperate. Collaboration has also been eased by continuity in the political leadership and foreign policy establishments of ASEAN countries, the limited role played by elected parliaments in the shaping of foreign policy, and the general acceptance of a number of rules of the game that emphasize achieving consensus, however slowly; noninterference in one another's domestic affairs; and civility and restraint in bilateral dealings.

Indochina

In this century, superior force has been required to establish organic linkages among Cambodia, Laos, and Vietnam—that of France in the colonial era and of Vietnam thereafter. To be sure, the sociocultural differences among the three are no greater than those among the ASEAN states. However, the common interests that have encouraged voluntary association in ASEAN have no counterpart in Indochina outside the ranks of the governing Communist parties. Equally, the intensity of Cambodian nationalist antagonism toward the Vietnamese has no counterpart in ASEAN.

Hanoi's drive toward hegemony reflected its security interests in the external policies of bordering states exposed by their weakness not only to Vietnamese ambitions but also, from Hanoi's perspective, to manipulation by hostile forces. Its most potent weapon has been military force. In the absence of large, occupying forces, pressures on Phnom Penh and Vientiane for conformity to Hanoi's wishes will lose some of their impact. This will be increasingly true as ideological bonds wither, new leaders emerge with fewer personal ties across national borders, and access to the wider world reduces dependency on Vietnam and enlarges opportunities for balancing relations. By the same token, nationalist resistance to Vietnamese claims is likely to assert itself more strongly. Vietnam's impressively larger size may induce caution in Vientiane. As history demonstrates, however, this will not necessarily be the case in Phnom Penh.

Recognition of Thailand's superior economic attractions will also encourage Lao and Khmer tendencies to move away from Vietnam. Thailand will welcome opportunities to expand its influence in these neighboring states, but if relations with Vietnam are equable, not at the expense of these relations.

Support from outside: The extraregional role.   Their desire for maximum autonomy notwithstanding, the members of both subsystems have looked to outside powers for help. The latter have felt impelled to respond, sometimes because of obligations assumed to former colonies, but more often because of their competition with one another, especially in the Cold War context. Outside powers have thus continued to play a very substantial role in the affairs of the region. Chinese and Soviet support contributed heavily to Hanoi's victory in Vietnam, but massive assistance from the United States failed to preserve the independence of South Vietnam. Western economic and security assistance, coupled with trade and investment, strengthened ASEAN and its members; Soviet support encouraged Vietnam to persist in its Cambodian venture.

The special ties of some ASEAN states with outside powers have generally served the interests of ASEAN as a whole; no ASEAN member has attempted to use such ties to influence or coerce a fellow member. This contrasts with the way in which Vietnam and Khmer Rouge Cambodia were reinforced in their struggle with one another by their respective Soviet and Chinese allies.

Reliance on outside power has not brought subordination. Regional governments have shown a shrewd appreciation of the leverage clients enjoy over patrons who are competing to advance their own strategic interests through winning the allegiance of smaller states. Fundamental decisions, including decisions on where to look for help, have been driven primarily by each government's conception of its interests in relation to its capabilities or ideological or ethnic affiliations. Nevertheless, if only because of their contribution to national capabilities, outside decisions influence regional behavior. Declining British and American interest and presence in Southeast Asia reinforced collaborative impulses in ASEAN; American support of right-wing governments in Laos and Cambodia was mirrored in Vietnamese support of their Communist opponents. The end of the Cold War and other aspects of the Gorbachev era have once again demonstrated the strong influence of global developments on Southeast Asian regional dynamics. Moscow's decision to end the drain on its resources caused by underwriting Hanoi's economy added to the strains that led Vietnam to withdraw the bulk of its military forces from Cambodia. Improved relations between Moscow and Beijing helped to encourage Vietnamese-Chinese reconciliation. Meanwhile, from Hanoi's perspective, rapprochement with China made military withdrawal from Cambodia a somewhat less risky course. The path to improved relations between Southeast Asia's two subregions was smoothed by this satisfaction of one of ASEAN's principal demands as well as by the efforts of the Indochina states—paralleling those of other socialist countries—to implement ASEAN-like open-market policies and to look to their neighbors and the West for help in economic development.

The economic factor. Economic considerations have not driven ASEAN very far or fast toward cooperative enterprise. They have been important, however, in increasing the value its members place on their organization's contribution to regional peace and stability. This contribution, they argue, has been important in enabling them to focus their attention and budgets on economic and social betterment and on attracting foreign investment. Similarly, conflict avoidance has been encouraged by the common ASEAN view of economic development as the prime national goal and source of political legitimacy.

The flow of commerce has also been important in affecting the external orientation of countries for whom trade has been the engine of growth and whose trade and investment ties (overwhelmingly with Japan, the United States, and the EC) make them an integral part of the Western trading system.

Balancing. Balancing has been a central concept in relations between the two subregions and external powers. Recognizing that the global balance of power, although it affects their well-being, is beyond their power to influence significantly, the ASEAN states have identified a strong U.S. position in the Pacific as an important element in their security. Regional balancing considerations are also important, given the inescapable nearby presence of the two East Asian great powers, China and Japan, both of which have records of expansionism. Relying on the United States and the West, ASEAN states also accepted the desirability of some balance in their Cold War relationships. They responded positively, although cautiously, to Russian and Chinese interest in improved political and economic relations. They also sought to balance their dealings with the two Communist powers, to avoid charges of favoritism.

Hanoi had to offset U.S. obstruction of its ambitions by relying on the Soviet Union and China while allowing neither to dominate its policy. As Sino-Soviet conflict became more intense and each side sought its own countervailing relations with the West, Hanoi's efforts to balance between them became more difficult and, in the end, impossible.

Foreign policy side effects of domestic politics. Domestic politics have played only a small part in foreign policy decisions. However, leaders cannot be as confident as in the past of their foreign policy monopoly as legislators become more assertive and the press more outspoken. In the Philippines, for example, the revival of legislative power and press freedom made the recent round of base negotiations with the United States even more difficult and contentious than the three previous rounds, when decision making was a Marcos monopoly. In addition, the rising foreign policy importance of trade issues has given influential interest groups a new stake in foreign policy decisions, pursued not only through their own direct pressures but also through the press and political parties.

Leaders also cannot ignore certain strong national emotions that they largely share but that can be exploited by political opponents. Sensitivity in domestic forums to evidence of "foreign domination" is heightened by the relative recency of the colonial era. Islam constrains the policies of Jakarta and especially of Kuala Lumpur. In Indonesia it is important to avoid moves that can be attacked as involving the country in a U.S.-dominated military alliance. In Vietnam, particularly because of the indigenous roots of the Lao Dong party and its long and remarkable history, ideology can be a potent factor in internal disputes over foreign policy, however pragmatic final decisions may be.

System change: Sources and prospects. Domestic political developments have contributed to regional system change. Sukarno's ouster made possible the establishment of ASEAN; in the almost thirty years of Suharto's New Order, his support for ASEAN has restrained tendencies among Jakarta's elite to assert a more dominant and perhaps disruptive Indonesian role. In Indochina, Sihanouk's overthrow ended prospects that Cambodia could fend off deeper involvement in the Indochina hostilities. Pol Pot's efforts to employ against the much stronger Vietnamese the same unmeasured brutality he inflicted on his helpless fellow countrymen ensured the forcible subordination of Cambodia to Vietnam, thereby transforming an uncertain Indochina-ASEAN relationship into a confrontational one.

The regional system has also been affected by regime changes of less consequence. Razak brought with him into office the commitment to neutralization that culminated in ZOPFAN; Chatichai, as prime minister, significantly speeded the pace of Thai-Vietnamese rapprochement; Nguyen van Linh's rise to power reflected the increased priority in Vietnamese policymaking of economic recovery and development and the consequent need to improve relations with ASEAN and the West.

In the ASEAN countries there is unlikely to be a repetition in the 1990s of the upheaval represented by the events of the mid–1960s in Indonesia. Even so, domestic developments could have systemic repercussions. In Indonesia, the succession process itself, as well as the character of the successor regime, could have an important bearing on ASEAN; the emergence of a far left Philippine regime strongly imbued with Maoist principles would cause intense uneasiness in the other ASEAN capitals; a violent Malay-Chinese clash in Malaysia would have disturbing implications not only for Singapore and Jakarta, but for the other ASEAN countries as well. In Vietnam and Laos real generational change is overdue and inevitable. The transformations now taking place elsewhere in the Marxist-Leninist world are increasing the likelihood that changes in personnel will bring changes in policy. Finally, to the extent that movement toward more open and participatory politics takes hold in ASEAN and even in Indochina, bilateral differences will be more difficult to deal with quietly, the number and volume of voices that must be heard will increase, and the process of mutual accommodation will become more difficult.

Although domestic political developments have helped mold re-gional systems, external forces have been even more influential and have combined with domestic drives and pressures to shape the policies of regional states. The pace at which Southeast Asia became a region of independent states was significantly speeded by Japan's victories in the Pacific and the weaknesses of the European colonial powers after World War II. Emergence into independence in the Cold War era affected both domestic politics and foreign relations. Cold War competition between the great power protagonists internationalized the Vietnamese civil war and helped involve Laos and Cambodia, brought outside support both to anti-Communist governments and to their domestic Communist enemies, and provided the context for the organization of ASEAN. Postwar economic developments (particularly the demand for raw ma-terials of Japan's resurgent economy and strong U.S. support for an open global market)—together with the pragmatic, development-ori-ented, and generally competent economic policies of ASEAN mem-bers—produced the high levels of growth that have contributed to regional cooperation. The Sino-Soviet dispute was important in inter-nationalizing the conflict in Cambodia, and China's role both brought Beijing into closer relations with the ASEAN states and caused differ-ences among them. Today the end of the Cold War and Sino-Soviet reconciliation have begun to change the parameters of Southeast Asian regional politics.

Without seeking to predict the outcome of still-changing circum-stances, the principal challenges to both ASEAN and Indochina fall into the following categories:

1. *Adjusting to changes in the Great Power environment.* Here caution is the watchword for both ASEAN and Hanoi—the concern not to abandon prematurely relationships that are susceptible of great future change but that are still useful. ASEAN has welcomed opportunities for more active relations with the Soviet Union and China, and although still apprehensive about the implications of an enhanced Japanese polit-ical role, has sought to shape and even encourage it. But still seeing the future as highly uncertain, ASEAN leaders continue to favor a strong U.S. security presence in the vicinity as a balance against the revival of old Soviet, Chinese, or Japanese threats or against new threats from an increasingly heavily armed India. ZOPFAN, and the Southeast Asia

Nuclear Weapons Free Zone more recently advanced by Indonesia, may find their place in some new Pacific order yet to come, but they remain only symbolic formulas today.

Hanoi's international orientation may well shift more than ASEAN's. The support it received from Moscow has already declined substantially and will continue to do so. Reconciliation with China has been eased by the fact that both have been similarly critical of Eastern European and Soviet departures from ideological purity. Meanwhile, economic compulsions are pressing Hanoi toward ASEAN and the West.

2. *Preserving subregional cohesion.* ASEAN's durability, the strength and prestige it has brought to its members, and the network of relationships it has inspired are impressive arguments for its survival. More than survival is at stake, however. ASEAN could lose some of its vitality without Cambodia and regional Cold War repercussions to inspire a common sense of threat. In their absence, sources of friction, old and new, could become more divisive; changes in national leadership, more unsettling; and the achievement of consensus, more difficult.

The future of Hanoi-dominated Indochina is much more uncertain. It will be affected by developments in Cambodia, the priorities Hanoi accords to its various interests, and the relations between Hanoi and ASEAN.

3. *Relations between the subregions.* Common aspirations toward strengthening regional autonomy will not quickly eliminate differences between the subregions. Hanoi, in continued pursuit of global respectability, is likely to press harder than ASEAN for new arrangements. ASEAN, well-entrenched in present relationships, will prefer a slow and cautious evolution; within ASEAN, consensus on the specifics of new arrangements with Hanoi may be hard to reach.

4. *Adjusting to a changing global economy.* Declining concern with military-security threats will intensify the pressures ASEAN faces for a more active effort to find ways beyond the bilateral to cope with unfavorable trends in the global market. Stronger pressures for economic cooperation may also be stimulated as the forum for Asian-Pacific Economic Cooperation (APEC) develops its role, one that ASEAN already fears will submerge its identity in that of a larger organization. Uniting on specific issues to put pressure on the extraregional powers who are its principal trading partners has brought some fruits in the past and fits well into the ASEAN process. To the extent, however, that ASEAN attempts even the most preliminary forms of economic integration, it will have to confront highly sensitive issues of national sovereignty and self-interest.

Economic cooperation will have little relevance to the fortunes of the

Indochina states, for whom economic relations with states outside the subregion, including ASEAN neighbors, will be of principal importance.

NOTES

1. Isolationist Myanmar (formerly Burma) is the only Southeast Asian country not included in either subsystem. Of its relations with its Southeast Asian neighbors, only those with Thailand are of any significance.

2. D. G. E. Hall, *A History of South-East Asia* (New York: St. Martin's Press, 1981), first published in 1955, remains the classic account, extending from prehistoric times to World War II. Milton Osborne's *Southeast Asia: An Introductory History* (Sydney: Allen and Unwin, 1979) is a brief but meaty survey. David Joel Steinberg, ed., *In Search of Southeast Asia* (Honolulu: University of Hawaii Press, 1987) focuses on Southeast Asia on the eve of the colonial era and on the impact of the West but includes several chapters on the period after World War II.

3. For a detailed discussion of the domino theory in American foreign policy, see Robert Jervis and Jack Snyder, *Dominoes and Bandwagons: Strategic Beliefs of Great Power Competition in the Eurasian Rimland* (New York: Oxford University Press, 1991).

4. Events in Southeast Asia between the end of World War II and the organization of ASEAN are the subject of a number of general studies, including John Bastin and Harry Benda, *A History of Modern Southeast Asia* (Englewood Cliffs, N.J.: Prentice-Hall, 1968); John F. Cady, *The History of Post-War Southeast Asia* (Athens: Ohio University Press, 1958); Michael Leifer, *Dilemmas of Statehood in Southeast Asia* (Singapore: Asia Pacific Press, 1973); and Milton Osborne, *Region of Revolt: Focus on Southeast Asia* (New York: Penguin Books, 1971).

5. Post–World War II Indonesia is discussed from various perspectives in Harold Crouch, *The Army and Politics in Indonesia* (Ithaca: Cornell University Press, 1978); Herbert Feith, *The Decline of Constitutional Democracy in Indonesia* (Ithaca: Cornell University Press, 1962); Karl D. Jackson and Lucian Pye, eds., *Political Power and Communications in Indonesia* (Berkeley: Institute of East Asian Studies, University of California, 1978); David Jenkins, *Suharto and His Generals* (Ithaca: Cornell University Press, 1984); George McT. Kahin, *Nationalism and Revolution in Indonesia* (Ithaca: Cornell University Press, 1952); Michael Leifer, *Indonesia's Foreign Policy* (London: Allen and Unwin, 1983); and Williams R. Liddle, ed., *Political Participation in Modern Indonesia* (New Haven: Yale University Press, 1973).

6. General studies include Barbara W. Andaya, *A History of Malaysia* (New York: St. Martin's Press, 1982); Stanley S. Bedlington, *Malaysia and Singapore: The Building of New States* (Ithaca: Cornell University Press, 1978); and R. S. Milne and D. K. Mauzy, *Malaysia: Tradition, Modernity, Islam* (Boulder, Colo.: Westview, 1986).

7. The official count—58 percent Malay—is reached by including in the Malay total Philippine and Indonesian Muslim immigrants and members of indigenous Borneo tribal groups. Without these additions, Malays are estimated to account for slightly less than 50 percent. The Indians, who make up the third significant ethnic community, account for 10 percent.

8. General studies include Bedlington, *Malaysia and Singapore*; Chan Heng Chee, *The Dynamics of One Party Dominance* (Singapore: Singapore University Press, 1976); and R. S. Milne and D. K. Mauzy, *Singapore: The Legacy of Lee Kuan Yew* (Boulder, Colo.: Westview, 1990).

9. David K. Wyatt, *Thailand: A Short History* (New Haven: Yale University Press, 1982) illuminates the background against which postwar institutions have developed. These are discussed in J. L. S. Girling, *Thailand: Society and Politics* (Ithaca: Cornell University Press, 1981); David Morell and Chai-anan Samudavanija, *Political Conflict in Thailand* (Cambridge, Mass.: Oelgeschlager, Gunn, & Hain, 1981); Clark D. Neher, ed., *Modern Thai Politics: From Village to Nation* (Cambridge: Harvard University Press, 1979); Somsakdi Xuto, ed., *Government and Politics of Thailand* (Singapore: Oxford University Press, 1987); and Somsakdi Xuto, *The Military in Thai Politics, 1981–1986* (Singapore: Institute of Southeast Asian Studies, 1987).

10. David Joel Steinberg, *The Philippines: A Singular and a Plural Place* (Boulder, Colo.: Westview, 1990) looks comprehensively at the influences, alien and indigenous, that have molded the contemporary Philippines and includes accounts of the Marcos era and the first years of the post-Marcos period. The events of the 1980s, their historical background, and their implications for the future are also discussed in John Bresnan, ed., *Crisis in the Philippines: The Marcos Era and Beyond* (Princeton: Princeton University Press, 1986), and Carl H. Landé, ed., *Rebuilding a Nation* (Washington, D.C.: Washington Institute Press, 1987). Robert Pringle, *Indonesia and the Philippines: American Interests in Island Southeast Asia* (New York: Columbia University Press, 1980) sheds penetrating light on the stresses and strains of the U.S.-Philippine relationship, and the history and status of the U.S. base presence are dealt with in detail in William E. Berry, Jr., *U.S. Bases in the Philippines: The Evolution of the Special Relationship* (Boulder, Colo.: Westview, 1989).

11. Ranjit Singh, *Brunei, 1839–1983: The Problems of Political Survival* (Singapore: Oxford University Press, 1984) provides unique, full-length coverage. The best sources for contemporary developments are the articles in the annual *Southeast Asian Affairs* published by the Institute of Southeast Asian Studies in Singapore.

12. J. A. C. Mackie, *Konfrontasi: The Indonesia-Malaysia Dispute, 1963–1966* (Kuala Lumpur: Oxford University Press, 1974) is the most comprehensive treatment of this subject.

13. Leifer, *Indonesia's Foreign Policy*, p. 119.

14. Charles Morrison and Astri Suhrke, *Strategies of Survival: The Foreign Policy Dilemmas of Smaller Asian States* (New York: St. Martin's Press, 1979), p. 170.

15. ASEAN's origins and early development are discussed in R. P. Anand, ed., *ASEAN Identity, Development, and Culture* (Honolulu: East West Center,

1981); Alison Broinowski, ed., *Understanding ASEAN* (New York: St. Martin's Press, 1982); and Centre for Strategic and International Studies, *Regionalism in Southeast Asia* (Jakarta, 1974).

16. Under the French, the Indochinese Union had six constituent elements. In Vietnam, these were Cochin China (a colony) and two protectorates, Annam and Tonkin, with the latter nominally under Annam's suzerainty. Cambodia was a protectorate, as was the Lao Kingdom of Luang Prabang; the rest of Laos was under direct French rule.

17. Arthur J. Dommen, *Conflict in Laos: The Politics of Neutralization* (New York: Praeger, 1971) focuses on the involvement of Laos in the Indochina wars from 1945 to 1969. The evolution of the relationship between the Lao and the Vietnamese Communists is examined in detail in McAlister Brown and Joseph J. Zasloff, *Apprentice Revolutionaries: The Communist Movement in Laos, 1930–1985* (Stanford, Calif.: The Hoover Institution, 1986), which deals also with the structure and policies of the Lao People's Democratic Republic, as does Martin Stuart-Fox, *Laos: Politics, Economics, and Society* (London: Francis Pinter, 1986).

18. David P. Chandler, *A History of Cambodia* (Boulder, Colo.: Westview, 1983) provides very useful background. More recent events are covered in David P. Chandler and Ben Kiernan, eds.,, *Revolution and Its Aftermath in Kampuchea: Eight Essays* (New Haven: Yale University Press, 1983), and in Karl Jackson, ed., *Cambodia, 1975–1978* (Princeton: Princeton University Press, 1989).

19. The literature on Vietnam is enormous, although much of it deals more with the American experience there than with Vietnam itself. Joseph Buttinger, *The Smaller Dragon: A Political History of Vietnam* (New York: Praeger, 1958), and his *Dragon Embattled*, 2 vols. (New York: Praeger, 1967), and Ellen J. Hammer, *The Struggle for Indochina, 1940–1955* (Stanford: Stanford University Press, 1966) are classic accounts of the period they cover. William J. Duiker, in *The Communist Road to Power in Vietnam* (Boulder, Colo.: Westview, 1981) provides a history of the Vietnamese revolutionary movement from 1900 to its victory in 1975; his *Vietnam: Nation in Revolution* (Boulder, Colo.: Westview, 1983) surveys the structure and policies of the SRV against a background of Vietnamese history and society.

20. For details of Chinese and Soviet assistance to Hanoi see Douglas Pike, *Vietnam and the Soviet Union* (Boulder, Colo.: Westview, 1987); Robert S. Ross, *The Indochina Tangle: China's Vietnam Policy, 1975–1979* (New York: Columbia University Press, 1988); and W. R. Smyser, *The Independent Vietnamese: Vietnamese Communism Between Russia and China, 1956–1979* (Athens: Ohio University Center for International Studies, 1980), which also contains an excellent analysis of Hanoi's efforts to balance between Moscow and Beijing and to maintain its independence.

21. General Le Duc Anh, quoted in Foreign Broadcast Information Service, *Daily Report, East Asia*, January 4, 1985.

22. The Vietnamese occupation of Cambodia, the events proceeding it, and Soviet and Chinese roles are covered in Nayan Chanda, *Brother Enemy: The War After the War* (New York: Harcourt Brace Jovanovich, 1986); David W. P. Elliot, ed., *The Third Indochina Conflict* (Boulder, Colo.: Westview, 1981); Pai Min-

Chang, *Kampuchea Between China and Vietnam* (Singapore: Singapore University Press, 1985); and Ross, *The Indochina Tangle*.

23. Leifer, *Indonesia's Foreign Policy*, p. 148.

24. Cited in Dick Wilson, *The Neutralization of Southeast Asia* (New York: Praeger, 1975), p. 4, which is the most comprehensive analysis of the ZOPFAN concept.

25. *New York Times*, May 13, 1975; Broinowski, *Understanding ASEAN*, pp. 32–33.

26. The Bali Summit is most fully covered by D. Irvine in Broinowski, *Understanding ASEAN*. Later ASEAN developments are treated in Karl D. Jackson and M. Hadi Soesastro, eds., *ASEAN Security and Economic Development* (Berkeley: Institute of East Asian Studies, University of California, 1984); Karl D. Jackson, Sukhumbhand Paribatra, and J. Soedjati Djiwandono, eds., *ASEAN in Regional and Global Context* (Berkeley: Institute of East Asian Studies, University of California, 1986); and Michael Leifer, *ASEAN and the Security of Southeast Asia* (London: Routledge, 1989).

27. The problems confronting ASEAN economic cooperation and its future prospects receive full and expert attention in Noordin Sopie, Chew Lay See, and Lim Siang Jin, eds., *ASEAN at the Crossroads: Obstacles, Options, and Opportunities in Economic Cooperation* (Kuala Lumpur: Institute of Strategic and International Studies, Malaysia, n.d.).

28. Cambodia as an issue between Vietnam and ASEAN is addressed in William S. Turley, ed., *Confrontation or Coexistence: The Future of ASEAN-Vietnam Relations* (Bangkok: Institute of Security and International Studies, Chulalongkorn University, 1985) and in Donald E. Weatherbee, ed., *Southeast Asia Divided: The ASEAN-Indochina Crisis* (Boulder, Colo.: Westview, 1985).

29. The figures are drawn from Frederick Z. Brown, *Second Chance: The United States and Indochina in the 1990s* (New York: Council on Foreign Relations Press, 1989), p. 50, which, together with a companion essay, *Cambodia and the Dilemmas of U.S. Policy* (New York: Council on Foreign Relations Press, 1991), provides a comprehensive account of Cambodian negotiating developments up to mid–1991.

30. The term aptly applied by Michael Leifer in *ASEAN and the Security of Southeast Asia*.

6

Conclusion

W. HOWARD WRIGGINS

Our examination of the four regional systems over the past forty years confirms the conclusion that most conflicts between regional states result from conditions embedded in each of the four regions. The major external powers have been "pulled" into the region by invitations from regional protagonists as much as they have "pushed" themselves in. External powers affect balances of capability between regional protagonists and the intensity of some of their rivalries. Their interventions sometimes decide local conflicts, but they have had little long-term effect on the direction of policy alignments or realignments among the regional states themselves. Nor have the superpowers, either singly or collectively, been able to impose themselves completely on the regions, replacing anarchy with hegemonic order.

In elaborating on these points, our conclusion first identifies important structural characteristics of the four regions and of the interstate relationships within those regions that limit what their statesmen (or stateswomen) can accomplish. It then considers the more dynamic factors deriving from fears and ambitions of the leading states, and from policies they and the smaller states may pursue in response. Examples of when conflict has been tamed, if not resolved, are examined. We then discuss the manner in which external major powers become drawn into regional affairs and the effects on regional relationships of their activities. We conclude with brief speculation about how the decline in Cold War competition may affect regional relationships.

Some Structural Characteristics

Brief Comparisons

The four regional security systems are very different; they represent four distinct types of international relationship, four contrasting anarchies. In South Asia, the asymmetry is so marked that India appears to be bent on establishing its predominance, and in the process discouraging the other states from security relationships with states beyond the region. In the Gulf, by contrast, more like the Western Europe of the past, several states compete for preeminence. Now one, now another aspirant pushes its entitlement, sometimes by unilateral force. Statesmen have shifted their friendships and their hostility with changing circumstances. The Horn is closer to a Hobbesian model, a world of all against all at both domestic and regional levels, where life is nasty, brutish and short. It is an immature anarchy reflecting the inchoate character of the member states and the lack of regional institutions or accepted norms. Southeast Asia has two sharply distinct subregions, one composed of the Indochina states organized hierarchically under Vietnam's control, the other of the ASEAN states, which have managed to subordinate their rivalries to levels of cooperation resembling the early stages of the movement toward the European Community, a markedly mature anarchy.

All are anarchies in that no single state or political entity has the right or effective capability to manage relationships among them. Anarchy does not imply chaos, however. Characteristic relationships give shape and durability to the way the regional states deal with one another. In these regional anarchies, similar strategies are pursued by states that on the surface seem to be very different from one another. The anarchic system in which each state is embedded narrows choices and often poses only unsatisfactory alternatives. Yet regional structures, different as they are, do not entirely predetermine what happens, since in important instances, as we have seen, changes in domestic political regimes or even leading personalities can lead to markedly different foreign policies that alter the configuration of the region.

Overall, the South Asian system has the simplest and most consistent structure. The long-standing, hostile, asymmetrical relationship between India and Pakistan dominates the region. By comparison, the Horn, the Gulf, and Southeast Asia are more complex and have experienced more marked changes in state-to-state relations. India and Pakistan have held contradictory conceptions of how the region should be organized. One stresses the prime state's responsibility, preferring bilateral dealings on controversial issues; the other stresses the sovereign equality of all the region's states, large or small. Each has at times hoped that the other's internal difficulties would decisively weaken its rival. Their relationship appears to entail unusual difficulties, partly because shadows of the past darkly color expectations and contradictory hopes for the future affect how contemporary issues are perceived by the contending states.

The Gulf security system has experienced more marked changes than any of the others in the past forty years, as British power withdrew and a succession of configurations developed, none of which has yet proved stable. Because the states are largely creations of the settlement of World War I and face competing bases of political allegiance, such as confessional affiliations and transnational programs (Arabism, Islam), their peoples are unusually susceptible to appeals that challenge each state's domestic legitimacy. Forming a three-cornered system, Iran (the largest) and Iraq (the most dissatisfied) have contended for predominance.

Saudi Arabia, the richest but least populous of the three, meanwhile has shifted its alignment, depending on which state has most threatened its domestic stability. Saudi Arabia also exploited the Iran-Iraq rivalry to develop special relations with those smaller neighbors that were more wary of either of the other two than of Riyadh. All three states have sought and received substantial support from the United States, the Soviet Union, or both.

The Horn of Africa represents the most primitive anarchic system, a world without agreed rules, where none of the states meet the Weberian criterion of having a "monopoly on the legitimate use of force." Most of the states lack cohesion, and ethnic differences have been acute. Domestic violence spills over into the international realm, as each state attempts to exploit domestic weaknesses elsewhere to offset its own internal divisions. The states differ fundamentally over the proper principles of statehood, and territorial issues bitterly divide them. Ethiopia, at the geographical center of the region, separates virtually all the others. Territorially based clan rivalries in Somalia in the early 1990s remind us that armed internal opposition can arise in response to authoritarian rule, even in the absence of sharp ethnic divisions. The peoples of Ethiopia, Sudan, and Somalia have all suffered grievously from the weaknesses of their states and the divisions in their populations.

Southeast Asia is the most complex regional system. Indochina, which assumed its Communist-controlled form little more than fifteen years ago, historically has been an imperium—highly asymmetrical, severely authoritarian, and dominated by Vietnam. ASEAN, in existence for almost a quarter of a century, is a consensual association. Underlying the willingness of its members to consider each other's interests and to cooperate as equals is the fact that despite marked differences in size, each of the members has significant strengths to contribute to the whole. The roughly commensurate capability of the member states thus helps induce a search for consensus, distinguishing this diplomatic community from all the other regional clusters we examine.

Embedded Cleavages

Each region is marked by a consistent, durable set of enmity-amity axes. Often these antagonisms have long roots and are well embedded in individual and group perceptions. Others derive from the way these states were incorporated into the international system during the colonial period. The dynamics of domestic politics are the principal engines of regional international politics, driving major foreign policy choices. They set limits to innovation; statesmen ignore them at their peril.

Each region and subregion has its own sources of interstate antagonism. In South Asia, grounds for interstate hostility include historic rivalries between Hindus and Muslims, past conquests of one group over the other, bitterness from the memory of partition, contention over specific territories such as Kashmir, constitutional principles that are mutually offensive, and recollections of three wars since independence. The stark, asymmetrical structure intensifies the security dilemma besetting them both.

In the Gulf, long-standing animosity among Arabs, Kurds, and Persians; rivalry between specific dynasties and personalities; bitter disagreements over arbitrary frontiers laid down by Europeans that affect oil rights and access to waterways; differences among Arab nationalists; modernizers and contending conservative or revolutionary interpreters of Islam; conflicts of interest on oil production and pricing issues; and the presence of thousands of embittered Palestinian refugees present grounds enough for difficulties between neighbors. More than the other regions, the Gulf is marked by political loyalties based on sectarian, linguistic, and familial affiliations that can undermine potential loyalties to existing states. Yet the states have been getting progressively more able to control their societies, building up their coercive and administrative capacities. The states are stronger, but they confront robust subnational and supranational identities. In addition, radical regimes organized around a single party challenge conservative regimes that are based on the claims of family inheritance.

The Horn, as already noted, has the least developed regional system. Bitter recollections of past conquests, long-standing Christian-Muslim rivalry, differing conceptions of the legitimate grounds for statehood, conflict over historic territorial disputes, and the precariousness of the principal states due in large part to the elementary level of political institutionalization and the important role played by dissident and secessionist movements have all contributed to nearly endless warfare or rebellion.

In Southeast Asia, the boundaries established by colonial powers have been an intermittent source of friction between Thailand and each of its neighbors, between Malaysia and the Philippines, and between Cambodia and Vietnam. As ASEAN's development has encouraged dialogue, cleavages stemming from conflicting territorial claims and religious and ethnic differences have been kept within manageable bounds. In Indochina, by contrast, conflicting border claims as well as traditional Khmer-Vietnamese antagonisms entered into the armed clashes that climaxed in the Vietnamese occupation of Cambodia. Thailand's anxieties, reflecting traditional rivalries with Vietnam for the control of the Mekong Basin and fears aroused by the loss of Cambodia as a buffer between them, contributed to the cleavage between ASEAN and Cambodia. Correspondingly, the withdrawal of Vietnamese troops, terminating their menacing presence on the Thai border, contributed to the peace-making process in Cambodia and the reduction of tensions between ASEAN and Hanoi.

Thus, regional conflict structures reflect many unique issues and perceptions. Other characteristics are found in more than one regional system.

The Security Dilemma Intensifies Mutual Fears

In all four regions, difficulties derive from the security dilemma, as prudent leaders seek to counterbalance apparent threats from across their immediate frontier. Each one's effort to gain a margin of safety appears to the other as an attempt to achieve predominance and must be dealt with, either through building internal strength or joining an external alliance.

In the Horn, Ethiopia and Sudan have each been caught in the dilemma, although as Lyons points out, in addition to a competitive arms buildup, they have exploited ethnic and secessionist movements in the other as unconventional ways of coping with it. In the Gulf, Iran, Iraq, and Saudi Arabia have similarly exploited domestic unrest across their borders. They also joined a conventional arms race, made easier by the returns from oil exports and the readiness of competing outside major powers to sell arms to their respective regional clients.

The security dilemma normally is seen as a two-party phenomenon. However, the dynamics in several of these regions suggest that it can often be driving more complex relationships. There are a number of instances where one state reacts to a sense of threat from a neighbor in such a way as to frighten a third. India and Pakistan worried about each other as each sought to improve its relative position with external support or by internal balancing. But for both of them, the threat of third parties complicated the difficulty. India's efforts to deal with the problems posed by China called for an internal buildup that intensified Pakistan's concerns, all the more so because the Soviet Union began providing India with sophisticated weapons and military coproduction facilities. Lacking persuasive Indian efforts to reassure Pakistan, these defensive measures so worried Pakistanis as to provoke them to precipitate the 1965 Indo-Pakistani war before India's defense build up became fully effective. In their turn, Pakistan's and China's cooperation intensified India's worries and made the link with the Soviet Union all the more desirable. Such dilemmas complicate relations and make predicting the other's behavior more difficult. They may increase tension, sometimes to the point of conflict. The following discussion of ASEAN reminds us, however, that under certain situational and leadership conditions, highly conflicted relationships can be transformed into cooperation.

Multiethnic States: Problems and Opportunities

In all four regions, the multiethnic character of these polities and the relative weakness of state institutions link the domestic politics of neighboring states, tempting statesmen to challenge frontiers and providing them with potential proxies useful for weakening their most worrisome neighbor. In many instances, borders were more fictions of European statesmen than expressions of political or administrative realities. The weakness of governments or the sheer numbers of peoples involved make frontier enforcement impossible. The weaker the states themselves, the more serious the problems resulting from this social fragmentation.

Cross-border and other ethnic identities affect the structure and international politics of the regions. In South Asia, ethnic and religious minorities in India, Afghanistan, Pakistan, and Sri Lanka seek help from ethnic brethren next door. India and Pakistan both accuse the other of encouraging ethnic dissidents within the other's borders (in India's Punjab and Kashmir and Pakistan's Sind). Millions of refugees fleeing Pakistan's 1971 crackdown in East Bengal and tens of thousands of Tamils fleeing 1983 race riots in Sri Lanka created the opportunity for Indian intervention. Similarly, millions of Afghans fleeing Soviet invasion and internal war gave Pakistan opportunities in Afghanistan.

In the Gulf, Iran used the Kurdish minority in Iraq to complicate Iraq's domestic problems, and Iraq tried to use Iran's Arab and Kurdish minorities for similar purposes. Revolutionary Iran's example as well as its efforts to inspire Shiites in Iraq, Kuwait, Bahrain, and Saudi Arabia were deeply disturbing to the regimes in those states, and pushed them together in an anti-Iranian alliance in the 1980s.

In the Horn, the Somali minority incorporated into Ethiopia with the Ogaden has been the cause of a war between Somalia and Ethiopia that led Ethiopia to appeal to the Soviet Union for massive military assistance. The Tigray autonomist and the Eritrean secessionist movements against Addis Ababa received arms and encouragement from Sudan and other Islamic states and eventually brought the Mengistu regime to its knees. In a tit-for-tat exchange, the southern Sudan resistance to Khartoum received similar support from Ethiopia.

Support for dissident minorities in neighboring countries has only rarely been employed as an instrument of national policy by Southeast Asian states. Their anxieties have focused more on China's ability to exploit the Overseas Chinese in their midst and members of tribal groups in China. However, Thailand has involved itself in hostilities between Burmese government forces and Burma's Karens and other minorities when their activities threatened the security of Thailand's frontiers. In line with its support of the Royal Lao government, Thailand supported the government's tribal allies while Hanoi, too, sponsored supporters among the hill peoples. Also, during the Vietnam War, the North Vietnamese (and the PRC) supported Thai Communist insurgency among Thailand's minorities in the north and northeast. Within Indochina, hostility between Hanoi and Khmer Rouge Phnom Penh was aggravated by the latter's brutal treatment of Vietnamese residents; more recently, Khmer apprehensions have been expressed in claims that Hanoi is resettling large numbers of Vietnamese in Cambodia. Within ASEAN, a dissident Muslim minority in Thailand has been a source of friction between Bangkok and Kuala Lumpur. Both Malaysia and Indonesia have shown the utility of ASEAN by tempering the Organization of Islamic Conference (OIC) response to Manila's efforts to frustrate Muslim secession.

Insecure Governments Cannot Accommodate One Another

Domestic politics can gravely impede governments that might otherwise want at least minimal accommodation and sometimes even cooperation with a neighbor. Where domestic support is uncertain or divided on foreign policy, leaders will hesitate to run the political risks that might result from accommodating a neighbor. The continued political backing of unreliable but indispensable domestic supporters may depend on a chauvinist stance toward that neighbor. Exaggerating the threat from next door may help shore up a shaky government or justify the use of authoritarian measures to impose order and weaken opponents. Differences in religious belief and expression, constitutional practice, or policy prevent mutual accommodation that might be commended on other grounds. Leaders in New Delhi or Islamabad; in Addis Ababa, Khartoum, or Mogadishu; or in postrevolutionary Teheran, to name but a few, have found that otherwise useful opportunities for reaching agreements with neighbors may have to be passed up because they risk splitting their domestic political following, provoking an officer corps, or alienating followers not yet ready for such a relaxation.

The domestic capacities of the states also greatly affect their freedom to maneuver in foreign policy. States that are better able, through their administrative and coercive structures, to govern their societies can improve their positions internationally and mobilize their resources for foreign policy goals. They can better fend off intrusions by foreign powers, be they direct military attacks or efforts to interfere in domestic politics. Thus, the problems presented by multiethnic societies for regional politics are most serious and prevalent on the Horn, where the states are least institutionalized; serious but more effectively countered in the Gulf and South Asia; and of little significance among the ASEAN states.

These underlying difficulties help define margins beyond which prudent statesmen can go only at grave risk. The comparative capabilities of states in any one region or subregion set outer limits to possibilities; the security dilemma besets them all. Moreover, the level of government institutionalization and multiethnicity in these societies affects the stability of all the regions.

On the other hand, these structural characteristics are not set in concrete. With great effort, the capabilities of states can be changed; the political significance of multiethnicity can sometimes be moderated or intensified by the actions of governments or secessionists; disruptive or overly ambitious governments may be followed by restrained successors. Such possibilities are exemplified by experience in the ASEAN subregion, where relatively stable and confident regimes, very much in charge of their foreign policy process and with their ambitions focused on positive-sum economic development rather than on zero-sum competition for power, have checked potentially explosive quarrels and emotions. Policy choices do make a difference.

Economic Links Within Each Region?

In all four regions economic relations between most of the states make up a remarkably small part of each state's total trade. Economic transactions, in fact, link them to far-away places; politics makes them concerned about relations with their near neighbors or with distant powers who can help them cope with the problems posed by those neighbors.

Regional Dynamics: Ambitions, Alignments, and Realignments

The dynamics of these regional systems are to be found in the interplay between the foreign policies of the principal states. These derive from intricate interrelationships between (a) the fears, ambitions, and interests of leaders of principal states, and limits or opportunities shaped for them by (b) the foreign policy behavior of neighboring states and (c) their own domestic politics. Certain characteristic patterns can be discerned.

Which State Shall Be the Region's Number One?

Within these regions are one or more prime states whose leaders have been tempted to claim regional preeminence. In the Horn, Ethiopia under both Haile Sellassie and Mengistu; in South Asia, India under the Nehrus; and in Southeast Asia, Indonesia under Sukarno have all acted as if they had an entitlement to manage the affairs of their neighbors. In the Gulf, Iran under both the shah and the ayatollah and Iraq under Saddam Husayn, each acted to assert such a claim.

Each had some reasons to aspire so high—by its size, by its greater military capability, or by its reading of the region's history. On the other hand, none of these contenders has been able to evoke the inspiration, muster the overwhelming military or economic power, or demonstrate the manifestly superior political wisdom that would make its predominant role unchallengeable. Indeed, opposition by the "smaller" states to such ambitions goes far to explain much of regional international politics. Such resistance is at the heart of the search for countervailing support, the key to the balancing process that explains much of regional alignments and most appeals to states beyond the region.

The Balancing Process: The Search for Regional Makeweights

In each of these regions, as in Western Europe's state system, leaders have responded to their sense of vulnerability by aligning themselves with those who might help them and who had compatible, if not identical, interests. However, fewer states were ready to form alliances with other regional states than European experience would suggest. Historical and ideological differences and structural problems sometimes prevented what would have seemed natural balancing alliances.

In South Asia, for example, the smaller states were worried about India, but there have been no open countervailing regional alliances against it. India's size, its central location in the region, its insistence on bilateralism in dealing with its smaller neighbors, and its predictable hostility to the idea made entering a countervailing regional alliance appear risky. "Alliances" carried a bad name in the Nonaligned Movement; they evoked memories of past imperial deals, and to formalize distrust of a fellow member courted opprobrium. Moreover, from the perspective of Pakistan, the only plausible organizer of such an effort, what could the smaller potential allies—Sri Lanka, Bangladesh, and Nepal—contribute?

There were no explicit countervailing regional alliances in South Asia. Nevertheless, the balancing process continued. Even though it was the Pakistan army that had tried to crush the Bangladesh independence movement, within three years of the liberation of Bangladesh with Indian assistance, Dakha's foreign policy veered sharply against friendship with India, seeking again collaboration with Islamabad. Similarly, until Sri Lanka's 1987 Accord with India, Pakistan and Sri Lanka helped each other when secessionists in East Pakistan and in the Jaffna Peninsula challenged their respective governments.

In the primitive anarchy of the Horn, similarly, the smaller states were not ready to combine in an attempt to balance the prime state. Even though both Somalia and Sudan were antagonistic to Ethiopia, Somalia's exaggerated ambitions led Sudan to refrain from cooperating with it against the country that separated them both, as balancing logic would recommend. Sudan found it more useful to back Ethiopia's separatist Eritreans and to reach beyond the region for support than to combine with the unpredictable Siad Barre. On the other hand, as if to confirm well-tried principles, Kenya found a traditional alliance arrangement with Ethiopia to be the best insurance against Somali ambitions toward Kenya's northern provinces.

Gause reminds us that statesmen in the Gulf have shown an acute sensitivity to balancing considerations. However, they have been as concerned about the disruptive potential of neighboring revolutionary regimes as about conventional power capabilities. When the Ba'thist government agitated against Saudi Arabia and the other conservative regimes in the Gulf, Riyadh perceived the smaller but revolutionary Iraq as a greater threat than the shah's Iran, internationally the most powerful state in the region. At the beginning of the Iran-Iraq war, when all the Arab states appeared to be threatened by a messianic and provocative Iran but Iraq temporarily had the upper hand militarily, Saudi Arabia and the shaykhdoms supported Iraq. To be sure, the smallest emirates prudently remained on the sidelines as best they could, cautiously moving between Saudi Arabia and Iran, neither joining the bandwagon nor balancing. Saudi Arabia saw Iraq's preoccupation with Iran as the time to shape the Gulf Cooperation Council, and the smaller Gulf states acquiesced, preferring a mild Saudi tutelage to exposure to Iran or Iraq. Iraq's invasion of Kuwait provoked a countervailing coalition, engaging Saudi Arabia and other Arab states in an unexpected politico-military collaboration with external powers.

In Southeast Asia, cooperation in ASEAN became more important to its members as North Vietnam's power increased, the United States abandoned its support for the Saigon government, and Hanoi's ambitions extended beyond Vietnamese reunification. Until they were displaced by Communist regimes, governments in Laos and Cambodia also sought makeweights against Hanoi. Even at the height of

ASEAN's confrontation with Hanoi, however, the countervailing view of Vietnam as a possible element in balancing against China and therefore a potential contributor to Southeast Asian regional autonomy kept the ASEAN door open to some future Vietnamese connection.

The Search for Ideologically Sympathetic Regimes

In each region new regimes, which often have seized power and pushed revolutionary change at home, have altered their foreign policy. They align with new partners not because other powers are rising and must be balanced, as balancing precepts would commend, but because they seek to distinguish themselves from their predecessors and to link with an alternative "partner" less likely to undermine them or more likely to provide support. On gaining power, Nimeiri, Suharto, Iraq's Ba'thists, and Lon Nol all sought new alignments with outside major powers. Ethiopia did so too when Washington withdrew and Moscow proved eager to replace it. The ayatollah was unique in rejecting any affiliations; all the others realigned their policies as soon as they could. They remind us that regional "structure" sets limits to statesmen's choice, but only to a degree. If the government is determined to change direction, domestic acquiescence is forthcoming, and other governments are ready to welcome their initiative, a new direction is possible.

Regional conflict is likely when a revolutionary regime becomes established amid states based on other principles of government. Violent political change in Iran and Iraq, South Yemen, Sudan, and Ethiopia and expanding Communist control in Indochina posed problems for their neighbors in all three regions. In each case, the other states saw the revolutionary regime as a threat to their domestic order as new government-society relationships were established. Since survival of "the revolution" may depend on similar changes in neighboring states, revolutionary states may actively encourage the subversion of their neighbors' governments. The Horn also shows that two neighboring regimes, both professing to be Marxist-Leninist, may have more profound grounds than ideology for defining their relationship. Kautilya would not have been surprised that the one notable example of interstate cooperation in the Horn has been between two states with very different ideologies—Ethiopia and Kenya. Sometimes, of course, the demonstration effect of the new regime next door is enough to weaken a neighboring government's ability to rule in the old ways. If, however, the new regime becomes a horrible example, it may confirm a familiar government's legitimacy.

In the Gulf, the Ba'thist victory in Iraq in the 1960s challenged Iran and all the neighboring Arab states. Both Riyadh and Teheran saw it as an active source of dissidence. Far more serious, the example of the 1979 revolution in Iran as well as the regime's active policy of subversion, it was feared, would promote opposition to neighboring regimes and encourage the demand for radical change. Shortly after its success in Aden, South Yemen's new regime quickly increased help to the Dhofar rebellion in Oman.

In Southeast Asia, ideology has been important in each subregion as both an integrating factor and a major cause of differences. Anti-Communism has linked ASEAN's governing elites, all survivors of assaults on their authority by insurgent local Communist parties. Marxism-Leninism linked the three regimes in Indochina, and shared reverence for Ho Chi Minh's contribution gave moral authority to Vietnamese dominance. As Hanoi's triumph over Saigon and the United States approached, its transformation in ASEAN eyes from a surrogate for Moscow and Beijing to a threat to the region in its own right was a further incentive to solidarity, as was, even more, the extension of Communist control over all Indochina in 1979.

Efforts to Improve Regional Cooperation and Emerging Rules of the Game

Scattered Efforts

Although the prospect of conflict appears to drive most significant relationships in the four regional systems, statesmen have made efforts to reduce it and promote cooperation. However, the four regions have shown marked differences in this respect.

As the British withdrew from South Asia and the Gulf, no overarching authority constrained conflicts. In South Asia, several summits drew leaders to deal with a number of specific difficulties. But periodic consultations between leaders of newly independent states that were not yet well consolidated, organized through foreign policy bureaucracies whose principal function appeared to be to prepare for possible conflict with the other, could not reduce suspicion. This was all the more the case when the conceptions of how the regional system should be organized were so mutually incompatible. Since each had an external patron who provided substantial military and economic assistance, there was little incentive to compromise. United Nations and Soviet mediation helped end two of the three wars but did not assuage the antagonism between the warring parties. Even the Soviet occupation of Afghanistan was not perceived as a sufficient threat to the independence of the region to help them overcome their differences. It did, however, contribute to the development of the South Asian Association for Regional Cooperation (SAARC), a beginning consultative arrangement that could improve the chances of mutual accommodation if it is taken seriously in the future.

In the Gulf there was even less commonality. The Gulf Cooperation Council was essentially a Saudi initiative to coordinate the security activities of its smaller neighbors and deliberately excluded the two most powerful regional states. The states of the Gulf communicate a good deal on economic issues, focusing on the pumping and pricing of oil in OPEC fora. But since they are divided among those with small populations and others with many people, consultations about petroleum policy contribute more to contention than to collaboration. Too many differences divide the states of the Gulf, and the competitive rivalry of external patrons up to 1990 only complicated matters. Only in the brief period of 1975–79 were there real consultations among the major regional powers on security issues. Those consultations were made possible because all the actors refrained from challenging the domestic political legitimacy of their neighbors and from interfering in their internal affairs. The Iranian revolution ended this period of moderation and respect for the norm of sovereignty in the Gulf.

In the Horn the parties differ on the principles of legitimate statehood. The protagonists have not tried to accommodate each other. There has been little communication between the leaders, and suspicion has remained high. The statesmen in this region have skillfully used ethnic and other divisions to weaken one another. Efforts to negotiate settlements between Addis Ababa and Mogadishu or Addis Ababa and Khartoum have been infrequent and the results meager. The OAU and a number of external powers have attempted to mediate major differences but without lasting success. Accordingly, the Horn has remained a region of destructive conflict, where no rules inhibit this acutely negative game and where the people have suffered gravely from the lack of mutual restraint and accommodation.

The ASEAN Model

In Southeast Asia, in sharpest contrast, the states of ASEAN have managed to change their international environment for the better.

To what extent was that unusual transformation the result of favorable system-level conditions or of the initiatives of individual leaders? The looming threat of a victorious Vietnam as American will faltered made mutual cooperation seem expedient. The states of the region considered that domestic dissidence and conflict between neighbors would lead to the still greater danger of external interference; moreover, the fact of their comparable international capability made consultation natural. That all the states had market economies steadied by government tutelage helped their leaders understand one another's specific interests. There were few competing territorial claims, and oceanic frontiers helped separate a number of the neighboring states. For much of the period, ideological differences were minimal. Stable governments, shielded from popular pressures on foreign policy both by political norms and by varying degrees of authoritarianism, found that regional cooperation had great practical advantages and that cooperation was made easier by the longevity of political leadership. Pragmatic and capable national leaders increasingly in touch with one another, and stable and sophisticated foreign policy bureaucracies showed notable flexibility. Moreover, the priority given to economic development was a disincentive to conflict; success in this endeavor increased the attractiveness of association with partners whose combined weight made ASEAN an increasingly effective instrument of regional interests.

Undoubtedly, statesmen's choices were also important. That Sukarno's successor had very different priorities than his predecessor proved to be critical. ASEAN statesmen worked their way toward policies that nurtured mutual collaboration. They devoted considerable time to gaining an in-depth understanding of each one's interests and needs, and they gradually institutionalized procedures of consultation that favored mutual accommodation and collaboration. The mutually agreed rules of the game include respect for the sovereignty of members' borders and domestic regimes, no group decisions except after substantial consultation and by consensus, and low-key, nonconfrontational public discussion of policy differences, if such discussion is to occur.

In this way, ASEAN became a security regime of collaboration, with understood norms, rules, and decision procedures, which gave due emphasis to interests shared, to well-understood constraints, and to collaborative processes for mitigating the worst effects of anarchy. The advantages of cooperation became apparent as the region became more predictable, as a smaller proportion of material resources had to be devoted to defense, and as the states became able to speak with one voice to such key market regions as Japan, the United States, and the EC. These advantages far outweighed the limited costs in terms of the right to sovereign self-assertion at the expense of their neighbors.

The contrast with developments in the other three regions needs no comment. For the future, the ASEAN combination faces a number of challenges. Will the coming generation of leaders who did not experience at firsthand the costs of regional strife be as careful to nurture collaboration as the present rulers? Will the reduction of concern with Communist threats—domestic or foreign—and the growing vigor of the Pacific Community weaken the unusual sense of interests shared by the ASEAN states?

The Role of External Powers

The Search for External Makeweights

None of these four regions stands alone. History has linked all four to Britain and other Western powers. Both history and geography have linked Russia and China to South Asia; Russia, to the Gulf; and China, to Southeast Asia. Their immediate neighbors to the south saw these great continental states as possible threats; and in a number of instances the states one tier further to the south saw them as possible friends, as Kautilya had predicted several millennia before. The United States was a relative newcomer, a distant and therefore relatively safe associate, with money and arms to distribute.

In all four regions, the fears and ambitions of regional states, as they dealt with their neighbors, drove them to seek assistance from external powers. That the three major powers relevant to the Indian Ocean rim often responded with alacrity and on occasion even offered help before being invited no doubt encouraged such invitations.

This process of seeking external makeweights best explains the ease with which these major powers could involve themselves in regional affairs. The "pull" of the invitations from the regional states was supplemented by the "push" of the external powers, either pursuing specific interests or playing out part of their mutual rivalry.

In South Asia, Pakistan's protracted search for help from Washington eventually succeeded, giving it a short-run boost. As a partial consequence, Pakistan was tempted to make a major try for Kashmir in 1965, before India's defense buildup became fully realized. In the long run it was more than matched by India's own costly military buildup and by Moscow's massive military supply to New Delhi. In the late 1980s renewed unrest in Kashmir underlined the hard fact that time elapsed does not necessarily mean problems resolved.

In a remarkable reincarnation of the Kautilyan checkerboard, India, the Soviet Union, Pakistan, and China formed two countervailing pairs of states. Both contenders within each of the regional pairs found support in their partner across the Himalayas. Each of the South Asian states received military and economic assistance from its central Asian patron, and each hoped that its patron would deter the patron of the other from providing critical support to its regional rival. Washington helped Pakistan militarily from 1955 to 1965 and after a fifteen-year hiatus, again from 1981 to 1990. These rivalries produced a regional arms race.

In the Horn, Ethiopia received diplomatic and economic backing from Washington, which helped Addis Ababa at the United Nations in its effort to incorporate Eritrea into an Ethiopian "federation" and promoted a modern military, economic growth, and educational change. Ethiopia's neighbor to the west, Sudan, received economic and military backing from the Soviet Union, as Khartoum claimed to be a socialist state and faced Ethiopia's and Libya's growing capabilities. American help to Addis Ababa eventually was more than matched by the Soviet response to Somalia, Ethiopia's neighbor to the east. Moscow provided enough military assistance to tempt Siad Barre to test conclusions in the Ogaden with a postrevolutionary Ethiopia in domestic disarray, which in turn led Addis Ababa to appeal to Moscow for help and opened the way to the 1975–78 diplomatic switch.

In the Gulf, the shah's Iran and Saudi Arabia succeeded in obtaining American backing, which reassured Iran as it faced the Soviet Union to the north and Saudi Arabia as it faced numerous regional challenges. Moscow responded to requests for help from Iraq, the odd man out between Saudi Arabia and Iran. Iraq eventually used its arms against Iran in the aftermath of the fundamentalist revolution there and then sought to annex Kuwait.

In Southeast Asia, the drive for help from outside the region against regional neighbors has been more compelling in Indochina than in ASEAN. Within ASEAN it was a fundamental principle that members did not call upon outside powers for help in quarrels with one another. On the other hand, in its relations with Vietnam on the Cambodian issue, ASEAN relied heavily on external powers to back up its diplomatic and economic pressures. The Indochinese countries, in contrast, often relied upon the assistance of outside powers in conflicts with their neighbors. As Cambodia's ruler, Sihanouk's fears of Thailand and Vietnam led him to tortuous balancing relationships with China and the United States. As leader of the Khmer resistance regime against the Vietnamese, he looked for support to the PRC and Thailand. Laos, before it came under Communist control, looked to the United States and Thailand for protection against Hanoi and its Lao Communist clients. South Vietnam relied on the United States for support against the North; Hanoi looked to Moscow and the Khmer Rouge to Beijing in their conflict with one another. In the broader international context, just as Hanoi looked for protection and support to fellow Communist countries, ASEAN looked to the West.

The fear of Communism that inclined non-Communist Asia to turn to the West was prompted at the outset by the policies and activities of the Soviet Union and China. Only later did they come to fear the future power of a unified Communist Vietnam. As the ASEAN states came together, their motives vis-à-vis outside powers were distinctly mixed. They wanted to reduce the frictions and disorders that might provide a pretext for outside intervention; they wanted their organization to be accepted as nonaligned. But they appreciated Philippine and Malaysian ties to the United States and Britain; and they wanted to reassure Washington, bruised by the recurrent failures of the government in Saigon, that their own capacity for stability and self-help would make Western assistance a good investment. Under such circumstances, categorical models do not adequately reflect the subtlety of the real world.

Accordingly, in three of our four regional systems, as major states worked up bilateral relations with external patrons, they really had an eye out primarily for their regional rivals. They were, in effect, triangulating, considering how a third party from beyond the region could help them cope with the immediate or the highest-priority long-run regional threat or concern. Southeast Asia is structurally different, since the role of China there has historically been so much greater than that of the Soviet Union or the United States in the other three regions. And in Southeast Asia, unlike in the other regions, external powers (notably France and the United States) actually fought protracted conflicts on the ground, giving them a more direct role than in any of the other regions until the Iraqi invasion of Kuwait.

In retrospect, one can give a reasonably neat account of these developments. But to the leaders involved, the future was often murky. Sometimes, such as Moscow's mid–1950s decision to cooperate with India or Washington's earlier decision to work with Iran, one sees strategic decisions. For the most part, however, a number of these relationships emerged incrementally, with openings that seemed to provide minimum-cost opportunities.

Regional Effects of Major Power Support

What were the regional effects of these patron-client relations with external powers? The following summary propositions are suggestive:

1. They altered regional balances in favor of the client, giving often temporary but sometimes decisive advantages to the client in its local rivalry. Weaker states were sometimes strengthened and better able to deter stronger neighbors from jeopardizing their security.
2. External assistance often encouraged the client's regional rival to seek help from the major power rival of its neighbor's patron.
3. Where external assistance was available from competing major power rivals, regional tensions were likely to be intensi-

fied. Indeed, large transfers of military equipment were likely to intensify the level of arms competition and might even provoke a regional arms race.

4. In all four regions there were instances where the military assistance provided from outside tempted regional leaders to attack a neighbor, particularly when domestic upheaval in the larger state provided the smaller neighbor with an unusual opportunity or when it could be done before the larger neighbor's intensified defense effort was completed.

5. Support from major external powers to states in the four regions prolonged stalemates, since when local rivals received assistance from competing patrons, neither regional state was under pressure to make concessions to the other.

6. Assistance was sought from outside not only by the smaller powers worried about their larger regional neighbor. In each region, the prime regional power (Ethiopia, Iran, India, and Indonesia) also sought outside assistance to improve its position with respect to its regional neighbors—and in the cases of Iran and India, against a neighboring major power.

7. Arms transfers also affected domestic politics, favoring the faction that received delivery, whether an established government, the chief of the army staff and minister of defense, or a revolutionary movement. They also strengthened the role of the military in the domestic political balance where civilian political institutions were not yet well established. However, too high a profile for military relationships with a major external power could lead to domestic opposition.

8. In each region there were significant instances when "clients" had substantial leverage in dealing with patrons who were competing for the allegiance of smaller states, as shown by Soviet experience with India, Somalia, and Vietnam and American experience with Pakistan, Iran, and South Vietnam.

9. Substantial changes in domestic political regimes were frequently followed by changes in alignments with major powers. A state could even switch superpower patrons, as Ethiopia and Somalia did, and thus realign itself in the global system, but do so to serve more consistent foreign policy interests of its own.

10. In some instances, external powers have helped moderate local conflicts. In the Gulf, where rivals Iran and Saudi Arabia both received assistance from a single power, the United States, the intensity of their rivalry was muted by the diplomatic activity of the supplier. In South Asia, the Soviet Union assisted India and Pakistan to reach agreement at Tashkent in

1966. However, Soviet efforts to moderate conflict between its clients—Ethiopia and Somalia—were no more successful than earlier British and American efforts to induce India and Pakistan to seek mutual accommodation.

11. Our evidence confirms the notion that the more intensely the external powers competed against each other, the more they were ready to respond favorably to opportunities provided by the regional rivalries along the Indian Ocean rim. On the other hand, a period of détente did not necessarily mean lessened efforts by the major powers to seek unilateral advantage. As Gause shows, during the Nixon-Brezhnev period of "détente" between the United States and the Soviet Union, Washington took exclusive advantage of the opportunities provided by the 1973 war to consolidate its position in the Gulf; Lyons shows that Moscow responded in a highly competitive way to opportunity in the Horn in 1978 despite (or perhaps because of) the "détente" with the Carter administration. Following the disintegration of Soviet power, however, Moscow simply watched as the Mengistu regime collapsed under pressure from the Tigray and Eritrean movements and as Washington's negotiators assisted the transition to its successor.

Responses of major powers to these regional invitations and their initiatives on behalf of their mutual rivalry, accordingly, have had a significant effect on regional international politics. What they have not done, however, was to alter the basic patterns of regional alignment and conflict within the region.

Which Variables Predominate?

From these explorations can one infer the circumstances that give greater or lesser weight to the different variables that have some explanatory power?

Most of the states acted as if they were following traditional balancing precepts. Familiar systemic responses were frequent. Formal alliances, however, were sought less often than European practice would suggest. And there were significant deviations from familiar interstate norms. Gause noted that because of legitimacy problems, states in the Gulf realigned more to counter perceived threats to their internal stability than to those based simply on military capabilities, at least until the invasion of Kuwait. In the Horn and South Asia, the smaller states, though perceiving their single major neighbor as a security threat, were not prepared to join together to oppose it, either because they were too small to make a difference or they feared the major state would take measures against them if they did.

Our explorations confirm the efficiency of applying the Kautilyan-Waltzian power-balancing model. The underlying interstate structure, such as the number of principal states and their relative international capability, is clearly of fundamental importance. Buzan's emphasis on enmity-amity axes proved to be a useful addition. Nevertheless, in these four regional systems, the domestic character of the states—their cohesion or fragmentation, the security of the leadership in the seats of power, the ability or inability of the state's agencies to control their societies and to extract resources and apply them to state purposes—limited the leader's range of choice. How individual leaders or their key decision groups operated within that range of choice to an important degree depended on their ideology and mindset. Looking at the extreme cases of the Horn and the ASEAN states, it would seem that the character of the state structures, their cohesion, and internal stability have much to do with their ability to accommodate each other. In ASEAN, moreover, there were five consequential states rather than two principals, an important structural point. At the same time, not until Sukarno passed from the scene and only after a substantial period of quiet effort did the region's statesmen learn the skills—and the utility— of mutual accommodation. That they actively pursued economic growth, a positive-sum effort rather than zero-sum power competition, no doubt contributed to their collaborative success.

Our explorations also suggest that in each of these different regional systems, different variables are crucial. However, given the complexity of these relationships, it is difficult to be sure to what extent in specific instances, superpower activities, system-level variables, or domestic characteristics of the states were dominant. Moreover, events may be more the result of statesmen who accept the range of policy choice provided them by their circumstances than the reflection of hard choices by leaders determined to turn these circumstances to a more constructive long-run future.

In South Asia, the huge difference in size and ultimate capability between India and Pakistan defines the limits of much else. Yet statesman's choices have made a difference to this imbalance. It was to be expected that India would sharply increase its defense expenditures after the 1962 Sino-Indian war, but it was not ordained that the momentum of India's buildup, particularly of air and naval power, become as marked as it did. It was understandable that Pakistan, like other states faced by larger neighbors, should seek support beyond the region. But the continued prominence of the Kashmir issue reflected political weaknesses of the Islamabad regime and ethnoreligious factors, not the inherent structure of the South Asian system. We have noted that different leaders did make a difference to their relationship. Yet we also can see that the limited cohesion of both states has made it more difficult for either to reach a modus vivendi with the other regardless of the proclivities of whoever was in charge. System, state structure, and leadership preferences are difficult to disentangle in actual practice.

In the Horn, by contrast, the inchoate condition of the principal states, and the secessionist movements that mark them affect much else. By 1991, both Ethiopia and Somalia had turned inward as the Mengistu regime collapsed under the combined onslaught from Tigray and Eritrea with support from Sudan and the Arab world, and Siad Barre's government was unseated by Somalia's clan rebellions. How the successor governments would deal with each other and with an independent Eritrea would depend in part on familiar structural variables. But the goals of the new leaders and their ability to manage each state's impact on the other would profoundly shape the developing configuration in the Horn. In the Gulf, huge resource flows to all states fed the driving ambitions of various leaders, each seeking regional predominance without decisively tipping the scale to any one. Such ambitions, all too familiar in state systems, led Iraq into two disastrous wars that deeply involved external powers and divided the Arab world. By contrast, in Southeast Asia, the relative equality of capability of the ASEAN states, the reliable command their governments have had, the priority they assign to economic performance, their intensifying search for ways to maximize their bargaining power in dealing with major trading partners and to exploit for their own benefit their very large combined market all induce the beneficent spiral of order, subregional cooperation, and predictability.

Moments of opportunity presented to ambitious leaders who possess substantial resources have also been consequential, beyond regional structure and state variables. The simultaneous moment of vulnerability in Ethiopia resulting from the revolutionary upheaval and of Somali strength resulting from large Soviet arms transfers provided Siad Barre with a temptation he could not resist. A similar combination of simultaneous weakness for Iran and apparent strength for Iraq provided Saddam Husayn with an analogous moment of opportunity.

No wonder, then, that a general theory continues to elude us.

Without the Cold War

A reduction in the Cold War will affect the way external powers deal with these regions.

1. Where *direct interests* of either of the nonregional states are engaged, they will react where and how they can, as President Bush and his coalition partners demonstrated when Iraq seized Kuwait and threatened Saudi oil production. With the collapse of the Soviet Union intervention in the region from the successor states will be limited. Indeed, as Gause suggests, Iran, Turkey, and the Gulf states may compete against one another for influence in the Muslim successor states. China can be expected to react if a resurgent Vietnam takes steps against its interests. Yet as Moscow no longer provides support to any of the Indochinese states, Beijing will have fewer competitive reasons for involving itself in Indochinese affairs, although it would face fewer risks of countervailing opposition if it chose to be more intrusive.

2. In regions where the interests of the external powers have been largely *derivative* of their mutual rivalry, one can expect a decline in their involvement. This will mean that the dynamics of the regional system will play more freely than when they were affected by the activities of external powers. Other things being equal, it can be expected that

a. In asymmetrical regional systems, as in South Asia, the aspiring preeminent regional power will pursue its goals with greater ease and that the smaller states will be more ready to acquiesce. However, other things never are equal. The virtual collapse of its Soviet makeweight will deeply trouble India's foreign policy establishment, which until recently had found Moscow such a reliable source of diplomatic support, military supply at bargain prices, and a ready market for goods that could not then be sold on the world market. Moreover, India's experience in Sri Lanka, persisting ethnic difficulties, and coalition government in New Delhi may reduce India's enthusiasm for testing the limits of its preeminence. Should India's leaders devote more imagination and effort to the skills of collaborative regional leadership than to the strategies of compulsion, relations with their smaller neighbors could improve substantially. Absent the familiar Soviet backup and with a new interest in a more open economy, yet worries about the growing solidarity of the EC, New Delhi can be expected to seek closer economic and political relationships with the United States. At the same time, it is likely that India, lacking Soviet backing, will be more ready to resolve its border problem with China, but whether China will reciprocate remains in doubt.

With lessened support from the United States, Pakistan can be expected to continue to maintain its links with the states of the Gulf, seeking their monetary and other support, perhaps in partial exchange for defense or other services. Continued domestic political uncertainty will impede Islamabad from reaching explicit compromise agreements with India should they be seriously proposed, but numerous tacit understandings on specific issues are not out of the question. Islamabad's links to China will remain important to Pakistan. Nevertheless, with lessened American backing, Pakistan's leaders may be less eager to incur risks on behalf of Kashmiris and more ready to respond constructively if India takes serious and persuasive steps toward confidence-building measures.

b. Similarly, in the Horn, since both external powers' interests were largely derivative of their competition, one can expect both to reduce their activity. Arms flows from the major external powers and the lethality of local conflict are likely to be reduced. On the other hand, since the protagonists in the Arab-Israeli competition and inter-Arab rivalries have come to see the Horn as a useful subsidiary arena, there is every reason to expect that contenders in the Horn will find external patrons even if the major external powers go home. Such support, nevertheless, is less likely to be decisive than when the Soviet Union so generously supported Somalia and then Ethiopia. The future of relations in the Horn will depend less on the activity of external powers and more on how successor regimes consolidate their hold and perceive and pursue their interests and the role of whatever secessionist movements achieve the statehood they had been fighting for.

c. The termination of the Cold War together with Sino-Soviet rapprochement have already brought significant changes to Southeast Asia. Both events, while reducing the strategic importance of Southeast Asia to the external powers, have contributed to the decline of Cambodia as a source of confrontation between ASEAN and Hanoi and reinforced the perception throughout the region that challenges for the future lie more in economics and trade than in military threats. ASEAN states can be expected to look to Vietnam for market ties and a cooperative relationship that they hope, over time, will establish the foundations of a broader regional comity. Hanoi has also been relieved of the burdens its close Soviet ties imposed. Its relations with China have improved markedly, and it more than reciprocates the interest of ASEAN countries in friendly and active relations.

The reduction of political-military threat perceptions could loosen ASEAN bonds and reduce the incentives for holding antagonisms and rivalries in check. The very effort to achieve higher levels of economic integration could cause considerable frictions. However, it is more probable that the advantages in their external dealings of maintaining a well-established comity among high-growth resource-rich states will continue to help ASEAN members overcome avoidable difficulties and differing national interests and sensitivities. Not yet sure that their great power neighbors have permanently renounced their ambitions nor willing to place themselves under Japanese protection, they will continue to seek an active American presence.

Our explorations confirm that if one wants to understand both regional conflicts and the foreign policy of specific Third World states one must look at the regional environment within which these states operate. Unlike the peculiar Cold War bipolar world of U.S.-Soviet relations, where the dynamics of relationships between the two often were independent of the regional surroundings of either, no Third World state can avoid the necessities imposed by its regional system of states. Each of the very different anarchies we have analyzed sets its own constraints around the states embedded in it, and offers opportunities to some as well. In addition, as we have seen, the types of states, the political circumstances, the range of effectiveness of their governments, and their ethnic structures impose further constraints. External states may help regional stability or intensify conflict, depending on how they affect the existing divisions and alignments.

Our review reminds us that Third World states have been by no means passive polities, waiting for encouragement or assistance from external powers, but that they have had their own ways of responding to their fears and pursuing their own interests and ambitions. The variegated repertoire of strategies and tactics open to states in these dynamic regions precludes the applicability of any simple model. International politics in these Third World regional systems, quite as much as in the more familiar world of "Western" states, provides a fascinating universe of "politics in the absence of government."

Different as these regions are from one another, we find familiar approaches to balancing. And in one important instance, we have seen how leaders of previously rivalrous states have managed to turn contention into collaboration of a sort and to change their insecure environment into one marked by greater predictability and prosperity. In an often tragic international world, where statesmen all too often appear locked into mutually destructive courses that they cannot or will not escape, instances in which policy choice leads to a more disciplined anarchy and even to the emergence of regimelike qualities deserve our careful attention.

Most international relations studies have focused on the dilemmas facing leaders representing the major external powers, for whom nuclear weapons have been the most chilling—and inhibiting—instruments of statecraft. We hope this study, in contrast, will encourage others to explore the dynamics of other regional systems. We believe that students of international politics will find through such studies a wider range of situations and a greater appreciation of the perplexities—and opportunities—that face most real-life statesmen.

Bibliography

Abrahamian, Ervand. *Iran Between Two Revolutions*. Princeton: Princeton University Press, 1982.

ACDA, *World Military and Arms Transfers, 1967–1976*. Washington, D.C., 1977; and *1974–1986* (1988).

Ahmed, Abdel Ghaffar M. and Gunnar M. Sorbo, eds. *Management of the Crisis in the Sudan: Proceeding of the Bergen Forum, 23–24 February 1989*. Bergen, Norway: University of Bergen Centre for Development Studies, 1989.

Akram, Lt. Gen. A. I. "South Asia and the Bomb." Islamabad, *Regional Studies*, 4(1) (Winter 1985):3–19.

Ali, Osman Sultan. "Djibouti: The Only Stable State in the Horn of Africa." *Horn of Africa* 5(2) (1982):48–55.

Alier, Abel. *The Southern Sudan: Too Many Agreements Dishonored*. Exeter, England: Ithaca Press, 1990.

al-Naqib, Khaldun Hasan. *Al-mujtamaʿ wa al-dawla fi al-khalij wa al-jazira al-arabiyya* [Society and state in the Gulf and Arabian Peninsula]. Beirut: Markaz Dirasat al-Wahda al-Arabiyya, 1987.

Anand, R. P., ed. *ASEAN Identity, Development, and Culture*. Honolulu: East West Center, 1981.

Andaya, Barbara W. and Leonard Y. Andaya. *A History of Malaysia*. London: Macmillan, 1982.

Anthony, John Duke. *Arab States of the Lower Gulf*. Washington, D.C.: Middle East Institute, 1975.

Arnold, Anthony. *Afghanistan: The Soviet Invasion in Perspective*. Stanford: Hoover Institute, 1985.

Asante, S. K. B. *Pan-African Protest: West Africa and the Italo-Ethiopian Crisis, 1934–1941*. London: Longman, 1977.

Assefa, Hizkias. *Mediation of Civil Wars: Approaches and Strategies—The Sudan Conflict*. Boulder, Colo.: Westview, 1987.

Assiri, Abdul-Reda. *Kuwait's Foreign Policy*. Boulder, Colo.: Westview, 1990.

Axelrod, Lawrence. "Saudi Oil Policy: Economic and Political Determinants, 1973–1986." Ph.D. dissertation, Columbia University, 1989.

——. *The Evolution of Cooperation*. New York: Basic Books, 1984.

Axelrod, Robert and Robert O. Keohane, "Achieving Cooperation Under Anarchy: Strategies and Institutions." *World Politics*, vol. 38, no. 1 (1985).

Ayele, Negussay. "The Horn of Africa: Revolutionary Developments and Western Reactions." *Northeast African Studies*, 2(3) (1980–1981), 3(1) (1981): 1–29.

——. "Somalia's Relations with Her Neighbors: From 'Greater Somalia' to 'Western Somalia' to 'Somali Refugees' to . . ." In Sven Rubenson, ed., *Proceedings of the Seventh International Conference of Ethiopian Studies*, pp. 659–60. Uppsala: Scandinavian Institute of African Studies, 1984.

Ayoob, Mohammed. "India, Pakistan, and Superpower Rivalry." *World Today*, 38(5) (1982):194–202.

——. "The Primacy of the Political: South Asian Regional Cooperation (SARC) in Comparative Perspective." In *Asian Survey*, 25(4) (April 1985):443–47.

Bakhash, Shaul. *The Reign of the Ayatollahs*. New York: Basic Books, 1984.

Barre, Abdurahman Jama. *Salient Aspects of Somalia's Foreign Policy: Selected Speeches*. Mogadishu: Ministry of Foreign Affairs, 1978.

Bastin, John and Harry Benda. *A History of Modern Southeast Asia*. Englewood Cliffs, N.J.: Prentice-Hall, 1968.

Beblawi, H. and G. Luciani, eds. *The Rentier State*. New York: Croon Helm, 1987.

Bedlington, Stanley S. *Malaysia and Singapore: The Building of New States*. Ithaca: Cornell University Press, 1978.

Bell, J. Boyer. "Endemic Insurgency and International Order: The Eritrean Example." *Orbis*, vol. 18, no. 2 (Summer 1974).

Berry, William E., Jr. *U.S. Bases in the Philippines: The Evolution of the Special Relationship*. Boulder, Colo.: Westview, 1989.

Bidwell, Robin. *The Two Yemens*. Harlow, Essex: Longman, 1983.

Bill, James A. *The Eagle and the Lion*. New Haven: Yale University Press, 1988.

——. "Resurgent Islam in the Persian Gulf." *Foreign Affairs*, vol. 63, no. 1 (Fall 1984).

Binder, Leonard. "The Middle East as a Subordinate International System." *World Politics*, 10(3) (1958):408–29.

Binyon, Michael. "West Acts as Midwife at Birth of New Leadership." *Times* (London), May 14, 1991.

Bokhari, Imtiaz H. "South Asian Regional Cooperation: Progress, Problems, Potential, and Prospects." *Asian Survey*, 25(4) (April 1985):371–90.

Bokhari, Imtiaz and T. P. Thornton, *The 1972 Simla Agreement: An Asymmetrical Negotiation*. Washington, D.C.: Foreign Policy Institute, SAIS, 1988.

Bradsher, Henry. *Afghanistan and the Soviet Union*. Durham, N.C.: Duke University Press, 1983.

Brecher, Michael. *Nehru: A Political Biography*. London: Oxford University Press, 1959.

——. "International Relations and Asian Studies: The Subordinate State System of Southern Asia." *World Politics*, 15(2) (1963):213–35.

Bresnan, John, ed. *Crisis in the Philippines: The Marcos Era and Beyond*. Princeton: Princeton University Press, 1986.

British Petroleum, *Statistical Review of World Energy* (London) (June 1988).

Broinowski, Alison, ed. *Understanding ASEAN*. London: Macmillan, 1982.

Brown, McAlister and Joseph J. Zasloff. *Apprentice Revolutionaries: The Communist Movement in Laos, 1930–1985*. Stanford, Calif.: Hoover Institution, 1986.

Bruce D. Porter, *The USSR in Third World Conflicts: Soviet Arms and Diplomacy in Local Wars, 1945–1980*. Cambridge: Cambridge University Press, 1984.

Bull, Hedley. *The Anarchical Society*. New York: Columbia University Press, 1977.

——, ed. *Intervention in World Politics*. Oxford: Clarendon, 1984.

Buttinger, Joseph. *The Dragon Embattled* (2 vols.). New York: Praeger, 1967.

——. *The Smaller Dragon: A Political History of Vietnam*. New York: Praeger, 1958.

Buzan, Barry. *People, States, and Fear: The National Security Problem in International Relations*. Chapel Hill: University of North Carolina Press, 1983.

——. "Regional Security." Copenhagen: CPSR, 1989.

——. "The Southeast Asian Security Complex." *Contemporary Southeast Asia*, vol. 10, no. 1 (June 1988).

Buzan, Barry and Gowher Rizvi, eds. *South Asian Insecurity and the Great Powers*. London: Macmillan, 1986.

Buzan, Barry, Gowher Rizvi, Charles Jones, and Richard Little. "The Logic of Anarchy: Neorealism Reconsidered." Working paper, 1988.

Cady, John F. *The History of Post-War Southeast Asia*. Athens: Ohio University Press, 1958.

Caldron, Lee. "Afghanistan in 1985: The Sixth Year of the Russo-Afghan War." *Asian Survey*, vol. 26, no. 2 (February 1986).

Cantori, Louis J. and Steven L. Spiegel. *The International Politics of Regions: A Comparative Approach*. Englewood Cliffs, N.J.: Prentice-Hall, 1970.

——. "The International Relations of Regions." *Polity*, 2(4) (1970):397–425.

Castagno, A. A. "The Somali-Kenya Controversy: Implications for the Future." *The Journal of Modern African Studies*, 2(2) (July 1964):165–88.

——. "Somali Republic." In James S. Coleman and Carl G. Rosberg, Jr., eds. *Political Parties and National Integration in Tropical Africa*. Berkeley: University of California Press, 1964.

Central Intelliegence Agency. *The World Factbook 1989* (CPAS WF 8–001, May 1989).

Chadda, Maya. "Domestic Determinants of India's Foreign Policy in the 1980's." *Journal of South Asia and Middle East Studies*, 11(1 and 2 (Fall/Winter 1987):21–36.

Chanda, Nayan. *Brother Enemy: The War After the War*. San Diego: Harcourt Brace Jovanovich, 1986.

Chandler, David P. *A History of Cambodia*. Boulder, Colo.: Westview, 1983.

Chandler, David P. and Ben Kernam, eds. *Revolution and Its Aftermath in Kampuchea: Eight Essays*. New Haven: Yale University Press, 1983.

Chang, Pao-min. *Kampuchea Between China and Vietnam*. Singapore: Singapore University Press, 1985.

Chaudhry, Kiren Aziz. "The Price of Wealth: Business and State in Labor Remittance and Oil Economies." *International Organization*, vol. 43, no. 1 (Winter 1989).

Chee, Chan Heng. *The Dynamics of One Party Dominance*. Singapore: Singapore University Press, 1976.

Chopra, Pran. *India's Second Liberation*. New Delhi: Vikas, 1973.

Choucri, Nazli. *Population Dynamics and International Violence*. Lexington, Mass.: Lexington Books, 1974.

Choudhury, G. W. *Pakistan's Relations with India*. Meerut, India: Prakashan, 1971.

Chowdhury, I. A. "Strategy of a Small Power in a Subsystem: Bangladesh's External Relations." *Australian Outlook* (April 1980).

Chubin, Shahram and Charles Tripp. *Iran and Iraq at War*. Boulder, Colo.: Westview, 1988.

Clapham, Christopher. *Transformation and Continuity in Revolutionary Ethiopia*. Cambridge: Cambridge University Press, 1988.

——. "Ethiopia and Somalia." *Conflicts in Africa*, Adelphi Paper no. 93 (1972).

——. "The Horn of Africa." In Michael Crowder, ed., *The Cambridge History of Africa*, vol. 8. New York: Praeger, 1977.

Cohen, Herman J. Statement of Assistant Secretary of State for African Affairs before the House Foreign Affairs Subcommittee on African Affairs hearing on the political crisis in Ethiopia, 18 June 1991.

Cohler, Larry. "House Memo Charges Israel Arms Ethiopian Regime." *Washington Jewish Week*, July 12, 1990.

Conference Paper. *Regionalism in Southeast Asia*. Jakarta, Indonesia: Centre for Strategic and International Studies, 1974.

Cottam, Richard. *Nationalism in Iran*. Pittsburgh: University of Pittsburgh Press, 1979.

Cottrell, Alvin, ed. *The Persian Gulf States: A General Survey*. Baltimore: Johns Hopkins University Press, 1980. Chapter by Keith McLachan, "Oil in the Persian Gulf Area."

Creed, John and Kenneth Menkhaus, "The Rise of Saudi Regional Power and the Foreign Policies of Northeast African States." *Northeast African Studies*, 8(2–3) (1986):1–22.

Crouch, Harold. *The Army and Politics in Indonesia*. Ithaca: Cornell University Press, 1978.

Crystal, Jill. "Coalitions in Oil Monarchies: Kuwait and Qatar." *Comparative Politics*, vol. 21, no. 4 (July 1989).

Dalvi, J. P. *Himalayan Blunder*. Bombay: Thacher, 1969.

David, Steven R. "Explaining Third World Alignment." *World Politics*, vol. 43, no. 2 (January 1991).

Davidson, Basil, Lionel Cliffe, and Bereket Habte Selassie, eds. *Behind the War in Eritrea*. Nottingham: Spokesman, 1980.

Deeb, Mary Jane. *Libya's Foreign Policy in North Africa*. Boulder, Colo.: Westview, 1990.

Dehio, Ludwig. *The Precarious Balance: Four Centuries of the European Power Struggle*. New York: Vintage, 1962.

Deng, Francis M. "The Identity Factor in the Sudanese Conflict." In Joseph V. Montville, ed., *Conflict and Peacemaking in Multiethnic Societies*. Lexington, Mass.: Lexington Books, 1989.

Deng, Francis M. and Prosser Gifford, eds., *The Search for Peace and Unity in the Sudan*. Washington D.C.: Wilson Center Press, 1987.

de Silva, K. M. *A History of Sri Lanka*. Delhi: Oxford University Press, 1981.

——. *Managing Ethnic Tensions in Multi-ethnic Societies: Sri Lanka, 1880–1985*. London: University Press of America, 1986.

Deutsch, Karl. *Political Community and the North Atlantic Area: International Organization in the Light of Historical Experience*. Princeton: Princeton University Press, 1957.

Dommen, Arthur J. *Conflict in Laos: The Politics of Neutralization*. New York: Praeger, 1971.

Donelan, Michael. *The Reasons of States: A Study in International Political Theory*. London: Allen and Unwin, 1978.

Donham, Donald and Wendy James, eds. *The Southern Marches of Imperial Ethiopia: Essays in History and Social Anthropology*. Cambridge: Cambridge University Press, 1986.

Drysdale, John. *The Somali Dispute*. London: Pall Mall Press, 1964.

Duiker, William J. *The Communist Road to Power in Vietnam*. Boulder, Colo.: Westview, 1981.

——. *Vietnam: Nation in Revolution*. Boulder, Colo.: Westview, 1983.

Economist Intelligence Unit. *Country Reports* for first quarter 1991.

——. *Country Report: Uganda, Ethiopia, Somalia, Djibouti*, vol. 4 (1988).

Ellingson, Lloyd. "The Origins and Development of the Eritrean Liberation Movement." In Robert L. Hess, ed. *Proceedings of the Fifth International Conference on Ethiopian Studies*, Part B. Chicago: University of Chicago Press, 1977.

Elliot, David W. P., ed. *The Third Indochina Conflict*. Boulder, Colo.: Westview, 1981.

Emerson, Donald K. "Southeast Asia: What's in a Name?" *Journal of Southeast Asian Studies*, vol. 15, no. 1 (March 1984).

Erlich, Haggai. *The Struggle Over Eritrea, 1962–1978*. Stanford, Calif.: Hoover Institution Press, 1983.

Falk, Richard and S. Mendlovitz, *Regional Politics and World Order*. San Francisco: Freeman Press, 1973.

Feith, Herbert. *The Decline of Constitutional Democracy in Indonesia*. Ithaca: Cornell University Press, 1962.

Fenet, Alain. "Djibouti: Mini-State on the Horn of Africa." In *Horn of Africa: From "Scramble for Africa" to East-West Conflict*, pp. 59–69. Bonn: Forschungsinstitut der Friedrich Ebert Stiftung, 1986.

Foreign Broadcast Information Service. *Daily Report—Middle East and Africa*, September 30, 1980; *East Asia*, January 5, 1985; *Near East and South Asia*, May 29, 1991.

Fox, William T. R. *A Continent Apart: The United States and Canada in World Politics*. Toronto: University of Toronto Press, 1985.

——. "Theories of International Relations." In Fox, ed., *Theoretical Aspects of International Relations*. Notre Dame, Ind.: University of Notre Dame Press, 1959.

Galbraith, Kenneth. *Ambassador's Journal*. Boston: Houghton Mifflin, 1969.

Gascon, Alain. "La Perestroïka à l'Ethiopienne: Le Pari de Mengistu." *Politique Africaine* 38 (June 1990):121–26.

Gasiorowski, Mark J. "The 1953 Coup d'Etat in Iran." *International Journal of Middle East Studies*, vol. 19, no. 3 (August 1987).

Gause, F. Gregory III. "British and American Policies in the Persian Gulf, 1968–1973." *Review of International Studies* (UK), vol. 11, no. 4 (October 1985).

——. *Saudi-Yemeni Relations: Domestic Structures and Foreign Influence*. New York: Columbia University Press, 1990.

Ghareeb, Edmond. *The Kurdish Question in Iraq*. Syracuse: Syracuse University Press, 1981.

Girling, J. L. S. *Thailand: Society and Politics*. Ithaca: Cornell University Press, 1981.

Gorman, Robert F. *Political Conflict in the Horn of Africa*. New York: Praeger, 1981.

Grier, Peter. "US Rethinks Africa Aid." *Christian Science Monitor*, July 12, 1990.

Gulhati, N. *Indus Water Treaty: An Experience in International Mediation*. Bombay: Allied Publishers, 1973.

Gulick, Edward V. *Europe's Classical Balance of Power*. New York: Norton, 1967.

Gurr, Ted. "Tensions in the Horn of Africa." In Feliks Gross, ed., *World Politics and Tension Areas*, pp. 316–65. New York: New York University Press, 1966.

Hagerty, Devin T. "India's Security Doctrine." *Asian Survey*, vol. 31, no. 4 (April 1991).

Hall, D. G. E. *A History of South-East Asia*. London: Macmillan, 1981.

Hamid, Muhammad Beshir. "The 'Findlandization' of Sudan's Foreign Policy: Sudanese-Egyptian Relations Since the Camp David Accords." *Journal of Arab Affairs*, vol. 2, no. 2 (1983).

Hammer, Ellen J. *The Struggle for Indochina, 1940–1955*, rev. ed. Stanford: Stanford University Press, 1966.

Harbeson, John W. *The Ethiopian Transformation: The Quest for the Post-Imperial State*. Boulder, Colo.: Westview, 1988.

Harden, Blaine. "Eritrean Rebels to Form Own Rule, Separate from Ethiopian Government." *Washington Post*, May 30, 1991.

Hardgrave, R. L. *India: Government and Politics in a Developing Nation*. New York: Harcourt Brace Jovanovich, 1970.

Harrison, Selig. *The Widening Gap*. New York: Free Press, 1978.

Hassan, Shauhat. *Indian-Bangladesh Political Relations During the Awami League Government—1972–1975*. Unpublished Ph.D. dissertation, Australia National University, Canberra, 1987.

Heikal, Mohamed Hassanein. "Egyptian Foreign Policy." *Foreign Affairs*, vol. 56, no. 4 (July 1978).

Henry, Neil. "Massacre in Somalia Spurred Shift in U.S. Policy." *Washington Post*, February 19, 1990;

Herz, John. *Political Realism and Political Idealism*. Chicago: University of Chicago Press, 1959.

Hicks, Irvin. Address by Deputy Assistant Secretary of State for African Affairs to the African American Institute 1990 Forum Series, November 18, 1990.

Holt, P. M. and M. W. Daly. *A History of the Sudan: From the Coming of Islam to the Present Day*, 4th ed. London: Longman, 1986.

Horn, Robert C. *Soviet Indian Relations: Issues and Influence*. New York: Praeger, 1982.

Hyder, Sajjad. "Pakistan's Afghan Predicament." *The Muslim* (Islamabad), February 5, 6, 8, and 10, 1984.

International Institute of Strategic Studies. *The Military Balance, 1985–86* (London, 1986), and other years.

———. *The Military Balance, 1990–91*. London: Brassey's for IISS, 1990.

International Monetary Fund. *International Financial Statistics Yearbook—1990*. Washington, D.C.: IMF, 1990.

Iraqi Embassy, Washington. Transcript of remarks by Saddam Husayn to U.S. Senate delegation, April 24, 1990.

Jackson, Karl D., ed. *Cambodia, 1975–1978: Rendezvous with Death*. Princeton: Princeton University Press, 1989.

Jackson, Karl D. and Lucian Pye, eds. *Political Power and Communications in Indonesia*. Berkeley: University of California Press, 1978.

Jackson, Karl D. and M. Hadi Soesastro, eds. *ASEAN Security and Economic Development*. Berkeley: University of California Press, 1984.

Jackson, Karl D., Sukhumbhand Paribatra, and J. Soedjati Djiwandono, eds. *ASEAN in Regional and Global Context*. Berkeley: University of California Press, 1986.

Jackson, Robert A. *Quasi-States: Sovereignty, International Relations, and the Third World*. Cambridge: Cambridge University Press, 1990.

Jackson, Robert Victor. *South Asian Crisis: India, Pakistan, and Bangladesh—a Political and Historical Analysis of the 1971 War*. New York: Praeger, 1975.

Jahan, Rounaq. *Pakistan: Failure of National Integration*. New York: Columbia University Press, 1972.

Jansson, Kurt, Michael Harris, and Angela Penrose. *The Ethiopian Famine*. London: Zed Books, 1987.

Jenkins, David. *Suharto and His Generals*. Ithaca: Cornell University Press, 1984.

Jervis, Robert. "Cooperation Under the Security Dilemma." *World Politics*, vol. 30, no. 2 (January 1978).

———. "From Balance to Concert: A Study of International Cooperation." *World Politics*, vol. 38, no. 1 (October 1985).

——. *Perception and Misperception in International Politics*. Princeton: Princeton University Press, 1976.

——. "Security Regimes." *International Organization*, vol. 36, no. 2 (Spring 1982).

Jervis, Robert and Jack L. Snyder, eds. *Dominoes and Bandwagons: Strategic Beliefs and Great Power Competition in the Eurasian Rimland*. New York: Oxford University Press, 1991.

Jha, C. S. *From Bandung to Tashkent: Glimpses of India's Foreign Policy*. New Delhi: Orient Longman, 1983.

Johal, Sarbjit Singh. *National Power and Regional Cooperation: Indo-Pakistan Relations, 1947–1983*. Unpublished Ph.D. dissertation, University of California, Santa Barbara.

Jones, Rodney. *Nuclear Proliferation: Islam, the Bomb, and South Asia*. Washington, D.C.: CSIS/Sage Publications, The Washington Papers, no. 82, 1981.

Jones, Rodney and S. A. Hildreth, *Modern Weapons and Third World Powers*. Boulder, Colo.: Westview, 1984.

Jook-Jok, Lim. *Territorial Power Domains: Southeast Asia and China—the Geostrategy of an Overarching Massif*. Singapore: Institute of Southeast Asia Studies, 1985.

Kahin, George McT. *Nationalism and Revolution in Indonesia*. Ithaca: Cornell University Press, 1952.

Kaiser, Karl. "The Interaction of Regional Subsystems." *World Politics*, vol. 21, no. 1 (October 1968).

Kalam, Abdul. "Cooperation in South Asia." *Regional Studies*, 6(3) (Summer 1988) (Islamabad):62–80.

Kapur, Ashok. "The Indian Subcontinent: The Contemporary Structure of Power and the Development of Power Relations." *Asian Survey*, 28(7) (July 1988):693–710.

Karsh, Efraim. "Military Lessons of the Iran-Iraq War." *Orbis* (Spring 1989).

Kasfir, Nelson. "One Full Revolution: The Politics of Sudanese Military Government, 1969–1985." In John W. Harbeson, ed., *The Military in African Politics*. New York: Praeger, 1987.

——. "Peacemaking and Social Cleavages in Sudan." In Joseph E. Montville, ed., *Conflict and Peacemaking in Multiethnic Societies*.

Kaul, Lt. Gen B. M. *The Untold Story*. Bombay: Allied Publishers, 1967.

Keddie, Nikki. *Roots of Revolution*. New Haven: Yale University Press, 1981.

Keerawella, G. B. "The Janatha Vimukthi Peramuna and the 1971 Uprising." *Social Science Review* (Colombo), vol. 2 (1989).

Keller, Edmond J. *Revolutionary Ethiopia: From Empire to People's Republic*. Bloomington: Indiana University Press, 1988.

"Kenya: How Long Can Moi Survive?" *Africa Confidential*, 31(14) (July 31, 1990):1–2.

Keohane, Robert. "Theory of World Politics: Structural Realism and Beyond." In his *International Institutions and State Power*. Boulder, Colo.: Westview, 1989.

Keohane, Robert O. and Joseph S. Nye. *Power and Interdependence*. Boston: Little, Brown, 1977.

Khadduri, Majid. *The Gulf War*. New York: Oxford University Press, 1988.

Khalifa, Mohammed. *The United Arab Emirates: Unity in Fragmentation*. Boulder, Colo.: Westview, 1979.

Khalilzad, Zalmay. "The Security of Southwest Asia." In Zalmay Khalilzad, Timothy George, Robert Litwak, and S. Chubin, eds., *Security in Southern Asia*, pp. 1–183, esp. 73–84. New York: St. Martin's Press, 1984.

Khan, Air Marshal (Ret'd) Zulfiqar Ali. "Afghanistan: The Refugees." *The Muslim*, (September 5, 1984).

Khan, Ayub. *Friends, Not Masters*. London: Oxford University Press, 1967.

Khar, G. M., "Four Choices Facing Front-Line Pakistan." *Economist* (London), October 31, 1981.

Kissinger, Henry A. *White House Years*. Boston: Little, Brown, 1979.

Kodikara, Shelton. *Foreign Policy of Sri Lanka: A Third World Perspective*. Delhi: Chanakya, 1982.

Korn, David. *Ethiopia, The United States, and The Soviet Union, 1974–1985*. Carbondale: Southern Illinois University Press, 1986.

Kramer, Martin, ed. *Shi'ism, Resistance, and Revolution*. Boulder, Colo.: Westview, 1987. See chapter by Joseph Kostiner, "Shi'i Unrest in the Gulf."

Krasner, Stephen. "Regimes and Limits of Realism: Regimes as Autonomous Variables." *International Organization*, 36(2) (Spring 1982):497–510.

——. "Structural Causes and Regime Consequences: Regimes as Intervening Variables." *International Organization*, 36(2) (Spring 1982):185–206.

Krauss, Clifford. "Conflicting Peace Plans Offered in Ethiopia Strife." *New York Times*, February 24, 1991, p. A11.

——. "Ethiopia and 3 Rebel Groups Look Toward U.S.-Led Peace Talks." *New York Times,* May 14, 1991, p. A6.

——. "Ethiopians Have New Rulers, but Famine's Specter Lingers." *New York Times*, June 14, 1991.

Laitin, David. "War in the Ogaden: Implications for Siyaad's Role in Somali History." *Journal of Modern African Studies*, vol. 17, no. 1 (1979).

Laitin, David D. and Said S. Samatar. *Somalia: Nation in Search of a State*. Boulder, Colo.: Westview, 1987.

Lebow, R. N. *Between Peace and War*. Baltimore: Johns Hopkins University Press, 1981.

Legum, Colin. "Communal Conflict and International Intervention in Africa." In Colin Legum, I. William Zartman, Steven Langdon, and Lynn K. Mytelka, eds., *Africa in the 1980s: A Continent in Crisis*. New York: McGraw-Hill, 1979.

Leifer, Michael. *ASEAN and the Security of Southeast Asia*. London: Routledge, 1989.

——. *Dilemmas of Statehood in Southeast Asia*. Singapore: Asia Pacific Press, 1973.

——. *Indonesia's Foreign Policy*. London: Allen and Unwin, 1983.

Lesch, Ann Mosely. "A View from Khartoum." *Foreign Affairs*, 65(4) (Spring 1987):807–26.

——. "Confrontation in the Southern Sudan." *Middle East Journal*, 40(3) (Summer 1986):410–28.

Levine, Donald N. "Ethiopia: Identity, Authority, and Realism." In Lucian W. Pye and Sidney Verba, eds., *Political Culture and Political Development*. Princeton: Princeton University Press, 1965.

——. *Greater Ethiopia: The Evolution of a Multiethnic Society*. Chicago: University of Chicago Press, 1974.

Lewis, I. M. *A Modern History of Somalia: Nation and State in the Horn of Africa*. London: Longman, 1980.

——. "The Ogaden and the Fragility of Somali Segmentary Nationalism." *African Affairs*, 88(353) (October 1989):573–84.

Liddle, William R., ed. *Political Participation in Modern Indonesia*. New Haven: Yale University Press, 1973.

Litwak, Robert. "The Soviet Union in India's Security Perspective." In Khalilzad et al., *Security in Southern Asia*.

Lyons, Terrence. "Post–Cold War Superpower Roles in the Horn of Africa." Paper presented at the Second Conflict Reduction in Regional Conflicts Conference, Bologna, Italy, May 1991.

——. "Reaction to Revolution: United States–Ethiopian Relations, 1974–1977." Ph.D. dissertation, Johns Hopkins University, 1991.

——. "The United States and Ethiopia: The Politics of a Patron-Client Relationship." *Northeast African Studies*, 8(2–3) (1986):53–75.

MacFarlane, S. Neil. "Africa's Decaying Security System and the Rise of Intervention." *International Security*, 9 (Spring 1984):129–30.

——. *Superpower Rivalry and Third World Radicalism: The Idea of National Liberation*. London: Croom Helm, 1985.

Mackie, J. A. C. *Konfrontasi: The Indonesia-Malaysia Dispute, 1963–1966*. New York: Oxford University Press, 1974.

Makinda, Samuel M. "From Quiet Diplomacy to Cold War." *Third World Politics*, vol. 4, no. 1 (January 1982).

——. "Sudan: Old Wine in New Bottles." *Orbis*, 31(2) (Summer 1987).

Malik, Hafeez. "Problems of Regionalism in Pakistan." In Howard Wriggins, ed., *Pakistan in Transition*. Islamabad and New York: University of Islamabad Press, 1975.

Mandelbaum, Michael. *The Nuclear Future*. Ithaca: Cornell University Press, 1983.

Manor, James, ed. *Sri Lanka in Change and Crisis*. London: Croon Helm, 1984.

Mansingh, Surjit. *India's Search for Power: Indira Gandhi's Foreign Policy 1966–1982*. New Delhi/Beverly Hills: Sage, 1984.

Marcus, Harold G. *Ethiopia, Great Britain, and the United States: The Politics of Empire*. Berkeley: University of California Press, 1983.

——. *Haile Sellassie I: The Formative Years, 1892–1936*. Berkeley: University of California Press, 1987.

——. *The Life and Times of Menelik II: Ethiopia, 1844–1913*. Oxford: Clarendon Press, 1975.

Markakis, John. *Ethiopia: Anatomy of a Traditional Polity*. Oxford: Clarendon Press, 1974.

——. *National and Class Conflict in the Horn of Africa*. Cambridge: Cambridge University Press, 1987.

Marks, Tom. "Counter Insurgency in Sri Lanka: Asia's Dirty Little War." *Soldier of Fortune*, 12(2) (February 1987):38–47, 82–84.

Marr, Phebe. *The Modern History of Iraq*. Boulder, Colo.: Westview, 1985.

Martin, Lenore G. *The Unstable Gulf*. Lexington, Mass.: D. C. Heath, 1984.

Marwah, Onkar. "India's Military Power and Policy." In O. Marwah and J. Pollack, eds., *Military Power in Asian States: China, India, Japan*. Boulder, Colo.: Westview, 1980.

——. "National Security and Military Policy in India." In L. Ziring, ed., *The Subcontinent in World Politics*. New York: Praeger, 1982.

Maxwell, Nevil. *India's China War*. London: Jonathan Cape, 1970.

McCann, James. *From Poverty to Famine in Northeast Ethiopia*. Philadelphia: University of Pennsylvania Press, 1987.

McGee, George. *Envoy to the Middle World*. New York: Harper & Row, 1983.

Mellor, John W., ed. *India: A Rising Middle Power*. Boulder, Colo.: Westview, 1979.

Menilek's 1891 circular letter to European heads of state. Printed in Richard Greenfield, *Ethiopia: A New Political History*, pp. 464–65. London: Pall Mall Press, 1965.

Michel, A. *The Indus River: A Study of the Effects of Partition*. New Haven: Yale University Press, 1967.

Migdal, Joel, *Strong Societies and Weak States: State-Society Relations and State Capitalism in the Third World*. Princeton: Princeton University Press, 1988.

Milne, R. S. and D. K. Mauzy. *Malaysia: Tradition, Modernity, Islam*. Boulder, Colo.: Westview, 1986.

——. *Singapore: The Legacy of Lee Kuan Yew*. Boulder, Colo.: Westview, 1990.

Modelski, George. "Kautilya: Foreign Policy and the International System in the Ancient Hindu World." *The American Political Science Review*, 58(3) (September 1964):549–60.

Morell, David and Chai-anan Samudavanija. *Political Conflict in Thailand: Reform, Reaction, Revolution*. Cambridge, Mass.: Oelgeschlager, Gunn & Hain, 1981.

Morrison, Charles and Astri Suhrke. *Strategies of Survival: The Foreign Policy Dilemmas of Smaller Asian States*. New York: St. Martin's Press, 1979.

Mullick, B. N. *My Years with Nehru: The Chinese Betrayal*. New Delhi: Allied Publishers, 1971.

Muni, S. D. "Building Regionalism from Below." *Asian Survey*, 25(4) (April 1985):391—404.

Mylroie, Laurie Ann. "Regional Security After Empire: Saudi Arabia and the Gulf." Ph.D. dissertation, Harvard University, 1985.

Najmabadi, Afsaneh. "Iran's Turn to Islam: From Modernism to Moral Order." *Middle East Journal*, vol. 41, no. 2 (Spring 1987).

Nakhleh, Emile. *The Gulf Cooperation Council: Policies, Problems, and Prospects*. New York: Praeger, 1986.

National Democratic Institute for International Affairs report. *1990 Pakistan National Assembly Elections*. Washington, D.C., 1991.

Nayar, Baldav Raj. "Regional Power in a Multipolar World." In J. W. Mellor, ed., *India: A Rising Middle Power*. Boulder, Colo.: Westview, 1979.

——. "Treat India Seriously." *Foreign Policy*, vol. 18 (Spring 1975).

Nayar, Kuldip. *Distant Neighbors*. New Delhi: Vikas, 1972.

O'Balance, Edgar. "Sri Lanka and Its Tamil Problem." *Armed Forces*, 5(12) (December 1986):542–43.

Obeysekere, G. "Some Comments on the Social Background of the April 1971 Insurgency in Sri Lanka (Ceylon)." *Asian Survey*, vol. 33 (1984).

Odhiambo, Atieno. "The Economics of Conflict Among Marginalized Peoples of Eastern Africa." In Francis M. Deng and I. William Zartman, eds., *Conflict Resolution in Africa*. Washington, D.C.: Brookings Institution, 1991.

Ododa, Harry. "Continuity and Change in Kenya's Foreign Policy from the Kenyatta to the Moi Government." *Journal of African Studies*, 13(2) (Summer 1986):52.

——. "Somalia's Domestic Policies and Foreign Relations Since the Ogaden War of 1977–78." *Middle Eastern Studies*, vol. 21, no. 3 (July 1985).

Osborne, Milton. *Region of Revolt: Focus on Southeast Asia*. Rushcutters, N.S.W., Australia: Pergamon, 1970.

——. *Southeast Asia: An Introductory History*. Sydney: Allen and Unwin, 1979.

Ottaway, Marina. "Eritrea and Ethiopia: Negotiations in a Transitional Conflict." Paper presented at a conference on Negotiations in Internal Conflicts, Johns Hopkins University–SAIS, Washington, D.C. (March 1990).

——. "Foreign Economic Assistance in the Horn: Does It Influence Horn Government Policies?" Paper presented at the Woodrow Wilson International Center for Scholars Conference on Crisis in the Horn of Africa: Causes and Prospects, Washington, D.C. (June 1987).

——. "Post-Numeiri Sudan: One Year On." *Third World Quarterly*, 9(3) (July 1987):891–905.

——. "State Power Consolidation in Ethiopia." In Edmond J. Keller and Donald Rothchild, eds., *Afro-Marxist Regimes: Ideology and Public Policy*. Boulder, Colo.: Lynne Rienner, 1987.

——. "Superpower Competition and Regional Conflicts in the Horn of Africa." In Craig Nation and Mark V. Kauppi, eds., *The Soviet Impact in Africa*. Lexington, Mass.: Lexington Books, 1984.

Oye, Kenneth A. "Explaining Cooperation Under Anarchy." *World Politics*, vol. 38, no. 1 (October .

Parmelee, Jennifer. "Angry Ethiopians Go On Anti-American Rampage." *Washington Post*, May 30, 1991.

Patman, Robert G. *The Soviet Union in the Horn of Africa*. Cambridge: Cambridge University Press, 1990.

Patnaik, Sivananda. "Sri Lanka and the South Asian Subsystem: A Study of Submacro International Politics." *India Quarterly*, 36(2) (April-June 1980):137–55.

Pelletiere, Stephen C. *The Kurds: An Unstable Element in the Gulf*. Boulder, Colo.: Westview, 1984.

Peterson, Erik R. *The Gulf Cooperation Council*. Boulder, Colo.: Westview, 1988.

Petterson, Donald K. "Somalia and the United States, 1977–1983: The New Relationship." In Gerald J. Bender, James S. Coleman, and Richard L. Sklar, eds., *African Crisis Areas and U.S. Foreign Policy*. Berkeley: University of California Press, 1985.

——. "Ethiopia Abandoned? An American Perspective." *International Affairs*, 62(4) (Autumn 1986):627–45.

Pike, Douglas. *Vietnam and the Soviet Union*. Boulder, Colo.: Westview, 1987.

Pipes, Daniel. *The Long Shadow: Culture and Politics in the Middle East*. New Brunswick, N.J.: Transaction Publishers, 1989.

Plascov, Avi. *Security in the Persian Gulf #3: Modernization, Political Development, and Stability*. London: Gower, for IISS, 1982.

Ponnambalam, Satchi. *Sri Lanka: The National Question and the Tamil Liberation Struggle*. London: Zed Books, 1983.

Pringle, Robert. *Indonesia and the Philippines: American Interests in Island Southeast Asia*. New York: Columbia University Press, 1980.

Pye, Lucian. *Asian Power and Politics: The Cultural Dimensions of Authority*. Cambridge: Harvard University Press, 1986.

Quandt, William B. *Saudi Arabia in the 1980s: Foreign Policy, Security, and Oil*. Washington, D.C.: University Press of America, 1983.

Raina, Asoka. *Inside RAW: The Story of India's Secret Service*. New Delhi: Vikas, 1981.

Rais, Rasul Bux. *China and Pakistan*. Lahore: Progressive Publishers, 1977.

Ramazani, R. K. *The Gulf Cooperation Council: Record and Analysis*. Charlottesville: University Press of Virginia, 1988.

——. *Revolutionary Iran: Challenge and Response in the Gulf*. Baltimore: Johns Hopkins University Press, 1986.

Reiss, Mitchell. *Without the Bomb*. New York: Columbia University Press, 1988.

Remnek, Richard B. "Soviet Policy in the Horn of Africa: The Decision to Intervene." In Robert Donaldson, ed., *The Soviet Union in the Third World*. New York: Praeger, 1981.

——. "The Soviet-Somali 'Arms for Access' Relationship." *Soviet Union/Union Sovietique*, 10, part 1 (1983):59.

Republic of Kenya. *Kenya-Somalia Relations: Narrative of Four Years of Inspired Aggression and Direct Subversion Mounted by the Somali Republic Against the Government and People of the Republic of Kenya*. Nairobi: Government Printer, 1967.

Republic of Somalia. *French Somaliland: A Classic Colonial Case*, n.d.

——. *Somalia: A Divided Nation Seeking Reunification*. Mogadishu: Ministry of Information, 1965.

Rizvi, Gowher. "The Role of the Smaller States in the South Asian Complex." In Buzan and Rizvi, eds., *South Asian Insecurity*.

Robertson, B. A. "South Asia and the Gulf Complex." In Buzan and Rizvi, eds., *South Asian Insecurity*.

Rose, Leo E. *Nepal: Strategy for Survival*. Berkeley: University of California Press, 1971.

Rose, Leo E. and John T. Scholz, *Nepal: Profile of a Himalayan Kingdom*. Boulder, Colo.: Westview, 1980.

Ross, Robert S. *The Indochina Tangle: China's Vietnam Policy, 1975–1979*. New York: Columbia University Press, 1988.

Rothchild, Donald and Naomi Chazan, eds. *The Precarious Balance: State and Society in Africa*. Boulder, Colo.: Westview, 1988.

Rothschild, Joseph. *Ethno-Politics: A Conceptual Framework*. New York: Columbia University Press, 1982.

Rubenson, Sven. *The Survival of Ethiopian Independence*. New York: Africana, 1976.

Rubin, Barnett R. *Never Content with a Master: The Struggle for the State in Afghanistan* (forthcoming).

——. "The Fragmentation of Afghanistan." *Foreign Affairs*, vol. 68, no. 5 (Winter 1989–90).

——. "Lineages of the Afghan State." *Asian Survey*, vol. 28, no. 11 (November 1988).

Rudolph, Lloyd and Susanne Rudolph. *The Regional Imperative*. Study originally commissioned by the Senate Foreign Relations Committee. Atlantic Highlands, N.J.: Humanities Press, 1980.

Ruggie, John. "International Regimes, Transactions, and Change: Embedded Liberalism in the Postwar Economic Order." *International Organization*, vol. 36, no. 2 (Spring 1982).

Rustow, Dankwart. *Oil and Turmoil: America Faces OPEC and the Middle East*. New York: Norton, 1982.

Safran, Nadav. *Saudi Arabia: The Ceaseless Quest for Security*. Cambridge: Harvard University Press, 1985.

Salih, Kamal Osman. "The Sudan 1985–9: The Fading Democracy." *Journal of Modern African Studies*, 28(3) (1990):199–224.

Samantar, Mohamed Ali. Comments printed in Foreign Broadcast Information Service, *Daily Report*, February 10, 1989.

Samaraweera, Vijaya. "Foreign Policy." In K. M. de Silva, ed., *Sri Lanka: A Survey*, pp. 330–52. Honolulu: University of Hawaii, 1977.

Samatar, Ahmed I. "Somalia's Impasse: State Power and Dissent Politics." *Third World Quarterly*, 9(3) (July 1987):871–90.

Schelling, Thomas. *The Strategy of Conflict*. New York: Oxford University Press, 1963.

Schilling, Nancy A. "Problems of Political Development in a Ministate: The French Territory of Afars and Issas." *Journal of Developing Areas*, 7(4) (July 1973):613–34.

Schwab, Peter. "Israel's Weakened Position on the Horn of Africa." *New Outlook*, 21(2) (April 1978):21–27.

Selassie, Bereket Habte. *Conflict and Intervention in the Horn of Africa*. New York: Monthly Review Press, 1980.

Selassie, Haile. *Important Utterances of H.I.M. Emperor Haile Selassie I, 1963–1972*. Addis Ababa: Imperial Ethiopian Ministry of Information, 1972.

Sen Gupta, Bhabani. *The Afghan Syndrome: How to Live with Soviet Power*. New Delhi: Vikas, 1982.

——. *Ethno-political Interstate Tensions and Conflicts in South Asia: Prognosis for the Next 15 Years*. New Delhi: Center for Policy Research, 1986 (mimeo).

——. "The Indian Doctrine." *India Today*, August 31, 1983, pp. 20–21.

——. "Waiting for India: India's Role as a Regional Power." *Journal of International Affairs* (Columbia University, SIA, 1975), vol. 29, no. 2.

Shamasastry, R. *Kautilya's Athasastra*. Mysore: Raghuveer, 1951.

Sick, Gary. *All Fall Down: America's Tragic Encounter with Iran*. New York: Random House, 1985.

——. "Trial by Error: Reflections on the Iran-Iraq War." *Middle East Journal*, vol. 43, no. 2 (Spring 1989).

Singh, Anita Inder. "The Superpower Global Complex and South Asia." In Buzan and Rizvi, eds., *South Asian Insecurity*, ch. 8.

Singh, Ranjit. *Brunei, 1839–1983*. New York: Oxford University Press, 1984.

Smith, Arnold. *Stitches in Time: The Commonwealth in World Politics*, with Clyde Sawyer. Don Mills, Ontario: General Publishing, 1981.

Smyser, W. R. *The Independent Vietnamese: Vietnamese Communism Between Russia and China, 1956–1969*. Athens: Ohio University Center for International Studies, 1980.

Snyder, Glenn. "The Security Dilemma in Alliance Politics." *World Politics*, 36(4) (July 1984):461–95.

Snyder, Jack. "Richness, Rigor, and Relevance in the Study of Soviet Foreign Policy." *International Security* (Winter 1985).

Solheim, Wilhelm. "What's in a Name? Another Point of View." *Journal of Southeast Asian Studies*, 17(1) (March 1986).

Sontag, R. E. and J. S. Beddie. *Nazi-Soviet Relations, 1939–1941*. New York: Didier, 1948.

Sopie, Noordin, Chew Lay See, and Lim Siang Jin, eds. *ASEAN at the Crossroads: Obstacles, Options, and Opportunities in Economic Cooperation*. Kuala Lumpur, Malaysia: Institute of Strategic and International Studies, 1987.

Spear, Percival. *India: A Modern History*. Ann Arbor: University of Michigan Press, 1961.

Spector, Leonard S. *Nuclear Ambitions*. Boulder, Colo.: Westview, 1990.

Spencer, John H. *Ethiopia at Bay: A Personal Account of the Haile Selassie Years*. Algonac, Mich.: Reference Publications, 1984.

Spykman, N. *America's Strategy in World Politics*. New York: Harcourt Brace Jovanovich, 1942.

Stein, Janice Gross. "The Wrong Strategy in the Right Place: The United States in the Gulf." *International Security*, vol. 13, no. 3 (Winter 1988/89).

Steinberg, David Joel. *The Philippines: A Singular and a Plural Place*, 2d ed., rev. and updated. Boulder, Colo.: Westview, 1990.

——., ed. *In Search of Southeast Asia*. rev. ed. Honolulu: University of Hawaii, 1987.

Stuart-Fox, Martin. *Laos: Politics, Economics, and Society*. London: Francis Pinter, 1986.

Subrahmanyam, K. "Dialogue with Pakistan." *Strategic Analysis* (New Delhi), vol. 6, no. 10 (January 1983).

——. "Pakistan's Nuclear Capability." In V. D. Chopra, ed., *Studies in Indo-Pakistan Relations*. New Delhi: Patriot Publishers, 1984.

Subramanian, R. R. *Proliferation in South Asia: Security in the 1980's*. Canberra: Papers on Strategy and Defense, no. 26, 1982.

Suchit, Bundongkam. *The Military in Thai Politics, 1981–1986*. Singapore: Institute of Southeast Asian Studies, 1987.

Swami, Subrahmaniam. "Pakistan Holds the Key to India's Security." *Sunday* (Calcutta), November 13, 1983.

Taheri, Amir. "Policies of Iran in the Persian Gulf Region." In Abdus Amiris, ed., *The Persian Gulf and the Indian Ocean in International Politics.* Teheran: Institute of International Political and Economic Studies, 1975

Tambiah, S. J. *Sri Lanka: Ethnic Fratricide and the Dismantling of Democracy.* Chicago: University of Chicago Press, 1986.

Teferra, Daniel. Letter to the editor. *Washington Post*, June 12, 1991.

Tereke, Gebru. *Ethiopia: Power and Protest.* Cambridge: Cambridge University Press (forthcoming).

Thomas, Raju. "India." In E. A. Kolodziej and R. E. Harkovy, eds., *Security Policies of Developing Countries.* Lexington, Mass.: Lexington Books, 1982.

——. "Strategic Consequences of Nuclear Proliferation in South Asia." *Journal of Strategic Studies*, vol. 8 (December 1985).

Thompson, Virginia and Richard Adloff. *Djibouti and the Horn of Africa.* Stanford: Stanford University Press, 1978.

Thompson, William R. "The Regional Subsystem: A Conceptual Explication and a Propositional Inventory." *International Studies Quarterly*, 17(1) (March 1973):89–117.

Thornton, Thomas P. "The Indo-Pakistan Conflict: Soviet Mediation at Tashkent, 1966." In Saadia Touval and I. W. Zartman, eds., *International Mediation in Theory and Practice*, pp. 141–75. Boulder, Colo.: Westview, 1985.

——. *Challenge to United States Policy in the Third World: Global Responsibilities and Regional Devolution.* Boulder, Colo.: SAIS, Westview, 1986.

Touval, Saadia. *The Boundary Politics of Independent Africa.* Cambridge: Harvard University Press, 1972.

Trevaskis, G. K. N. *Eritrea: A Colony in Transition.* London: Oxford University Press, 1960.

Trimingham, J. Spencer. *Islam in Ethiopia.* London: Oxford University Press, 1952.

Turley, William S., ed. *Confrontation or Coexistence: The Future of ASEAN-Vietnam Relations.* Bangkok: Institute of Security and International Studies, Chulakongkorn University, 1985.

United Nations, *World Demographic Estimates and Projections, 1950–2025* (New York, 1988):246.

United States Arms Control and Disarmament Agency. *World Military Expenditures and Arms Transfers.* Washington, D.C.: The Agency, 1989.

United States Department of Energy, Energy Information Administration. *Monthly Energy Review*, April 1987.

Vali, Ferenc A. *Politics of the Indian Ocean Region: The Balances of Power.* New York: Free Press, 1976.

Vayrynen, Raimo. "Regional Conflict Formations: An Intractable Problem of International Relations." *Journal of Peace Research*, 21(4) (1984):337–59.

Venkateshwar Rao, P. "Ethnic Conflict in Sri Lanka: India's Role and Perceptions." *Asian Survey*, 28(4) (April 1988):419–37.

Vertzberger, Y. I. *The Enduring Entente: Sino-Pakistan Relations, 1960–1980.* New York: Praeger, 1983 (CSIS, The Washington Papers, no. 95).

——. *Misperceptions in Foreign Policy Making: The Sino-Indian Conflict, 1959–1962.* Boulder, Colo.: Westview, 1984.

Visalakshmi. *India and Iraq: From Cordial Political Relations to Close Economic Relations.* Unpublished dissertation, University of Hyderabad, India, 1981.

Voll, John O. "Northern Muslim Perspectives." In Joseph E. Montville, ed., *Conflict and Peacemaking in Multiethnic Societies.* Lexington, Mass.: Lexington Books, 1989.

Voll, John O. and Sarah Potts Voll. *The Sudan: Unity and Diversity in a Multicultural State.* Boulder, Colo.: Westview, 1985.

Wai, Dunstan. "Revolution, Rhetoric, and Reality in the Sudan." *Journal of Modern African Studies,* 17(1) (March 1979):71–93.

Walt, Stephen M. *The Origins of Alliances.* Ithaca: Cornell University Press, 1987.

——. "Testing Theories of Alliance Formation: The Case of Southwest Asia." *International Organization,* 42(2) (Spring 1988):275–317.

Waltz, Kenneth, N. "Anarchic Orders and Balances of Power." In R. Keohane, ed., *Neorealism and Its Critics.* New York: Columbia University Press, 1986.

——. *Theory of International Politics.* Reading, Mass.: Addison-Wesley, 1979.

——. "Reflections on Theory of International Politics: A Response to My Critics." In R. Keohane, ed., *Neorealism and Its Critics.*

Wariavwalla, Bharat. "Wary Neighbours." *The Illustrated Weekly of India,* June 11, 1989.

Waterbury, John. *Hydropolitics of the Nile Valley.* Syracuse: Syracuse University Press, 1979.

Weatherbee, Donald E., ed. *Southeast Asia Divided: The ASEAN-Indochina Crisis.* Boulder, Colo.: Westview, 1985.

Weiner, Myron. "International Migration and Development: Indians in the Persian Gulf." *Population and Migration Review,* 8(1) (March 1982):1–36.

——. "The Macedonian Syndrome: An Historical Model of International Relations and Political Developments." *World Politics,* 23(4) (July 1971):665–83.

Whiting, Allen. *The Chinese Calculus of Deterrence.* Ann Arbor: University of Michigan Press, 1975.

Wight, Martin. "The Balance of Power and International Order." In Alan James, ed., *The Bases of International Order: Essays in Honour of C. A. W. Manning.* London: Oxford University Press, 1973.

Wilson, Dick. *The Neutralization of Southeast Asia.* New York: Praeger, 1975.

Wirsing, Robert G. "The Arms Race in South Asia: Implications for the United States." *Asian Survey,* 25(3) (March 1985):270–71.

Wolde-Mariam, Mesfin. *The Background of the Ethio-Somalia Boundary Dispute.* Addis Ababa: Berhanena Selam, 1964.

——. "The Horn of Africa: Ethnoconflict Versus Development." Paper presented at the International Symposium on the African Horn, University of Cairo, January 1985.

——. *Somalia: The Problem Child of Africa.* Addis Ababa: Artistic Printing Press, 1977.

Wolfers, Arnold. *Discord and Collaboration.* Baltimore: Johns Hopkins University Press, 1962.

Woodward, Peter. *Sudan, 1898–1989: The Unstable State*. Boulder, Colo.: Lynne Rienner, 1990.

World Bank, *World Development Report, 1985*. New York: Oxford University Press, 1985): table 1, "Basic Indicators."

——, *1989*. New York: Oxford University Press for World Bank, 1989.

Wriggins, Howard. "The Balancing Process in Pakistan's Foreign Policy." In L. Ziring, R. Braibanti, and H. Wriggins, eds., *Pakistan: The Long View*. Durham, N.C.: Duke University Press, 1977.

——. *Ceylon: Dilemmas of a New Nation*. Princeton: Princeton University Press, 1960.

——. "Pakistan's Search for a Foreign Policy After the Invasion of Afghanistan." *Pacific Affairs*, 57(2) (Summer 1984):284–303.

——. *The Ruler's Imperative*. New York: Columbia University Press, 1969.

——. "South Asia and the Gulf: Linkages, Gains, and Limitations." *Middle East Review*, 18(2) (Winter 1985/86):25–37.

——. "Youth Cohorts, Population Growth, and Political Outcomes." Vienna, International Institute for Applied Systems Analysis, July 1989, working paper.

Wriggins, Howard and James Guyot, eds. *Population, Politics, and the Future of Southern Asia*. New York: Columbia University Press, 1973. See chapter 10, "Youth Protest in Sri Lanka."

Wyatt, David K. *Thailand: A Short History*. New Haven: Yale University Press, 1982.

Xuto, Somsakdi, ed. *Government and Politics of Thailand*. Singapore: Oxford University Press, 1987.

Yergin, Daniel. *The Prize*. New York: Simon and Schuster, 1991.

Young, Oren. "Political Discontinuities in the International System." *World Politics*, 20(3) (1968):369–92.

——. "Regime Dynamics: The Rise and Fall of International Regimes." *International Organization*, vol. 36, no. 2 (Spring 1982).

Zahlan, Rosemarie Said. *The Origins of the United Arab Emirates*. London: Macmillan, 1978.

Zartman, I. William. "Introduction." In I. William Zartman, ed., *Negotiations in Internal Conflict* (forthcoming).

——. "The Political Analysis of Regionalism" (unpublished paper).

——. *Ripe for Resolution: Conflict and Intervention in Africa*. New York: Oxford University Press, 1985.

Zartman, I. William and W. Scott Thompson. "The Development of Norms in the African System." In Yassin El-Ayouty, ed., *The Organization of African Unity After Ten Years*. New York: Praeger, 1975.

Zelniker, Shimshon. *The Superpowers and the Horn of Africa*. Center for Strategic Studies Paper No. 18, Tel Aviv University, September 1982.

Selected Bibliography for Further Reading

THEORETICAL STUDIES

Ayoob, Mohammed. "The Security Problematic of the Third World." *World Politics*, 43(2) (January 1991):257–83.

——. "The Third World in the System of States: Acute Schizophrenia or Growing Pains" *International Studies Quarterly*, 33(1) (March 1989):67–79.

Bull, Hedley. *The Anarchical Society*. New York: Columbia University Press, 1977).

Bull, Hedley and Adam Watson, eds. *The Expansion of International Society*. New York: Oxford University Press, 1984.

Buzan, Barry. *Peoples, States, and Fear: The National Security Problem in International Relations*. Chapel Hill: University of North Carolina Press, 1983, esp. ch. 4.

Buzan, Barry and Gowher Rizvi, eds. *South Asian Insecurity and the Great Powers*. London: Macmillan, 1986.

Buzan, Barry, Gowher Rizvi, Charles Jones, and Richard Little. "The Logic of Anarchy." Working paper, 1988.

Cantori, Louis J. and Steven L. Spiegel, *The International Politics of Regions: A Comparative Approach*. Englewood Cliffs, N.J.: Prentice-Hall, 1970.

David, Steven R. "Explaining Third World Alignment." *World Politics*, 43(2) (January 1991):233–56.

Dehio, Ludwig. *The Precarious Balance: Four Centuries of the European Power Struggle*. New York: Vintage, 1962.

Deng, Francis M. and I. William Zartman, eds. *Conflict Resolution in Africa*. Washington, D.C.: Brookings Institution, 1991.

Donelon, Michael. *The Reasons of States: A Study in International Political Theory*. London: Allen & Unwin, 1978.

Fox, W. T. R. *Theoretical Aspects of International Relations*. Notre Dame, Ind.: University of Notre Dame Press, 1959.

Jackson, Robert H. *Quasi-States: Sovereignty, International Relations, and the Third World*. New York: Cambridge University Press, 1990.

Jackson, Robert H. and Carl G. Roseberg. "Why Africa's Weak States Persist: The Empirical and the Juridical in Statehood." *World Politics*, 35(1) (October 1982):1–24.

Jervis, Robert. "From Balance to Concert: A Study of International Cooperation." *World Politics*, vol. 38, no. 1 (October 1985).

——. *Perception and Misperception in International Relations*. Cambridge, Mass.: Harvard University Press, 1976.

Jervis, Robert and Jack Snyder. *Dominoes and Bandwagons: Strategic Beliefs of Great Power Competition in the Eurasian Rimland*. New York: Oxford University Press, 1991.

Keohane, Robert. *International Institutions and State Power*. Boulder, Colo.: Westview, 1989.

——, ed. *Neorealism and Its Critics*. New York: Columbia University Press, 1986.

Maoz, Zeev. "Joining the Club of Nations: Political Development and International Conflict, 1816–1976." *International Studies Quarterly*, 33(2) (June 1989):199–231.

Rothchild, Donald and Naomi Chazan, eds. *The Precarious Balance: State and Society in Africa*. Boulder: Westview, 1988.

Ryan, S. "Explaining Ethnic Conflict: The Neglected International Dimension." *Review of International Studies*, 14(3) (July 1988):161–77.

Thompson, William R. "The Regional Subsystem: A Conceptual Explication and a Propositional Inventory." *International Studies Quarterly*, vol. 17, no. 1 (March 1973).

Touval, Saadia. *The Boundary Politics of Independent Africa*. New York: Oxford University Press, 1985.

Walt, Stephen M. *The Origins of Alliances*. Ithaca: Cornell University Press, 1987.

Waltz, Kenneth W. *Theory of International Relations*. Reading, Mass.: Addison-Wesley, 1979), esp. chs. 5 and 6.

Weiner, Myron. "The Macedonian Syndrome." *World Politics*, vol. 23, no. 4 (July 1971).

Wight, Martin. "The Balance of Power and International Order." In Alan James, ed., *The Bases of International Order: Essays in Honour of C. A. W. Manning*. London: Oxford University Press, 1973.

Wolfers, Arnold. *Disaccord and Collaboration*. Baltimore: Johns Hopkins University Press, 1962, esp. ch. 8.

THE GULF
Recommended readings other than those listed in notes.

Iran

Akhavi, Shahrough. *Religion and Politics in Contemporary Iran: Clergy-State Relations in the Pahlavi Period*. Albany: State University of New York Press, 1980.

Arjomand, Said Amir. *The Turban for the Crown: The Islamic Revolution in Iran.* New York: Oxford University Press, 1988.

Khomeini, Ruhollah. *Islam and Revolution.* Translated and annotated by Hamid Algar. Berkeley, Calif.: Mizan Press, 1981.

Ramazani, Rouhollah K. *Iran's Foreign Policy, 1941–1973.* Charlottesville: University Press of Virginia , 1975.

Zonis, Marvin. *Majestic Failure: The Fall of the Shah.* Chicago: University of Chicago Press, 1991.

Iraq

Al-Khalil, Samir. *Republic of Fear: The Politics of Modern Iraq.* Berkeley: University of California Press, 1989.

Baram, Amatzia. *Culture, History, and Ideology in the Formation of Ba'thist Iraq, 1968–1989.* New York: St. Martin's Press, 1991.

Batatu, Hanna. *The Old Social Classes and the Revolutionary Movements of Iraq.* Princeton: Princeton University Press, 1978.

Farouk-Sluglett, Marion and Peter Sluglett. *Iraq Since 1958: From Revolution to Dictatorship.* London: KPI, 1987.

Khadduri, Majid. *Republican Iraq: A Study in Iraqi Politics Since the Revolution of 1958.* New York: Oxford University Press, 1969.

——. *Socialist Iraq: A Study in Iraqi Politics Since 1968.* Washington, D.C.: Middle East Institute, 1978.

Saudi Arabia

Al-Yassini, Ayman. *Religion and State in the Kingdom of Saudi Arabia.* Boulder, Colo.: Westview, 1985.

Field, Michael. *The Merchants: The Big Business Families of Saudi Arabia and the Gulf States.* Woodstock, N.Y.: Overlook Press, 1985.

Halliday, Fred. *Arabia Without Sultans.* London: Penguin Books, 1974.

Helms, Christine Moss. *The Cohesion of Saudi Arabia.* Baltimore: Johns Hopkins University Press, 1981.

Holden, David and Richard Johns. *The House of Saud.* New York: Holt, Rinehart and Winston, 1981.

Lackner, Helen. *A House Built on Sand: A Political Economy of Saudi Arabia.* London: Ithaca Press, 1978.

Niblock, Tim, ed. *State, Society, and Economy in Saudi Arabia.* London: Croon Helm, 1982.

Salameh, Ghassan. "Political Power and the Saudi State." *MERIP Reports,* no. 91 (October 1980).

Troeller, Gary. *The Birth of Saudi Arabia.* London: Frank Cass, 1976.

Kuwait

Crystal, Jill. *Oil and Politics in the Gulf: Rulers and Merchants in Kuwait and Qatar.* New York: Cambridge University Press, 1990.

Ismail, Jacqueline S. *Kuwait: Social Change in Historical Perspective.* Syracuse: Syracuse University Press, 1982.

Rumaihi, Muhammad. *Beyond Oil: Unity and Development in the Gulf.* London: Al Saqi Books, 1986.

Bahrain

Khuri, Fu'ad I. *Tribe and State in Bahrain*. Chicago: University of Chicago Press, 1980.

Lawson, Fred H. *Bahrain: The Modernization of Autocracy*. Boulder, Colo.: Westview, 1989.

Nakhleh, Emile. *Bahrain: Political Development in a Modernizing Society*. Lexington, Mass.: Lexington Books, 1976.

United Arab Emirates

Heard-Bey, Frauke. *From Trucial States to United Arab Emirates*. New York: Longman, 1982.

Khalifa, Ali Mohammed. *The United Arab Emirates: Unity in Fragmentation*. Boulder, Colo.: Westview, 1979.

Zahlan, Rosemarie Said. *The Origins of the United Arab Emirates*.New York: Macmillan, 1978.

Oman

Allen, Calvin H. *Oman: The Modernization of the Sultanate*. Boulder, Colo.: Westview, 1987.

Peterson, John E. *Oman in the Twentieth Century*. New York: Barnes and Noble Books, 1978.

Townsend, John. *Oman: The Making of a Modern State*. London: Croon Helm, 1977.

Wilkinson, John. *The Imamate Tradition of Oman*. New York: Cambridge University Press, 1987.

Kurds

Chaliand, Gerard, ed. *People Without a Country: The Kurds and Kurdistan*. London: Zed Books, 1980.

Ghareeb, Edmund. *The Kurdish Question in Iraq*. Syracuse: Syracuse University Press, 1981.

Pelletiere, Stephen C. *The Kurds: An Unstable Element in the Gulf*. Boulder, Colo.: Westview, 1984.

SOUTH ASIA

Spear, Percival. *India: A Modern History*. Ann Arbor: University of Michigan, 1961.

Regional International Politics

Barnds, William J. *India, Pakistan, and the Great Powers*. New York: Praeger, 1972.

Choudhury, G. W. *Pakistan's Relations with India*. Meerut, India: Prakashan, 1971.

Ganguly, Sumit. *Origins of War in South Asia: Indo-Pakistan Conflicts Since 1947*. Boulder, Colo.: Westview, 1988.

Kodikara, Shelton. *Foreign Policy of Sri Lanka: A Third World Perspective*. New Delhi: Chanakya, 1982.

Mansingh, Surjit. *India's Search for Power: Indira Gandhi's Foreign Policy, 1966–1982*. New Delhi/Berverly Hills: Sage, 1984.

Rose, Leo E. *Nepal: Strategy for Survival*. Berkeley: University of California Press, 1971.

Tahir-Kelhi, Shirin. *The United States and Pakistan: The Development of an Influence Relationship*. New York: Praeger, 1982.

Tharoor, Shashi. *Reasons of State: Political Development and India's Foreign Policy Under Indira Gandhi*. New Delhi: Vikas, 1982.

Vertzberger, Y. I. *Misperceptions in Foreign Policy Making: The Sino-Indian Conflict, 1959–1962*. Boulder, Colo.: Westview, 1984.

India

Asia Society. *India Briefing*. Boulder, Colo.: Westview, 1987.

Akbar, M. J. *The Siege Within*. New York: Viking, Penguin, 1985.

Brass, Paul. *The Politics of India Since Independence*. New York: Cambridge University Press, 1990.

Kholi, Atul. *India's Democracy: An Analysis of Changing State-Society Relations*. Princeton: Princeton University Press, 1990.

Rudolph, Lloyd I. and Susanne Hoeber Rudolph. *In Pursuit of Lakshmi: The Political Economy of the Indian State*. Chicago: University of Chicago Press, 1987.

Weiner, Myron. *Sons of the Soil: Migration and Ethnic Conflict in India*. Princeton: Princeton University Press, 1978.

Pakistan

Baxter, Craig. *Zia's Pakistan: Politics and Stability in a Frontline State*. Boulder, Colo.: Westview, 1985.

Burke, S. M. and Laurence Ziring. *Pakistan's Foreign Policy*, 2d ed. London: Oxford University Press, 1972.

Burki, Shahid Javed. *Pakistan: Continuing Search for Nationhood*. Boulder, Colo.: Westview, 1991.

Burki, S. J. and Craig Baxter, *Pakistan Under the Military: Eleven Years of Zia ul Haq* (Boulder: Westview, 1991).

Callard, Keith. *Pakistan, A Political Study*. New York: Macmillan, 1957.

Cohen, Stephen P. *The Pakistan Army*. Berkeley: University of California Press, 1984.

Gardezi, Hassan and Jami Rashid, eds. *Pakistan Roots of Dictatorship: The Political Economy of a Praetorian State*. London: Zed Press, 1983.

Bangladesh

Jahan, Rounaq. *Pakistan: Failure of National Integration*. New York: Columbia University Press, 1972.

Khan, Ziller Rahman. *Leadership in the Least Developed Nation: Bangladesh*. Syracuse, N.Y.: Maxwell School, 1983.

Sri Lanka

Coomeraswamy, Radhika. *Sri Lanka: The Crisis of the Anglo-American Constitutional Traditions in a Developing Society*. New Delhi: Vikas, 1984.

de Silva, K. M. *A History of Sri Lanka*. Berkeley: University of California Press, 1981.

——. *Managing Ethnic Tensions in Multi-ethnic Societies: Sri Lanka, 1880–1985*. New York: University Press of America, 1986.

Jiggins, Janice. *Caste and Family in the Politics of the Sinhalese*. New York: Cambridge University Press, 1979.

Manor, James. *Sri Lanka in Change and Crisis*. London: Croom Helm, 1984.

Pffenberger, Bryan. *Caste in Tamil Culture: The Religious Foundations of Sudra Domination in Tamil Sri Lanka*. Syracuse, N.Y.: FACS Publications, 1983.

Ratnatunga, Sinha. *Politics of Terrorism: The Sri Lanka Experience*. Belconnen, Australia, International Fellowship for Social and Economic Development, 1988.

Tambiah, S. J. *Sri Lanka: Ethnic Fratricide and the Dismantling of Democracy*. Chicago: University of Chicago Press, 1986.

Nepal
Rose, Leo and John Scholz. *Profile of a Himalayan Kingdom*. Boulder, Colo.: Westview, 1980.

HORN OF AFRICA
Clapham, Christopher. *Transformation and Continuity in Revolutionary Ethiopia*. Cambridge: Cambridge University Press, 1988.

Donham, Donald and Wendy James, eds. *The Southern Marches of Imperial Ethiopia: Essays in History and Social Anthropology*. Cambridge: Cambridge University Press, 1986.

Drysdale, John. *The Somali Dispute*. London: Pall Mall Press, 1964.

Erlich, Haggai. *The Struggle Over Eritrea: 1962–1978*. Stanford: Hoover Institution Press, 1983.

Harbeson, John W. *The Ethiopian Transformation: The Quest for the Post-Imperial State*. Boulder, Colo.: Westview, 1988.

Holt, P. M. and M. W. Daly. *A History of the Sudan: From the Coming of Islam to the Present Day*, 4th ed. London: Longman, 1986.

Keller, Edmond J. *Revolutionary Ethiopia: From Empire to People's Republic*. Bloomington: Indiana University Press, 1988.

Korn, David. *Ethiopia, the United States, and the Soviet Union, 1974–1985*. Carbondale: Southern Illinois University Press, 1986.

Laitin, David D. and Said S. Samatar. *Somalie: Nation in Search of a State*. Boulder: Westview, 1987.

Levine, Donald N. *Greater Ethiopia: The Evolution of a Multiethnic Society*. Chicago: University of Chicago Press, 1974.

Lewis, I. M. *A Modern History of Somalia: Nation and State in the Horn of Africa*. London: Longman, 1980.

Marcus, Harold G. *Ethiopia, Great Britain, and the United States: The Politics of Empire*. Berkeley: University of California Press, 1983.

Markakis, John. *Ethiopia: Anatomy of a Traditional Polity*. Oxford: Clarendon Press, 1974.

——. *National and Class Conflict in the Horn of Africa*. Cambridge: Cambridge University Press, 1987.

Ottaway, Marina, ed. *The Political Economy of Ethiopia*. New York: Praeger, 1990.

Thompson, Virginia and Richard Adloff. *Djibouti and the Horn of Africa*. Stanford: Stanford University Press, 1978.

Voll, John O. and Sarah Potts Voll. *The Sudan: Unity and Diversity in a Multicultural State*. Boulder, Colo.: Westview, 1985.

Woodward, Peter. *Sudan, 1898–1989: The Unstable State*. Boulder, Colo.: Lynne Rienner, 1990.

SOUTHEAST ASIA
In addition to the works cited in the notes, the following are noteworthy sources for the subjects listed.

Foreign and Security Policy

Alagappa, Muthiah. *The National Security of Developing States: Lessons from Thailand*. Dover, Mass.: Auburn House, 1987.

Scalapino, Robert A., Seizaburo Sato, Jusuf Wanandi, and Sung-joo Han, eds. *Asian Security Issues: Regional and Global*. Berkeley: Institute of East Asian Studies, University of California, 1988.

Snitwongse, Kasuma and Sukhamband Paribatra, eds. *Durable Stability in Southeast Asia*. Singapore: Institute of Southeast Asian Studies, 1987.

Wurfel, David and Bruce Burton, eds. *The Political Economy of Foreign Policy in Southeast Asia*. New York: St. Martin's Press, 1990.

The Military Role

Djiwandono, J. Soedjat and Yong Mun Cheong, eds. *Soldiers and Stability in Southeast Asia*. Singapore: Institute of Southeast Asian Studies, 1988.

Hoadley, J. Stephen. *Soldiers and Politics in Southeast Asia: Civil Military Relations in Comparative Perspective*. Cambridge, Mass.: Schenkman, 1975.

Wah, Chin Kin. *Defense Spending in Southeast Asia*. Singapore: Institute of Southeast Asian Studies, 1987.

Zakaria, Haji Ahmad and Harold Crouch, eds. *Military-Civilian Relations in South-East Asia*. Singapore: Oxford University Press, 1985.

Communist and Ethnic Dissidence

Brimmell, J. H. *Communism in Southeast Asia: A Political Analysis*. London: Oxford University Press, 1959.

Jeshurin, Chandran, ed. *Governments and Rebellions in Southeast Asia*. Singapore: Institute of Southeast Asian Studies, 1985.

Lim, Joo-Jock. *Armed Communist Movements in Southeast Asia*. New York: St. Martin's Press, 1984.

Lim, Joo-Jock and S. Vann, eds. *Armed Separatism in Southeast Asia*. Singapore: Institute of Southeast Asian Studies, 1984.

Van Der Kroef, Justus. *Communism in Southeast Asia*. London: Macmillan, 1981.

China and the Overseas Chinese

Cushman, Jennifer and Wang Gungwu. eds. *Changing Identities of Southeast Asian Chinese Since World War II*. Hong Kong: Hong Kong University Press, 1988.

Kallgren, Joyce K., Noordin Sopie, and Soedjati Djiwandono. *ASEAN and China: An Evolving Relationship*. Berkeley: 1988.

Lim, Linda and Peter Gosling, eds. *The Chinese in Southeast Asia*, 2 vols. Singapore: Maruzen Asia, 1983.

Purcell, Victor. *The Chinese in Southeast Asia*. London: Oxford University Press, 1951.

Somers-Heidhues, Mary F. *Southeast Asia's Chinese Miniorities*. Melbourne: Longman, 1974.

Taylor, Jay. *China and Southeast Asia*. New York: Praeger, 1976.

Index

Nimeiri and, 179; Ogaden and, 164; overthrown, 160, 191; Qadhafi and, 186; Sudan and, 167; unification efforts of, 159–60; U.S. and, 189, 198; Yemen and, 188

Halabja, 65

Hashemi-Rafsanjani, Ali Akbar, 66, 67

Hashemite monarchy, 34, 35

Heng Samrin, 245, 256

Hinayana Buddhism, 237

Hindus, 96, 99, 128

Hobbesian model, 7, 277

Ho Chi Minh, 242, 246

Ho Chi Minh trail, 244–45

Horn of Africa regional politics, 16–17, 153–209, 196–202; antagonisms in, 280; balancing in, 286; Cold War termination of, 299; cooperation, lack of, and, 289; cross-border ties and, 282; external powers and, 183–96, 292; ideology and, 287; predominating variables, 172, 279–80, 296–97; relational patterns in, 172–83, 297; security dilemma in, 281; state capability and, 157–58; structure of, 155–72, 279; superpowers and, 183, 184, 188–96, 197–98, 299

Hostage crisis, 53, 55

Hun Sen, 257, 259–60

Husayn, Saddam: ʿAziz and, 51; Baʿth party and, 30; conspiratorial fears of, 69, 87n81; Iranian revolution and, 52, 56; Iraq-Iran war and, 68, 76, 87n66; Iraq-Kuwait crisis and, 69–70, 71; Khumayni and, 60; Security Council resolution 598 and, 87n77; superpowers and, 28; survival of, 73

Hyderabad, 97

Ibadis, 32–33

Ideologies, 287–88; *see also* Transnational ideologies

India, 92; Afghanistan invasion and, 127–30; and balancing process, 104–5; Bangladesh and, 120–21; China and, 105–8, 131, 145–46n48, 51; defense budget of, 104, 106–7; "expansionism" of, 120, 134; external powers and, 104–5; Iran and, 112; Iraq and, 111–12

—— Pakistan and, 96–120, 135–36; Afghanistan invasion and, 128–29, 140; American aid and, 103–4; Bangladesh secession and, 140; China and, 108, 115;

comparative military strength in, 103; contrasting perceptions, 97–98; cooperation in, 115–20, 132, 148n72; domestic politics and, 99–101; ethnic regionalism and, 101; external influences on, 102–13, 139–40; Gulf states and, 111–13; history of, 96–99; nuclear dimension of, 114, 148n71; regional structure and, 92–103, 278; SAARC and, 119, 132–33, 136; security dilemma in, 97, 98–99, 144n22, 281; Soviet Union and, 127–28, 138; Sri Lanka and, 123, 140; superpowers and, 103, 108, 109; triangulation in, 107, 117; warfare between, 97, 107, 109, 136, 281

Indian National Congress, 131

India Northeast Frontier Agency, 127

Indian Peace-Keeping Force, 126

India Research and Analysis Wing, 125

Indochina, 236–46, 264; ASEAN and, 253–61, 267, 268–70; Cold War and, 218; cross-border ties and, 283; external powers and, 292; Vietnamese dominance of, 261

Indochina Special Relationship, 237, 244–46

Indochinese Union, 236, 272n16

Indonesia, 220–22; ASEAN and, 230–33, 260, 267; China and, 231, 235; development and, 229; entitlement, 285; independence of, 217; Malaysia and, 229, 260; Singapore and, 236, 250–51; Western ties of, 235

Indo-Sri Lanka Accord, 124, 133

Indus Waters Agreement, 117–18

Intergovernmental Authority on Drought and Development (Africa), 201

Internal balancing, 10, 102, 106, 110

International Monetary Fund, 166

Iran, 29; Bahrain and, 36, 38; Dhufar rebellion and, 45, 46; Egypt and, 51; extraregional links of, 78; GDP of, 83n7; India and, 112; Iraq and (*see under* Iraq); Iraq-Kuwait crisis and, 71–72, 73; oil boom and, 42–43; Pakistan and, 100, 111; Qajar Persian Empire and, 34; revolution in, 50–55, 76, 81; Saudi Arabia and, 48, 49, 51, 52, 62; Soviet Union and, 34, 36, 53, 59; U.S. and, 34, 36–37, 40, 41, 56, 66

"Iran-Contra" affair, 63

Iranian hostage crisis, 53, 55

Iraq, 29–30; arms sources of, 82; Britain